❖

Shakespeare and national culture

❖

edited by
John J. Joughin

Manchester University Press
Manchester and New York

distributed exclusively in the USA by St. Martin's Press

Published by Manchester University Press
Oxford Road, Manchester M13 9NR, UK
and Room 400, 175 Fifth Avenue,
New York, NY 10010, USA

Distributed exclusively in the USA
by St. Martin's Press, Inc.,
175 Fifth Avenue, New York, NY 10010, USA

British Library Cataloguing-in-Publication Data
A catalogue record for this book is available from the British Library

Library of Congress Cataloging-in-Publication Data
Shakespeare and national culture / edited by John J. Joughin.
        p.   cm.
    Includes index.
    ISBN 0-7190-4888-5 (hardback). — ISBN 0-7190-5051-0 (pbk.)
    1. Shakespeare, William, 1564–1616—Appreciation—Foreign
countries. 2. Shakespeare, William, 1564–1616—Study and teaching—
Foreign countries. 3. Shakespeare, William, 1564–1616—Stage
history—Foreign countries. 4. National characteristics, English,
in literature. 5. English drama—Appreciation—Foreign countries.
6. Civilization, Modern—English influences. 7. Communication,
International. 8. Great Britain—In literature. 9. Nationalism in
literature. I. Joughin, John J.
PR2971.F66S48 1997
822.3'3—dc20   96–30812
                                                                  ‑   CIP

ISBN 0 7190 4888 5 *hardback*
ISBN 0 7190 5051 0 *paperback*

First published in 1997

01 00 99 98 97   10 9 8 7 6 5 4 3 2 1

Printed in Great Britain
by Redwood Books, Trowbridge

Contents

❖

Notes on contributors

❖

Francis Barker is Professor of Literature at the University of Essex. His many publications include *The Tremulous Private Body: Essays on Subjection* (London, Methuen, 1984) and *The Culture of Violence: Essays on Tragedy and History* (Manchester, Manchester University Press, 1993).

Simon Barker is senior lecturer in English at Cheltenham and Gloucester College of Higher Education. Recent publications include a new edition of John Ford's play *'Tis Pity She's a Whore.*

Curtis Breight is Assistant Professor of English at the University of Pittsburgh. His work has appeared in *Critical Quarterly* and *Shakespeare Quarterly*, among other journals and collections. His *Surveillance, Militarism and Drama in the Elizabethan Era* is forthcoming (Basingstoke, Macmillan, 1996) and he is currently working on a book on Shakespeare and film entitled *Elizabethan World Pictures.*

John Drakakis is a Reader in English Studies at the University of Stirling, where he teaches Shakespeare and Renaissance Drama. He has edited *Alternative Shakespeares* (London, Routledge, 1989), *Shakespearean Tragedy* (Harlow, Longman, 1991) and the New Casebook of *Antony and Cleopatra* (Basingstoke, Macmillan, 1994). He is currently the General Editor of Routledge English Texts and The New Critical Idiom, and has just edited the first quarto of *Richard III* for the Harvester Shakespeare Originals series. He is the author of numerous articles on Shakespeare and is currently at work on a book entitled *Shakespearean Discourses.*

Thomas Healy is Reader in Renaissance Studies at Birkbeck College,

London. He is the author of *Richard Crashaw* (Medieval and Renaissance Author Series, Leiden, Brill, 1986), *New Latitudes: Theory and English Renaissance Literature* (London, Edward Arnold, 1992), *Christopher Marlowe* (Plymouth, Northcote House, 1994) and editor (with Jonathan Sawday) of *Literature and the English Civil War* (Cambridge, Cambridge University Press, 1990). He is currently writing a book on the aesthetics of sectarianism in early modern England.

Graham Holderness is Professor of Cultural Studies and Dean of Humanities and Education at the University of Hertfordshire. His many publications include *The Shakespeare Myth* (Manchester, Manchester University Press, 1988) and *Shakespeare Recycled: The Making of Historical Drama* (Hemel Hempstead, Harvester Wheatsheaf, 1992).

John J. Joughin teaches critical and cultural theory at the University of Central Lancashire where he is senior lecturer in the Department of Cultural Studies. His book *Shakespeare in the Spirit of Modernity* is forthcoming.

Ania Loomba is Associate Professor of English at Jawaharlal Nehru University New Delhi. She is author of *Gender, Race, Renaissance Drama* (Oxford, Oxford University Press (India), 1992) and various articles on Renaissance theatre, post-colonial theory and culture, and feminist theory. At present she is working on a full-length study of the shaping of English Renaissance drama by travels to the East Indies.

Willy Maley is a lecturer at the University of Glasgow. He is the author of *A Spenser Chronology* (Basingstoke, Macmillan, 1993) and co-editor of *Representing Ireland: Literature and the Origins of Conflict, 1534–1660* (Cambridge, Cambridge University Press, 1993). He is currently working on a study of Spenser and colonial identity and a collection of essays on Ireland in the English Renaissance.

Andrew Murphy is lecturer in English at the University of Hertfordshire. He has published articles on Renaissance and Irish topics. His work has appeared in *Textual Practice* and *Literature and History*, among other journals and collections.

Martin Orkin is the author of *Drama and the South African State* (Manchester, Manchester University Press, 1991). He has recently edited *At the Junction* (Witwatersrand, Witwatersrand University Press, 1995), a collection of South African plays. At present he teaches at the University of the Witwatersrand, Johannesburg.

Robert Weimann is Professor of Drama at University of California, Irvine. His many publications include *Shakespeare and the Popular Tradition in the Theater: Studies in the Social Dimension of Dramatic Form and Function* (Baltimore, Johns Hopkins University Press, 1978) and *Structure and Society in Literary History: Studies in the Theory of Historical Criticism* (Baltimore, Johns Hopkins University Press, 1985).

Richard Wilson is Professor of English at the University of Lancaster. He is author of *Julius Caesar* in the Penguin Critical Studies Series (Harmondsworth, Penguin, 1992) and *Will Power: Essays on Shakespearean Authority* (Hemel Hempstead, Harvester Wheatsheaf, 1993). He is also co-editor of *New Historicism and Renaissance Drama* (Harlow, Longman, 1992).

❖

Introduction

❖

John J. Joughin

The formation of a national culture is dependent upon, and often invokes, a particular version of the past which it would then either reaffirm or deny. With these heterogeneous associations, at the moment of its emergence, nationhood articulates a double move-ment. Not just a sense of beginning, but also a sense of return and beginning over again. This collection of essays attempts to reprob-lematise perhaps one of the most traditional of all cultural recursions – the turn to Shakespeare.

If the Shakespearian mediation of the national is very much part of our persistent need to situate the past in order to comprehend the present then many would argue that its neutrality on these matters has stood in question for long enough. And though it is apparent that for some 'Shakespeare' merely continues to signify 'Englishness', the papers gathered here testify that the playwright has featured in the construction, refashioning and articulation of a diverse range of other cultures and identities too. Indeed, Shake-speare has become the national poet of a variety of countries in particular forms. There is, and was, a German Shakespeare (East and West); there is the contested legacy of a colonial Shakespeare in former British possessions; there is the post-national 'Shakespeare' who has served to focus debates concerning multi-culturalism etc. It becomes clear that, amidst this process of reappropriation, just as Shakespeare has often been co-opted to secure nationalism, then he has also continued to contest and transform it in complex and contradictory ways too.

Nationalism has many places – real and illusory – and this volume cannot claim to inhabit them all. Nor do its separate thematic parts make a whole. Paradoxically, the symbology of a nation's idealised construction and its imagined community is often secured by its very intangibility.[1] It follows that although the nation is an entity against which individuals define themselves it often simultaneously resists definition itself, even as its abstract necessity is likely to be reinforced by an altogether more substantial apparatus of uniformity – passport, green card, border guard etc. Nationalism's productive lack of fixity is part of a problem which can engender the most dangerously dominative forms of solution and in this sense the current intervention cannot be considered wholly exempt in its inevitable partiality. At an academic distance, the arrangement of the volume's various sections no doubt reinforces restrictions and assumptions which, even in their more futuristic or liberationist strains, are indirectly complicit with the forms of identity thinking they would otherwise oppose. Any hierarchisation of Shakespeare's ability to compartmentalise currents of political and social change will necessarily reinscribe something of the logics of differentiation which so often secures nationalism's ongoing claim to validity. In focusing on the extraordinary diversity of liaisons, actual and imagined, between 'Shakespeare' on the one hand and various national cultures on the other, *Shakespeare and National Culture* aims to forge new interconnections in a global perspective, whilst simultaneously attempting to maintain a historically attuned sense of vigilance concerning the gradations of inequality which such a wide-ranging disarticulation of national identity inevitably helps to secure.

Shakespeare's English

It was perhaps inevitable that British contributions to a volume which raises the issues of nationalism and its culture in such close proximity were going to be shaped, to some extent, by the aftermath of the controversy which arose in the early 1990s involving the Tory government's attempt to implement an integrated core curriculum for English in schools – a move which, at the time, amply illustrated the desire of the British state to enforce a traditional adherence to the values of 'great literature' and the virtue of 'English'. It is to these and related concerns that Graham Holderness and Andrew Murphy speak in the opening chapter of the present volume, 'Shakespeare's England: Britain's Shakespeare', as they recall the powerful alliance of over five hundred teachers and scholars who rallied to oppose publicly the government's policy and its proposal to introduce compulsory tests on three of Shakespeare's plays.

That this political matter should have located Shakespeare at the centre of its ideological contestation is, as they remind us, wholly predictable and merely the last in a long history of disputes about the status of the Bard and the proper role of literary criticism. In this 'national' context Shakespeare has in fact been reappropriated by left, centre and right alike ever since the early seventeenth century.[2] And faced with such an uneven genealogy the projected return to the basics of 'canonicity' and 'standard English' is far more problematic than the Tory government might have supposed. Not least, in that, as Holderness and Murphy demonstrate, Shakespeare's 'English' precedes the invention of standard 'English' and is an altogether less disciplined affair, comprising a mixture of regional and class dialects as well as exhibiting instability of spelling, pronunciation and syntax. Yet the system of privileging standard English via Shakespeare is facilitated by a long-standing editorial consensus, which has effectively settled the instabilities of the Shakespearian corpus by 'translating' Shakespeare into modern English. In order to break with this reductive author-centred system and the editorial practices which continue to sustain it, they propose what amounts to a form of materialist bibliography. Such a project would redisperse notions of authorship and authority within a wider social matrix of relations, by resituating the production and reproduction of the variant 'Shakespearian' texts within their specific historical and institutional conditions and alongside other forms of writing and cultural practice.

While it's arguable that a nation is nothing more or less than a product of its culture, this is never merely a retroactive process. The furore over the national curriculum confirmed the power of Shakespeare's figuration in its more immediate vicinity, as it stirred the strongest emotions in the cause of control and centralisation. It is with an informed sense of the practical dilemmas faced by those who are on the receiving end of such a drive towards 'standardisation' that Simon Barker reminds us of the ever expanding market of up-to-the-minute examination guides and student 'aids', whose increase, as he wryly observes, is 'in direct proportion to the contraction in the resource bases of the institutions in which most of these students study' (p. 43). In 'Re-loading the canon: Shakespeare and the study guides' Barker interrogates the failure of this material to impart what he loosely terms 'critical theory' to the students in question. While he concedes the occasional permeability of some 'How to Study Guides' to theoretically informed perspectives, it is the broad implication of his brief survey that, despite the proliferation of research activity and published work that was made possible by utilising the tools of analysis which were provided by theoretical developments within post-structuralism, this success has not been matched by the realisation of any appreciable advance in terms of making a radical critical apparatus available at the chalkface.

Barker's chapter locates a series of significant strategical conundrums which implicitly inform several of the contributions to the current volume. As he notes, in a British context, early 1980s initiatives like Literature Teaching Politics and the Essex Soc. Lit. conferences seemed to promise much in terms of formulating an interventionist strategy which would breach the divide between theory and practice. How did the bold innovatory momentum of these projects become so thoroughly outflanked in terms of the allocation of material resources? Why, towards the end of the same decade, after the prompt dispatch of idealist criticism and essential humanism, did so many of us find ourselves clinging to a life-raft which sought to save the humanities? It is evident that despite the scaremongering of those who would oppose it, a Political Shakespeare has not yet come to pass.

It has long been part of a radical pedagogical approach to Shakespeare (cultural materialism's included) to emphasise the relevance of studying the plays in performance and in their theatrical context, and this is a project to which many of the contributors ascribe to a greater or lesser extent, either by taking account of the material process of the production of the Shakespearian text in its early modern context, or by examining the process of its appropriation and recirculation via theatre practices past and present. Part I closes with a chapter which actively opposes the powerful collusion of Shakespeare and education in the shaping of a national culture, and in doing so produces a resounding polemical counterblast with which to upbraid the prevailing anti-intellectualism of Britain's theatre establishment. In 'NATO's pharmacy: Shakespeare by prescription', Richard Wilson suggests that the Royal Shakespeare Company has become nothing less than the stalking horse of the political right. Indeed it is the thrust of his argument that the company has collaborated in constructing Shakespeare as a kind of panacea for our national ills. So that in the words of the RSC's present director Adrian Noble the answer to an education system bedevilled by political dissent lies in 'teaching the teachers' how to teach Shakespeare. It turns out that Noble's 'prescription' serves as a shorthand for what is in effect the company's mission statement, and quite fittingly so, for, as Wilson demonstrates, the organising metaphor of the contemporary discourse which empowers and informs the RSC's evaluation of Shakespeare's role in education is both medicinal and quasi-religious. Wilson traces this curative project, which privileges the purgational power of theatre in the belief that it will instil the right type of 'social and emotional experience', to its earliest incarnation in the theatre theory and practice of Peter Brook, in many ways the founding father of the formation under discussion.

As Wilson notes, the evolving ideological function of the education programmes and workshops currently peddled by our theatre companies discloses a still more material history. In the process of its financial transition from state subsidy to commercial funding during the 1980s, Wilson argues that the RSC was caught in the conflicting ideological currents of what Perry Anderson has termed 'A Culture in Contraflow'.[3] Wilson's redeployment of Anderson's analysis is persuasive and suggests that, along with other institutions in a hitherto leftward leaning public service sector, the RSC was directly compromised by the prevailing logic of the marketplace in which it was forced to operate. Meanwhile the rise of the political right also produced a 'cultural drift to the left' whose vociferous opposition merely served to symptomatise its disempowerment in real terms. So it is that, sadly, Wilson's reading provides still further confirmation, if we needed it, of a disabling wedge between the political and intellectual worlds of the radical British critical problematic which continues to secure a gulf between theory and practice of a type which we have already had cause to notice.

Contesting the colonial

Needless to say, the necessity of disconcealing the political agenda which informs the fabrication of Shakespearian culture is not restricted to its English or its British context but is still more likely to be situated somewhere between the confusion of the two. Indeed, the chapters in Part I serve to suggest that the homogenising cultural identity of 'Britain' has operated to occlude the acutely uneven relations of power which obtain between its constituent parts and continues to subsume crucial differences of race, region, religion, class, subculture etc.

In this, its colonial context, British national identity has always been part of a more deeply rooted and potentially conflictual condition which embraces or contests a particular state of belonging or being, viz.: the experience of being 'English', or 'Irish', or 'Scottish', or 'Welsh', or 'British', or somehow each of these, and other, at a certain moment of time. It clearly matters which. So long as this is the case, the experiential nexus of 'being British' (whatever that is) will remain indeterminate and confusing. By way of beginning to unravel something of the complexity of these heterogeneous forms of political and cultural identity, Willy Maley's chapter on ' "This sceptred isle": Shakespeare and the British problem' directs us to related aspects of their uneven development. Despite its historical diversity Maley demonstrates that the dominant construction of Britain's cultural identity remains English. Yet, as such, 'England' is a part that stands for the whole. Or, as Willy Maley puts it, still more succinctly 'England' functions as a 'simplifying synecdoche' for the British state. Meanwhile, historiography old and new has continued (with a few notable exceptions) to perpetuate the 'Englishing of the British state'; not least in its revisionist construction of an English Civil War. Towards breaking the grip of this broadly influential paradigm Maley proposes that we direct our attention to reconfiguring the multi-national complexity of the 'British problem', in order to make room for a new approach to 'English culture in the early modern period, and Shakespeare in particular' (p. 92). In the process Shakespeare's 'Englishness' is revealed as contingent, simultaneously constructed within a British context and *against* other national identities.

The interpenetration of national identities is also very much the locus for Ania Loomba's chapter, 'Shakespearian transformations', as she focuses on the cross-cultural adaptations of the Elizabethan dramatist on the Parsi stages of Bombay from the mid nineteenth century onwards. Her chapter usefully combines a survey of theatre history with a theoretical exposition of the current limitations of post-colonial approaches to Indian culture. As she demonstrates, the Parsi theatre companies embodied a complex and often irreverent transformation of Shakespeare in production, as, in what was very much a two-way street, performances drew simultaneously on an already hybrid ensemble of indigenous traditions in the process of their assimilation of many of the material practices and conventions of the European theatre. Loomba's reading usefully locates something of the potential heterogeneity of a 'national' culture, which as she notes in its 'Third World' context is all too often shorthanded reductively as anti-colonial. In contradistinction the Parsi performances underline the importance of considering a dominant alien culture within the parameters of its own historical and cultural specificity. Indeed it is the implication of her reading that such phenomena are especially useful, precisely because the complexity of their repositioning resists containment, or any easy formulaic subsumption within a polarity between 'us' and 'them', anti-colonial and colonial. Rather, by accentuating the contradictions which inform what she terms 'the travels of Shakespeare abroad' (p. 139) cross-cultural performances often symptomatise the possibility of change and transformation which resides in the relationship between an 'original' and its appropriations.

The potential promotion of cultural transformation and social change is the shared concern of Martin Orkin's 'Whose things of darkness? Reading/representing *The Tempest* in South Africa after April 1994'. Orkin's chapter opens with a résumé of the mainstream conservatism which currently holds sway in the South African academy, where the standing of Shakespeare is predominantly anglocentricised and bardolatrous. If language is still the instrument of empire (and Orkin's account leaves us in little doubt that it is), then for the old guard of South African scholarship this 'civilising mission' is at one with the wider policy of a neo-apartheid education system, where the study of indigenous forms of writing is explicitly discouraged, and an old style of literary awareness is inculcated, which replaces, and thereby displaces, the formation of more enabling forms of consciousness, political or otherwise. The focus of Orkin's attention is on *The Tempest*, where the use of language and the implementation of political order are powerfully conjoined. Orkin proceeds to disconceal the often ambivalent function of figures of speech in the play, which in their attempt to secure textual unity often succeed only in doubling back upon themselves, thus undermining the exploitative power relations which they seek to uphold.

In exploring the possibilities of resistance to apartheid, in its wider context, Orkin is concerned to supplement his exposition of colonialist discourse by locating elements in its presentation which might facilitate what he terms, pace Alan Sinfield, a 'dissident understanding' of Shakespeare's text. As Sinfield suggests, the opportunity for such a reading arises precisely because the dominant culture of a complex society is necessarily heterogeneous in its make up, and so must also accommodate a vulnerable awareness of the disruptive potential of the various layers and interests of its own intricate structuration.[4] Building on this conjecture, Orkin suggests that elements of subordinate representation in *The Tempest* have the potential to illuminate and contest the faultlines which necessarily inform the dominant social order. Howsoever the play is re-read and represented in the new South Africa, those charged with implementing the delicate transition to a non-apartheid system of democracy would do well to heed its achieved failure to accommodate the production of difference within the exclusionary demands of a dominant culture.

Shakespeare at the heart of Europe

Along with so many of the transformations plotted in the volume, the defining feature of the prevailing discourse of European identity is that it is Janus-faced. On the one hand the West looks forward to the demise of nationalism, and contemplates the prospect of forging a new alliance of European federalism. Meanwhile, in Central and Eastern Europe, the aftermath of the dissolution of the Soviet bloc and the collapse of totalitarianism brings with it the spectre of the rebirth of nationalism, either in its 'progressive' form as a democratic break with the bad totalities which preceded it, or, by way of a relapse to still older forms of racial and ethnic collectivity which are reactivated in its wake.

Nowhere are the issues of unification and diversity forced more urgently or in closer constituency than in Germany, where the recent process of reunification breaches the former front-line of cold war opposition and, in the process of relocating the shared cultural roots which preceded it, constellates a series of newly conceived relations between past, present and future. Of course in some respects, and certainly since the formative cultural context of the late eighteenth century, 'Shakespeare' has long had a part to play in the forging of a German identity. Yet as Robert Weimann suggests in his 'A divided heritage: conflicting appropriations of Shakespeare in (East) Germany', the genealogy of this assimilation is by no means a straightforward one. As Weimann demonstrates, the shifting adaptation and appropriation of the Shakespearian text needs to be situated in its more material and interactive relations, with the inconsistencies and contradictions which structure the social process itself. Amidst the tangled relations of the East German problematic, Weimann's chapter identifies two related yet contradictory currents of cultural practice which have informed the criticism and theatrical production of Shakespeare in the former GDR for almost thirty years: on the one hand, the orthodox party-line of 'Positive Heritage' and on the other, the less uniform alternative of what Weimannn aptly terms 'Conjunctural Appropriation'. The former bears a resemblance to the empty homogeneity of historicism's grand narrative, and conjoins with a classical tradition, which emphasises Shakespeare's humanism, and foregrounds utopian notions of continuity, culminating in eventual emancipation through socialism, while the latter is more likely to remark a discrepancy between Shakespeare's 'past significance and its present meaning'.

With its complex sense of the lack of continuity between 'then' and 'now', and its incredulity towards the unilinear metanarrative of a positivistically grounded heritage, it will be apparent that the 'Conjunctural' version of historical criticism outlined by Weimann has much in common with the diacritical concept of historicity, which has emerged as a result of a critical encounter between Marxism and post-structuralism, and helped to shape and change the field of Renaissance studies in the West. Yet, importantly, in its East German variant, Weimann traces a configuration of the past/present correlation which precedes both the arrival of post-structuralism and the more recent, and newly critical, 'return to history' witnessed in Anglo-American versions of historicism.

The articulation of the divided legacy which Weimann traces

provides illuminating confirmation of the potentially fruitful ambiguities which can arise, when, by granting Shakespeare the totemic
significance of a civilising influence, an appropriating culture or
regime can unwittingly accommodate and promote the very contradictions it seeks to resolve. Located at the site of national consciousness, the cultural critic can fashion a role of resistance precisely
because she retains a privileged position of involvement within the
state apparatus of education. In these circumstances, even in a
coded form, the disarticulation of a critique demands a high level
of methodological resourcefulness and frequently yields advances
in terms of theoretical innovation. In the event, Robert Weimann's
seminal work on *Shakespeare and the Popular Tradition in the
Theater*, first published in the GDR in 1967,[5] had decisive ramifications for the development of Shakespeare studies, East and West.
But viewed in terms of the originating conditions of its production and reception, perhaps its greatest significance was that in its
articulation of a position of relative autonomy it exemplified the
potential of cultural criticism to accommodate the formation of an
oppositional identity within the constraints of an overbearingly
authoritarian regime.

Yet however productive the polarities of internal dissent are,
other more reactionary forms of political independence and self-
determination will remain intact. There has been a tendency,
especially on the part of Western commentators, to view the
phenomenon of resurgent European nationalism through the rose-
tinted shades of nineteenth-century Enlightenment and liberal
democracy. Yet this brand of celebratory internationalism exagger-
ates the solidity of pre-communist democratic traditions only by
virtue of disregarding the atavistic forms of religious intolerance
and racial persecution which precede and survive them, and which
are now in danger of resurfacing once again in the guise of post-
communist nationalism. Thomas Healy's 'Past and present Shakespeares: Shakespearian appropriations in Europe' grapples with the
latent complexity of these neglected but still remembered forms of
cultural identity; and explores their potential to interrogate our
own complacent and overfamiliarised sense of an endlessly rein-
vented 'Shakespeare', which despite, and indeed partly because of,
its reproducibility, is in danger of losing its sense of political specificity. In a brief overview of recent trends in Shakespeare criticism

Healy argues that while, on the one hand, our appreciation of 'a multitude of Shakespeares' has undoubtedly helped to disrupt and contest the deployment of Shakespeare as a unifying and restrictive instrument with which to police national conformity, European or otherwise, an emphasis on appropriation and difference has also simultaneously helped to produce an homogenised version of 'Shakespeare', which is available for exchange and consumption in the universalising sphere of the academic marketplace. Nor, as Healy demonstrates, is radical criticism exempt from this charge of homogenisation, in that it too often relies on a radically selective recycling of the past to ratify its preferred political interpretation of the present, thus leaving itself open to the accusation that it merely rehearses another brand of the critical bias which it would otherwise claim to oppose.

As Healy demonstrates, an emphasis on the social and political continuities which make Shakespeare 'our contemporary' is a prime component in the history of European appropriation(s). For here also, there is a tendency to forge cultural identity by retrospectively prescribing a past for the present, and refashioning the history of national identity 'up time' by writing history 'toward a moment of origin'.[6] In the circumstances, merely remembering that which was forgotten is not enough. It is at least as important to mark the return of that which we are in danger of forgetting in our preoccupation with remembering. As we survey the historical deployment of 'Shakespeare' in its wider European context, Healy argues that we must learn to recognise that the recovery of an unfamiliar or alien culture can simultaneously relocate a different sense of that which we considered ours. An awareness of the sectarian positions which multiple Shakespeares occupy will enable us to confront the categories and structures through which we have sought to understand or dismiss them, in order to reclaim otherness otherwise, and thus acknowledge the cultural diversity of European difference.

It is the search for conceptual origins, or rather the relation between this quest and the actual context of origin seeking itself, which concerns Francis Barker in his 'Nationalism, nomadism and belonging in Europe: *Coriolanus*'. The resonance of Barker's chapter is political rather than merely philosophical, as he invokes Martin Heidegger's *An Introduction to Metaphysics*, which opens

with the question of the question of authenticity itself – 'why are
there things which are; why is there anything; why isn't there
simply nothing at all?' If, in strictly philosophical terms, the answer to Heidegger's questioning of Being is destined to remain
deferred, the historical destination of its final solution was, as Barker implies, all too readily to hand. In its original attempt to solicit
an answer for 'this most fundamental of all questions', the question
itself is located at a threshold of enormous consequence for Germany, coinciding as it does with the dawn of National Socialism,
and converging still more decisively in what Heidegger goes on to
term 'the historical destiny of the West'.

Now, more than half a century later, just as a preoccupation
with European identity returns to haunt us, we might well appre-
hend its recurrence as constituting a warning sign at a moment of
danger. For, as Barker reminds us, the integration promised by the
contemporary rhetoric of a 'new Europe' belies the destructive
potential of the resurgent nationalisms which it must also necessarily accommodate. In order to illuminate further the structural
complexities which currently inform the cultural ideal of nationalism and its discourse, Barker returns to Shakespeare's *Coriolanus*,
where, at a precarious founding moment, the figuration of national
identity locates the site of a problematic textual and ideological
contradiction. Here, as elsewhere, to sustain the illusion of national
embodiment, is, as Barker demonstrates, to confront a considerable dilemma. As, somewhat paradoxically, in order to secure its
empowerment, and in its desire for solidarity, nationalism must
also hold within itself a moment of separation which sanctions a
discriminatory and divisive system of identifying and eliminating
difference.

Again, as with Weimann and Healy, the insistence of Barker's
argument is conjunctural; in that by locating the emergence of
'thinking the national' in the early modern period, and disconcealing
its instabilities, we may critically reflect on, and where necessary
resist, the destructive centrifugal forces of 'newly energised nationalisms' as they re-emerge in our own threshold moment. In this
respect, the most pressing problem in the new Europe, will be, as
Barker puts it, to 'imagine community' without beginning 'the war
against the others' (p. 259). Towards realising this objective he
proposes the theorisation and, in time, the practical implementation of a form of 'post-territorialism'.

Shakespeare and transnational culture

We live within the shifting boundaries of a shrinking world, where particular localities and cities are reintegrated via computer networks and electronic media which bypass national frontiers. The acceleration of information and communication technology and the associated developments within video, film and television, CD ROM, virtual reality, etc. that go with them have already had a considerable effect in terms of the construction and reconceptualisation of our cultural identities, and they will therefore also continue to have an impact on the traditional pedagogical practices and educational structures of the humanities. It's clear that 'Shakespeare' is very much part of this virtual world, configuring a transnational corporate matrix which Gary Taylor has termed 'Shakesperotics' and Terry Hawkes has labelled more succinctly 'Bardbiz'.[7] The volume concludes with two chapters which address contrasting dimensions of Shakespeare's redispersal beyond traditional limits and within an emergently global context.

In 'Shakespeare, national culture and the lure of transnationalism' John Joughin argues that, amidst the discrepancy configured by the apparent deregulation provided by the new forms and permutations of cultural criticism, we should not underestimate the capacity of the new media to interarticulate (on a national as well as a transnational scale) with residual structures of institutional conformity. Just as contemporary forms of Shakespearian criticism appear to confirm a shift to a decentred paradigm whose transition has been noticed on a more general level as part of the necessary move from literary to cultural studies, Joughin argues that this breach between disciplines in the humanities symptomatises domination even as it apparently heeds alterity. By way of developing this thesis, he notes that a focus on interdisciplinarity and a collapse in the distinction between the inside and the outside of the institution has also been one of the organising features of the so-called culture wars in its British context. Amidst currently resurgent notions of a leftish pedagogy and discussions surrounding the question of the 'political correctness' of Shakespeare criticism, Joughin argues that if Shakespeare criticism is to retain its vital relevance in the struggle against a breach in the humanities which might yet prove to be critical, we need a topology of Shakespeare studies which will hold the centre.

In 'Elizabethan world pictures' Curt Breight takes a more expansionist perspective than Joughin, as he suggests a connectedness between the triumphant globalism of America's recent military adventurism and the cultural imperialism evidenced by the proliferation of a new wave of multi-national cinematic adaptations of Shakespeare. Breight proposes that there is valuable ground to be won amidst this process of international cinematic (re)canonisation, in so far as a postmodern 'ShakeCinema', and its interpretation, has the potential to reconfigure the dominant representations of imperial history, and contest their claim to authority. The focus of his attention is on Gus Van Sant's *My Own Private Idaho* (1991). In pursuit of its anti-imperial theme, Van Sant's film reprocesses iconic images culled from the wider reaches of Renaissance culture and sets them alongside the excesses of imperial Rome and the exploitation suffered by those who currently inhabit a decaying American heartland. Breight argues that the early modern component of the film mediates a cultural continuum of oppression, and thus confronts us with the awareness that we ourselves are implicated within a society and a culture that is still engaged in imperial domination. By emphasising the links between the political and the personal, whilst also celebrating the resilience of those who survive the extremes of socio-political alienation which constitutes the dystopic reality of 'America the Beautiful', Shakespeare's text is effectively re-situated as a critique of 'contemporary institutional exploitation'.

Whatever the role of Shakespearian criticism in the new world order, the fact that Joughin and Breight offer opposed models of oppositionality suggests that here, as elsewhere in the volume, cultural transformation is shaped by a complex interweaving of contradictory currents of change and continuity. If attempts to construe 'Shakespeare' within a transnational frame of significance continue to disclose their entwinement with what Robert Weimann terms culture's 'divided heritage', then this doubtless marks a legacy for the future as well as the past. As nationalism variously begins and ends again, the range and diversity of contributions in the current volume suggest that in its global context 'Shakespeare' continues to constitute one of the most culturally heterogeneous sites for its articulation. The continued dependency of our academic practice upon Shakespeare's irreducibility indirectly acknowledges not just a critical awareness of its facility to accommodate ever more diverse forms of cultural reappropriation, but also confirms its potential to shape and know new territories altogether and to illuminate fresh grounds for their inquiry.

Notes

I am indebted to Francis Barker whose early support helped to initiate this volume and greatly assisted in the subsequent clarification of its project. Thanks are also due to John Banks for his assiduous attention to detail in the process of copyediting the volume, and also to MUP's anonymous reader for helping to locate the volume and suggesting a number of valuable revisions to its Introduction.

1 This formulation, by now ubiquitous in our understanding of the fictional 'past-times' which secure national identity, finds its most memorable exposition in Benedict Anderson's *Imagined Communities: Reflections on the Origin and Spread of Nationalism* (London, Verso, 1983), to which I am indebted here and throughout.
2 Criticism is growing apace in this particular area. Among recent interventions compare especially Gary Taylor, *Reinventing Shakespeare: A Cultural History from the Restoration to the Present* (New York, Weidenfeld and Nicolson, 1989; Oxford, Oxford University Press, 1991); Jean I. Marsden, ed., *The Appropriation of Shakespeare: Post-Renaissance Reconstructions of the Works and the Myth* (Hemel Hempstead, Harvester Wheatsheaf, 1991); and Michael Dobson, *The Making of the National Poet: Shakespeare Adaptation and Authorship, 1660–1769* (Oxford, Oxford University Press, 1992).
3 Perry Anderson, *English Questions* (London, Verso, 1992), pp. 199–200.
4 A. Sinfield, *Faultlines: Cultural Materialism and the Politics of Dissident Reading* (Oxford, Oxford University Press, 1992), pp. 45–6.
5 *Shakespeare and the Popular Tradition in the Theater: Studies in the Social Dimension of Dramatic Form and Function* (Baltimore, Johns Hopkins University Press, 1978).
6 See Anderson, *Imagined Communities*, especially pp. 187–206.
7 See Taylor, *Reinventing Shakespeare*, pp. 298–372; and Terence Hawkes, *Meaning by Shakespeare* (London, Routledge, 1992), pp. 141–53.

Part I

❖

Shakespeare's English

❖

1

✤

Shakespeare's England: Britain's Shakespeare

✤

Graham Holderness and Andrew Murphy

I

> It is not eafy to difcover from what caufe the acrimony of a fcholiaft can naturally proceed. The fubjects to be difcuffed by him are of very fmall importance; they involve neither property nor liberty; nor favour the intereft of fect or party.[1]

So Samuel Johnson wrote in the introduction to his edition of Shakespeare. Whatever the applicability of Johnson's sense of the role and importance of the scholar (and, more particularly, of the literary critic and textual editor) to the world of the century in which he himself wrote, clearly, in the closing years of our own century, the business of scholarship has come to be seen as being of very particular importance, precisely because it has, in recent years, been viewed as involving crucial issues of liberty, and of being very deeply furrowed by what Johnson terms 'the intereft[s] of fect[s] or part-[ies]'. As a result, the academy has become something of a battle-ground for competing ideological positions. In the USA, for instance, conservative commentators such as Allan Bloom have imagined a left-wing hegemony within the academic realm which threatens the very future of civilisation as we know it.[2] In the UK, the conflict has been played out in an even more public arena, as the school-teachers' professional organisations have endeavoured, over a long period of time, to resist the efforts of the Conservative government to refashion the educational system according to its own image

– reimposing on English teachers and their students notions of, for instance, canonicity and 'standard English'.

It is English, indeed, which has been at the centre of so many of these disputes encompassing the political and academic realms. Terry Eagleton once wrote of the enormous self-centralising power of an emergent new criticism that 'in the early 1920s it was desperately unclear why English was worth studying at all; by the early 1930s it had become a question of why it was worth wasting your time on anything else'.[3] One might wonder, of course, whether this is still true for *students* today, but, at any rate, the discipline of English seems of late to be attracting a very great deal of attention from politicians and their attendant satellites. A particularly good example of this new centrality of English could be seen at the 1993 Conservative Party conference in the UK, when the British Prime Minister, in the midst of his annual keynote address to the party faithful, took the time to launch a counter-attack against a group of some five hundred academics who had published a letter in the British press condemning the government's policies on the study of literature. Mr Major, waving a copy of the letter in the air, and pledging to speak to such academics in a language of which they themselves might approve, declared resolutely: 'Me and my party ain't going to take what them on the left says is OK. Right?'[4]

The letter in question had addressed, among other things, the issue of how and when Shakespeare should be taught in British schools, with the original writers of the letter registering their opposition to the government's policy that the study of Shakespeare be a mandatory part of the curriculum for students from an early age.[5] Shakespeare, indeed, has always been of centrally strategic importance in the battleground formed by the intersection of education and politics. In August 1993, the British Sunday newspaper *The Observer* ran a lengthy feature article in its Review section under the headline ' "Presume not that I am the thing I was" ' and subtitled 'The battle of the Bard'. In this article, the journalist Peter Watson traces the rise, within Shakespeare studies, of the related critical strategies of new historicism and cultural materialism and charts the reactions which these approaches have provoked among conservative critics. 'The battle and the bitchiness are far from over', Watson writes, 'the Bard is still up for grabs.'[6] It is the contention, of course, of many scholars that 'the Bard' has, in fact, always been up for grabs. Since the first wave of British cultural

materialist Shakespeare criticism redrew the theoretical map in the
mid-1980s, subsequent writers – in particular Gary Taylor in
Reinventing Shakespeare, Michael Bristol in *Shakespeare's America,
America's Shakespeare*, and Jean Marsden in *The Appropriation
of Shakespeare* – have produced cultural histories of the ways in
which Shakespeare has, ever since the seventeenth century, been
constituted and reconstituted, fashioned and refashioned to serve
political and ideological ends – on both sides of the Atlantic.[7]
Those who accuse radical critics of somehow 'misappropriating'
Shakespeare for their own nefarious ends thus fail to see that
Shakespeare has *always* been the subject of appropriations of one
sort or another. Indeed, we will recall that in the dramatist's own
lifetime his work was deployed for explicitly political ends on at
least one occasion, when the supporters of the Earl of Essex commissioned a special performance of *Richard II* on the eve of their
rebellion against Elizabeth in 1601.

But, of course, we might also question in this context the conservative assumption that there does in fact exist in the work of
Shakespeare something coherent, stable and unitary which is *capable* of being 'mis'appropriated by the cultural materialists, and,
conversely, which can, in turn, be restored to an original pristine
self, if only the defacing graffiti of a radical critical practice could
be expunged from its surface. It is not just a matter of interrogating the conservative assumption that there is a transcendent and
universal meaning which inheres in the works of Shakespeare, a
meaning to which we must somehow 'return', eschewing the wil-
ful 'mis'reading of the radicals. We must also interrogate the prior
assumption which lies behind this conservative view: that the works
in question themselves constitute a unitary and coherent set of
entities, whose material stability is safely to be taken for granted.

II

Such a confidence in the unity and stability, both of 'Shakespeare'
and of the Shakespeare text, certainly lies at the heart of conservative thinking as it manifests itself in promotion of the British Government's 'National Curriculum for English'. Shakespeare, according
to the proponents of the National Curriculum, remains an indispensable component of the latter as a consequence of his centrality to the 'literary heritage'. There exists something of value,

literature, that descends from the past and is inherited in the present. Although that object of value is a common inheritance, theoretically available to all, not everyone who is entitled to claim it (as is often the case with state social security benefits) does, despite the existence of a nominal universal right, actually do so. From this idea derives the concept of the National Curriculum as an 'enabling curriculum', facilitating access to their inheritance for those who would otherwise remain disinherited.

Shakespeare, together with a strikingly narrow range of Victorian and Edwardian classics, represents this literary heritage in exemplary form. In 1992 British secondary schools were required to ensure (at absurdly short notice) that 14-year-olds would study one of three prescribed Shakespeare plays (*Julius Caesar*, *A Midsummer Night's Dream* and *Romeo and Juliet*), and be tested on what they had studied. So your heritage doesn't come to you automatically, any more than do state benefits or the contents of a will: you are required to *prove* your title to that inheritance in exactly the same way (via the system of *probate*, a term derived from the Latin *probare*, to test or prove) as you have to prove your title to private property.

The process by which your inheritance can be claimed, as the metaphor begins to disclose its true contents, is therefore less about possession and more about establishing entitlement; less of a free bequest and more about requirement, imposition, testing and proof. 'English' is in this way used in much the same way as Latin was used in the British grammar school system: to assess levels of cultural competence; to identify those who are worthy of the literary heritage; and to differentiate them from those who are patently unfit to inherit. The crucial difference is, of course, that Latin as employed in the grammar school system was a dead language, a specifically literary rather than an oral form, which even in the time of its currency bore an oblique relation to its own equivalent vernacular; and which naturally bore a precisely negative relation to the contemporary vernacular within which it operated (indeed still operates) in grammar schools. Contemporary English is a language in use; in continual exchange and change; dynamic and developing; adapting to new relations of cultural exchange as new social and political relations evolve. Moreover, there is not of course only one English, but many: class and regional dialects; all the Englishes of the large anglophone world. In terms of the population of Britain itself, English has long co-existed with other languages such as Welsh and Gaelic, and with the languages of all the other language groups that make up the global population of a multi-cultural society. The difficulties entailed in using this language, as an equivalent of Latin, to express and embody standards of linguistic acquisition and performance will be self-evident.

This problem is solved by the privileging of one form of English, a particular class-dialect, as the dominant form: standard English. Standard English, the educated language of the ruling class, derived from a particular regional dialect of early English, is now declared the universal *lingua franca* of all classes, races and creeds. Standard English, though 'owned' in terms both of speech and writing by a privileged few, is none the less nominally available to all: a common inheritance, a universal right. Standard English may not be the language you learn 'naturally' from family and immediate social environment; but it is there as a linguistic standard to which you may aspire, promising the rewards of intelligibility, freedom of speech and communication, educational and social advancement.

Standard English is also declared the common language of the literary inheritance; the language of the Bible and of Shakespeare: a language exemplifying a cultural continuity through the process of historical and political change. We who speak the tongue that Shakespeare spake (sorry, *spoke*) enter in that process of linguistic transaction a cultural continuum continually demonstrated by the palpable contemporary existence of the literary heritage.

The key ideas outlined here are all linked in an ideological ensemble purporting to represent a coherent, organically unified cultural 'core'. The literary heritage, based upon a notion of classic writing narrowly selected from a vast range of possibilities, and including an indispensable, unavoidable component – Shakespeare – is made possible and exemplified by standard English, the universal dialect of a linguistic and literary common inheritance. Language acquisition and literary education are seen as a seamless continuum, each an inevitable condition of the other. Literary and linguistic competence, demonstrable via certain media of academic performance, can be tested against the same measurable performance indicators. The ability to speak and write, clearly and confidently, standard English; and the capacity to demonstrate an acceptable level of understanding *vis-à-vis* Shakespearian drama, are in the National Curriculum system regarded as interdependent and reliably measurable by common criteria. In order to speak the tongue that Shakespeare spake/spoke, we are obliged to frequent the writing which embodies that speech.

But much of our 'literary heritage', including the work of the one writer regarded as indispensable, was of course written long before the invention of standard English. The process of systematising the English language, establishing principles of correctness in relation to its grammar and syntax, determining conventions of regularity in relation to spelling and punctuation, which can be said to have commenced in the eighteenth century, was not accomplished, and certainly not disseminated through the educational system, before the nineteenth. Early modern English, the English of the sixteenth and seventeenth centuries, was in many ways quite unlike standard English: in some ways more systematic – enjoying for example a much wider range of usable grammatical forms than those available to modern standard English – and in some ways, especially in relation to spelling and punctuation, far less regularised. The continuing availability into the seventeenth century of Latin as a medium of writing indicates that English had not at that stage of its development achieved complete cultural dominance. English was still sufficiently 'emergent' as a language for its written usage to be closely linked with the linguistic variety of the vernacular.

Shakespeare's English was therefore very obviously a non-standard English, both structurally and contextually very different from its modern counterpart: with a different grammatical system, different rules of spelling and punctuation; with a different set of relations between written and spoken language; with a different relationship, among the educated classes, with other languages. English was in that early modern period a dynamic and developing language, characterised by diversity and change, the very opposite of a fixed, regularised and systematised form such as standard English. Indeed the historical and political processes that made standard English possible and necessary – the emergence from medieval Catholic Europe of England/Britain as an independent national state, and the eventual rise of that state to imperial domination – were only just beginning. In the plays of Marlowe, Shakespeare and their contemporaries English is frequently marked off from other languages, other regional and class-dialects, as a distinct linguistic medium: but that evidence of linguistic differentiation only indicates that the process of shaping within the language a national identity was at an early stage of development.

How is it possible then to use the work of an early modern dramatist, written long before the language was regulated and codified into what we now know as standard English, to exemplify that linguistic form? Simply, the answer is, by translation. Even a cursory glance at a manuscript record or printed text from the early modern period would be sufficient to convince the reader that the writing of that period does not exemplify standard English usage. But this incontrovertible documentary evidence is of course not normally available to the modern reader – often not even to the university student of literature, and certainly not to the school student reading a Shakespeare play within the context of the National Curriculum for English – since Shakespeare is not read in early modern English, but in modern 'translation'.

Many modern readers of Shakespeare, particularly younger readers, lulled by long-established editorial traditions into an implicit confidence in the object of their attention, probably have little idea of what a sixteenth-century printed play text actually looked like. Confronted with an example, she or he could be forgiven for recoiling before the intimidating display of linguistic and visual strangeness – antique type, non-standardised spelling, archaic orthographic conventions, unfamiliar and irregular speech prefixes, oddly placed stage directions, and possibly an absence of act and scene divisions. 'It looks more like Chaucer than Shakespeare', said one sixth-former, presented with a facsimile of an Elizabethan text, neatly calling attention to the peculiar elisions by which Shakespeare is accepted as modern, while Chaucer is categorised as ancient. Yet Shakespeare too is read in modernised forms. A student reading Chaucer in modern translation knows that the text is a contemporary version, not a historical document. But the modern translations of Shakespeare which universally pass as accurate and authentic representations of an original – the standard editions – offer themselves simultaneously as historical document and accessible modern version, like a tidily restored ancient building.

The standard modern editions of Shakespeare, much more obviously compatible with the conventions of modern standard English than the original printed texts, thus operate continually to foster the illusion that these writings of the late sixteenth and early seventeenth centuries effortlessly prefigured the grammatical system, syntactical conventions, rules of spelling and punctuation characteristic of standard English. The modern Shakespeare edition thus seems anachronistically to exemplify that standard English that was invented centuries after the initial production and performance of the plays. With its regularisation of spelling and punctuation, together with editorial systematisation of whatever appears 'irregular' in the original texts, whether that be a matter of grammar, stage directions, structural divisions into act and scene, the standard modern edition presents to the reader a Shakespeare which, smoothly translated into a familiar modern idiom, seems to present far fewer problems of comprehension even to the relatively unsophisticated reader. The modernised edition of Shakespeare thus performs an essential service to the National Curriculum, by completing the continuum of language and literature, speech and writing, past and present, and enabling a transhistorical 'Shakespeare', purged of all disconcerting historical difference, to stand as an incontrovertible demonstration of the 'greatness' embodied in 'English' – whether that nomenclature is employed to signify a literature, a language, a culture or a political state.

Inheriting Shakespeare through the National Curriculum, we may well feel disposed to believe that, as fortunate beneficiaries of a generous bequest, we have come into possession of a valuable antique. But barely concealed beneath the patina of antiquity we can discern the varnish of novelty. This is not an antique but an imitation, perfectly adapted to the conveniences of modern living: 'repro Shakespeare'.

III

When the British Education Secretary insists that schoolchildren be compelled to read Shakespeare, the presumption that there exists such a thing as a coherent 'Shakespeare' 'text' for them to read is manifestly demonstrated by the unassailed supremacy of the modern edition. British schoolchildren and their teachers are spoilt for choice of such texts, as is evidenced by the recent publication of a volume entitled *Which Shakespeare?* – a sort of 'consumer's guide' to the major available editions of Shakespeare's plays, which aims to assist the teacher and scholar in making an informed choice among competing flocks of Penguins, Bantams, Signets, Ardens, Cambridges and Oxfords.[8] All of these editions of Shakespeare are much the same. Or rather, they are simultaneously the same and yet not the same. The texts of Shakespeare commonly available in major editions differ little enough from each other in substance, because they have all been produced under the guiding principles of a textual theory which came into prominence among editors of early modern texts in the early decades of the twentieth century – a theory derived in the first instance (appropriately enough, conservatives would no doubt say) from the realm of biblical studies. What these texts *do* differ from, however (and often differ from very significantly indeed), is the texts of the same plays as they were first published during Shakespeare's own lifetime, or in the years immediately following his death in 1616.

The text, then, the government would have the British schoolchild read is, in fact, not a text that would have been familiar to Shakespeare's own contemporaries. Take the instance of *Hamlet*. Three texts of a play with that name somewhere in the title (and all attributed to Shakespeare as author) were published within two decades of each other at the beginning of the seventeenth century: individual quarto editions in 1603 and 1604/5 (Q1 and Q2 respectively) and the First Folio text of 1623 (F), as part of Heminge and Condell's edition of the collected works of Shakespeare. All three texts differ substantially from each other. Q1 is a short text, comprising some 2,200 lines. Q2 is the longest version, yielding approximately 3,800 lines. F is about 230 lines shorter than Q2, but also includes some seventy lines not present in that text. But *Hamlet*, in fact, provides just one example of the convoluted history of the process of transmission of Shakespeare's texts. Many of the other plays are equally problematic, and problematic in different ways. The first publication of *The Taming of the Shrew*, for instance, was in the 1623 Folio collection. But almost three decades earlier, in 1594, a play entitled *The Taming of a Shrew* had appeared in print, with no authorial attribution offered on the title page. The relationship between the two texts is complex and, finally, indeterminate: 'A *Shrew* has sometimes been regarded as the source for *The Shrew*; some scholars have believed that both plays derive independently from an earlier play, now lost; it has even been suggested that Shakespeare wrote both plays.'[9]

Where, then, in all of this, is the body of the individual Shakespeare play? How do we deal with this proliferation of early modern Shakespeares? In the opening decades of the present century, the new bibliographers, building on the work of such eighteenth-century Shakespeare editors as Edward Capell and Edmond Malone, essayed a solution to these problems.[10] Drawing on theories of textual transmission developed in the realm of biblical studies by scholars such as Karl Lachmann, the proponents of the new bibliography foregrounded a narrative of textual history which posited a stable, coherent authorial text which had been 'corrupted' in the process of entering the printed state. The morally charged lexicon of the new bibliographers is perhaps not so surprising, given the original provenance of the theories which they deployed. For example, in *Textual and Literary Criticism*, Fredson Bowers writes:

> The most important concern of the textual bibliographer is to guard the purity of the important basic documents of our literature and culture. This is a matter of principle on which there can be no compromise. One can no more permit 'just a little corruption' to pass unheeded in the transmission of our literary heritage than 'just a little sin' was possible in Eden.[11]

The new bibliographers seemed to regard the printed state of a text as a sort of post-lapsarian realm – to be born into print was in some sense necessarily to carry a stigma of corruption. The objective of the new bibliographers was to save such fallen texts and restore them to the wholesome state they had been in immediately when their authors' hands had finished fashioning them. In the process, the wayward text is retrieved and restored to something akin to a state of grace.

The views of the new bibliographers have had a profound impact on the practice of textual editing. The effect of the deployment of their theories in the field of Shakespeare editing has led to the raising of relatively uniform and unitary editions from the multiplicity and polyvocality of the set of original texts from which these modern editions have been compiled. Where multiple contemporary editions of a play exist (as they do in the case of some nineteen plays from the Shakespeare canon), the individual contemporary texts have been sorted, and subjected to a process of conflation and consolidation, whereby a particular copy text is added to (and, sometimes, subtracted from) in order to arrive at the best possible text. As Bowers puts it: 'the immediate concern of textual bibliography is only to recover as exactly as may be the form of the text directly underneath the printed copy'.[12]

One problem with this approach is that 'the text directly underneath the printed copy' is entirely notional, since, in Shakespeare's case, none of these manuscript texts has survived.[13] So the conflationary endeavour is an exercise in attempting to get back to an ideal 'original', but an original of which no direct knowledge can ever be possible. As we have noted elsewhere:

> The object of which we can have direct knowledge, the printed text, is judged to be corrupt by conjectural reference to the object of which we can by definition have no direct knowledge, the uncorrupted (but non-existent) manuscript. The procedure is self-contradictory, since the historical document is being compared with an 'original' that can be speculatively reconstructed only from the evidence of the historical document itself.[14]

The new bibliographic enterprise has been criticised on other grounds also. It presumes, for instance, that, given a set of diverse early modern editions of a particular play, the editor's task is to discover among those texts a single set of 'correct' readings which can (and must) be privileged above all other possibilities. If a line or a speech or an entire scene exists in two or more versions, the editor labours to determine which is the correct form of the text – which is, in Charlton Hinman's words, 'the most authoritative possible [text] of Shakespeare', which is his definitive version 'just as he meant [it] to stand'.[15] Editing becomes, within this regime, an extended process of separating the textual sheep from the textual goats and of shepherding back into the control text any stray sheep which may have wandered off and turned up in the chronologically neighbouring fields of another edition. This process precludes the possibility that more than one reading may, in fact, be admissible. As Gary Taylor writes in *William Shakespeare: A Textual Companion*, under these circumstances, 'faced with two sheep, it is all too easy to insist that one *must* be a goat'.[16]

The dominance of new bibliographic practice in editing Shakespeare has been seriously challenged over the course of the past two decades, initially on the basis of variations on the 'two sheep' (or even three sheep) textual hypothesis. In 1975, Michael Warren submitted a paper to the Modern Language Association's journal (*PMLA*) in which he discussed the relationship between two early texts of *King Lear* – the first quarto edition (Q) printed in 1608 for Nathaniel Butter, and the First Folio text of 1623 (F). *Lear*

had always represented a particularly troublesome case for editors
of Shakespeare. As Stanley Wells notes:

> The most striking [difference between F and Q] is the presence [in
> F] of short passages amounting to more than 100 lines of text which
> are not in the Quarto. The Folio also lacks close on 300 lines which
> *are* in the Quarto; several speeches are differently assigned; and there
> are more than 850 verbal variants, some of them obviously the
> correct version of manifest errors in the Quarto, others offering an
> alternative sense.[17]

The traditional practice of editors had been to combine the two
texts, so that all of the available material was united into a single
entity. Warren, in his paper, suggested an alternative possibility,
arguing that the two texts represented distinct independent versions of the play and proposing that, in fact, Shakespeare had
systematically revised the play so that, far from having one *King
Lear*, we actually have two, each of equal authority. The *King* was
seen, as it were, to have two bodies.

Warren's paper was not well received in 1975. *PMLA* rejected
it; a report on the article from one of the journal's readers con-
cluded: 'This paper ought not to be published anywhere.'[18] Within
five years, however, Steven Urkowitz was advancing a similar argument in his 1980 book *Shakespeare's Revision of King Lear*.
Urkowitz was supported not just by Warren but also by a group
of other Shakespeare scholars, including Gary Taylor, Peter Blayney
and Randall McLeod. In 1982 Blayney further advanced the revisionist cause in his *The Texts of King Lear* and the following year
Taylor and Warren published, as co-editors, *The Division of the
Kingdoms: Shakespeare's Two Versions of King Lear* – a ground-
breaking collection of essays, each drawing out different aspects of
the two text hypothesis.[19]

The revisionist position became enshrined in a major edition of
Shakespeare's works in 1986 when Gary Taylor and Stanley Wells,
as joint general editors, elected to include separate texts of both
versions of *King Lear* in the new edition of the Oxford *Complete
Works*, offering the reader both *The History of King Lear* (based
on the 1608 Quarto text) and *The Tragedy of King Lear* (based
on the 1623 Folio text).[20] Wells declared subsequently, in an article
in *New Theatre Quarterly*, that 'once the hypothesis of revision
is accepted, conflation becomes a logical absurdity . . . I believe
that the conflated text has had its day.'[21]

That the overall effect of the edition was unsettling is evidenced by the reaction which the *Complete Works* encountered on publication. David Bevington, who had himself acted as editor for one of the single volume texts of the Oxford edition, reviewed the project in *Shakespeare Quarterly*. While praising much of the work produced by Wells and Taylor, he professed himself disquieted by 'something that is now awesomely present on the textual scene: the phenomenon of indeterminate Shakespeare', and he opened his review with a parable and a plea:

> A few years ago, when Coca-Cola introduced its ill-starred new Coke with considerable fanfare announcing to a skeptical world that the time had come for a big change, a *New York Times* reporter asked a man on the streets of Atlanta (where Coca-Cola is headquartered) what he thought of the idea. 'They done fixed something that warn't broke!' was his memorable way of putting what so many devoted customers felt. And it pretty well expresses what this devoted reader of Shakespeare feels about the revisionist parts of the new Oxford Shakespeare. . . . Coca-Cola soon admitted its mistake and brought back Classic Coke. Let us hope that the Oxford Press, which has presided so long and with such dignity over the concept of the standard author, will sooner or later bring back Classic Shakespeare.[22]

There is, it must be said, a certain irony in the fact that Bevington's reaction to the *Complete Works* should have taken the particular form that it did. While the Wells and Taylor volume was indeed innovatory and provocative,[23] the one thing which it emphatically did not call into question was Bevington's cherished 'concept of the standard author'. Wells and Taylor may well have effected a distancing of their readers from certain aspects of individual texts, but the centrality of 'Shakespeare' to the entire enterprise was in no way questioned. In fact, if anything, the final effect of the revisionist project generally was to extend to Shakespeare an even greater centrality than he had ever before possessed. As Margreta de Grazia and Peter Stallybrass have noted with regard to the entire revisionist project in a valuable recent article: 'The recognition of multiple texts and variant passages is compromised by a theory of revision that ends up unifying and regulating what it had dispersed and loosened: all intertextual and intratextual variants are claimed in the name of a revising Shakespeare.'[24] De Grazia and Stallybrass further note that, within the revisionist framework, 'each multiple text constitutes a canon in miniature in which the

author's personal and artistic development can be charted from revision to revision'. David Bevington's fears notwithstanding, then, it
is clear that what Wells and Taylor (and the other revisionists)
present is not at all an image of 'indeterminate Shakespeare', since
Shakespeare for the revisionists is, in fact, something very like a
determining principle, a guarantor of authority and meaning – the
fixed and stable point through which a clear relationship among
multiple texts can be drawn.

Coca-Cola's recognition in the 1980s that their 'new formula'
had not been a success and their decision to revert to the tried and
trusted in 'Classic Coke' may well have signalled a victory for the
conservative American palate. But it should be noted here that the
word 'classic', in this context, has a rather odd valence to it. For
the Coca-Cola company was reverting not to its *original* formula
but simply to the penultimate version of that formula. The original Coke had, we remember, famously been so named because
it contained cocaine, and the product had been promoted initially
on the strength of its medicinal value, presented virtually as a 'rare
extraction, that hath only power to disperse all malignant hum-
ours that proceed either of hot, or cold, moist, or windy causes'.[25]
But the long history of the product itself and of the company
which produces, promotes and profits from it is elided in the
narrative of the simple battle between the 'new formula' version
of the product and its supposedly 'classic' predecessor. The difference between the two recent versions of the product is (with all
due deference to The Man On The Streets Of Atlanta and his compatriots) largely insignificant – certainly in the light of the difference between both contemporary incarnations and the original
recipe. The much-heralded return to origins is a return, in effect, to
a misremembered recent past, nostalgically reconstructed as a site
of authenticity. In the process, the deep institutional past is quite
and quietly forgotten.

David Bevington's analogy between the Shakespearian world
and the world of Coca-Cola is, then, as it turns out, quite appos-
ite. The battle between 'Classic Shakespeare' and the Oxford Shakespeare is a battle between variations on the same fundamental
entity: a set of texts all predicated on a single source of meaning
and authority.[26]

Just as the narrative of the free consumer choice between a
new formula Coke and Coca-Cola Classic elides the complex and

extended institutional history of the product on offer, so too does the centring of the business of textual production on a single unitary figure called 'Shakespeare' serve to obscure the institutional history of the production and dissemination of those texts which are united under his name. Ironically, both the new bibliographers and the Oxford editors have been among those who have placed a great deal of emphasis on the excavation and bringing to prominence of the material and institutional conditions of the texts which they have edited. In *On Editing Shakespeare and the Elizabethan Dramatists*, for example, Fredson Bowers contrasts the materialist approach of the bibliographer with the 'unscientific' efforts of the literary critic:

> Bibliography may be said to attack textual problems from the mechanical point of view, using evidence which must deliberately avoid being colored by literary considerations. Non-bibliographical textual criticism works with meanings and literary values. If these last are divorced from all connections with the evidence of the mechanical process that imprinted meaningful symbols on a sheet of paper, no check-rein of fact or probability can restrain the farthest reaches of idle speculation.[27]

In this spirit the new bibliographers initiated the field of 'compositor study', meticulously combing through texts in an effort to unravel the history of, for example, the passage of the First Folio through William and Isaac Jaggard's printing house.[28] Likewise, Wells and Taylor have laid great emphasis on the theatrical context of the plays, stressing their function as performance scripts.[29]

The ultimate effect of such work has been, however, to constellate the material conditions of production, distribution and performance around the unitary figure of Shakespeare, or rather, more accurately, to establish a hierarchy of production and dissemination with Shakespeare at the summit, as the overweening source of meaning and authority. This can be seen, for instance, in the approach of W. W. Greg to the interrelation of the different hands participating in the manuscript copy of *Sir Thomas More*. Hand D, it has been suggested, belongs to Shakespeare. Hand C (which, as it happens, bears a strong resemblance to Hand D) 'worked over various parts of the manuscript, stitching together passages from the others, copying . . . correcting some stage directions, and getting the thing into shape for the actors to work on'.[30] Greg cast Hand C as a 'playhouse functionary' and, as Scott McMillin has observed:

> The model that produces this distinction is the model of literary can-
> onization, which gives the privilege of genius to authors and holds
> those responsible for the material conditions of literature – actors,
> for example, but also printers, scribes, stationers, and paper manufac-
> turers, just to name those whose work Shakespeare would have valued
> – as more or less contemptible.[31]

By contrast with this approach, an alternative view of the process of literary production has been advanced by Jerome J. McGann,
initially in his 1983 *Critique of Modern Textual Criticism*. In the
Critique McGann advances what has since come to be characterised as a 'social theory of texts', arguing that 'Authority is a social
nexus, not a personal possession; and if the authority for specific
literary works is initiated anew for each new work by some specific artist, its initiation takes place in a necessary and integral
historical environment of great complexity.'[32] In *The Textual Condition*, McGann further observes that 'texts are produced and
reproduced under specific social and institutional conditions, and
hence . . . every text, including those that may appear to be purely
private, is a social text'.[33] McGann thus stresses the inextricable
interlacing of the author into a greater social matrix. In McGann's
model, the social nexus serves collaboratively in the process of
generating and disseminating meaning, in contrast to the traditional view which would see the author as the unique source of a
meaning that is carried by the channels of production and distribution, acting merely as subordinate agents of transmission.

Of course, McGann, as a textual critic writing his *Critique* in the
early 1980s, was advancing a theory of authorship and authority which, while at odds with the views of many of his colleagues
in the world of textual scholarship, would have been perfectly
intelligible to other contemporary literary theorists. Some fifteen
years before the *Critique* appeared in print, Roland Barthes had proclaimed, in 'The death of the author', that 'to give a text an Author
is to impose a limit on that text, to furnish it with a final signified,
to close the writing'.[34] Foucault also interrogated the concept of
authorship and the privileging and centralising of the author with
regard to the text in his seminal essay 'What is an author?' Like
Barthes, Foucault saw the invocation of the concept of the author
essentially as the deployment of a strategy of containment, whereby
meaning is delimited, divided and constrained: 'the author does
not precede the works; he is a certain functional principle by which,

in our culture, one limits, excludes, and chooses; in short, by which one impedes the free circulation, the free manipulation, the free composition, decomposition, and recomposition of fiction.'[35]

The pertinence of these remarks to the field of traditional Shakespeare editing should be readily apparent. For the new bibliographers, faced with a plurality of texts all purporting to be incarnations of a single particular work, the objective was to discover within their dispersed parts the single coherent text which Shakespeare truly intended. Once this ideal text was arrived at, all other meanings were to be rigorously excluded. The revisionists, by contrast, admitted the possibility of multiple versions and of a plurality of meanings, but they insisted on referring this multiplicity back always to the unifying figure of Shakespeare, as the single source of the texts' polyvocality. In the case of both the new bibliographers and the revisionists, then, Shakespeare becomes precisely what Foucault has characterised as a functional principle of limitation, exclusion, and choice: Shakespeare is engaged as a means of limiting the field of potential readings, excluding from the set of available meanings those which are deemed not to be truly 'authorial'.

IV

That which withers in the age of mechanical reproduction is the aura of the work of art . . . the technique of reproduction detaches the reproduced object from the domain of tradition. By making many reproductions it substitutes a plurality of copies for a unique existence.[36]

It is a mark of the essential unity of approach of the new bibliographers and the revisionists that the latter, while setting themselves up in opposition to their bibliographic predecessors, should have accepted virtually without question certain of the new bibliographers' foundational assumptions, including, most notably, the sorting of the earliest Shakespeare texts into sets of 'good' and 'bad' quartos.[37] The 'good' quartos are those which can be considered 'authentically' 'Shakespearian', by contrast with the 'bad' quartos, which are characterised as being imperfect, pirated copies of the true Shakespeare originals (patched together, in the narrative of 'memorial reconstruction', from memory by actors who had participated in performances of the plays).[38] As long ago as 1982, Random Cloud (Randall McLeod) criticised this practice of sorting texts into morally charged categories, observing in 'The marriage of good and bad Quartos' that 'employing moral categories in textual work obliges one to choose: to reject Evil once and for all, and to strike out toward Goodness (and toward Shakespeare, who is a Good writer)'.[39] McLeod registers here the imposition of constraints on the greater circulation of meaning which Foucault sees as being characteristic of the author function generally. The invocation of the concept of authorial authenticity serves as a principle for privileging one set of texts, to the exclusion of others.

Jonathan Goldberg has noted the intersection of the concerns of post-revisionist textual theorists with the parameters of the general post-structuralist project, observing that 'post-structuralism and the new textual criticism coincide, historically – and theoretically. Both have called the criterion of authorial intention into question, thereby detaching the supposed sovereign author from texts open to and constituted by a variety of interventions.'[40] The implications of this intersection have yet to be fully appreciated. A clear imperative now exists for the working through of a new conception of editorial and of critical practice in the light of this interconnected theoretical framework. If we are indeed to pursue the pathway which Goldberg charts as the 'detaching [of] the supposed sovereign author from texts open to and constituted by a variety of interventions', then clearly we must make a break not only with the conflationary texts of the new bibliographers but also with the author-centred texts of the revisionists. This requires the abandonment of such morally charged notions as the division of the kingdom of writing into good and bad texts. In the case of the 'Shakespeare' canon, all of the relevant texts must be opened up to analytical scrutiny, as historical documents of interest and importance in their own right.[41]

To propose turning attention to these texts is not to call for a Bowersesque redemptive mission whereby the bad quartos, having long fallen by the wayside, will now be lifted up into glory. Nor is the point of the exercise to reverse the value judgement traditionally passed on these texts by suggesting that, far from being 'bad' texts, they are in fact just as good as their supposedly authentic fellows. The point is, rather, to move *beyond* the application of the criterion of value to the project of literary scholarship, and to continue the process, most recently foregrounded by new historicism/cultural materialism, of questioning the very notion of a category of literature which is distinct and separable from all other forms of writing.[42]

We have come a long way, then, from the letter-waving, jeering-demotic assurance of the British Prime Minister and his Cabinet colleagues, who would insist on making Shakespeare a mandatory part of every British schoolchild's education. For the 'Battle of the Bard' entails more than just a debate over the ways in which Shakespeare may (or may not) be interpreted, but extends to the question of what constitutes not just that centralising force labelled Shakespeare but also the very materiality of the texts united under that identity.

As a final thought, we might do well to remember that politicians are, in any case, notoriously liable to be caught wrong-footed when it comes to invoking Shakespeare. In the Clarence Thomas confirmation hearings in the USA in 1992, one of the senators on the committee set up to examine the allegations of sexual harassment brought against Thomas by his former co-worker, Anita Hill, proclaimed, for the benefit of the committee, a recitation of the 'Good name in man and woman' speech from *Othello*, apparently unaware that the speech was that of a character described in the 'Names of the Actors' in the First Folio as 'a Villaine'. Perhaps he, like his counterparts in the UK, should have read his texts of *Othello* more carefully.

Notes

1 From Samuel Johnson's edition of *Shakespeare* (London, 1765), p. lvii.
2 See Allan Bloom, *The Closing of the American Mind* (New York, Simon and Schuster, 1987).
3 Terry Eagleton, *Literary Theory: An Introduction* (Oxford, Basil Blackwell, 1983).
4 Patrick Wintour and Stephen Bates, 'Major goes back to the old values', *The Guardian* (9 October 1993), p. 6. There is a certain odd irony at the heart of Major's parodic adoption of this 'demotic' register – he himself has few academic qualifications and is not university-educated, a fact much trumpeted on his accession to the leadership of the Conservative Party and during the course of the 1992 General Election, when he was presented as the embodiment of a modern, democratic, 'class-less' conservatism.
5 The letter was originally drafted by a group of twenty-one professors

of English, including Alan Sinfield, Lisa Jardine and Catherine Belsey. It was published in *The Times Higher Education Supplement* (20 November 1992). Subsequently, the letter was circulated to English departments throughout the country and it garnered a further five hundred signatures. The original letter, together with a list of the further signatories, is reprinted in the *THES* (11 June 1993), p. 15. This same issue of the *THES* also includes a 'Perspective special', consisting of a selection of articles on 'the forces fighting in the field of English', p. 17.

6 *The Observer* (22 August 1993), pp. 37–8. For further articles of a similar kind, see 'To see or not to see', 'Brush up your Shakespeare' and 'Bard folk' in *The Guardian* (2) (13 October 1994), pp. 2–4 and 'Was Shakespeare really a genius' in *The Guardian* (2) (8 March 1995), pp. 10–11.

7 See Jonathan Dollimore and Alan Sinfield, eds, *Political Shakespeare: New Essays in Cultural Materialism* (Manchester, Manchester University Press, 1985; second edition, 1994); John Drakakis, ed., *Alternative Shakespeares* (London, Methuen, 1985; new edition forthcoming); Graham Holderness, ed., *The Shakespeare Myth* (Manchester, Manchester University Press, 1988); Gary Taylor, *Reinventing Shakespeare* (New York, Weidenfeld and Nicolson, 1989; Oxford, Oxford University Press, 1991); Michael Bristol, *Shakespeare's America, America's Shakespeare* (London, Routledge, 1990); Jean I. Marsden, ed., *The Appropriation of Shakespeare: Post-Renaissance Reconstructions of the Works and the Myth* (Hemel Hempstead, Harvester Wheatsheaf, 1991); and Michael Dobson, *The Making of a National Poet: Shakespeare, Adaptation and Authority, 1660–1769* (Oxford, Clarendon, 1992).

8 Ann Thompson, Thomas L. Berger, A. R. Braunmuller, Philip Edwards and Lois Potter, *Which Shakespeare?: A User's Guide to Editions* (Milton Keynes, Open University Press, 1992).

9 Stanley Wells and Gary Taylor, eds, *William Shakespeare: The Complete Works Compact Edition* (Oxford, Clarendon, 1988), p. 25.

10 On the significance of Malone's edition as a watershed text in the editorial tradition, see Margreta de Grazia's compelling and persuasive *Shakespeare Verbatim: The Reproduction of Authenticity and the 1790 Apparatus* (Oxford, Clarendon, 1991).

11 Fredson Bowers, *Textual and Literary Criticism* (Cambridge, Cambridge University Press, 1966), p. 8.

12 Fredson Bowers, *Bibliography and Textual Criticism* (Oxford, Clarendon, 1964), p. 8.

13 The one possible exception is the 'Hand D' contribution to the manuscript of *The Book of Sir Thomas More*, but even this is questionable – see Scott McMillin, *The Elizabethan Theatre and The Book of Sir Thomas More* (Ithaca, Cornell, 1987), especially pp. 135–59.

14 Graham Holderness and Bryan Loughrey, 'Text and stage: Shakespeare,

bibliography, and performance studies' in *New Theatre Quarterly*, 9:34 (1993), pp. 187–8.

15 Charlton Hinman, *The First Folio of Shakespeare* (New York, Norton, 1968), p. xi. This text is, in itself, a most extraordinary example of conflation in action. Setting out to produce a facsimile edition of the 1623 Folio, Hinman quickly abandoned the established practice of reproducing one of the particular extant copies of the text, opting instead to produce a text which consisted of an assemblage of the best pages drawn from thirty of the eighty copies of the First Folio held in the collection of the Folger Shakespeare Library in Washington DC. He thus 'sought', as he observes, 'to give concrete representation to what [had] hitherto been only a theoretical entity, an abstraction: *the* First Folio', p. xxii.

16 Gary Taylor, 'General introduction' in Stanley Wells, Gary Taylor, John Jowett and William Montgomery, *William Shakespeare: A Textual Companion* (Oxford, Clarendon, 1987), p. 18.

17 Stanley Wells, 'The once and future King Lear' in Gary Taylor and Michael Warren, eds, *The Division of the Kingdoms: Shakespeare's Two Versions of King Lear* (Oxford, Clarendon, 1983), p. 6.

18 Quoted in Taylor, *Reinventing Shakespeare*, p. 358. Warren did, however, present a version of the paper at the World Shakespeare Congress in Washington DC, in the following year. For this version of the paper, see 'Quarto and Folio *King Lear* and the interpretation of Albany and Edgar' in David Bevington and Jay L. Halio, eds, *Shakespeare: Pattern of Excelling Nature: Shakespeare Criticism in Honor of America's Bicentennial* (Newark, University of Delaware Press, 1978), pp. 95–107.

19 Urkowitz has continued to work on the revision issue. See, in particular, ' "Well-sayd olde mole": Burying three *Hamlets* in modern editions' in Georgianna Ziegler, ed., *Shakespeare Study Today* (New York, AMS, 1986), pp. 37–70; and ' "Brother, can you spare a paradigm?": textual generosity and the printing of Shakespeare's multiple-text plays by contemporary editors', *Critical Survey*, 7:3 (1995), pp. 292–8. See also Random Cloud (Randall McLeod), 'The marriage of good and bad quartos', *Shakespeare Quarterly*, 33:4 (1982), pp. 421–31. For a comprehensive review of the theory and history of revision, see Grace Ioppolo, *Revising Shakespeare* (Cambridge, Mass., Harvard University Press, 1991).

20 Three years later Michael Warren published his *Complete King Lear 1608–1623* (Berkeley, University of California Press, 1989), consisting of three discrete photoduplicated texts: Q1 (1608), Q2 (1619), F and a parallel text of Q1 and F. In 1991, Paul Bertram and Bernice Kliman published *The Three-Text Hamlet: Parallel Texts of the First and Second Quartos and First Folio* (New York, AMS, 1993).

21 Stanley Wells, 'Theatricalizing Shakespeare's text', *New Theatre Quarterly*, 7:26 (1991), p. 186.
22 David Bevington, 'Determining the indeterminate: The Oxford Shakespeare', *Shakespeare Quarterly*, 38:4 (1987), pp. 501–2.
23 Or rather 'volumes', since the *Complete Works* was packaged in a variety of different formats, ranging from the single volume to the 'compact edition', to an elaborately bound three-volume boxed set aimed at the book club market.
24 Margreta de Grazia and Peter Stallybrass, 'The materiality of the Shakespearian text', *Shakespeare Quarterly*, 44:3 (1993), p. 279. For a response to this article, see Graham Holderness, Bryan Loughrey and Andrew Murphy, ' "What's the matter?" Shakespeare and textual theory', *Textual Practice*, 9:1 (1995), pp. 93–119.
25 Ben Jonson, *Volpone* in *Three Comedies*, ed. Michael Jamieson (Harmondsworth, Penguin, 1966), II.i.91–3.
26 To say this is not at all to slight the very real and worthy achievements of the Wells and Taylor edition, which has provided the stimulation for much valuable discussion and debate within the realm of textual scholarship since its first appearance just a decade ago.
27 Fredson Bowers, *On Editing Shakespeare and the Elizabethan Dramatists* (Philadelphia, University of Pennsylvania Library, 1955), p. 35. The tone of Bowers's comment on literary critics is characteristic. Elsewhere, in *Textual and Literary Criticism* he writes: 'it is still a current oddity that many a literary critic has investigated the past ownership and mechanical condition of his second-hand automobile, or the pedigree and training of his dog, more thoroughly than he has looked into the qualifications of the text on which his critical theories rest', p. 5.
28 For a good example of the great early summation of such work, see W. W. Greg's *The Shakespeare First Folio: Its Bibliographic and Textual History* (Oxford, Clarendon, 1955).
29 It is a mark of this theatrical emphasis that the Oxford texts are heavily supplemented with speculative stage directions and that the visual representation of the act and scene divisions has been diminished in order to suggest, as far as possible, a single continuous performance text.
30 McMillin, *The Elizabethan Theatre*, p. 154.
31 *Ibid.*
32 Jerome J. McGann, *A Critique of Modern Textual Criticism* (Charlottesville, University of Virginia Press, 1992; first published University of Chicago Press, 1983), p. 21.
33 Jerome J. McGann, *The Textual Condition* (Princeton, Princeton University Press, 1991), p. 21.

34 Roland Barthes, 'The death of the author' in *Image Music Text*, trans. Stephen Heath (London, Flamingo, 1984), p. 147.

35 Michel Foucault, 'What is an author?' in Paul Rabinow, ed., *The Foucault Reader* (New York, Pantheon, 1984), pp. 118–19.

36 Walter Benjamin, 'The work of art in the age of mechanical reproduction' in *Illuminations*, trans. Harry Zohn (New York, Schocken, 1969), p. 221.

37 For the origins of this division, see Alfred W. Pollard, *Shakespeare Folios and Quartos: A Study in the Bibliography of Shakespeare's Plays, 1594–1685* (London, Methuen, 1909), especially p. 80.

38 For the first outlining of a theory of memorial reconstruction, see the introduction to W. W. Greg's edition of *The Merry Wives of Windsor* (Oxford, Clarendon, 1910), pp. xxvii–xli.

39 McLeod, 'The marriage of good and bad quartos', p. 421.

40 Jonathan Goldberg, 'Textual properties', *Shakespeare Quarterly*, 37:2 (1986), p. 213. McGann has also noted this intersection, observing in the Preface to the 1992 edition of his *Critique* that: 'Whereas textual theory had previously been the province and interest of a small group of scholars who generally confined themselves to technical and editorial studies it is now one of the liveliest arenas of general critical studies. Theory, textual scholarship, and interpretation no longer operate in their separate but (un)equal worlds', p. xxii.

41 Work of this kind has already been undertaken by a number of scholars. See in particular Annabel Patterson's chapter on the texts of *Henry V* in *Shakespeare and the Popular Voice* (Oxford, Blackwell, 1989) and Leah Marcus, 'Levelling Shakespeare: local customs and local texts', *Shakespeare Quarterly*, 42:2 (1991), pp. 168–78. See also forthcoming work by Marcus on orality and writing in the various texts of *Hamlet*.

42 See, for example, Alan Sinfield and Jonathan Dollimore's 'Foreword' on cultural materialism in their Manchester University Press Cultural Politics series, where they note that, in cultural materialist analysis, '"high culture" is taken as one set of signifying practices among others'.

2

✤

Re-loading the canon: Shakespeare and the study guides

✤

Simon Barker

This chapter is a version of a paper delivered at the Shakespeare and the Teaching of English conference held at the University of Central Lancashire in April 1993. The conference sought to bring teachers with an interest in Shakespeare from the compulsory school sector together with those from higher education in order to initiate a dialogue over a range of issues affecting the teaching of the work of the single most important figure of the traditional canon. The aims and scope of the conference were impressive, partly because these two groups of teachers rarely meet (although they often claim a knowledge of each other's work) and partly because the proceedings were informed and defamiliarised by the presence of teachers from non-British cultures and traditions, as well as by teachers of drama.

The impact of the critical theory of the last twenty years or so upon teaching at all levels was apparent in both the formal and informal discussions, questioning the relationship between Shakespeare and issues of nationalism and gender, canon and methodology. Although these issues have long combined to interrogate the principles governing the teaching of Shakespeare's texts (and even whether they should be taught at all), the conference was also influenced by a range of topical, passing references to Shakespeare in the media and by the more sustained concerns of government policy. Public debate over the provision of a National Curriculum was thus linked to the Major government's curious 'Back to Basics' moral/pedagogic crusade which advocated a restoration of standard English, the literary classics, good manners and some rather bizarre visions of a pastoral England 'at peace with itself', a peace immediately interpreted for many attending the conference in terms of the battle the government was waging with schoolteachers over the imposition of compulsory testing for school students at frequent intervals in their careers.

A number of these topical references may be found in what follows, ranging from Norman Tebbit's memorable testing of the loyalty to the Crown of the families of colonial immigrants against their loyalty to national cricket teams, to Kenneth Branagh's recently released and controversial film version of *Henry V*.

Although some of these topical references will have faded with time since the conference, my feeling is that they will only have been replaced by a new but similar matrix of popular allusion, governmental decree and nationalistic fantasy, so the reader should be able to supply alternatives – evidence of the continuing, pervasive nature of 'Shakespeare' in the twentieth century, ranging, as it were, from educational Kitchener to contemporary *kitsch*.

The paper started with a quotation usually associated with a more liberating discourse, that of the relationship between gender and identity in the Shakespeare text:

> If it be true that good wine needs no bush 'tis true that a good play needs no epilogue. Yet to good wine they do use good bushes; and good plays prove the better by the help of good epilogues. What a case am I in then, that am neither a good epilogue nor can insinuate with you in the behalf of a good play?
>
> (*As You Like It*, V.v.200–4)

The boy actor's epilogue to Shakespeare's *As You Like It* forges a link between the market and the aesthetic; a link which is never far away from the dogma of the present Conservative government. In this context it is not surprising to see that students at work in schools and in higher education looking for introductions to Shakespeare's plays are subject to an expanding and fiercely competitive market in study guides, specialised editions of the plays and such eye-catching titles as *How to Study a Shakespeare Play*.[1] It might be said that the range of this material has expanded in direct proportion to the contraction in the resource bases of the institutions in which most of these students study. We might even look

back with something approaching nostalgia to those innocent days
when copies of Coles, Brodie's or Longman's notes circulated
amongst middle-class schoolchildren as a kind of forbidden fruit,
supplemented at college or university level by things like Macmillan's Casebook series. In the present climate a quick visit to the
bookshop reveals shelf upon groaning shelf of this material, and
my idea here is to raise some questions about what I find significant in the relationship between these guides and what I shall
loosely call 'critical theory' in the general context of teaching early
modern culture. My particular concern is, of course, how we should
see this relationship in terms of questions about 'curriculum and
canon' in view of the government's continuing rightward march
towards a particularly strident form of cultural nationalism.

First I need a kind of taxonomy of the study guides – one which
roughly corresponds to the various sectors at work in Shakespeare
scholarship and teaching. *Brodie's Notes* and Longman's *York Notes*
series are still going strong (even if *Coles Notes* have retreated in
the face of competition to the shores of their native Canada), and
along with other series are aimed primarily at GCSE and A level
students. Such series seem quite adequately to have survived something approaching parody in the public imagination, and have
easily resisted the efforts of academics concerned to expose their
Leavisite underpinning. Alongside these long-established series has
grown a range of imitations, together with special editions of the
plays themselves and altogether new kinds of guide, usually tailored
specifically to Shakespeare's fortunes in the ever-changing curriculum – a site of ideological contest currently equated with Tory
ideas on 'returning to basics' in terms of English language teaching.

More often it seems to me that the Bard's fate is linked to whatever kind of disaffected chatter the latest Secretary of State for Education has picked up at the golf club the previous weekend. This
is the work of a *laudator temporis acti*: nationalistic, uncompro-
mising, hierarchical and scornful of those at work in the cultural
cost-centres of secondary education. All this re-affirms a public
role for Shakespeare and has produced something of a crisis in the
schools.

Beyond the sets of notes produced for school students, the 'How
to Study' volumes form a second category of study guide, are
generically more varied and are principally aimed at the non-
compulsory sector. Here it is indeed possible to trace the impact

of 'critical theory', though sometimes by default. Embarrassed by theory, but disinclined to ignore the work of the last twenty years or so, these books make a rather insignificant adjustment to theory's terminology. The authors of these kinds of texts are like atheist drivers who give way to members of the clergy at junctions – just in case there's something in it after all. But these texts really supply little beyond a theoretical gloss to what is basically new critical analysis. There is also a delayed reaction: theory is still 'structuralism', and although it has to be 'worked with', it is finally wrestled to the ground in the name of 'common sense'.

Thirdly, there is a significant and in many ways respectable enough project in which the progress of theory is more clearly recorded. Notable in this category is the collection of critical essays or extracts – characteristically edited these days by one of the names we associate with the term 'cultural materialism'.[2]

Knowledge, like history, does not all come at once, so I am by no means against some aspects of study guide publishing since it is easy to see that the central concerns of much of the last fifteen years of Shakespearian criticism – those of gender, class, race and ideology – are being made accessible to a wider and younger audience.

However, leaving aside books such as *How to Study a Shakespeare Play*, which fall into my second category, I want to concentrate on the quiet collusion between the kinds of student guide aimed at school students and those which specifically marshal developments in theory for students in higher education. Where one might have hoped for dialogue and influence as a result of the high hopes expressed for an exchange of views between teachers in the compulsory sector and in higher education when some of us were 're-reading English' and going to Literature Teaching Politics conferences in the heady days of the early 1980s, we find instead a curious mutual commitment to a traditional canon, sadly demonstrating how little impact has been made by those critics who sought to redefine not only the canon but the whole category of 'Literature' itself.[3]

Taking the National Curriculum models first, an optimistic view would be that the radical work on early modern culture has effected something of a revolution in the politics of Shakespearian criticism – the methodologies we employ and the assumptions we challenge – and that this has affected and even transformed the politics of

Shakespeare teaching in the secondary school. This is an uneven terrain since it is still the case that any number of National Curriculum books reinforce notions of plot and character, Shakespeare's unique grasp of a timeless and causal human nature, his overriding commitment to a national identity and the usual idealised view of the English Renaissance which we might associate with the work of critics like E. M. W. Tillyard. Shakespeare's role in determining Englishness rolls on – timelessly. Yet, just occasionally, it is possible to find some unease, some subversive strands of historicism that would have been quite unthinkable a couple of decades ago. There are guides for young students that introduce ideas of the materiality of Shakespeare's theatre, emphasise the uncertainty of the times in which he lived and generally resist the kind of 'Golden Age' view of the Renaissance which was for a long time the orthodox one. Some throw in, and not just for good measure, an acknowledgement that although Shakespeare was top dog he was by no means the only dramatist writing at the time.

In January 1993 *The Daily Telegraph* gave a summary of examiners' alleged unease at the influence of radical literary theory:

> For the first time, 'A'-level examiners have expressed concern that the literary theories of Left-wing academics are influencing the way pupils are being taught English literature in schools. They said: 'some candidates seemed convinced that every piece of writing must have some hidden meaning which is very different from what the words actually say, and that this meaning will usually be the expression of a political protest of some kind. The fact that this approach was typical of groups of candidates from particular schools suggests that it derived from the way they had been taught.'[4]

This is evidence of debate within Shakespeare teaching at the secondary level and whilst it is true that examinations often shape this teaching, and A level questions were exposed long ago, it is also true that the space given to project work in GCSE has created some opportunities for radical teachers to explore some really alternative Shakespeares – and against the tremendous odds (financial and ideological) described by Nigel Wheale in *Shakespeare and the Changing Curriculum*:

> The English political élite has cynically administered the decline of public sector education in response to short-term budgetary objectives and for its own narrow ideological reasons. At the same time it

has insulated itself from consequent damage through use of private education and the most privileged areas of the university system. And let's be clear: Shakespeare is expensive to teach, because our pupils need to spend time with the language and conventions that are now quite alien . . . it is not fanciful to imagine a division of cultural knowledge that will widen, as the privileged insist on knowing what they choose to term their heritage, and which they can afford to internalize, while the rest of us are left to cope with life skills and contemporary studies. The continuing divisive effects of the English class-cum-education system will not be solved by the National Curriculum proposals.[5]

I have to assume that these 'school points' are of concern for those of us active in degree work, favouring a pedagogy that proceeds from what is known to what is knowable. The alternative is a complacency which idealises our teaching against the cultural and ideological preparation that students have had before matriculation. And even if our fantasies were true, I suspect that they will not be in a few years' time.

By comparison with what is on the agenda being established by the present government, the *Cox Report* seems today a conciliatory document, acknowledging something of the accumulated challenges to Shakespeare's universality that have been made by teachers in the name of multi-culturalism, taking, perhaps as I do, the word 'universal' to mean global as well as transhistorical. The report remarked in 1989:

Many teachers believe that Shakespeare's work conveys universal values, and that his language expresses rich and subtle meanings beyond that of any other English writer. Other teachers point out that evaluations of Shakespeare have varied from one historical period to the next, and they argue that pupils should be encouraged to think critically about his status in the canon.[6]

Despite the continuing efforts of schoolteachers in offering a critique of the content of the new curriculum while at the same time having to oppose the quite odious introduction of systems of testing in the schools (an issue which threatens to make teachers the next group of workers to be arguably criminalised for their dissent), a knowledge of Shakespeare still seems set to qualify, along perhaps with Norman Tebbit's cricket loyalties, as a test of citizenship in a government effort at redefining the equation between education and Englishness which sets Kingman and Cox alongside Arnold and Newbolt. By comparison with the present government's 'philosophy' the position taken by these education-alists and their reports seems rather more liberal than is acknow-ledged by some sections of the left.[7] I certainly do not want to seem like an apologist for the *Cox Report*, but it is true that the situ-ation has worsened significantly since 1989. It is a measure of this that even Cox himself, notorious in the late 1960s for his reaction-ary *Black Papers*, recently remarked in *The Times*/Channel 4 lec-ture that

> The danger is now from the right-wingers. They want to return to the so-called golden days of the 1950s or the 1930s. How have the extreme rightwingers managed to take over education? In July 1991 Kenneth Clarke, then the education secretary, removed from their posts the chairmen and chief executives of the National Curriculum Council and Assessment Council. They were men with consider-able experience of educational administration. They were replaced by David Pascall, an oil executive who had once worked in Margaret Thatcher's policy unit at No. 10, and Lord Griffiths of Fforestfach, previously her policy adviser on education. Both had strong links with the rightwing Centre for Policy Studies, a think-tank with frankly absurd views about how English should be taught.[8]

My real concern is not so much with schoolteachers, or even some of the publications aimed at their students, but with a dis-continuity announced in the direction taken by some of us work-ing in the higher education sector – in our teaching and publishing – and specifically in our relations (or lack of relations) with those teaching in the compulsory sector.

This is partly exemplified in the many new series of critical essays, but also by any number of broadly radical guides for under-graduate students. Our project is, of course, very different from that outlined by Cox in his interview with Susan Leach in her book *Shakespeare in the Classroom*. Leach explained that Cox had

> four main reasons for wanting Shakespeare in the National Curric-ulum: first, the belief that the kind of 'great' literature written by Shakespeare encompasses wisdom; second, that 'these great works' are part of our cultural heritage, are central to our culture, and that every child has the right to be introduced to them; third, that Shake-speare 'uses language in a way beyond that of any other writer, and his language has been influential beyond that of any other writer.' Lastly, that Shakespeare has greater insight into human character

than other writers. Additional reasons are that the history of the development of the English language is intimately bound up with Shakespeare's language.

As Leach remarks:

> a plethora of questions is provoked by these views: Whose culture? What wisdom? Who defined it as wisdom? In what ways are these works central to our culture? What does Professor Cox mean by cultural heritage – the heritage of which people? How has this language of Shakespeare been influential? The juxtaposition of notions of 'cultural heritage', 'birthright', 'greatness' and Standard English imply their own ideological provenance and, at a time of anxieties about standards, ideas of national identity and access to a universally understood version of English, indicate a paternalist, establishment perspective on contemporary challenges.[9]

In response to these kinds of question the theoretical influences of the last twenty years or so have produced a new script, so to speak, which, as far as some guides are concerned, involves those ideological questions of gender, class, race and ideology that I mentioned before. But the characters remain the same: Shakespeare is still top dog, surrounded by the familiar entourage of Danish Princes, assorted English and Scottish Kings, star-crossed lovers and the occasional comic turn.

It may be that this is the right way to proceed, working slowly from the familiar to the obscure. Yet, in another way, these guides and collections simply mimic the established canon. It might even be said that they simply occupy the ground already given by the *Cox Report* in its assertions about 'evaluation' and 'history'.

What has been lost for undergraduates – and undoubtedly for school students as well – is the sheer force of the debate about Shakespeare, the canon and Englishness that seemed to promise so much a few years ago.[10] The kind of literary historiography that quite seriously seemed to challenge the canon itself seems to have been reduced to the familiar and surely, in the end, rather facile remarks about Shakespeare's appearance on credit cards and beermats.

I say this not because I don't enjoy a little Bard-bashing myself (and if I drink a pint of Flowers Beer – I'm always careful to eat the beermat afterwards), but because this seems sometimes to be all that is left of a project which at one time announced plans for

a quite fundamental shift in the cultural topography of the early
modern. And, if this is the case, then it is no wonder that the kind
of Tory dream referred to in the early 1990s by Simon Shepherd
has a very real chance of succeeding, combining as it does the
new-right fiscal with the old-right philosophy of heroes and heritage. Shepherd has recalled the now infamous *Late Show* discussion in 1988 in which

> the then secretary of State for education, one Kenneth Baker, had a
> dream, a dream in which Shakespeare was central to the curriculum
> and chunks of bardic verse were memorized in tiny heads. Shakspere
> [*sic*] learnt by rote: a cultural recipe for Tory civilisation. It's a tasty
> model of the individual mind's relationship to central authority. . . .
>   The politician's academic fantasy is ferociously underpinned by a
> systematic reduction in educational budgets, with consequent demoli-
> tion of staffing and resources provision. The material cut-back creates
> the problems to which the fantasy of rote learning becomes a 'feas-
> ible' solution. If chunks of text are learnt by heart who needs whole
> books, let alone new ones?[11]

How accurate this dystopian view was in the context of the government's contention that only some classes of pupils (class being the
operative word) would study a whole Shakespeare play, while others
would merely study what my historian friends call 'gobbets'.

It is not that I am not one of the many admirers of Graham
Holderness's *The Shakespeare Myth* – but I am also aware of the
possibility of Shakespeare studies being reduced to a rather casual
acknowledgement of 'Shakespeare as cultural icon' and that, if this
is the case, and the debate continues along these attractive but easy
lines, then views such as those advanced by Baker on *The Late
Show* will ultimately triumph.[12] For these reasons it seems to me
that there remains some purchase in the idea of revitalising a project that would seek to subvert the canonised *nomenclature* that is
almost irresistibly linked to the kinds of cultural value that are advanced by the conservative educationalists with respect to writers
of the early modern period. I see this as the most decisive of a
number of deliberate acts of transgression in terms of the contours
that map out the cultural topography of the early modern.

Clearly we need to re-load the Shakespearian canon itself.
Although it might be argued that Shakespeare is in many ways too
far gone, too saturated with the ethic of nationalism (and much
else) to be redeemed, it is also the case that those in charge of

dreaming up the kind of Shakespearian landscape fit for the student heroes of a triumphant post-Thatcher Toryism are certainly very cautious in the choice of plays for the curriculum. For those of us who still have a little choice as to what we teach there is work to be done with texts beyond the established entourage of plays such as *Julius Caesar, A Midsummer Night's Dream* and *Romeo and Juliet* which so happily coincide with current Tory thinking on the state, on class and on the family. Or if we work in sectors where specific texts are already prescribed in order to maintain the health of the subject then we can learn new ways with them. I agree with Isobel Armstrong that 'it is not really necessary to ditch the category of literature and abandon Shakespeare just because they are fetishized by liberal humanists and manipulated by an élitist ideology'.[13]

And I also applaud, quite literally, the work of theatre groups like Cheek by Jowl and the English Shakespeare Company which have demonstrated the sense of Armstrong's remark by producing some really quite alternative Shakespeares in a medium which for a long time was used as an ideological stick to beat back the claims of theory, rubbishing its methodologies by showing how 'obviously' Shakespeare demonstrated timeless verities when his work was presented in its 'proper' environment – on the stage.

Yet there is also the more familiar 'line of value' which has condemned Shakespeare's contemporaries to the seeming backwaters of Deptford while the Bard himself goes swanning up the Avon. There is another environment for Shakespeare that is achieved by abolishing that particular category of literature which ignores the local conditions under which Shakespeare's plays were produced. In other works, it is clear that he wrote in the context of a vastly complicated theatrical institution in which a number of hands were at work, as Douglas Bruster has recently shown so eloquently in *Drama and the Market in the Age of Shakespeare*.[14] My only problem with this approach is that, although it gives fruitful airing to the kind of running commentary made on Shakespeare's plays by his contemporaries, it also hints, as the boy actor in *As You Like It* does, of 'the marketplace' and of 'competition', and there is a danger that the Tories, sensing 'market forces' at work in the actual production of early modern plays, might produce a new framework in which to teach Shakespeare. Beyond the present absurdities of 'timeless verities' and the Shakespeare text

as guarantee of a form of 'Quality Assurance' in terms of the
teaching of the English language, we might find Shakespeare newly
'taken on board', but only, of course, if there is a 'level playing field'
for the Bard and his competitors. Of the traditional 'ringfencing'
of Shakespeare, government ministers would have to say 'enough
is enough' since, as we know ('at the end of the day'), this is the
kind of newspeak that passes for political discourse these days
among those very politicians who are so anxious to halt a seeming
decline in the use of the English language. One is tempted to ask
whether this is the same group of people which says that the
working class speaks in clichés. Whose language, we must wonder, is the more impoverished?

This nightmare aside, and to examine the issue in another way,
I want to explain what happened when a group of my students
looked at some recent criticism of *Henry V*. I have written elsewhere about this group's reaction to a tantalising misprint in the
opening pages of Donald G. Watson's recent book on Shakespeare's early history plays where reference is made to the Arden
edition of *King Henry III*. Although one member of the group of
final-year students to which I brought this remarkable discovery
claimed to have been reading the play in bed the night before, an
interesting discussion arose concerning the kinds of cultural assumption that would help define the reception of a new Shakespeare play.[15] The group's speculation was informed by its general
reading in literary theory, that 'applied' specifically to the history
plays and upon reactions to the occasional attribution of fragments
of verse to Shakespeare. The students argued that the authentica-
tion of a new play by Shakespeare would clearly be an issue of public concern, guaranteed to claim the attention of the mass media
as something of national moment at the very least. If the group
was right, then this public and national sense of Shakespeare would
inevitably shape interpretation of the newly discovered play, placing
it firmly in the hands of the right. Despite this, there was intense
speculation over the possibility of an undiscovered play that would
be so radical that it would undermine the dominant cultural values
attached to Shakespeare.

It was a group well versed in the dynamics of critical theory and
so, turning back to the more familiar *Henry V*, it had begun to
look at critical issues which would remove the play from the value
assumptions they had found in the *York Notes* series which had

stated that 'One of the things the play does, then, is to arouse and focus feelings of patriotism. National feeling is linked to war, and the patriotism is military.'[16]

The students had justifiably asked, in their search for the kind of aesthetic judgement suggested here, whether they had *necessarily* to end up with such a unproblematic and univocal reading of *Henry V* as part of a nationalist symbolic order. On whose behalf does such a reading work, and is there anything in the text that works against such a reading?

They had examined the old historicism established by critics such as E. M. W. Tillyard, Wilson Knight and others, which conjured this particular image of the Elizabethan era as one of organic cohesion rendered through a hierarchical apprehension of the world by participating subjects in a kind of 'Golden Age' of history and literary production. They had also brought themselves up to date with arguments concerning the relationship between 'new historicism' and 'cultural materialism' by looking at Hugh Grady's book *The Modernist Shakespeare.*[17] Here they had discovered the revealing notion that in the United States British 'cultural materialism' was defined against the given American model of new historicism as a 'family relation' which held overtly political credentials that the 'family' clearly took exception to. They had weighed up Grady's remark that 'British cultural materialism has roots in an activist British Left that give it different qualities, different strengths and weaknesses, from the much more academically orientated American new historicism', and that 'The connections to a political Left bring with them, along with passion and commitment, occasional suggestions of the familiar Left vices of dogmatism and sectarianism.' By contrast, it seems 'There is a sense of passion and commitment quite different from, say, Greenblatt's personal but unpolitical accents.'[18]

It was difficult to think of Greenblatt's work as either personal or unpolitical, but, concluding that issues of race, class and gender had seemingly disappeared in the USA, the students decided that they were against the kind of politics of power outlined in new historicist readings – the sort of deeply pessimistic 'containment' reading which presented subversion as a regenerating *product* of power and left the reader simply to admire its smooth aesthetic.

Instead, the group had worked through critical accounts of Elizabethan historiography and questions of bibliographical accuracy

to discover the instability of the fixed artefact we know as *Henry
V* – given the disparities between the Folio and the Quarto. An
examination of the function of the Chorus in the play led the students to look at the kinds of assumption that have been made about
the relationship between the early modern spectator and the theatre
as a place of artifice and convention in terms of the materiality
of work itself, forging for the audience the link between a 'made'
history and the construction of a place for Essex in the contemporary *realpolitik* of the Elizabethan state and its relationship with
Ireland. The way that Henry's right to rule and to wage war against
France is continually reinforced in the play had been investigated
in terms of the 'naturalness' of his position in the context both of
his God-given lineage and hierarchy and the much discussed 'democracy' of his relationship to the common people of his country.
This was extended into further discussions of warfare which suggested that Shakespeare was keying *Henry V* into a substantial
body of contemporary thought, the focus of which was to idealise
militarism in a state which, according to many writers, had neglected
a tradition of arms viewed as having reached a high point in the
battles undertaken by the real Henry V. Furthermore the relationship between the act of marriage and territorial ambition was
studied in the light of the play's suggestion that 'The king hath
granted every article: / His daughter first, and then in sequel all, /
According to their firm proposed natures' (V.ii.350–2).

As well as this, all those 'legs and arms and heads chopped off'
had been weighed against the play's acclaimed univocal patriotism
and celebration of the just war.

Yet none of this finally satisfied a group still intrigued by the
fantasy of a lost radical play entitled *Henry III* which would over-
turn all the rhetoric distilled from generations of critical readings,
blended by Branagh, served up with (but surpassing) Mark Antony,
and overreaching Richmond at Bosworth.

The students finally found what they were looking for by search-
ing beyond Shakespeare's *Henry V* to another play, later than the
histories but contemporary with *Coriolanus*, in which issues of
nationhood, patriotism, warfare and economics were equally to
the fore. This parody and inversion of Shakespeare gave a new context in which to read Shakespeare and restored questions of canon
and aesthetics by showing that these were actually raised *at the time*
when Shakespeare was still writing.

The scene is the Mile End Road and the business is the recruitment of soldiers for foreign and domestic service; the speech that
follows should ideally be judged in the light of all the Henry plays,
Julius Caesar, Coriolanus, Richard II, Richard III, the opening
of Sidney's *An Apology for Poetry* and the complete works of
Machiavelli!

> Remove and march. Soft and fair, gentlemen, soft and fair! Double
> your files! As you were! Faces about. Now, you with the sodden
> face, keep in there. Look to your match, sirrah, it will be in your
> fellow's flask anon. So, make a crescent now; advance your pikes;
> stand and give ear! Gentlemen, countrymen, friends, and my fellow
> soldiers, I have brought you this day from the shops of security and
> the counters of content, to measure out in these furious fields honour
> by the ell, and prowess by the pound. Let it not, o, let it not, I say,
> be told hereafter the noble issue of the city fainted, but bear your-
> selves in this fair action like men, valiant and freemen. Fear not the
> face of the enemy, not the noise of the guns, for believe me, breth-
> ren, the rude rumbling of a brewer's car is far more terrible, of
> which you have a daily experience; neither let the stink of powder
> offend you, since a more valient stink is nightly with you. To a
> resolved mind, his home is everywhere. I speak not this to take away
> the hope of your return; for you shall see, I do not doubt it, and that
> very shortly, your loving wives again, and your sweet children, whose
> care doth bear you company in baskets. Remember then, whose cause
> you have in hand, and like a sort of true-born scavengers, scour me
> this famous realm of enemies. I have no more to say but this: stand
> to your tacklings, lads, and show to the world you can brandish a
> sword as shake an apron. Saint George, and on, my hearts!
>
> (*The Knight of the Burning Pestle*, V.v.45–66)

In conclusion, it is worth mentioning that many of the group of
students that re-read Shakespeare in the light of Beaumont and
Fletcher's play were planning to be teachers themselves, some of
English and others of drama. And I think that it is only from these
preliminary moves – re-locating the canon as well as re-loading it
– that we can proceed to the kind of utopian thought Shepherd
has spoken of in his desire for

> alliances with teachers in all sectors, a familiarity with some of the
> new readings and none of the new practices, an angry awareness of
> the marginalization of drama work within universities, a lack of ex-
> perience of drama in schools, a responsibility for teaching people who
> will end up working in the schools of which I have no experience.[19]

This sentiment I endorse: it includes, for example, making links with drama departments of all kinds. The government's scorn for drama in terms of the National Curriculum and (for a long time) as a suitable degree subject, is not just an economic one. If it is thought that drama is the last outpost of socialism, celebrating diversity and pluralism, then supporting it is almost a political practice in itself.

Finally, I would say that, above all, we need to address the question which drifted around the Essex conferences and the LTP project long ago. What are schoolteachers' attitudes to us, and ours to them? The test of a political theory rests with its ability to survive beyond a line constructed by the institutions' selectivity in terms of class and race. This accounts in part for the better reputation enjoyed by feminist theory amongst schoolteachers and, indeed, amongst European scholars looking across at work undertaken in Britain with occasional bafflement.

If our teaching really has a part to play in confronting what I think is only the beginning of a trend towards almost unprecedented levels of dictatorship in education (and elsewhere), with notions of performance-related pay and assessment to the fore, then the line which divides us from those who will people this new land may be the one we have to cross first.

Notes

1 John Peck and Martin Coyle, *How to Study a Shakespeare Play* (London, Macmillan, 1985).
2 An example would be Macmillan's New Casebooks series.
3 The Literature Teaching Politics conferences of the early 1980s provide a model for the kind of development which might grow from the Shakespeare and the Teaching of English conference and the present volume. A specific aim was to provide a dialogue between teachers and lecturers around the politics of critical theory. This ideal was achieved in part, although for financial and other reasons the conferences tended to remain in the hands of those working in higher education. Despite an increasing formality and glossiness (and evidence of financial dependence upon publishers' advertisements) the *LTP* journal retained a grass-roots feel and for many represented an accessible and overtly political reflection of what was happening in critical theory by linking it with, and testing it against, learning environments already deeply affected by government cuts and ideological intervention.

I am indebted to Catherine Belsey for helping with an archaeology of the *Literature Teaching Politics* journals.

4 *The Daily Telegraph* (29 January 1993).

5 Lesley Aers and Nigel Wheale, eds, *Shakespeare and the Changing Curriculum* (London, Routledge, 1991), p. 8.

6 Department of Education and Science, *English for Ages 5 to 16*, Cox Report (London, HMSO, 1989).

7 I am grateful to Tony Crowley for reminding me of just how liberal Kingman and Cox are by comparison with what emerged in the final form of the National Curriculum and that it would be a mistake to reject all their conclusions and recommendations without recognising an inherent critique of some of the baser assumptions about education held by the government at the end of the last decade.

8 Brian Cox, 'The right is wrong on English teaching', *The Times* (1 March 1993).

9 Susan Leach, *Shakespeare in the Classroom* (Buckingham, Open University, 1992), pp. 22–3.

10 This sense of loss depends upon the notion that theory comes to school students through those teachers who were taught it themselves as undergraduates.

11 Simon Shepherd, 'Acting against bardom; some utopian thoughts on workshops' in Aers and Wheale, eds, *Shakespeare and the Changing Curriculum*, p. 88.

12 Graham Holderness, ed., *The Shakespeare Myth* (Manchester, Manchester University Press, 1988).

13 Isobel Armstrong, 'Thatcher's Shakespeare?', *Textual Practice*, 3:1 (1989), pp. 1–14 (p. 13).

14 Douglas Bruster, *Drama and the Market in the Age of Shakespeare* (Cambridge, Cambridge University Press, 1992).

15 Donald G. Watson, *Shakespeare's Early History Plays* (London, Macmillan, 1990), p. ix. The reference is a misprint for Anthony Hammond's Arden edition of *King Richard III* (London, Methuen, 1981). See Simon Barker, '"But you must learn to know such slanders of the age": literary theory in the study of Shakespeare' in J. M. Q. Davies, ed., *Bridging the Gap: Literary Theory in the Classroom* (West Cornwall, CT: Locust Hill Press, 1994), pp. 219–44.

16 Charles Barber, *York Notes on Henry V* (London, Longman, 1983), p. 50.

17 Hugh Grady, *The Modernist Shakespeare* (Oxford, Clarendon Press, 1991).

18 *Ibid.*, pp. 231–2.

19 Shepherd, in Aers and Wheale, eds, *Shakespeare and the Changing Curriculum*, p. 90.

3

✤

NATO's pharmacy:
Shakespeare by prescription

✤

Richard Wilson

'The key to teaching Shakespeare is teaching the teachers', the RSC's supremo, Adrian Noble, remarked when he was asked by *The Independent* in 1992 whether he had 'crept unwillingly to school' to study the plays. At Chichester High School, O level *Macbeth* had been 'a miserable affair', but he 'saw masses of Shakespeare' at the Festival Theatre, including Olivier's *Othello* when he was 12. Confronted by the Bard in class, 'I just rushed off', Noble gloated, 'to see what was missing from the text we'd been given'. Here – with the legend of a *wunderkind* who discovers truth unaided – is the paradoxical power of those who teach the teachers Shakespeare: that the prescription is made not as an aid but as the answer to education, since, as Noble swears, without 'live theatre, I'd have been a clerk in the council offices, or at best a teacher'.[1] The relations between thespians and teachers have seldom been better skewered than with this gaffe, which Noble compounded with an interview in the same newspaper in 1993, when he proposed that 'every child should be taken to the theatre twice a term' for a 'social and emotional experience' to counteract those 'voices of dissent, phrase it how you like, [for which] I hold drama schools responsible. Most drama schools today don't teach acting – they teach behaviour.' Sponsors need have no qualms about his RSC, he insinuated, for 'Though we did have a subversive, left-wing image, the flag we fly now is quite reactionary: the need for a strongly articulated classical tradition in the midst of our culture. . . . I'm a classicist, a traditionalist', he explained, whose vital role was 'conducting tutorials for the country's leading directors on how to speak the verse'.[2] Himself addicted to indigestion pills as a remedy for choked emotion, according to Kenneth Branagh,[3] Noble prescribed Shakespeare's 'verbal and emotional articulacy' as a medicine to cure what he called 'this dreadful reduction of the English vocabulary' by those who taught the Bard as 'an anti-feminist, imperialist'.[4]

On 29 October 1992 it was announced that the RSC summer school would receive 'royal lessons on the Bard' from its President, the Prince of Wales. Though a Palace spokesman added that 'It is difficult to talk about the what, where, and when' of the royal timetable, it was not hard to see what united Prince and Noble.[5] It had been at Stratford on Shakespeare's Birthday in 1991 that Britain's most 'virulent late-developer' launched his crusade against 'so-called experts' blamed for 'marginalising Shakespeare' with the '*extraordinary* argument that he is elitist';[6] and like Noble, Charles thought teaching the Bard too crucial to be left to teachers, noting how he himself 'never understood the plays when taught them at Gordonstoun, but only when he saw them performed by Branagh'.[7] So, the Prince hardly needed his secret Shakespeare seminar – Brian Cox, Moelwyn Merchant, the Headmaster of Eton and Sir Peter Parker – since his school record, Cambridge degree and distrust of educationists matched those of his adopted profession so completely. For when other RSC and National Theatre directors were polled, they too complained that at Sherborne (Richard Eyre), Magdalen College School (John Caird) or the Perse (Peter Hall) they 'didn't learn much about Shakespeare', except that, in Hall's words, 'Shakespeare has to be taught as theatre. Sitting children down to study Shakespeare is like trying to come to grips with Bach without letting people hear it.'[8] When Prince Edward could become a West End angel, there seemed no reason, then, why his brother should not act at Stratford: a fantasy rehearsed in 1995 when he was allowed to play Hal to Robert Stephens's Falstaff. But what this billing at the Memorial Theatre in fact exposed was the ideological function of the school trip and theatre workshop in postwar British education. For if the supermarket chain Sainsbury's was happy to donate £100,000 to Kickstart, the RSC education unit, this was with confidence that, as Prince and Noble blurted, Royal Shakespeare was not a catalyst but the antidote to 'voices of dissent' in lecture halls and staff rooms.

It was as an intellectual purgative that Shakespeare featured in the 'great debate' about the core curriculum. The Prince had traced the scandal that 'In Shakespeare's England . . . thousands of children have never seen a Shakespeare play', to 'shadowy experts' who 'disapprove of the Bard'; leaving these phantoms to be identified by hacks such as Brian Appleyard in *The Sunday Times*, who explained that English had been 'compromised by high-theory trickling down into the classrooms when a whole generation of thinkers – Derrida, Barthes, Foucault – discovered literature was dead'.[9] Likewise, Professor of Cultural History Jeffrey Richards informed readers of *The Daily Mail* that 'a stew of continental isms – Marxism, Freudianism, modernism, post-modernism, structuralism, post-structuralism – overlaid with a paralysing custard of political correctness have stifled Britain's greatest heritage', and that 'The pitiful state of literature teaching in today's schools' would be relieved only by prescribing works like Shakespeare's, which 'exalt the warrior, explorer, gentleman, and adventurer, at the expense of the wilting provincial spinster'. Richards's anathema was wilder than the Prince's, and included Leavis, damned for neglecting 'robust, masculine and direct' authors such as Kipling; but his invective was similar as he scorned academic colleagues as 'ageing Sixties' trendies in jeans and pullovers who tell us Shakespeare is no longer relevant'.[10] To hand Marx or Saussure to such a 'low grade educational establishment', Appleyard jeers, 'is like giving a Kalashnikov to a four-year old',[11] for is there not, as United States Republican candidate Pat Buchanan swears, truly a cultural war on? *The Independent* thinks so, and on 13 June 1992 targeted its smart weapons on English at Loughborough University, in reprisal for its 'surreptitious' annexation of Shakespeare to a syllabus that was clearly 'not about poetry, but politics', as it incorporated 'books written by women and homosexuals'.[12] If these were, indeed, the first shots of a new *kulturkampf*, the RSC had clearly aligned itself with a rhetorical *blitzkrieg*.

On the very day that Prince Charles unleashed this campaign for 'real Shakespeare' two other news items put the battle in perspective, when the Under-Secretary for Education announced that by April 1992 all secondary schools would have bank accounts 'to tighten the grip on costs'; and the Inspectorate reported that 'the encouraging quality of English teaching' was being undermined because 'schools could not afford to buy sufficient books'.[13] This was, therefore, in a true cultural materialist sense, a struggle for possession of the text; but, as Appleyard countered, 'the educational establishment will focus on "resources". What they will not do is accept their cataclysmic failure to transmit the most glorious cultural heritage in the world.'[14] By this reasoning, it did not matter that buildings leaked, providing the 'trickle' of theory was plugged; nor that meals were cut, so long as the 'stew' and 'custard' of radical criticism was trashed. Even books would be shown as immaterial, when the Education Secretary, John Patten, revised his controversial English tests to prescribe just one Shakespearian passage for examination at Key Stage Three (at age fourteen): Jacques's corporatist sermon, 'All the world's a stage'. It was 'Patten's hand, if not his pen' which was reported to be behind the Prince's lambasting, in May 1994, of 'fashionable theorists in the English faculties of our universities who try to tear apart our wonderful poets, novelists, and playwrights because they do not fit the abstruse theories of the day', when the animus against the 'trendy dogma of single-issue fanatics' would be seconded by even liberal journalists with nostalgic memories of reading English under Leavis.[15] For what *did* matter, *The Independent* argued in a triumphalist editorial entitled 'A dead male playwright', was *how* pupils were taught to 'come to grips with such a crucial part of the nation's cultural heritage', since the first thing teachers had to learn was that there was nothing 'questionable' or 'difficult' about the Bard:

> Shakespeare was, indeed, a white, middle-aged male. But good teachers are able to bring out the excitement and fun of his plays. *Hamlet*, for instance, is far more than a study of regicide. It is a timeless drama of teenage angst. It concerns a boy coming to terms with sexuality. *Macbeth* is a play about the price people pay as they claw to the top of any organisation. And *Julius Caesar* is about the assassination of a noble Father of the Nation. . . . Many youngsters whose parents came to this country from former colonies will have family tales of the night the president was shot and the soldiers took to the streets. Any child who has witnessed the violent collapse of Communism on television news will know that power does not always pass via the ballot box. In addition to being rattling good yarns, Shakespeare's plays have great contemporary resonance. . . . The key to

teaching his works is to remember that Shakespeare did not write
texts to be pored over. He wrote vibrant verse to be exclaimed out
loud and exulted in. The first essential is that children should get out
of school and attend performances . . . John Patten has identified the
popular mood.[16]

With its complacency about British institutions, condescension
towards multi-culturalism and dancing on the grave of commun-
ism, *The Independent* was here spelling out the prescription for
Shakespeare teaching in the 1990s, but underlining that the plays
were to be administered only in controlled doses: like all laxat-
ives, their cathartic content would be diluted. If Shakespeare was
indeed so powerful, its toxicity would need to be strictly licensed;
and the editor's insistence that it was more important for children
to see the plays on stage than study them historically, and to 're-
enact them for themselves, than be led to literary analysis', helps
explain the current flood of sponsorship for theatre-in-education
programmes, such as that of the English Shakespeare Company by
IBM. Once more, it was the Prince who announced this scheme in
a speech at Salford in October 1992, when he linked it to his own
Compact plan for partnership between business and schools, as
evidence of how commerce could 'promote the spiritual side of a
technological society' by investing in 'our extraordinarily rich
cultural heritage'.[17] What Charles and the leader writers candidly
expect from TIE schemes, then, is precisely that they will transform history into 'heritage' by diverting schools from 'poring over
texts' to 'rattling' out 'good yarns', with the express aim of producing a generation of Bard-happy consumers to rid us of the current
one of turbulent priests. For, as Noble testified, 'The Prince of Wales
is extraordinarily keen about what Shakespeare can give young
people, [which is] verbal articulacy . . . a play gives words to the
wordless. We should give young people this mighty experience.'[18]

Prince Charles, who was ambiguously reported by Noble to be
'mad about Shakespeare', might himself have been the ideal gradu-
ate of the de-historicised Bard, since as late as September 1993 he
expressed himself sincerely astonished on being told that female
parts were performed at the Globe by boys.[19] In the new educational order the history of Shakespeare's theatre will be rigorously
evacuated from Shakespeare's words. So, where one Dr Bertolt
Trumptup, Professor at Revision University, and the typical 'progressive educationist' (according to yet another acid editorial in

The Times), would argue that 'The catalogue of this dead white English male is too long for tender minds',[20] the RSC will help the young to rejoice in Shakespeare by teaching them simply how to 'exclaim' his 'vibrant verse out loud'. This is the Pentacostalist euphoria of the *Cambridge School Shakespeare* series, which sets out to supersede the Arden, its editor Rex Gibson states, by encouraging pupils 'to make their own discoveries without having interpretations forced on them'. Inspired by techniques of RSC coaches such as Kristin Linklater, who sincerely imagines she can 'free Shakespeare's voice' from inside an actor's possessed and ventriloquised body, Gibson's 'Shakespeare and Schools' project is charismatically anti-intellectual in its exhortation to joy, though his instructions to pupils sound like matron's most muscular injunctions to swallow the medicine whole:

> The best way into *Romeo and Juliet* is simply to read it straight through. Don't pause to discuss. Just go straight through to line 189 on page 63. Enjoy yourselves! This Shakespeare aims to be different from other editions. It invites you to bring the play to life in your classroom, hall or studio through enjoyable activities. Whatever you do, remember that Shakespeare wrote his plays to be acted, watched and enjoyed. . . . Do you believe in love at first sight? Talk together about what happens when in that electrifying moment two people fall head over heels in love.[21]

Music and movement in the aisles is the sugar that makes the bitter pill go down in Gibson's regime, which seems a perfect prescription for schools compelled by law to study Shakespeare yet starved of funds for critical or historical support, since, as *The Guardian* admiringly exclaimed, 'In this edition the play is the thing. There is no elaborate critical introduction. . . . Instead pupils are encouraged to split speeches between themselves, pick out words, find lines which use only monosyllables, to take possession of Shakespeare's language and worry the meaning out of it.'[22] So, when Gibson gave evidence to the working group on the English National Curriculum chaired by Brian Cox he inducted them, the newspaper marvelled, into an impromptu workshop and 'had the academic worthies on their feet exploring the Prospero–Caliban exchanges in ways they never did at school'. The picture of the dance around, under and on top of Professor Cox's table is, perhaps, an apt one for the *ressentiment* that drives the counter-revolution against the lecturers on what one article called 'Rex's magic island'. For this acclaimed 'guru of active Shakespeare' makes no bones about his aim in 'getting pupils away from their desks and up on their feet', which is to prise the plays from the detested 'educationists' to liberate them from 'interpretation': 'We want to introduce young-sters to the imaginative world of Shakespeare so they experience it in their hearts and bodies', he affirms, 'and no one tells them that that is what they should think.'[23]

Orchestrating classes to 'Sit facing each other [as] one student reads the lines aloud [and] another echoes certain words', Gibson, who as an editor is unabashed when 'he doesn't know' what Shakespeare means, induces his choristers, he believes, to 'dis-cover' the essential Shakespeare 'for themselves'. There is, argu-ably, nothing wrong with this mission to 'worry' the historical meaning out of Elizabethan texts, except that, as *The Guardian* noted, 'It's an approach which demands an intelligent and imagin-ative response, with Gibson ever present as guide and mentor.'[24] At its climax, his project takes the teachers away from school for a term to a utopia purified of 'prejudices and inhibitions'; 'Yet he would be King on't': the latter end of Rex's commonwealth for-gets the beginning. So, the Kent teacher who described in *The Independent* on 11 February 1993 how, enthused by 'Active Shake-speare', she had marched her 14-year-olds around the classroom chanting lines from *Julius Caesar* 'to the tune of "Abide with Me", so as to get the feel of the iambic pentameter', while they imagined 'how we might publicly murder the headmaster', re-vealed the political naivety of this uprising against the 'academic elitists' with their 'bookshelves of cribs'; for 'Would [a revolution] work?' her class was forced to ask, 'Would the governors appoint one of us as head?'; and 'Of course not', they were prompted, supposedly by their own imagination: 'It was a flawed plan from the start.'[25] Like every peasants' revolt, the moral economy of Gibson's insurrection turns out to be conservative; for, whether conscious or not, the rhetoric of this children's crusade to rescue Shakespeare from the Shakespearians chimes exactly with the reactionary populism of Britain's Tory administration.

'People say there is too much jargon in education', John Major ironised to the Conservative Women's Conference in June 1993, 'so let me give you my own: Discipline, Tables, Sums, Dates, Shakespeare.'[26] In the Back to Basics campaign waged by the gov-ernment in its poujadist fourth term it became axiomatic that, as the Prime Minister bewailed to the Carlton Club, 'we have been bombarded by the arrogant claims of those who believe the glories of British history, the plays and sonnets of Shakespeare, the novels of Trollope, even poor old Winnie the Pooh, are irrelevant to the modern child'.[27] Thus, the diatribe with which the right-wing Michael Portillo unmasked his bid for the premiership in January 1994 attributed 'the Poison of a new British Disease' to 'cynics, egalitarians, and socialists', who had 'corrupted' the universities with their nihilism, for which the antidote was Shakespeare's lesson that 'When degree is shaked, / Which is the ladder to all high designs, / The enterprise is sick'.[28] It had been the same Ulyssean homily on obedience which had been lifted out of context by the Chancellor of the Exchequer, Nigel Lawson, in 1983, to philosophise that because 'Shakespeare was a Tory', who wrote 'from a Tory point of view', Tory values were universal too,[29] and the syllogism provided the classic instance of what Pierre Bourdieu has described as the 'symbolic violence' of pedagogic action: the circular logic 'whereby power relations are perceived not for what they objectively are, but in a form that renders them legitimate in the eyes of the beholder'.[30] For when Portillo castigated the 'so-called sophisticated . . . the chattering classes and pressure groups', for 'whingeing about Britain', and 'sneering at and tearing down British achievements' (such as Shakespeare), his rebuttal of the 'opinion-formers within the British élite' was, of course, self-validated by his quotation of Shakespeare.

Symbolic violence, according to Bourdieu, is that process by which the arbitrariness of a culture is misrecognised as universal, for behind all culture lurks 'pure *de facto* power'.[31] It was a power that was nearly naked, however, in Portillo's co-option of Shakespeare to his threat that 'We must temper tolerance when confronted by those whose stock-in-trade is to belittle and undermine the fabric of our society'; and that was blatant when within hours of his tirade *The Evening Standard* raised a hue and cry against Jane Brown, the head of a Hackney primary school who had allegedly denied pupils tickets to the Royal Ballet on grounds that *Romeo and Juliet* was 'entirely about heterosexual love'.[32] Brown's mistake, it seems, had been to take the directive that 'Shakespeare was a Tory' literally; but in the ensuing witch-hunt, when she was scapegoated by Labour councillors for 'ideological idiocy and cultural philistinism',[33] and vilified as a lesbian in the tabloids, it was clear her crime had been, in the words of Hackney's Director of Education, 'to bring a wholly inappropriate ideological question' to 'this great play', which the local Labour leader promised he would stage at his own school.[34] That the story was leaked months after the event from the office of Ingrid Haitink, daughter of the Glyndebourne conductor, confirmed the forces ranged against the hapless teacher; for the entire press echoed Major when he told the Commons she had shown why 'political correctness' was detested by parents 'who want children taught the basics to equip them for adulthood'.[35] In fact, the Hackney parents loudly endorsed Brown; but the violence invested in Shakespeare was now such that a public recantation of heresy was demanded of the woman who had, as *The Guardian* smirked, 'Barred the Bard'.[36] Televised images of her humiliation as she 'apologised' on her school steps, reading from a dictated text how she hoped 'the opportunity to see *Romeo and Juliet* will arise again',[37] brought home with a vengeance the intolerance intended by Portillo when he had prescribed Shakespeare as the nation's purge.

'You want to do something really radical', demands Camille Paglia:

> read Shakespeare. . . . We need back-to-basics reform on every level of education. Let us put an end to the yuppie buffet, piss-poor Molotov cocktails served with French canapés. Enough of Derrida and Foucault poured like ketchup . . . or these Marxists, like Terry Eagleton. Do you know the salary that man makes? That is why he has to wear jeans.[38]

These are the ravings that remind us that there is, indeed, a kind of holy war on, and that Professor Trumptup, the straw man on the bonfire of books, is the composite author of *Radical Tragedy, Alternative Shakespeares, Political Shakespeare, The Shakespeare Myth, Still Harping on Daughters, The Matter of Difference, Rewriting the Renaissance, The Subject of Tragedy* and *Colonial Encounters*. Dr Trumptup is that historicist critic who for the last ten years has been exploring not the factitious relevance of *Shakespeare Our Contemporary* but real continuities between the Shakespearian text and its modern actors, such as the one dramatised in a non-examined play when the Kent ancestors of those very students who were taught to translate a revolution into the Cup Final betrayed their own leaders and murdered Jack Cade. What is at stake in the struggle over the teaching of Shakespeare, as the Prince and the editors at least admit, is the radicalisation of criticism in the 1980s; but to remind ourselves of that fact is instantly to raise the question of how it is that such a well-intentioned movement as 'Shakespeare and Schools' has come to collaborate in a moral panic fomented by Tory ministers; and how it is that the RSC has become a Trojan Horse in the counter-insurgency waged by Fleet Street on the 'politically correct'. How is it that an organisation which was founded 'to question everything and disturb its audience', in the words of the then-radical Hall,[39] and which, as Noble says, had for so long 'beliefs and ideals that were left of centre',[40] should now join the purge against the 'voices of dissent' in universities, colleges and schools?

In his essay on 'Royal Shakespeare' Alan Sinfield has analysed the evolving ideology of the RSC as the company negotiated the transition from an era of public subsidy to an age of private sponsorship, and he describes the early radicalism of Stratford as a function of the rapidly expanding education opportunities of the 1960s. A new university-educated middle class of teachers, media workers and local government officials found its combination of dissidence and dependence mirrored in productions like the epic Brechtian cycle of *The Wars of the Roses* and performances like David Warner's rebellious Hamlet, as the company 'felt its way towards this class fraction'.[41] But with the breakdown of consensus under Heath the RSC backed away from its Brechtian style, and Hall's successor, Trevor Nunn, was at pains to state he was 'not a political animal'.[42] Torn between social concern and fear of union militancy, the RSC of the 1970s reflected its fragmenting public with confusing spectacle, as in Nunn's Roman plays or John Barton's *Troilus and Cressida*, where ignorant armies clashed by night. After the oil crisis, however, the withdrawal of state funds and hiked seat prices forced the company to court business patrons with productions that emphasised collective purpose, such as Terry Hands's *Henry V*. Employing six hundred people, the RSC had become, so Hall believed, the ICI of the theatre, but, like the board of some imperial pharmaceutical company, its directors were now made to feel that their responsibility was not so much to their consumers as their shareholders, and that what counted was the return on investment, rather than the ideological composition of the product.[43] The turning-point was the election of the

Thatcher government, with its doctrinaire commitment to commercial funding; a moment of truly Shakespearean ambivalence after the famous 'winter of discontent', recorded by Hall in successive entries to the diary he soliloquised from his eyrie as director of the National Theatre, a post he held while maintaining his associate directorship at Stratford:

> May 2 1979: I fear for the Tories getting in because it could make the way easier for Tony Benn in five years time; but I also fear if they don't, because the present decline into a land without opportunity will continue. So, on balance, I am voting Tory. Just. But that's tomorrow. . . .
>
> May 3: It wasn't at all difficult this morning to vote Tory. In fact, it felt good, wanting change, and we have to change. . . . The election was fascinating television. . . . Thatcher is in with a majority of over forty: a resounding victory. The newspapers are very favourable to her. The press likes to be on the winning side.[44]

Editors were not alone, of course, in relishing the company of wolves. When he compiled his survey of the RSC in 1985 Sinfield was doubtful that the 'radical edge' of subsidised theatre could survive the onslaught from sponsors like the company chairman who protested that Shakespeare was to be played 'with the actors dressed in boiler suits or similar garb. I cannot believe that this is true for such a performance, especially with royalty present.'[45] The heyday of the donor would justify such fears, with notorious interventions like that of Guinness, which withdrew its backing from the National Theatre's production of *'Tis Pity She's a Whore* in 1990, after its chairman's wife had unsuccessfully lobbied to euphemise Ford's embarrassing title. And, locked into partnership with commerce through its tenancy of the Barbican Theatre in the finance district of the City, the RSC was now physically, as well as ideologically, cut off from its original audience of public sector workers and students. Dependent on tourism as the company had thereby become, 'terrorism, football hooliganism, the miners' strike, and Wapping' were estimated to have cost it £1.3 million in lost receipts, according to Hands's frantic 1987 report; so the schizophrenia of his reign was as much a reflex of conflicting interests within the structure as of his obvious personal incoherence. As *The Daily Telegraph* cruelly records: 'paranoia stalked the corridors of the RSC. The top brass adopted a siege mentality, the actors were bolshy, and there was a great deal of press sniping, not just from theatre critics, but from pundits who thought the organisation had got too big for its boots and was constantly whingeing about money.'[46] Desperation was the mark of Hands's last production, *Coriolanus* in 1990, when the Tribunes were hammed as Scargill stooges to Charles Dance's Tarzan hero, who received empathy one night from the person of Michael Heseltine. Their mutual admiration was spoiled only, *The Evening Standard* reported, by the grinning of Tory Chairman Kenneth Baker in the next row, 'a well-read fellow' who knew the plot.[47] Evidently, the RSC had built its hopes on an audience as ruthless as Aufidius, and paid the price when it was shortly forced by lack of funds to close its operations for four months.

Reading these fraught events back into Sinfield's essay, we can see how they bear out his thesis that the fate of the RSC cannot be dissociated from that of welfare and what he calls 'culturalism': the Keynesian belief that a wider distribution of high culture is good for people and must be paid for by the state. As a flagship of the Welfare State, the RSC and its managers were being subjected to the same blandishments and blackmail from Tory ministers as the managers of the great teaching hospitals; and this was surely only just for an institution that dated its origin from the moment when English spas declined, and, in place of hydropathy, the hoteliers of Cheltenham, Leamington and Bath inaugurated at Stratford in 1879 our modern – but no less tonic – therapeutic regimen of the arts festival. In any event, if the RSC became confused about its identity and audience during the 1980s, this was because, like the hospitals, market logic deposited it within the conflicting ideological currents of the leftward-leaning public service professions and a new rightward-bound financial élite. This was the peculiar British contradiction Perry Anderson describes in his book *English Questions* as 'A Culture in Contraflow':

> [when] an original Marxist culture of the Left gained ground against a backdrop of campus unrest and industrial militancy; a combative culture of the Right emerged to wipe the slate clean of them; and a traditional culture of the Centre was ruffled into an unaccustomed *fronde* by the outcome. The net balance of the shifts was ... [that] the political and intellectual worlds went in opposite directions, [as] a regime of the radical Right part confronted, part created an overall cultural drift to the Left. Prompted by social resentment and doctrinal animus, its purge of the academy tended to raise up the very

adversaries it sought to stamp out, even as its drive to impose the values of the counting house and constabulary on society swept forward elsewhere.[48]

Caught in this rip-tide between finance and education, the RSC was faced with a momentous choice when Hands retired in 1991. From the left perspective of its vestigial teaching constituency, the likeliest successor was David Thacker, director of the Young Vic, who built a radical reputation with productions such as a Civil War *Julius Caesar*, with Corin Redgrave as a Cromwellian Brutus, and co-opted Vanessa Redgrave and Arthur Miller to his inner city theatre. A pioneer of mixed-race casting, Thacker earned sneers for a *Macbeth* which was 'a delight to the race relations board';[49] but grudging respect when he directed Rudolph Walker as the first black Othello seen in London since Paul Robeson. No one had tried harder to respond to the advent of political criticism with historically pointed productions. In the event, however, the trustees promoted the in-house Noble, the son of an undertaker, to direct what many feared must be an imminent demise. From his first Stratford offering of *King Lear* in 1982, Noble's work was shaped by the pageantry he learned on Chichester's open stage; but his flair for spectacle was unmatched by intellectual insight: as Sinfield noted, the politics of his apocalyptic *Lear* were 'contradictory . . . without much attempt to develop a new analysis'.[50] In fact, all his comments emphasise a refusal of such analysis and a nostalgia for the celebratory arena of his youth: 'the big stage where Olivier and Gielgud performed'. Having 'discussed with Prince Charles how to make the plays more inspirational', he derides critical theories as 'ways for the young to get better marks and jobs'. So, his preferred critic remains Jan Kott; and it is an echo of the mysticism of the 1960s when he declares: 'We have to show the young Shakespeare's language is an imagistic language, and imagistic language in the modern world is like someone inventing the colour green if you live in the inner city.'[51] If the Prince hears a hint of his own Laurens van der Post in this casual disparagement of urban life, that may be because it is the rhetoric of a similar guru of eco-spiritualism: Peter Brook.

'Shakespeare is a piece of coal. One knows the whole process of the primeval forest and one can trace the history of coal; but the meaningfulness of a piece of coal starts and finishes in combustion, giving out the light and heat we want':[52] through gnomic

utterances such as this, Brook became the exemplary Stratford
director whose charisma legitimates the apostolic succession to
Noble from Hall. For if Noble has positioned the RSC within the
stream of right-wing ideology which flows from ministers, finance
and the Tory press, the manoeuvre has been justified as a return
to the primitive church of Brook. Nor is this specious, since all the
myths of today's Shakespeare revivalists are prefigured in the
master's gospel: that teaching is deadly; history bunkum; Shakespeare magic; and language god. It is his career which establishes
the rule that the Shakespeare prodigy should treat teachers with
'detached compassion', like Christ among the elders, as he did his
at Westminster School, when they destroyed *As You Like It*, he
recalls, by reducing its 'miracle' to 'a nightmare School certificate
blur'.[53] His whole dramaturgy can be seen as revenge for this
primal scene of pedagogic coercion, when 'deadlines' became 'dead-
liness', and his reaction, he says, was to ask, 'who is the culprit?'.
The answer he gives in *The Empty Space* might have been sup-
plied by Prince Charles: it is 'the deadly scholar, who emerges
from the Deadly Theatre smiling because nothing distracted him
from confirming his pet theories, and who confuses intellectual
satisfaction with true experience'.[54] When Brook praised Kott,
therefore, it was as an anti-academic, whose 'title of "Professor"
sat ill on him', because he knew the Bard 'from direct experience':
'Kott makes one aware', he exulted, 'how rare it is for a pedant
sheltered behind ivy-covered walls to experience Shakespeare's
passions.' If this 'quick-witted combative man', with 'a beautiful
girl' beside him in a Warsaw night club, was really an Elizabethan,
you were to understand, this was precisely because he was *not*
your British 'educationist'.[55]

Of all the 'great white gods' of modernism who promulgated
the theorem that 'less is more' – Mies van der Rohe, Le Corbusier,
Rothko, Beckett, Cage – Brook alone remains immune to challenge. When *The Observer* series 'The experts' expert' canvassed
theatre directors in 1989 the result was unique for unanimity:
every one of those questioned agreed with the National Theatre's
Richard Eyre, that 'the director I admire most and regard as inspirational is Brook, both as guru and showman'. For Michael
Bogdanov he is 'a master' of 'deep insight'; for Hands 'half a body
above anyone else' for his power to 'uncover the true essence of
the play'; for Thacker, one who is 'way ahead' for 'an ability to

uncover things in the text other people would not have known
were there'; and for Noble, a 'tower' and 'fearless explorer of
uncharted ways. A missionary', whose work 'made me want to
join the RSC'. For depth, height and transcendence, it seems,
nobody can compare with Brook who, in Nunn's encomium, holds
the secret patent for a 'self-purgation' that is 'inspirational, unlike
the usual adrenaline-based excitements of conventional theatre'.[56]
If the RSC, which depends for much of its funding on the deter-
gents giant Unilever, really is the theatrical ICI, then these tributes
were like the advertisements for soap powder analysed by Barthes
in *Mythologies*, which proclaim redemptive qualities for their products, in contrast to the usual chlorine-based excitements: pow-
ders which 'liberate objects from circumstantial imperfection' by
'driving dirt through the textile', to uncover the true essence of
'the fine immaculate linen'. '*Brook* Whiteness', these jingles chime,
'cleans in depth', thereby restoring to textures a dimension no one
previously thought they had.[57] The adverts were boosting, that is
to say, Brook's own lavatorial metaphysics of presence, which
assume that 'what passed through the body of this man Shakespeare and came into existence on sheets of paper is different from
any other author's work',[58] because 'the real richness of the writing exists at a deep level, underneath the words, where there is
nothing but the vibration of a great potential force':

> Directing Shakespeare is a matter of letting forms spring up of their
> own accord [from] what might be called 'the secret play'. Beneath
> the play one reads on the page, there is another play, which is hid-
> den and resists analysis, but whose presence can be felt. A director
> can only enter this zone with actors, who are sharp and penetrating
> instruments. If it is possible to listen to the invisible movements that
> flow behind each phrase . . . then, with much patience, unexpected
> forms appear. These must be weighed, rejected. The forms which
> arise from the external play can be discovered quickly, but long,
> rigorous work is necessary before they are impregnated by the spirit
> of the hidden play.[59]

'Ideas', Brook inveighs, 'are not worth the paper they are written on. It is necessary for such an old-fashioned idea as the importance of ideas to be swept away.'[60] No wonder Eagleton comments
on the 'dismally regressive opinions' of 'the top dogs, the manag-
ing directors of the whole shebang' of Stratford.[61] His depression
is warranted by the earnestness with which Brook's claque credits

such effusions. If Aristotle defined tragedy as *katharsis*, which Milton glossed as a homeopathic purge,[62] Brook's chemical theatre literalises the metaphor of defecation. Here the script is indeed a *pharmakon*: a cathartic to purify the essence of the 'hidden play' of its excremental forms. A poison that cures, Shakespeare's text consists of 'radioactive points',[63] in Brook's imagination, which must be rationed, since 'the dosage is so subtle it is impossible to establish the exact formula'.[64] Like 'marijuana and LSD', he holds, Shakespeare 'destroys the word', and 'penetrates deeper', to reveal 'sacred invisibility [in] a theatre working like the plague, by intoxication, by infection, by magic: a theatre in which the play itself stands in place of the text'.[65] To read this pharmaceutical fantasy after Derrida's deconstruction of Plato's myth of writing as supplement of the *logos* is obviously to consign Brook and his dispensary to the dustbin of phonocentrism. Yet, as new historicism notices, the place of the stage has always been that of the *pharmakos*, the druggist licensed to administer a lesser evil to cast the greater out;[66] and what counts in all such myths of writing is the question Derrida asks: 'What is the evil' inscribed on the despised paper; and 'What has been invested in the "living word" to make writing intolerable?'[67] What is this 'deadly business' Brook hopes 'the public is smelling out'; the 'debris in the system' his theatre will 'clear', when, 'like all purgations, its catharsis makes all clean and new'?[68] Of what faecal matter must 'the empty space' be flushed, before it can become the sanitised, pristine cubicle of Brook's *Dream*? The answer, of course, is what he calls the filthy 'grossness' of politics,[69] the dirt of history itself.

'History is a way of looking at things', Brook concedes, 'but not one that interests me. I'm interested in the present. Shakespeare doesn't belong to the past. If his material is valid, it is valid now.'[70] This refusal of history has been repeated by a generation of Stratford directors, who admit to having 'no interest in politics',[71] nor 'any sense of history as a reality';[72] and its finality confirms that Brook's function has been to neutralise the influence of Brecht. It was a role he fulfilled in *Marat/Sade* by incorporating Brechtian devices into a representation of revolution as a madhouse; and in *US* by reducing Vietnam (as Charles Marowitz objected) into 'a nightmare of contradictions we can never disentangle'.[73] In Shakespeare, evasion meant excluding issues that would 'turn the plays into mirrors of our preoccupations: feminism,

colonialism, homosexuality, which have become automatic, establishing new stereotypes'.[74] His escapology was virtuoso – as in the
pauses of his rococo *Love's Labour's Lost*; the halo shone around
the Duke in *Measure for Measure*; or the ritual that turned *Titus
Andronicus* into an Eisenstein procession – but the outcome was
always to preserve the Holy Theatre of the invisible from the
Rough Theatre of commitment. Brook accepts that not all of 'Shakespeare's stars' were accessible to his magic (*Romeo and Juliet* was
telescoped; and *Hamlet* and *Antony and Cleopatra* collapsed into
mere star vehicles); but those that did 'swing close' promised an
escape from history, even if, like *The Tempest*, they had to be
translated into French.[75] The vista offered by Time in *The Winter's Tale* was indicative: a snowstorm, like Citizen Kane's globe.
If the English hesitated to accept, wrote Brook's amanuensis, David
Selbourne, this was because 'they lack understanding of his priestly
theatre of ultimate truth'. As 'a radical of the right', Brook was
taking audiences back to Stravinsky's *Rite of Spring*, fifty years
after the event.[76] The analogy was apt: when Brook's *King Lear*
toured Russia he finally recognised his own history in the Siberia
he had staged:

> At that moment I felt the audience was moved by something much
> more considerable than the sentimental image of a poor old father
> howling. Lear was suddenly the figure of old Europe, tired, and
> feeling that after the events of the last fifty years people had borne
> enough, that some kind of respite was due.[77]

Although Stravinsky used every modern musical means, Adorno
observed, his quest for primitive forms and eternal truths remained
the revanchism of the White Russian émigré;[78] and when Brook
set *Timon of Athens* in the gutted shell of a *belle epoch* theatre,
he also revealed his reactionary nostalgia for a lost world. 'The
deeper you go into Europe and countries that have known revolution', he likes to think, 'the more related Elizabethan plays are to
history';[79] and what he restores by purging Shakespeare of fifty
years of modern meaning is thus inevitably his own image of 'old
Europe' as his 'poor old father': Simon Brook, the Menshevik
agitator who fled Russia after the 1905 Revolution, and exchanged
socialism for capitalism in Chiswick. There is a famous anecdote
which suggests how much British theatre owes to this paternal
retreat from politics, which has the businessman presenting the

6-year-old boy wonder with an expensive toy theatre; but Brook's biographer recounts what may have been an equally formative scene, when he first saw the display in a chemist's shop. J. C. Trewin is at a loss to know what to make of young Brook's wonder at the bright prescriptions;[80] but his later pharmaceutical jargon provides a clue. The toy theatre had been bought with the first profits of his father's company, floated in 1931 with the irresistibly Shakespearian name of Westminster Laboratories, and very soon one of Britain's main suppliers of drugs to schools. Brook's precocious theatrical career was literally funded on a generous dispensation of medicine to children, and his subsequent 'experimental laboratory' would always pay symbolic dues. Nor is the nexus so surprising, for as Peter Burke observes: 'The combination of healer and entertainer is an extremely old one. Healing was, and in some parts of the world still is, a social drama involving elaborate ritual.' Because of his Orthodox religion and Russian background, Brook has often been seen as a Siberian shaman; but his father's firm reminds us that in the West the showman who peddles pills has also been known as a charlatan.[81]

'Once, theatre could begin as magic', Brook recalls, 'but today . . . we must open our empty hands and show that there is nothing up our sleeves. Only then can we begin.'[82] It is a complex cultural moment when the Emperor of Russia declares he has no clothes, for which, however, Roy Porter provides a context in his book *Health for Sale*, when he relates how quackery split at the end of the last century, as chemists established Allen & Hanburys or Boots, and mountebanks the music halls.[83] The Brook brothers would be paid on both sides, for while Peter assumed command of the Memorial Theatre, 'like a high-pressure executive', Tynan said, 'arriving to take over a dying business',[84] Alexis qualified as a doctor. Neither, however, sustained the firm, which their father sold in 1961 to Reckitts. There is a photograph showing him as the grim patriarch at his last management board, and this furnishes an exact analogue of his son's *King Lear*. For the purpose of staging Shakespeare, Brook maintains, is to release 'the long chain of words' from history into 'the world'; and what more universal language exists than that into which the name of Westminster was dissolved: the Esperanto of Reckitt, Colman, and (since 1982) of the Swiss trust Sandoz, with all their household avatars of Exlax, Dettol, Windolene, Ovaltine and Delysid (also called LSD)?[85] It would be

interesting to know how Brook's anality accommodates the environ-
mental disaster that occurred in 1986, when the conglomerate in
which his family product merged excreted a deluge of chemicals into
the Rhine, killing river-life throughout Germany and the Nether-
lands. In reality there is no magic purge from the faeces of history;
but if Shakespeare is indeed a quintessential commodity, as Eagleton
suggests, 'at once ever new and consolingly the same',[86] then Brook's
market mission, we see, has been, by de-historicising the plays, to
transfer them on to a plane where, as Barthes writes, Ariel, Daz
and Persil are all one and the same: the united colours of the
multi-national.[87]

After his French *Tempest*, Brook announced that he would direct no more Shakespeare. Instead he would concentrate on medical dramas, such as a staging of Oliver Sacks's neurological
casebook of *The Man who Mistook his Wife for a Hat*. When this
opened in 1993, however, the critics worried that he seemed more
interested in amnesia than its cure.[88] For Brook's formula worked
only to erase the sense of history. Like a true son of the father to
whom he lavatorially dedicated *The Empty Space*, he had cathected
the juice of Shakespeare's 'purple flower' into a substance he called
Orghast and marketed at Persepolis to the petro-chemical industry
and the Shah. Its toxicity is identical to that of the family's other
patent drug, which is also sold in a hundred countries, wrapped
with a picture of the globe, as both 'The British laxative' and simultaneously 'The laxative of choice all over the world'. 'Not just
our British' favourite prescription, then (as Prince Charles puffs
Shakespeare), 'but the world's', the success of Brook's cash chemistry is to export the Westminster product as a medicine 'so universal' (according to the royal testimonial) 'that we recognise its effect
alive in us today, every day of our lives';[89] and on the selfsame pitch:
that 'waste products must be excreted if the organs are to function
at their best'. Likewise composed of scientifically controlled dosages
of ninety per cent cocoa and ten per cent cathartic, BROOKLAX
is the name of the brand; and, to make it palatable to children, it
is available over the counter as both Brooklax Chocolate Laxative
and Bonomint Chewing Gum. But in whichever form it is administered, its chemistry is apparently the same, being based on a
colonic stimulant called phenolphthalein; which is derived from
benzine; which Simon Brook refined from coal: which is, of course
(or so his son says), simply Shakespeare by another name.[90]

Notes

A version of this chapter was given as a lecture to the conference on Shakespeare and the Teaching of English at the University of Central Lancashire in April 1993.

1 'Tales out of school', *The Independent* (11 July 1992).
2 'Young actors not tutored in Shakespeare', *The Independent* (2 February 1993).
3 Quoted in 'How to make the best of a bad job: a profile of Adrian Noble', *The Daily Telegraph* (14 December 1992).
4 *Ibid.*
5 'Teachers get royal lessons on Bard', *The Guardian* (29 October 1992).
6 C. Windsor, 'Shakespeare birthday lecture', *The Times* (23 April 1991).
7 'Prince urges moral aspect to education', *The Times* (29 October 1992).
8 *The Independent* (11 July 1992). For Prince Charles's 'secret conclave', see 'Class war: can Prince Charles save our schools?', *The Sunday Times* (28 April 1991).
9 *The Times* (23 April 1991); B. Appleyard, 'The revolution that turned education sentimental', *The Sunday Times* (28 April 1991).
10 J. Richards, 'Censors stifling Britain's greatest cultural heritage', *The Daily Mail* (15 June 1992).
11 Appleyard, 'The revolution'.
12 'English as she should be taught?' *The Independent* (13 June 1992).
13 'Schools ordered to open bank accounts' and 'Reading lessons unsatisfactory', *The Independent* (23 April 1991).
14 *The Sunday Times* (28 April 1991).
15 'Charles's charmed circle: his ayes and ears', *The Guardian* (27 June 1994); 'Prince enrages the left with attack on "trendy dogma"', *The Times* (5 May 1994).
16 'A dead male playwright', editorial, *The Independent* (2 July 1992). But cf. 'The Bard, by order', editorial, *The Guardian* on the same day: 'Mr Patten's insistence that 14-year-olds should face tests on Shakespeare . . . will bring apprehension to good teachers as well as bad.'
17 *The Times* (29 October 1992).
18 *The Daily Telegraph* (14 December 1992).
19 'Comment: Richard Ingrams', *The Observer* (12 September 1993).
20 'Dropping the Bard', editorial, *The Times* (23 April 1991).
21 E. Pilkington, 'Making a drama out of a stasis', *The Guardian* (7 January 1992); K. Linklater, *Freeing Shakespeare's Voice: Actors Guide to the Talking Text* (New York, Theatre Communications Group, 1993); R. Gibson, 'Introduction' in R. Gibson, ed., *The Cambridge School Shakespeare: 'Romeo and Juliet'* (Cambridge, Cambridge University Press, 1991), quoted in *The Observer* (12 September 1993).

22 *The Guardian* (7 January 1992).
23 'Rex's magic island', *The Guardian* (3 April 1990).
24 *The Guardian* (7 January 1992).
25 'Shakespeare brought to life by murder most foul', *The Independent* (11 February 1993).
26 Quoted in 'Much ado about a liberal playwright', *The Guardian* (22 January 1994).
27 *Ibid.*
28 'Right hails Portillo as next Prime Minister', and 'Poison of a new British disease: the speech', *The Independent* (16 January 1994).
29 'The Terry Coleman interview', *The Guardian* (5 September 1983). Lawson subsequently made the Degree speech the theme of his autobiography.
30 P. Bourdieu and J.-C. Passeron, *Reproduction in Education, Society and Culture* (London, Sage, 1977), p. xiii.
31 *Ibid.*, p. xi.
32 'Londoner's diary', *The Evening Standard* (18 January 1994).
33 'Jane Brown's schooldays: Head on the block', *The Guardian* (27 January 1994).
34 'Teacher in "Romeo and Juliet" row apologises', and 'The play's the thing: but is it ideologically sound?', *The Independent* (21 January 1994).
35 'Bard barred as Verona meets Hackney in clash of cultures', *The Guardian* (20 January 1994); 'Head sorry for refusing "Romeo and Juliet" trip', *The Guardian* (21 January 1994).
36 *The Guardian* (20 January 1990); 'Parents praise efforts of school', and 'Improved schools retain "loony left" slur', *The Guardian* (21 January 1994); '"Romeo" row draws in Patten', *The Guardian* (26 January 1994).
37 'Head sorry for refusing "Romeo and Juliet" trip', and 'Editorial: sorry, sorry, sorry', *The Guardian* (21 January 1994); also cf. *The Guardian* (27 January 1994).
38 Camille Paglia, *Sex, Art, and American Culture* (Harmondsworth, Penguin, 1992), pp. 241, 255 and 288.
39 Quoted in D. Addenbrooke, *The Royal Shakespeare Company* (London, Kimber, 1974), p. 66.
40 *The Independent* (2 February 1993).
41 A. Sinfield, 'Royal Shakespeare: theatre and the making of ideology' in Jonathan Dollimore and Alan Sinfield, eds, *Political Shakespeare: New essays in Cultural Materialism* (Manchester, Manchester University Press, 1985), p. 167.
42 *Ibid.*, p. 169.
43 *Ibid.*, p. 172..

44 Peter Hall, *The Peter Hall Diaries: The Story of a Dramatic Battle*, ed. J. Goodwin (London, Hamish Hamilton, 1983), pp. 434–5.

45 Quoted in Sinfield, in Dollimore and Sinfield, *Political Shakespeare*, p. 173.

46 *The Daily Telegraph* (14 December 1992).

47 'Londoner's diary', *The Evening Standard* (15 May 1990).

48 Perry Anderson, *English Questions* (London, Verso, 1992), pp. 199–200.

49 *The Evening Standard* (23 October 1984).

50 Sinfield, in Dollimore and Sinfield, *Political Shakespeare*, p. 171.

51 *The Independent* (2 February 1993).

52 Peter Brook, *The Shifting Point: Forty Years of Theatrical Exploration: 1946–1987* (London, Methuen, 1988), p. 96.

53 J. C. Trewin, *Peter Brook: A Biography* (London, MacDonald & Co., 1971), p. 14; Brook, *The Shifting Point*, p. 75.

54 Peter Brook, *The Empty Space* (Harmondsworth, Penguin, 1972), pp. 12–13.

55 Peter Brook, Preface to J. Kott, *Shakespeare Our Contemporary*, trans. B. Taborski (London, Methuen, 1965), pp. ix–xi.

56 ' "The Experts" expert: direct hit', *The Observer Magazine* (5 March 1989).

57 Roland Barthes, *Mythologies*, trans. A. Lavers (London, Paladin, 1972), pp. 36–7.

58 Brook, *The Shifting Point*, p. 76.

59 Peter Brook, 'Sharing Shakespeare with the world', *The Guardian* (2 November 1990).

60 Peter Brook, 'Theatre with a message? The very idea!', *The Independent* (28 October 1990).

61 Terry Eagleton, 'Afterword' in Graham Holderness, ed., *The Shakespeare Myth* (Manchester, Manchester University Press, 1988), p. 207.

62 Aristotle, *Poetics*, 6:2; John Milton, Preface, *Samson Agonistes*, in D. Bush, ed., *Milton: Poetical Works* (Oxford, Oxford University Press, 1966), p. 517. For the history of the medical analogy, see S. H. Butcher, *Aristotle's Theory of Poetry and Fine Art* (repr. New York, Doner, 1951), pp. 240–59.

63 Brook, *The Shifting Point*, pp. 93–4.

64 Brook, *The Empty Space*, p. 13.

65 *Ibid.*, pp. 41 and 54–5.

66 Steven Mullaney, *The Place of the Stage: License, Play, and Power in Renaissance England* (Chicago, The University of Chicago Press, 1988), pp. 42–5.

67 J. Derrida, *Of Grammatology*, trans. G. C. Spivak (Baltimore, Johns Hopkins University Press, 1976), p. 41. See also 'Plato's pharmacy',

in P. Kamuf, ed., A *Derrida Reader: Between the Blinds* (Hemel Hemp-stead, Harvester Wheatsheaf, 1991), pp. 124–37.

68 Brook, *The Empty Space*, pp. 12 and 153.

69 *The Guardian* (2 November 1990).

70 Brook, *The Shifting Point*, p. 95.

71 Terry Hands interviewed in Holderness, ed., *The Shakespeare Myth*, p. 123.

72 Peter Brook interviewed in R. Berry, ed., *On Directing Shakespeare* (London, Croom Helm, 1977), p. 129.

73 C. Marowitz, 'US: a review' in D. Williams, ed., *Peter Brook: A Theatrical Casebook* (rev. edn London, Methuen, 1991), p. 107.

74 *The Guardian* (2 November 1990).

75 Brook, *The Shifting Point*, p. 91.

76 D. Selbourne, *The Making of A Midsummer Night's Dream: An Eye-Witness Account of Peter Brook's Production* (London, Methuen, 1982), p. 29.

77 Brook, *The Shifting Point*, p. 93.

78 T. Adorno, 'On the social situation of music' (1932), quoted in S. Buck-Morss, *The Origin of Negative Dialectics: Adorno, Benjamin and the Frankfurt Institute* (Hassocks, Sussex, Harvester Press, 1977), pp. 38–9.

79 Brook, *The Shifting Point*, p. 92.

80 Trewin, *Peter Brook*, p. 14.

81 Peter Burke, *Popular Culture in Early Modern Europe* (London, Temple Smith, 1979), p. 95.

82 Brook, *The Empty Space*, pp. 108–9.

83 R. Porter, *Health for Sale: Quackery in England, 1660–1850* (Man-chester, Manchester University Press, 1989), pp. 222–35.

84 Kenneth Tynan quoted in Trewin, *Peter Brook*, p. 15.

85 *The Guardian* (2 November 1990). I am grateful to Mr G. E. Ste-phenson, archivist of Reckitt and Colman Products Limited, for assist-ance in researching the history of Westminster Laboratories and the career of Simon Brook.

86 Eagleton, in Holderness, ed., *The Shakespeare Myth*, p. 207.

87 Barthes, *Mythologies*, p. 38.

88 M. Billington, 'Disability as a family affair: A review of "L'Homme Qui"', *The Guardian* (13 March 1993).

89 *The Times* (23 April 1991).

90 Reckitt and Colman archives; J. G. Lewis, *Therapeutics* (London, Hodder & Stoughton, 1980), pp. 180–1; J. A. Whiting, 'Phenols', in D. Burton *et al.*, *Comprehensive Organic Chemistry: The Synthesis and Reactions of Organic Compounds* (Oxford, Pergamon, 1979), pp. 707–8.

Part II

❖

Contesting the colonial

❖

4

❖

'This sceptred isle': Shakespeare and the British problem

❖

Willy Maley

> And some I see
> That two-fold balls and treble sceptres carry.
> (Macbeth, IV.i.119–20)

A scepter is one thing and a ladle another.[1]

This Shakespeared isle

In the summer of 1941 the eminent Shakespearian critic G. Wilson Knight staged a special Shakespeare revue entitled 'This Sceptred Isle' at Westminster Theatre in London. Billed as a 'Dramatisation of Shakespeare's call to Great Britain in time of war', the performance was in three parts. The first, headed 'St. George for England', opened with Faulconbridge's lines from the conclusion of *King John*. This was followed by John of Gaunt's 'sceptred isle' oration from *Richard II*, Richard III's speech before the Battle of Bosworth against 'those bastard Britains', and Henry V's pronouncements before and during Agincourt. After a ten-minute interval, Part Two, 'Patriotism is not enough', comprised two soliloquies from *Hamlet*, Macbeth's vision of a line of British monarchs stretching out to 'the crack of doom', and three scenes from *Timon of Athens*, showing Timon's encounters with Alcibiades and his army, with the bandits, and with the Senators of Athens. A further interval of five minutes preceded the third and final act, 'The Royal phoenix', which consisted of two excerpts from *Henry VIII*, Buckingham's farewell and Cranmer's prophecy. The performance was rounded off with Queen Elizabeth's address to English troops at Tilbury before the Spanish Armada. A notice in *The Times* had reservations about Knight's acting, but praised the event:

> the whole unusual production firmly establishes his conception of Shakespeare as the poet and prophet of a free and virile people united under a benevolent monarchy and determined to fight in themselves the evils of greed and corruption and to take up arms against tyranny and the lust for power in others.[2]

It was fitting that this call to arms should open with a bastard and end with a virgin. England was of uncertain parentage, but relied on a myth of purity of origins. It was also appropriate that the performance drew on material from a variety of genres, and that the series of dramatic monologues culminated in a 'historical' speech.

The closing speech from *King John* contains several recurring features of English nationalism: a siege mentality, England backed into a corner by Europe; the myth of an expatriate culture – specifically a monarchical culture – repatriated; a defiant claim to global power; and a sense of identity and a claim of right to self-determination that transcends unions and empires:

> This England never did, nor never shall,
> Lie at the proud foot of a conqueror.
> But when it first did help to wound itself.
> Now these her princes are come home again,
> Come the three corners of the world in arms,
> And we shall shock them. Naught shall make us rue,
> If England to itself do rest but true.

> (V.vii.112–18)

Reflecting, in the wake of the Falklands War, on this wartime production, Wilson Knight wrote: 'I have for long accepted the validity of our country's historic contribution, seeing the British Empire as a precursor, or prototype, of world-order.'[3] 'This Sceptred Isle' summed up Wilson Knight's approach to Shakespeare's texts, which he saw as 'royal propaganda'. Out of that wartime production grew an essay of the same name on 'the British Crown' and 'Shakespeare and the nation'.[4] Remaining within the realm of Knight, this 'Shakespeared Isle' – the first British Empire – and the place of England's national bard within it is the subject of this essay.

The British problem

'No man can, by care taking, as the Scripture saith, add a cubit to his stature, in this little model of a man's body: but in the great frame of kingdoms and commonwealths, it is in the power of princes or estates, to add amplitude and greatness to their kingdoms' (Bacon, 'Of plantations'). The nation, of course, is always a metonymy of one sort or another – a privileged part made to stand for an imaginary whole.[5] England and English have long functioned as metonymies for Britain and British. In 1975, J. G. A. Pocock made a plea for a non-anglocentric British history, 'the plural history of a group of cultures situated along an Anglo-Celtic frontier and marked by an increasing English political and cultural domination'.[6] The history of this domination is also the reason for its limited representation in historiography, or in literary criticism.

English Renaissance literature has resisted a broad-based British perspective. Its investment is in England and Englishness. A. J. P. Taylor, commenting on Pocock's plea, declared: 'British and its variants now dominate most political institutions except the queen. English dominates the culture and most of the past.'[7] Shakespeare's corpus undergirds the Englishness of British literary culture, and his work is often enlisted in the service of a conservative English nationalism. Yet the Bard was preoccupied with putting the problems of the state on to the stage. His representations of the history, formation and future of the British state are complex and heterogeneous. We find an elaboration of the British problem in the plays of Shakespeare, works which, owing to their position within the canon of *English*, are read historically as a contribution to the making of a national literature rather than the critique of a multi-national state. Indeed Shakespeare's texts offer a much more fragmented picture of British politics than that adumbrated by some radical English critics. In the Foreword to *Political Shakespeare*, Jonathan Dollimore and Alan Sinfield set out the method by which 'cultural materialism' approaches a text:

> A play by Shakespeare is related to the contexts of its production –
> to the economic and political system of Elizabethan and Jacobean
> *England* and to the particular institutions of cultural production (the
> court, patronage, theatre, education, the church). Moreover, the rel-
> evant history is not just that of four hundred years ago, for culture

is made continuously and Shakespeare's text is reconstructed, reap-
praised, reassigned all the time through diverse institutions in specific
contexts.[8]

The history of four hundred years ago, history today and the history that informs Shakespeare's plays, from *Cymbeline* to *Henry
VIII*, impinge upon parts of the British Isles other than England.
Cultural materialism, which has a more palpable identity in English Renaissance studies than Scotland, 'registers its commitment
to the transformation of a social order which exploits people on
grounds of race, gender and class'.[9] But Britain, a site of contested
identities in the early modern period, and in Shakespeare's plays,
manifests itself in *Political Shakespeare* either as Elizabethan or
Jacobean England, or as contemporary Britain. Paul Brown's essay
on *The Tempest* and Irish colonial discourse is a notable exception, but then, as Dollimore and Sinfield remark elsewhere, 'Ireland was the great problem'.[10] I submit that Britain was the great
problem. To naturalise Britain while retaining Ireland as a colonial or semi-colonial other is to reproduce the post-1603 ideological reification of political relations in the British Isles. In fact, it is
to forget the origins of Partition, which lie in the Anglo-Scottish
plantation alluded to in Brown's suggestive essay.[11] The four hundred years of history between Renaissance England and contemporary Britain are leapt over lightly in any critical discourse that
can say of the 'state' with respect to *Henry V* that 'Ireland was,
and remains, its bad conscience'.[12] The so-called National Curriculum in Britain covers England, Wales and Northern Ireland. It
does not apply in Scotland. Yet Alan Sinfield's article on Shakespeare and education slips easily between 'English' and 'British'.[13]
Ironically entitled 'Give an account of Shakespeare and education,
showing why you think they are effective and what you appreciate about them. Support your comments with precise references',
this essay answers the question it poses very successfully. Shakespeare is effective in the Englishing of the British state, and in
protecting that state from constitutional interrogation, from a questioning that goes to its heart, excepting occasional references to
Ireland.

Shakespeare, for half of his literary career, lived in a polity that
consisted of England, Wales and – contested – Ireland. The royal
house was of Welsh provenance, and the Irish wars were the most
pressing contemporary political conflict. For the remainder, he

wrote in the context of an enlarged state presided over by a Scottish king, a state whose most significant events, provoking crises of representation, were union and plantation. Neither cultural materialism nor new historicism has shown itself to be sensitive to the conflictual British context of Shakespeare's texts. Ireland is a late entry to English Renaissance criticism, and its position within a simple oppositional model of Irish versus English, or British versus Irish, owes more to contemporary politics than to the vicissitudes of the early modern British state.

It is worth remembering that Jonson's famous poem addressed to Shakespeare and prefixed to the first Folio edition of 1623, having first proclaimed Shakespeare's exalted position among authors domestic and foreign, goes on specifically to situate the Bard in a British context – the words 'English' and 'England' do not appear in the poem. While the line which is most often quoted declares that Shakespeare was 'not of an age, but for all time!' the preceding couplet contradicts that claim to transcendence and universality: 'Triumph, my Britain; thou hast one to show, / To whom all scenes of Europe homage owe.'[14] The Bard of Britain, in the wake of Anglo-Scottish Union and the subjection of Ireland, is set favourably against European literary figures both contemporary and classical. The subsequent reference to 'those flights upon the banks of Thames, That so did take Eliza and our James' reinforces the notion that Shakespeare is the poet of the British state, of two monarchs and four nations, whose power, artistic and administrative, centres on London. The 'rise of English' in the nineteenth century would reclaim Shakespeare as narrowly English. By the eighteenth century, with the Union of Parliaments in 1707 stripping Scotland of a further layer of political identity, and with the Ascendancy in Ireland at the height of its powers, the triumph of English literary culture rather than the triumph of Britain was the cultural claim. Samuel Johnson provides an instructive update on Ben Jonson's judgement. In 1765, Johnson could complain, with special reference to *King Lear*, perhaps Shakespeare's most British play, that Shakespeare 'commonly neglects and confounds the characters of ages, by mingling customs ancient and modern, English and foreign'.[15] Between Jonson and Johnson, Shakespeare has gone from being both British and for all time to forming the cornerstone of an emerging English canon, and any mingling of 'English and foreign' is viewed as a dramatic and generic failing. Given the difference between Jonson and Johnson, it is disappointing to see John Drakakis, in the Introduction to *Alternative Shakespeares*, compound the two.[16] Chris Norris, in the same volume, accurately touches on Johnson's 'determination to hold Shakespeare up as the naturalized voice of a peculiarly *English* character and style'.[17] In the gap between Jonson and Johnson, the new word order of literature and language placed the term 'English' at the heart of *culture*, and reserved the epithet 'British' for *politics*.

Shakespeare is our contemporary exactly because the British problem has the same currency, indeed, the same urgency, that it possessed when he grappled with it. Not all natives of English were, or are, unequivocally devoted to the political unification of the British Isles. The gradual displacement of English nationalism by British unionism was a painful process. The expansion of English sovereignty into other parts of the British Isles entailed a loss of sovereignty, not merely for Ireland, Scotland and Wales but for England itself. This loss was also, paradoxically during the Renaissance, a loss of European identity, a loss for all the nations of the British Isles and a loss for Europe. Graham Holderness, in a brilliant essay on the continuing relevance of Shakespeare's treatment of national identities, expresses this tension succinctly: 'The interesting combination, on the part of Britain's Tory Government, of pro-European commitment and chauvinistic resistance to European union, testifies to the problem facing British national ideology.'[18] That the British government had to resort to an electoral pact with Ulster Unionists in 1993 to get agreement on the Maastricht Treaty points up the way in which the Tory Party – still known in Scotland as the Conservative and Unionist Party – sees Britishness as a buttress against Europe and a means of sustaining its grip on 'the Nation'. Yet 'one-nation conservatism' is not the sole province of the Tory Party.

In essence, the history of the emerging British state in the early modern period revolves around three overlapping themes: political unification; the supplantation of Celtic cultural forms by Anglo-Norman administration; and the anxieties aroused by the opposition of lowland and highland social structures. The Reformation put Union high on the agenda, as England began the retreat into Britain, a retreat from Europe that was also a westward and northward expansion of Englishness.

The 'British problem' as currently conceived in English historiography refers specifically to recent responses to the log-jam of the 1640s.[19] There had been overproduction in terms of historical accounts of the events leading up to the execution of Charles I and beyond to the Restoration of the monarchy, the period traditionally referred to as the 'English Revolution' or the 'English Civil War', followed from 1649 to 1660 by the 'Republic' or the 'Interregnum'. Whatever the political preferences of particular historians, the emphasis was always on England and the struggle for English sovereignty between Crown and Parliament. Then the sources became exhausted, as did the source-miners. English historians looked about them and saw that Scottish and Irish scholars in particular had been doing some interesting work on the same period.[20] They remembered that the British state was a multiple monarchy. They recalled that the invasion of England by Scotland in 1638 and the Ulster Rising of 1641 had some considerable bearing on events in England in the 1640s. The much-vaunted 'English Revolution' was always 'Cogadh na dTrí Ríocht' for Gaelic annalists, and 'The War of the Three Kingdoms' for earlier English commentators. The Englishing of those crucial politico-cultural experiences was a piece of modern revisionism. The current shift by English critics towards a British perspective sees in the process of union, conquest and plantation that constituted the state a problem, rather than the solution to a problem, which is how it came to be represented in a dominant English historiography. Episodes enacted on the margins of English society can no longer be regarded as irrelevant, inconsequential or tangential to events unfolding at its centre, not least of all because the 'centre' of English culture, its pretensions to statehood, is located precisely in those margins. England was the gun, and Ireland and Scotland the hammer and trigger.

As well as focusing attention on the political complexities of a multi-national state, the British problem also raises the question of British relations with Europe and the rest of the world. Ireland functioned in the period as a repository of expatriate Englishness, nascent Britishness and colonial otherness. It was represented at one and the same time as a back-door for Spain, an outpost of barbarity, the last port of call for Renaissance humanism and a staging-post for America. It was the Achilles' Heel of the multiple monarchy, since geographically it was situated outside the sceptred isle.

The encounter with other cultures is the key to cultural identity, and tangential texts and experiences can tell us something about mainstream literature and history. The colonial margins are crucial sites of struggle in the construction of metropolitan identity. Indeed, it is the non-English elements of the British Isles, represented as colonies or regions, that define and circumscribe Englishness. The largest country in any union has a tendency to dominate, for example Russia in the former Soviet Union. In the case of Britain, England has long functioned as a simplifying synecdoche for the complex whole that is the British state.

In 'Certain considerations touching the plantations in Ireland (1606)', Francis Bacon, addressing James I, the first (historical) king of Britain, declared that 'unions and plantations are the very nativities or birth-days of kingdoms'.[21] In 'On the Union', Ben Jonson employs the metaphor of marriage:

> When was there contract better driven by Fate?
> Or celebrated with more truth of state?
> The world the temple was, the priest a king,
> The spoused pair two realms, the sea the ring.[22]

Plantation suggests birth, and union marriage, but the offspring of this particular union, the Plantation of Ulster, has ensured that the marriage is an unhappy one. Ireland is born out of wedlock – outside the sea's ring. In fact, Ireland is a child by a previous marriage, Henry II having been granted the lordship of Ireland by a papal bull of 1172. The Anglo-Scottish settlement annulled that previous bond. The fates of the three kingdoms are bound up together. In *Macbeth*, Duncan's sons find succour in the other two kingdoms:

> *Malcolm*: I'll to England.
> *Donalbain*: To Ireland I.

> (II.iii.3–4)

Macbeth, something of a Scottish nationalist, observes: 'We hear our bloody cousins are bestowed / In England and in Ireland' (III.i.29–30). In *King Lear* there is an attempt to make England's Celtic neighbours subject nations, but when you have only daughters, or when there is a woman on the throne as with Elizabeth, then there is a risk that the Celtic nations will subject England. Goneril is wedded to Albany (Scotland) and Regan to Cornwall, while Cordelia goes off with France. But in one of the sources of Shakespeare's play, *The True Chronicle Historie of King Leir*, the third Celtic neighbour – besides Cambria (Wales) and Cornwall – is Ireland, not France. Cordelia is betrothed to 'the rich King of Hibernia'. Shakespeare's substitution of France for Ireland echoes that in *Henry V*. In the *True Chronicle* the purpose of the proposed marriages of Ler's daughters is explained by a noble:

> To match them with some of your neighbour Kings,
> Bordring within the bounds of Albion,
> By whose united friendship, this our state
> May be protected 'gainst all forrayne hate.[23]

The neighbouring kingdoms are to act as buffer zones between England and Europe. The main plank of policy in the Union of the Crowns was the Ulster plantation, which resolved the competing claims to Ireland put forward by England and Scotland. An Elizabethan commentator had suggested that 'her Majesty shall make Ireland profitable unto her as England or mearly a West England'.[24] Edmund Spenser, speaking of Ulster in *A View of the Present State of Ireland*, thought that 'the chiefest caveat and provision in reformation of the north, must be to keep out those *Scottes*'.[25]

One of the English objections to the Union was that the country would be swamped with Scots, in the same way that 'sheep or cattle, that if they find a gap or passage open will leave the more barren pasture, and get into the more rich and plentiful'.[26] Francis Bacon, speaking in defence of the Union, countered this particular fear in three ways. Firstly, he suggested that Scottish migration would be limited by the fact that 'we see it to be the nature of all men that they will sooner discover poverty abroad, than at home'. So much for Scottish fortune-hunters. Secondly, he claimed 'that this realm of England is not yet peopled to the full', and could thus afford to accommodate any such prospective Scots invasion.[27] Finally, Bacon put his finger on a key feature of the Union, its third term, as it were – the mutually profitable carve-up of Ireland:

> there was never any kingdom in the ages of the world had, I think, so fair and happy means to issue and discharge the multitude of their people, if it were too great, as this kingdom hath, in regard of that desolate and wasted kingdom of Ireland; which being a country blessed with almost all the dowries of nature, as rivers, havens, woods,

quarries, good soil, and temperate climate, and now at last under his
Majesty blessed also with obedience, doth, as it were, continually
call unto us for our colonies and plantations.[28]

In the event, the (relative) surplus population of Scotland was
planted in Ulster under Anglo-Scottish/British jurisdiction. Ireland
earthed the political energy generated by the Union.

We 'other' Elizabethans

'This Shakespearian royalty, conceived in the reign of Elizabeth I,
is not dead; it has lived since, within the story of Great Britain;
and it is alive today, in the reign of Elizabeth II.'[29] What I want
to attempt here is a kind of critical cartography, a provisional
mapping-out of a problem I believe to be central to Shakespeare's
texts, and to the culture that sustains, and is sustained by those
texts, upholding their exemplary status and their claims to universality. There are, traditionally, two ways of looking at Elizabethan
society, as a beleaguered nation, insular and defensive, or as the
embryo of an aggressively expansionist British Empire, as England
writ large, England plus the 'National Regions' – to use contemporary BBC-speak. Both of these positions, Great British and Little English, elide the complexities of the British state. Few scholars
engage with the British state as an entity made up of four nations
and many nationalities. My thesis is that the so-called 'British
problem', a new way of thinking about English history of the
seventeenth century, can usefully be generalised as an approach to
English culture in the early modern period, and Shakespeare in
particular. The history of the formation of the British state, the
national and colonial struggles that brought it into being, can
backlight not simply the histories but the later tragedies, those
plays written after the Tudor myth had outlived its usefulness.
Because this problematic British history is also a volatile political
present, it cannot be confined to an Elizabethan World Picture.
We 'other' Elizabethans inhabit a new World Picture, or order,
that is both distant and derived from the first. The terms 'Elizabethan' and 'English' are obviously not coterminous. One rarely
hears of 'Elizabethan Wales', although such a thing must have
existed. 'Elizabethan Ireland' has been the subject of much historical attention, but the best book on the subject is called *The*

Elizabethans and the Irish, as though Elizabethans were not Irish.[30] There was no Elizabethan Scotland. The first Elizabethan state excluded Scotland. Indeed, from a Scottish perspective there can be no Elizabeth II, since there was no Elizabeth I of Scotland – just as there were two James I's. We 'other' Elizabethans are re-living the reign of Elizabeth I. When England was Elizabethan, Scotland was Jacobean. Jacobean Scotland and Elizabethan England coincided historically. The time is out of joint. Scotland had no place in the Tudor state. When England and Ireland and Wales were Tudor, Scotland was Stuart. Ulster and the Anglo-Scottish frontier were the two areas where Elizabethan England and Jacobean Scotland clashed, and these disputed territories were reinscribed into a British polity after 1603.

There is a tendency to view Renaissance England as a flat homogeneous whole, whether in the idealised form of 'Merry England' or in the old historicist terms of the 'Elizabethan World Picture'. Jonathan Dollimore and Alan Sinfield have pointed out both the initial value of Tillyard's historicism over the universalising theories to which it was opposed, and its ultimate recuperation of that pervasive humanism.[31] The 'Jacobean World Picture' never caught on in quite the same way.

To focus upon the matter of Britain is not to lose sight of the continent, but to cut through the fog that obscures the English Channel. It is one of the paradoxes of English Renaissance culture that a period characterised by Europeanisation can be viewed as a time in which England virtually turned its back on the continent in order to concentrate on matters 'domestic', in order, in fact, to domesticate the British Isles in the interests of English sovereignty. The Reformation isolated England from Catholic Europe. The Celtic fringe had to be tamed, brought under English jurisdiction, or it would offer access to Spain, by way of Ireland, or France, through Scotland. Shakespeare's histories deal with the problem of civil strife and foreign conflict, with English expansionism abroad and consolidation at home. But these terms, 'home' and 'abroad', are especially fraught in a British context, and it is difficult, and not necessarily desirable, to separate the question of English aggrandisement within the British Isles from the issue of war, and, by extension, competition for territory with its European neighbours. One thinks here immediately of John of Gaunt:

> This royal throne of kings, this sceptred isle,
> This earth of majesty, this seat of Mars,
> This other Eden, demi-paradise,
> This fortress built by nature for herself
> Against infection and the hand of war,
> This happy breed of men, this little world
> This precious stone set in the silver sea,
> Which serves it in the office of a wall,
> Or as a moat defensive to a house
> Against the envy of less happier lands.
> This blessed plot, this earth, this realm, this England.
>
> (*Richard II*, II.i.40–50)

This is described – in my edition – as 'one of Shakespeare's most moving speeches', and it is moving, because it moves the map of England north and west to obliterate Scotland and Wales, which are no doubt included in the list of 'less happier lands' waiting to jump the moat. To Shakespeare's little Latin and less Greek, we must add, in the margin of this nascent National Curriculum, under Geography, 'Could do better'. But before we blame the Bard for a map of misreading we ought to recall that the tendency to see England as an island, and as Britain, is part of a long historiographical tradition.[32] It is also the stuff of Shakespeare studies. A typical title would be *Shakespeare's Eden: The Commonwealth of England*.[33] The compilers of *Who's Who in Shakespeare's England* include an entry on James I, who 'reigned as James VI of Scotland from 1567, coming to the *English* throne in 1603'.[34]

There is a tension between the Little England speech delivered by John of Gaunt in *Richard II* and the imperialist rhetoric it serves. The supreme irony of this passage is that Richard II's downfall was tied to his failed expedition to Ireland, an island in itself, but a lordship of the English Crown in Richard's day, and a subordinate kingdom in Shakespeare's time. Of course, there's never been an England in the sense suggested by John of Gaunt in this moving speech. When England was not a colony of Rome or France, it held colonies itself – Ireland from the twelfth century, Wales from the thirteenth – and was thus always something more or less than self-contained, never quite at home. England had entertained hopes of a continental empire in the fifteenth century, possessing Gascony, Normandy and Calais. Indeed, the infant Henry VI had been crowned King of France in 1422. As well as the other countries of the British Isles, England had to contend with Cornwall and the ubiquitous 'North' – anywhere north of Stratford. There was also the matter of the Western Isles, Orkney, the Shetland Isles, the Isle of Man, the Isle of Wight and the Channel Islands. The northern isles were controlled by Denmark until 1470. When Gaunt laments: 'That England that was wont to conquer others, / Hath made a shameful conquest of itself', he is pointing up the vulnerability and instability of England as a geopolitical unity. England exists here only as conqueror or conquered, not as a nation in its own right. What others had England been wont to conquer in 1399? Or 1591, for that matter? Post-Reformation England had to buttress itself against Europe. Thomas Churchyard, in a text unambiguously entitled *The Miserie of Flaunders, Calamitie of Fraunce, Missfortune of Portugall, Unquietness of Irelande, Trowbles of Scotlande: And the blessed State of ENGLANDE*, rehearsed the dual position of the Elizabethan state as an island cut off from Europe, an island that both includes and excludes Scotland, Ireland and Wales:

> This ILE is kirnell of the Nutte,
> and those that neare us dwell,
> (Our forraine neighbours rounde aboute,)
> I counte them but the shell:
> That holdeth in this kirnell sweete,
> as Nature hath asciende.
> And as some shells worme eaten are,
> yet kirnell sounde we finde.[35]

Islands beget islands. In *The Tempest*, ownership of the island, disputed by Prospero the planter and Caliban the native ('This island's mine'), is resolved by the claim of the Duke on behalf of the metropolis:

> *Sebastian*: I think he will carry this island home in his pocket, and give it to his son for an apple.
> *Antonio*: And sowing the kernels of it in the sea, bring forth more islands.

> (II.i.89–92)

The island-empire of England, the first 'British' Empire, what has been called 'the Atlantic archipelago', was fundamentally an anti-European phenomenon.[36]

In the Afterword to *Political Shakespeare*, perhaps the most influential collection of essays on Shakespeare to emerge in recent years, Raymond Williams recounts his experience of coming face-to-face with the volume and diversity of scholarship on the Bard in Cambridge University Library.[37] There is a sense in which no study of Shakespeare can be considered too eccentric. His inclusiveness, though, is not as democratic as it might appear at first glance. Certain presuppositions underpin the majority of work on Shakespeare: that Shakespeare is English; that the language of the plays is English; that he is, by and large, sole author of the corpus that bears his name.

'Shakespeare's English' is a phrase which both names the language and literature he helped shape and give international prestige to, and fixes his nationality. Shakespeare is English. English is Shakespeare. This tautology lies at the heart of the dramatist and the discipline. To begin to question Shakespeare's Englishness, to see it as part of the problem rather than part of the solution to his cultural centrality, is to tamper with the landscape of 'this sceptred isle'.

'Shakespeare's English' is part of that universalising humanist discourse that sees the language as belonging to the playwright, rather than the other way round. By reading it as 'Shakespeare is English', we lay stress upon the specificity of Shakespeare's national identity, but underplay the degree to which he lived and worked through the formation of a British political system. Shakespeare is English, and his canonisation went hand-in-hand with the naturalisation of the English language, a process that heralded, amongst other great things, the complex political struggle that saw the triumph of English as the dominant language of the British Isles. In 1500, half of the British Isles was Celtic-speaking. By 1650 only one-tenth was Celtic-speaking. But Shakespeare's British, too. His *genus* is as important as his genius.

W. F. Bolton, in a recent study called *Shakespeare's English*, opposes the scene in *Henry V* in which Catherine's tutor, Alice, coaches her ward in English, and the exchange on the battlefield 'where all speak English, but none share a native tongue . . . the "international" scene with Gower, Fluellen, Macmorris, Jamy and their cacaphonic regional varieties of English, Welsh, Irish, Scots'.[38] Already we can see the familiar slippage between nation and region that characterises anglocentric British discourse. Within a page these 'cacaphonic regional varieties of English, Welsh, Irish, Scots' have become 'regional varieties of English'.[39] Gower's language, far from being a regional variety of English, becomes the standard against which others are measured. The problem here is that there are Celtic languages – Welsh, Irish, Scots – which are not 'regional varieties of English'. The 'Franglais' spoken by the King, and by Pistol to M. Fer, is further evidence of the flexibility of English, its ability to cut the throat of other languages. As Terence Hawkes has observed, 'the language of British society has never been, and is not now, simply English'.[40]

It is one of the paradoxes of English Renaissance culture that a period characterised by Europeanisation can be viewed as a time in which England virtually turned its back on the continent in order to concentrate on matters 'domestic'. The Reformation isolated the English nation from Catholic Europe. England had declared itself an 'empire' in the Act of Restraint of Appeals in 1533, a word which in this context 'designated a sovereign territorial state which was completely independent of the pope and all foreign princes'.[41] In order to turn this 'empire' into an 'imperial monarchy', Henry VIII declared himself King of Ireland in 1541. The 'inland enemy', too, had to be eliminated. There had been an English pale in Scotland in the fifteenth century, but the loss of Roxburgh in 1461 and Berwick in 1482 had put paid, temporarily, to English aspirations in Scotland. Scotland invaded England in 1513. In 1521, a Scottish humanist intellectual based in France wrote in Latin a proto-unionist *History of Greater Britain*, which argued that although there were two kingdoms on the island, all of its inhabitants were basically Britons. Published in Paris, the work was punningly known as *Britannicus Major*, after its author, who, by a curious quirk of history, bears the same name as the later Prime Minister.[42]

English investment in France effectively ended with the loss of Calais in 1558. The peace of Câteau Cambrésis in March 1559, and the departure of French troops from Scotland with the treaty of Edinburgh in July 1560, ensured that, if England was going to be out of Europe, then Europe was going to be out of the British Isles. The end of the 'auld alliance' between Scotland and France, known as 'the bridle of England', was forced home by London. The Battle of Kinsale in 1603 put paid to Spanish influence in Ireland, and with Anglo-Scottish Union the same year the first phase of England's shift from Europe to Britain was completed.

Henry V is a telling instance of a play ostensibly reconstructing a famous victory for England over France, which constructs the Elizabethan conquest of Ireland both as a lesser form of that victory, a variation on the imperial theme, and as a necessary prerequisite for the repetition of such a famous victory. Ireland, the ruin of Richard II, whose usurpation by Bolingbroke led ultimately to Henry's vanquishing of the French, returns as the 'second' of France. Yet Henry's Agincourt and Essex's Ireland were two quite different episodes. When Henry promises Catherine: 'England is thine, Ireland is thine, France is thine' (V.ii.230) we can spot the odd one out. What have Henry, formerly Prince of Wales, now King of England, and Catherine, the daughter of the king and queen of France, to do with Ireland? Ireland is the battlefield in *Henry V*. While the interaction of the four nations that make up the nascent British state is figured, significantly, at the siege of Harfleur – a scene thought to have been especially written *after* James's accession as King of Britain – the nexus of British identity is not France but Ireland. There is, as Gary Taylor points out, the 'revealing textual error' that substitutes Ireland for France: 'So happy be the issue, brother Ireland' (III.vii.51–5).

The histories suggest themselves as the most obvious repository of material on the formation of the British state. The questions of sovereignty and succession that are the stuff of both the 'Tudor myth' and the 'Elizabethan World Picture' are raised explicitly in the two tetralogies. Indeed, the fact that these plays can be grouped together suggests a dramatic history of a process, or problematic, being worked out in the 1590s. In the first two tetralogies the 'civilising' of intra-British conflict, its representation as a threat to the 'nation', as equivalent to inter-English disputes, rather than as a challenge to the constitution of the state, is one of the most successful of Shakespeare's political ruses. Neither in the period in which the plays are set nor in the period in which they were staged is the unified Britishness invoked as anything other than wishful thinking. The dramatic domestication of Ireland, Scotland and Wales prefigured their political domestication. The histories are prophesies.

1 Henry IV opens with the king extolling the virtues of a holy war as an alternative to civil war. Westmoreland interrupts to say that 'a post from Wales' has brought 'heavy news':

Whose worst was that the noble Mortimer –
Leading the men of Herefordshire to fight
Against the irregular and wild Glendower –
Was by the rude hands of that Welshman taken,
A thousand people butchered,
Upon whose dead corpses there was such misuse,
Such beastly shameless transformation
By those Welshwomen done, as may not be
Without shame retold or spoken of.

(I.i.38–46)

The king is compelled to postpone the crusade: 'It seems then that the tidings of this broil / Brake off our business for the Holy Land' (I.i.57–8). Again, as with *Henry V*, the impression is given that intra-British conflict, like inter-English struggle, is an obstacle in the path of grander enterprises. But the 'tidings' that 'Brake off our business for the Holy Land' are yesterday's news. That business was, remember, intended as a diversion, to give the state a breathing space. This sceptred isle is an ill-sheathed knife, sitting uneasily in the scabbard. Hot on the heels of the post from Wales comes Sir Walter Blunt 'new lighted from his horse', with word from the North. Scots and English forces, under the Earl of Douglas and Harry Hotspur, have clashed, leaving: 'Ten thousand bold Scots . . . / Balked in their own blood' (*1 Henry IV*, I.i.67–9). For me, this is one of Shakespeare's most moving speeches, although editors rarely accord it the same emotional impact as Gaunt's lament for Little England. In *Macbeth*, we get a defence of English intervention in Scottish affairs when Malcolm declares: 'Gracious England hath lent us . . . ten thousand men' (IV.iii.189–90). Presumably as a replacement for those lost in the earlier play. In *1 Henry IV* Westmoreland says of the slaughter of the Scots: 'It is a conquest for a prince to boast of' (I.i.77). Hotspur, son of the Earl of Northumberland, is the hero of the hour. The king expresses regret that his own son, Prince Henry of Wales, is not similarly heroic.

This short scene sets out, in sharp relief, the issues that will dominate this tetralogy, and indeed Shakespeare's histories as a whole. 'Civil' strife has to be suppressed by seeking an 'external' enemy. Unruly subjects, together with Welsh, Scots and Irish forces, pose a problem for the English polity. In *Henry V* it is worth recalling that when the Irish officer Macmorris first appears he is in the company of the Scottish Captain Jamy. The heated exchange between Macmorris and Fluellen broaches the question of national identity:

> *Fluellen*: Captain Macmorris, I think, look you, under your correction, there is not many of your nation –
> *Macmorris*: Of my nation? What ish my nation? Ish a villain and a bastard and a knave and a rascal? What ish my nation? Who talks of my nation?
>
> (III.iii.61–5)

Gower, the English captain, interjects with 'Gentlemen both, you will mistake each other' (III.iii.74). In Essex's *Lawes and Orders of Warre* for the conduct of the service in Ireland, item number seven stated that there were to be 'No violent private quarrels in Campe or Garrison upon paine of death'.[43] Fluellen's breach of military etiquette, in selecting to debate military strategy in the field, undercuts his claim to 'know the disciplines of war' (III.iii.79).

Richard II's mistake was to do the British business without a sideline in foreign quarrels. He mortgaged the realm to fund his Irish expedition: 'From whence he, intercepted, did return / To be deposed, and shortly murdered', as Northumberland reminds us (*1 Henry IV*, I.iii.148–50). Conversely, Henry V is seen to harness the Irish in the service of an overweening Englishness. Ironically, the latter play coincides with Elizabeth's costly campaign to quell Tyrone's rebellion, and contains the only contemporary reference in all of Shakespeare's works, if one accepts a stultifyingly narrow conception of contemporary reference. As Gary Taylor says: 'Reflections of contemporary history have been suspected in many of Shakespeare's plays, but the allusion to the Irish expedition in 5.0.29–34 is the only explicit, extra-dramatic, incontestable reference to a contemporary event anywhere in the canon'.[44] This suggests an approach to drama, text and history that limits all three. The passage in question traverses such categories. There are at least three different kinds of history at work here. Henry's return to London is first compared with Caesar's to Rome, then, less enthusiastically, with Essex's anticipated arrival from Ireland:

> As, by a lower but high-loving likelihood,
> Were now the general of our gracious empress
> (As, in good time, he may) from Ireland coming,

Bringing rebellion broached on his sword,
How many would the peaceful city quit,
To welcome him! Much more (and much more cause)
Did they this Harry.

(V.Chorus.29–35)

This is British mythology at its most powerful. First there is the appeal to classical precedent, in this case imperial Rome, then the anti-European perspective, embodied in the defeat of the French, and finally the restless natives, Irish 'rebels' in this instance. The insistence that broaching Irish rebellion ranks lower in importance than the putative conquest of France ignores the reality of British state-formation. The juxtaposition of 'gracious empress' and 'peaceful city' suggests that colonial adventures and domestic order are intimately associated. Four different histories intermingle here. There is the history of a past investment in France, an investment that reached its zenith with Agincourt, and its nadir with the relinquishing of Calais in 1558, the year of Elizabeth's accession. There is the history of the Roman Empire, which England wishes to emulate. There is the 'contemporary' history of the Irish wars, whose successful conclusion, in a move of ideological deprecation, is described as 'a lower but high-loving likelihood' in comparison with Henry's triumph over the French. There is, too, the hopeful history of an empire for the 'gracious empress', an empire which consisted at Shakespeare's time of writing of France (wishful thinking), Ireland (not quite), and Virginia (in progress). Wales was not listed as part of the Crown's possessions, since the House of Tudor was of Welsh provenance. England also had a stake in Greenland at this juncture. Hardly the stuff that Rome was made of. But the British myth – Tudor, Stuart, Hanoverian and Windsor – depends upon just this disavowal of so-called 'internal colonialism' – indigenous indigestion – its rhetorical relegation to a side-show whose main event is empire proper, a staging post to global influence. Ireland – together with Scotland and Wales – has to be 'put down' in more ways than one, silently incorporated, demeaned, absorbed, rather than trumpeted as part of an imperialist project. Alluding to empire abroad is the best way of concealing empire-building at home. In 1599, France was a competitor, not a colony. The siege of Harfleur had less significance than events in the Welsh marches, the Irish pale and the Scottish frontier. The nostalgia for territories lost or forfeited goes hand-in-hand with the deliberate, strategic diminution of the Irish conquest. This is today's history, too. British sovereignty is threatened from within, by demands for Irish, Scottish and Welsh independence, and from without, by the prospect of European unification.

Richard's mistake was to concentrate the attention of his subjects on Ireland. Henry – and Shakespeare – averts the gaze, directs it to France. Richard articulated in too bold a fashion the project of the Tudor state-in-progress:

> Now for our Irish wars.
> We must supplant those rough rug-headed kerns
> Which live like venom where no venom else
> But only they have privilege to live.
>
> (*Richard II*, II.i.155–8)

The other nations of the British Isles were presented as a thorn in the side of England's imperial ambitions, when in fact they were the root and branch of England's imperial ambitions. Two common sayings of the time were 'England's difficulty is Ireland's opportunity', and 'If that you will France win, Then with Scotland first begin', which an English lord recites at the opening of *Henry V*, elaborating thus:

> For once the eagle England being in prey,
> To her unguarded nest the weazel Scot
> Comes sneaking, and so sucks her princely eggs.
>
> (I.ii.169–71)

William Hazlitt pointed out the hypocrisy in this: ' "The eagle England" has a right to be in prey, but "the weazel Scot" has none "to come sneaking to her nest", which she has left to pounce upon others. Might was right, without equivocation, in that heroic and chivalrous age.'[45] In a variation on the theme, Diego Ortiz, in 1567, declared that 'There is an English proverb in use among them which says – "He who will England win, / In Ireland must begin" '.[46] All of these proverbs were reversible, but the basic point remained that between England and Europe lay the other nations of the British Isles. Once again the British myth constructs a history in which the threat from its neighbours, north and west, is a barrier to English aspirations. The subordination of the non-English nations of the British Isles is posited as an essential prerequisite of empire rather than an act of empire in itself. The British Empire is first and foremost the British state, which represents the political subjection of the British Isles under English supremacy. 'England' and 'Empire' are the twin umbrellas that adumbrate the British problem. England is substituted for the British state, and the empire is exoticised, oriented elsewhere, made foreign, represented as being otherwise occupied than with, say, Ireland, or Scotland or Wales. The use of 'empire' to mean extra-British activity overlooks the imperialism implicit in Britishness itself.

Contradictions abound, but they are constantly resolved by appealing to the British myth, an origin-myth of 'national' unity that regionalises dissent. Brian Levack has analysed attempts made in the seventeenth century to convert the emerging British state into a British nation.[47] The process is uneven. Wales had the Tudors, Scotland the Stuarts, but Ireland's entry to the state was not preceded by the gift of a royal house. The only prince of Ireland was Tyrone, and Essex could not broach his rebellion.

Being British is above all a matter of flexibility and incorporation. In *Henry V*, the Welsh Captain Fluellen appeals to the King's Welsh origins:

> *Fluellen*: And I do believe your majesty takes no scorn to wear the leek upon Saint Tavy's day.
> *King Henry*: I wear it for a memorable honour,
> For I am Welsh, you know, good countryman.
> *Fluellen*: All the water in the Wye cannot wash your majesty's Welsh plood out of your pody, I can tell you that; God pless it, and preserve it, as long as it pleases his grace, and his Majesty too!
> (V.vii.101–8)

When Williams enters in pursuit of the previously disguised King, Henry asks if the one he seeks is an 'Englishman'. Here, Henry has assumed another mask, that of Welshman. It pleases his majesty to 'preserve' his 'Welsh plood' no longer than is politically expedient. His earlier battle cry: 'God for Harry! England and Saint George!' made no mention of Wales or Saint David. When Henry goes among his men he hides his regal identity but reveals his ethnic origins:

> *Pistol*: What is thy name?
> *King Henry*: Harry *le roi*.
> *Pistol*: Leroi? A Cornish name. Art thou of Cornish crew?
> *King Henry*: No, I am a Welshman.
> (IV.i.49–52)

Henry is something of a chameleon. What is *his* nation? The French envoy Montjoy had addressed him as 'Harry of England' (III.vi.118), and he had appeared to Williams 'but as a common man' (IV.viii.50). This is the same Hal who 'can drink with any tinker in his own language' (*1 Henry IV*, II.iv.18). The would-be British monarch presents himself as classless and multi-national.

With the passing of the Tudor regime, claims to Welshness lost their currency, and Wales was silently absorbed into Greater England, not meriting a mention in Great Britain. In 'Zeale', a poem addressed to James I, Thomas Dekker and Ben Jonson wrote: 'And then so rich an Empire whose fair breast / Contains four kingdoms by your entrance blest'.[48] The 'four kingdoms' are not the four nations of the British Isles represented in *Henry V*. One foot is kept on the continent as France takes the place of Wales.

We ought to recall that Essex did, in a sense, bring back rebellion broached on his sword – his own rebellion. The Essex rebellion can be viewed as a displacement of Elizabeth's Irish war. Ireland could function as an alternative power-base. This was Richard's ploy in 1399 and Charles I's in the 1640s. But if that base failed, then the so-called 'mainland' or 'metropolis' would suffer.

History is not to be found exclusively in the histories, nor do we have to confine the question of contemporary reference to that allusion to Essex's Irish venture by the Chorus in *Henry V*. The politics of genre – and the question of history's relation to the present – is rather more complex than the accepted classification of the plays will allow. By categorising as tragedies those later histories which deal with an earlier period in the development of the British polity, we deprive them of their historical specificity. *Macbeth*, *King Lear* and *Cymbeline* address the fresh issues confronting the emerging British state in the light of Anglo-Scottish Union. The violence of the triple monarchy is displaced on to a mythical Scottish past, the Stuart succession is vindicated, and, by extension, the Union. Ancient British history is rewritten in order to emphasise the dangers inherent in dividing the kingdom. Recent work on these plays goes some way towards establishing a British milieu. One thinks here, among others, of Paul Brown's excellent article on *The Tempest*, supplemented by an informed reading from Francis Barker and Peter Hulme; Donna Hamilton's incisive analysis of *Cymbeline*; Terence Hawkes's energetic piece on *King*

Lear; and the historically grounded essays on *Macbeth* by David Norbrook and Alan Sinfield.[49]

By the Bishops' Order of June 1599 histories were proscribed: 'noe English historyes be printed excepte they bee allowed by some of her majesties privie counsel.'[50] After 1603, the Tudor myth, instituted in order to justify the reign of Elizabeth, was no longer necessary. With the accession of James I, and a new royal house, it was replaced by a Stuart myth of British 'national' unity, in which England's British problem, the problem of internal colonialism, had been momentarily resolved by the union with Scotland and the military defeat of Ireland. *King Lear* and *Macbeth* belong to a different *genre* from *Henry V*, not merely in the conventional sense – as tragedy rather than history – but as British rather than English texts.

These two powerful Jacobean dramas are, crucially, sites for the construction of a Britishness which is represented as both the fulfilment of a prophecy and the restoration of a fallen state. Lear's 'darker purpose', and the catastrophic consequences of his division of the kingdom, can be juxtaposed with Macbeth's vision of 'twofold balls and treble sceptres'. English sovereignty was simultaneously undermined and enhanced by the Elizabethan reconquest of Ireland, Anglo-Scottish union and the Ulster plantation which followed on from these two events. Undermined, in so far as English cultural specificity was rendered diffuse by the 'island empire'. Post-Reformation self-determination coincided with the birth of a modern Britishness. Enhanced, because England, as the dominant nation in the new political arrangement, with the biggest cut in the division of the kingdom, gained most from the concomitant loss of sovereignty implicit in the act of union.

The British problem is above all a problem of representation, political and aesthetic. The tensions it produces can be seen in terms like 'internal colonialism', 'home internationals', and the BBC's oxymoronic 'national regions'. English literature offers a way of preserving a national identity within a unionist framework. Between British studies and English studies lies the British problem. The loss of national identity – arguably an originary loss – is compensated for by the institution of a national culture. It is a mark of the split between culture and politics that John of Gaunt's speech continues to dominate the canon of English literature, while Lear's 'darker purpose' haunts the British state. The canon, being

English, tends to gloss over other national identities, as well as eliding the differences between nationalists, unionists and republicans. Ben Jonson's position as an advocate of Union is well documented, although even there we find ambiguity and opportunism. Shakespeare's politics, his conception of 'this sceptred isle', despite Wilson Knight's conviction, are harder to pin down. Patriotism is not only 'not enough'. It is often 'too much'.

Notes

I would like to record a debt here to Terence Hawkes, whose lively and suggestive treatment of Shakespeare and national identity has informed, at almost every stage, my own work on this topic.

1 G. Herbert, 'Outlandish proverbs' in A. B. Grosart, ed., *The Complete Works in Verse and Prose of George Herbert* (London, 1874), 3, no. 514.

2 G. Wilson Knight, *Shakespearian Production* (London, Routledge, 1968), p. 313.

3 Cited in Terence Hawkes, *That Shakespeherian Rag: Essays in a Critical Process* (London, Methuen, 1986), p. 68.

4 G. W. Knight, *The Sovereign Flower* (London, Methuen, 1958), pp. 11–91.

5 On the nation as a philosophical concept see Jacques Derrida, 'Onto-theology of national-humanism (prolegomena to a hypothesis)', *Oxford Literary Review*, 14 (1992), pp. 3–23.

6 J. G. A. Pocock, 'British history: a plea for a new subject', *Journal of Modern History*, 47:4 (1975), pp. 601–28.

7 *Ibid.*, p. 623.

8 Jonathan Dollimore and Alan Sinfield, eds, *Political Shakespeare: Essays in Cultural Materialism* (Manchester, Manchester University Press, 1985), p. viii; my emphasis.

9 *Ibid.*, p. viii.

10 Jonathan Dollimore and Alan Sinfield, 'History and ideology: the instance of *Henry V*' in John Drakakis, ed., *Alternative Shakespeares* (London, Methuen, 1986), p. 224.

11 See Paul Brown, ' "This thing of darkness I acknowledge mine": *The Tempest* and the discourse of colonialism' in Dollimore and Sinfield, eds, *Political Shakespeare*, pp. 48–71.

12 Dollimore and Sinfield, in Drakakis, ed., *Alternative Shakespeares*, p. 226.

13 A. Sinfield, 'Give an account of Shakespeare and education, showing why you think they are effective and what you appreciate about them.

Support your comments with precise references' in Dollimore and Sinfield, eds, *Political Shakespeare*, pp. 134–57.

14 G. Parfitt, ed., *Ben Jonson: The Complete Poems* (London, Penguin, 1975; rpt 1984), p. 264.

15 Cited in M. H. Abrams, ed., *The Norton Anthology of English Literature* (New York and London, Norton, 1993), 1, pp. 2402–3.

16 Drakakis, in Drakakis, ed., *Alternative Shakespeares* (London, Methuen, 1985), p. 24.

17 Chris Norris, 'Post-structuralist Shakespeare: text and ideology' in Drakakis, ed., *Alternative Shakespeares*, p. 50.

18 G. Holderness, ' "What ish my nation?": Shakespeare and national identities', *Textual Practice*, 5:1 (1991), pp. 74–93.

19 See for example C. Russell, 'The British problem and the English civil war', *History*, 72 (1987), pp. 395–415.

20 D. Stevenson, 'The century of the three kingdoms' in J. Wormald, ed., *Scotland Revisited* (London, Collins and Brown, 1991), pp. 107–18.

21 J. Spedding, R. L. Ellis and D. D. Heath, eds, *The Works of Francis Bacon* (London, 1857–74), 11:4, p. 114.

22 Parfitt, ed., *Ben Jonson: The Complete Poems*, p. 36.

23 G. Bullough, ed., *Narrative and Dramatic Sources of Shakespeare* (London, Routledge, 1973), 7, p. 338.

24 D. B. Quinn, ' "A Discourse of Ireland (circa 1599)": a sidelight on English colonial policy', *Proceedings of the Royal Irish Academy*, 47:3 (1942), 166.

25 E. Spenser, 'A View of the State of Ireland' in J. Ware, ed., *Two Histories of Ireland* (Dublin, 1633), pp. 79–80.

26 J. Spedding, ed., *The Life and Letters of Francis Bacon* (London, 1861–74), 10:3, p. 310.

27 *Ibid.*, p. 312.

28 *Ibid.*, p. 313.

29 Knight, *The Sovereign Flower*, p. 13.

30 D. B. Quinn, *The Elizabethans and the Irish* (Ithaca, NY, Cornell University Press, 1966).

31 Dollimore and Sinfield, in Drakakis, ed., *Alternative Shakespeares*, pp. 206–7.

32 See C. Z. Weiner, 'The beleaguered isle: a study of Elizabethan and early Jacobean anti-Catholicism', *Past and Present*, 51 (1971), pp. 27–62.

33 B. L. Joseph, *Shakespeare's Eden: The Commonwealth of England* (London, Blandford Press, 1971).

34 A. Palmer and V. Palmer, *Who's Who in Shakespeare England* (Brighton, Harvester, 1981), p. 131; my emphasis.

35 T. Churchyard, *The Miserie of Flaunders, Calamitie of Fraunce, Missfortune of Portugall, Unquietness of Irelande, Trowbles of Scotlande: And the blessed State of ENGLANDE* (London, 1579), E3.

36 See K. G. Robbins, 'Insular outsider?: "British history" and European integration' (Reading, University of Reading, Stenton Lecture, 1990), pp. 3–16.

37 Raymond Williams, 'Afterword' in Dollimore and Sinfield, eds, *Political Shakespeare*, pp. 231–2.

38 W. F. Bolton, *Shakespeare's English: Language and the History Plays* (Oxford, Blackwell, 1992), p. 244.

39 *Ibid.*, p. 246.

40 Hawkes, *That Shakespeherian Rag*, p. 69.

41 B. Levack, *The Formation of the British State: England, Scotland, and the Union, 1603–1707* (Oxford, Clarendon Press, 1987), p. 2.

42 See A. Constable, ed. and trans., *John Major's History of Greater Britain* (Edinburgh, Scottish History Society, 1892), p. 10.

43 R. Devereux, Second Earl of Essex, *Lawes and orders of Warre, established for the good conduct of the service in Ireland* (London, 1599), A2.

44 Gary Taylor, ed., *Henry V* (Oxford, Oxford University Press, 1982; 1984), p. 7.

45 Cited in M. Quinn, ed., *Henry V: A Selection of Critical Essays* (London, Macmillan, 1983), pp. 37–8.

46 J. A. Froude, *The History of England from the Fall of Wolsey to the Defeat of the Spanish Armada*, 12 vols, (London, 1856–70), 10, p. 480.

47 Levack, *The Formation of the British State*, pp. 169–213.

48 *Ibid.*, p. 2, n. 4.

49 See Francis Barker and Peter Hulme, 'Nymphs and reapers heavily vanish: the discursive con-texts of *The Tempest*' in Drakakis, ed., *Alternative Shakespeares*, pp. 191–205; D. B. Hamilton, *Shakespeare and the Politics of Protestant England* (London, Harvester Wheatsheaf, 1992); T. Hawkes, 'Lear's Maps' in *Meaning by Shakespeare* (London, Routledge, 1992), pp. 121–40; D. Norbrook, '*Macbeth* and the politics of historiography' in K. Sharpe and S. N. Zwicker, eds, *Politics of Discourse: The Literature and History of Seventeenth-Century England* (Berkeley, University of California Press, 1987), pp. 78–116; Alan Sinfield, '*Macbeth*: history, ideology and intellectuals' in C. MacCabe, ed., *Futures for English* (Manchester, Manchester University Press, 1986), pp. 63–77.

50 Cited in Annabel Patterson, 'Censorship and the 1587 "Holinshed's" Chronicles' in Paul Hyland and Neil Sammels, eds, *Writing and Censorship in Britain* (London and New York, Routledge, 1992), pp. 23–35.

5

✜
Shakespearian transformations
✜

Ania Loomba

Travelling with Shakespeare

In Heywood's *The Fair Maid of the West Part 1* (1631), Bess Bridges, an English lass, travelling to Fez upon a trading vessel called *The Negro*, asks her boatswain to entertain his subordinates: 'with musicke cheare up their astonisht soules, / The whilst the thundring ordnance beare the Bass.'[1] Performances – musical and theatrical – were an integral part of Renaissance voyaging. Four musicians were taken along on John Davis's voyage of 1585, their role being to 'mollify the Eskimos with their sweet airs'.[2] Martin Frobisher too provided himself with musicians on the second voyage to discover the North-west passage, aware that 'music purges melancholy, out of which come quarrels, mutinies, and seditions'. Humphrey Gilbert realised that music could be used in a more direct way for colonisation: 'Besides, for the solace of our people, and allurement of the Savages, we were provided of Musike in good variety: not omitting the least toyes, as Morris dancers, Hobby horsse, and Maylike conceits to delight the Savage people, whom we intended to winne by all faire means possible.'[3] Renaissance, especially Shakespearian, drama was later to be deployed far more widely than music, and with far more long-lasting effects, as a means of winning over the 'Savage' peoples of the empire. The stories of Shakespeare's imperial travels are tales of colonial formations, of decolonisation, national cultures, post-colonialism and even the new world order. These are often sad tales, in which the 'delight' of 'savage peoples' in Shakespeare is bought at the expense of their own stories.[4]

Without minimising the decimation of native cultures by colonial encounters or the repressive effects of colonial domination, I want to focus on a different version of the 'Shakespeare among the Savages' narrative. Performances of 'Shakespearian' plays on the Parsi stages of Bombay, from the middle of the nineteenth century to the early decades of the twentieth, literally transformed both Shakespeare and the idea of an Indian public theatre. Both these transformations depended on each other, and are testimonials to the power of colonial culture, and to the resilience, as well as creativity, of the cultures it seeks to penetrate. Recent post-colonial theory has, following Frantz Fanon, underlined the 'hybridity' that is put into play by colonial encounters: a hybridity constituted by a clash of foreign and indigenous cultures within the psyche of the colonised – black skins, white masks. But because the study of dominant cultures is far fuller than that of its 'native' counterpart, analyses of 'hybridity' are in danger of turning into accounts of simple *displacement* of native languages and culture by those of the rulers, both at an individual level and on the 'national' scale. Such a move makes it difficult to think about oppositions to colonial rule, without understanding them as an effect of the slips and cracks within dominant ideology itself. On the other hand, a reverse simplification is also possible, whereby anti-colonial consciousness is romanticised as the effects of some pure indigenous cultures and knowledges. The problem in either case is that the colonial relationship is isolated from the workings of class, or gender, or other cultural tensions and fictions. Thus, for all its apparent sophistication, 'hybridity' can sometimes work to posit a rather reductive notion of the culture of the oppressed (variously labelled 'colonised', 'Third World' or 'post-colonial').

In this chapter, I want to emphasise an alternative aspect of colonial hybridity – one which highlights the *multiple* relationships to the dominant alien culture that can and do exist within any 'colonised' society. 'National' culture, in the case of 'Third World' societies, is all too often understood as constituted by the overtly anti-colonial. Thus, in relation to colonised or post-colonial societies, the terms 'national' and 'nationalist' are taken to be identical. As Aijaz Ahmad has pointed out, the pressures of colonialism and imperialism have been such that 'nation' as the site of our collectivity, and 'nationalism' as its necessary ideological accompaniment, have been privileged and valorized to a degree that these categories appear to transcend all others. . . . anti-colonialism has been only one of the many sites at which the discourse of nationhood and nationalism is constructed.[5]

Shakespeare is a tenuous link between the three different kinds of performative spaces I will discuss in this paper – all spaces that were opened upon during the years of Indian decolonisation. By discussing 'his' relationship to all three, I hope to discuss both the relationship of Shakespeare and 'national' culture, and differences between the national and the nationalistic in this period. But first, I want to briefly turn back several centuries to the moment when Shakespeare first travelled to India.

The third voyage sponsored by the East India Company to the East Indies set sail in March 1607 under the command of Captain William Keeling. It consisted of three ships, the *Dragon*, the *Hector* and the *Consent*, which got scattered almost immediately after their journey began. The *Consent* set out for Bantam and the Moluccas; the other two were beset with storms and had to be anchored off Sierra Leone for almost six weeks. The *Hector* was commanded by William Hawkins, who was on his way to the court of the 'Great Mogol', while the *Dragon* was captained by Keeling himself. The editor of an 1849 publication of the Hakluyt Society, *Narratives of Voyages towards the North-west 1496–1631*, Thomas Rundall, quoted certain intriguing portions of Captain Keeling's journal of the voyage according to which two performances of Shakespeare took place aboard the *Hector* while the two ships were anchored at Sierra Leone:

1607 September 5th
I sent the interpreter according to his desier abord the Hector whear he brooke fast and after came abord me wher we gave the tragedie of Hamlett.
September 30
Captain Hawkins dined with me wher my companions acted Kinge Richard the Second.
September 31
I invited Captain Hawkins to a ffishe dinner and had Hamlet acted abord me wch I p'mit to keepe my people from idleness and unlawful games or sleepe.

These portions of Keeling's journal were not published by its first editor Samuel Purchas, who clearly did not attach much significance to sailors enacting Shakespeare in their journeys towards profit and empire. But the entries were subsequently challenged on various grounds. In an entry in *Notes and Queries* (21 July 1900), the prominent editor and commentator of Indian colonial papers, Sir William Foster, defended Rundall from the charge of forgery levelled against him by Sidney Lee in his *Life of Shakespeare*. Lee had alleged that the pages Rundall quoted from were missing from the *Journal of William Keeling* in the India Office and that therefore the Shakespeare entries could never be corroborated. Foster argued that Lee had taken his cue from the historian Clements Markham, another editor of the early voyages for the Hakluyt Society. Markham, said Foster, was mistaken in thinking that Keeling's journal was still there in the India Office with only a few pages missing. The entire journal had been destroyed, and the one with the missing pages was a different one altogether (no. IV of the India Office Marine records) kept aboard the sister ship, the *Hector*, not by the captain but by a subordinate factor. Foster added that there were other reasons to believe 'that the plays were acted on board the East India Company's ships in their tedious and lengthy voyages'.[6] Another journal, kept by Benjamin Greene, a factor on board the *Darling* in the sixth voyage under Henry Middleton, included a fragment which lists the cast of characters and the opening lines of a play.

The controversy flared up again, fifty years later. In a letter to *Notes and Queries* dated 5 August 1950, Sydney Race again maintained that the Shakespeare entries were forged, although he shifted the blame from Rundall to J. P. Collier. What is interesting for us is the grounds on which the charge of fabrication rests:

It is fantastic to think that in a crew of rude sailors, of the early years of the 17th century, could be found amateur players capable of producing Richard the Second one night and Hamlet the next, a task that no professional company would attempt nowadays. What opportunities would the men on board a small and overcrowded ship have of memorizing two of Shakespeare's most difficult plays, what unnamed man of genius played the part of Hamlet, and who was the young sailor who took the part of Ophelia? Was the play performed with or without costumes, scenery and properties? The Dragon had indeed an unusually docile crew if in the heat of Sierra

Leone they were prepared to listen to Hamlet rather than to indulge
in 'unlawfull games or sleepe'. Could the like be found nowadays?[7]

Race's objections are informed by the assumption that Shakespeare is 'above' ordinary folk – a belief that animated colonial
educators and indeed English literary studies in general. Later editors
of Keeling accept without any question that the performances were
designed to keep sailors in their place.[8] Both assumptions – flip
sides of the same coin – were to operate as the basis for the institutionalisation of English literary studies at the turn of this century.
As Chris Baldick has shown at some length, English literature
(and especially Shakespeare) was regarded as simultaneously beyond the comprehension of the lower orders (which included
colonised subjects, women and the poor) and necessary for their
schooling.[9] William Foster was still alive to reply to Race's letter.
Once again he argued against the charge of fabrication although
he agreed

> with Mr. Race that it is almost incredible that Keeling's illiterate
> sailors could have produced, in however elementary a fashion, two
> of Shakespeare's plays (especially the long and difficult *Hamlet*); but
> the conclusion I draw is, not that the passages describing them are
> forged, but that they have been misinterpreted. Neither Keeling nor
> Rundall mentioned Shakespeare at all in this connexion; and I am
> convinced that what the sailors performed were their own rough
> versions of the *stories* of Hamlet and Richard II – stories which were
> widely known and had doubtless been made still more popular by
> Shakespeare's use of them. Such versions would have a minimum of
> dialogue (perhaps largely extempore) and a maximum of action; and
> they would be much on a par with the play presented by Bottom and
> his associates before Duke Theseus, as portrayed in *Midsummer
> Night's Dream*.[10]

Thus the elevated status of Shakespeare is preserved. Here I am
not interested in examining the 'truth' status of Keeling's journal
entries. Rather, my point in pursuing these elusive first records of
a travelling Shakespeare is to indicate how archival differences are
submerged in a common understanding that lowly sailors cannot
perform the real Shakespeare. And yet, it is Shakespeare's use of
stories already in circulation that prompts the sailors to enact his
plays. Shakespeare is simultaneously both popular and aristocratic
– he embodies 'national' culture.

It is curiously appropriate that these initial Shakespearian travels should have to contend with a debate about 'authenticity', for the export of Shakespeare necessarily inaugurated a history of 'inauthentic' performances. The plays were performed abroad by English people who were not quite proper players, often to keep the sense of home alive in their compatriots. The performances of English plays by Anglo-Indian communities, as E. M. Forster was later to show in his *A Passage to India*, literally enacted the cultural differences between them and the Indians. But since English literature was a useful way of conveying to 'natives' how inadequate their own culture was, English plays were also taught and performed within educational institutions set up by the British. Such apparently contradictory moves are of course familiar in diverse colonial histories. The performances of Shakespeare by Indians and other 'natives' pushed the idea of the 'inauthentic' even further. They marked both the cultural success of imperialism and, by initiating the transformation of the colonial cultural icon itself, its failure.

Transformation scenes

From about the 1850s, travelling theatre companies run by the Parsis became extremely popular not only in their home town of Bombay but all over Maharashtra, Gujarat, Punjab and as far afield as Calcutta and Madras. One such troupe, managed by Balliwala, even ventured as far as Rangoon, Singapore and London.[11] Parsis are Zoroastrian émigrés from Persia, long settled in India but distinct as a community on account of their religion, their wealth and their supposed Westernisation. The theatres financed by them embodied colonial negotiation, theatrical transformations and cross-cultural adaptations at their most complex and hilarious. I hope my account will highlight the variety of Shakespearian transformations within a colonial/post-colonial arena, and also indicate how these are site-specific. Not only do these transformations comment on the nature of colonial exchanges and cultures but, like all adaptations, they also reflect on the form as well as conditions of production of the Shakespearian theatre which they so colourfully mutate.

The Parsi theatre companies were the result of astonishingly heterogeneous heritages. They developed from Parsi-organised amateur groups in Bombay, like the Elphinstone Club, which were directly related to British-run schools and colleges. In such clubs and in educational institutions all over colonial India, both English and Indian dramatic classics were performed, with Shakespeare and Kalidasa jostling for popularity among audiences that consisted largely of students, Anglo-Indians and some royal or élite Indians. Their co-existence was not coincidental. British administrators in India were divided about how best to educate the natives. Orientalists argued that it was important to 'revitalise' Indian culture by reviving its classical heritage; Anglicists had emphasised the need for implanting Western education instead. It has been pointed out that the debates between them belie their 'common method of governance: in both an influential native class was to be co-opted as the conduit of Western thought and ideas'.[12] And both treated contemporary Indian culture as impoverished, in need of a cultural boost from either its own forgotten past or a more alive Western tradition. In the middle of the nineteenth century, theatres in various parts of the country had these two models available to them – 'one, the modern European drama as it had developed since Shakespeare and Molière, and two, the virtually forgotten corpus of Sanskrit drama, now restored to a reputation of classical excellence because of the praises showered on it by Orientalist scholars from Europe'.[13]

According to at least one critic, the Parsi companies all mushroomed from the Bombay Theatre established in 1849 on Grant Road in Bombay, where English, Parsi and other English-educated Indians mingled to produce English-language plays. From this company was born the 'Hindu Dramatic Corps' whose aim was to enact the same kind of plays but in Indian languages, and which produced its first play in March 1853 in Marathi. It went on to stage Gujarati and then Urdu plays, all with the help of some English company or clubs.[14] At the same time, companies such as the Hindu Dramatic Corps were also inspired by the Bhave players of Maharashtra – a troupe assembled in 1842 at the directive of the ruler of Sangli who had seen plays performed by travelling 'Kanarese' players. After the death of Vishnupanth Bhave, their original director and manager, this troupe turned professional and began to travel. Such groups cross-bred with the Parsi companies, each learning the tricks of the other. Of course, the development of a formal public theatre varied enormously in different parts of the country – this chapter deals largely with the Bombay theatrical companies, which are significant to a discussion of 'national culture' because of their widespread influence all over the country, as they performed in many languages and were intricately connected with the birth of Indian cinema. As Lakshminarayan Lal suggests, 'Parsi theatre' does not connote a particular kind of theatrical content or style so much as the ownership of the theatrical companies by Parsis of Bombay.

The original Bombay Theatre had been established as far back as 1770, and European amateurs used to perform Shakespearian plays as well as musical comedies, farces and pantomimes there. But the Parsi stage was different from such theatres in Bombay or Calcutta: it enlarged its scope beyond the obviously colonial circle of Europeans, Anglo-Indians and educated Indians and drew a more plebeian audience as well. Its other progenitors were the *jatra* theatre,[15] the *Ramalila*[16] and other mythological dramas. Corresponding to the *jatras* of Bengal were other forms of musical folk drama in various parts of India: the *ojapali* of Assam, the *jashn* of Kashmir, the *kathakali* of Kerala, the *leela* of Orissa, the *swang* of Punjab. When a new Indian theatre began to develop in the nineteenth century it drew upon the reservoir of these folk-drama forms with their variegated traditions of song and dance.[17] Many of these forms were kept alive by travelling players who were to be found all over the country, and who often survived through the patronage of local rulers, although they usually did not travel as far afield as the Bombay companies did. If this heritage seems fraught with contradictions, it has to be said that the Parsi theatre embraced them with energy and exuberance. The fact that the burgeoning new theatres, not only in Bombay but also elsewhere, drew upon these folk forms and mythological dramas indicates how they exceeded the two models placed before them by colonial education – those of Western and Sanskrit drama. The literary criteria were thus insufficient for, and implicitly critiqued by, the public theatres.[18]

Dozens of companies sprang up across the country, all attaching the phrase 'Of Bombay' to their names, and financed by Parsi businessmen who were theatre buffs. Many of the leading actors, also Parsis, held shares in these companies and, in time, went on to form their own. Khurshedji Balliwala, the famous comic, founded the Victoria Theatrical Company in 1877, while in the same year

Khawasji Khatau, the 'Irving of India', established the rival Alfred
Theatrical Company. Muslims, Anglo-Indians and some Hindus
joined the companies, but the organisational reins remained largely
in Parsi hands. For almost a century, the dramas staged by these
companies were the primary form of dramatic entertainment consistently available to urban audiences in greater India. They ex-
erted a major influence on Marathi and Gujarati theatres as well
as on new drama in Hindi, Bengali, Tamil and other regional languages. The language of performance varied from Urdu, Hindi or
Gujarati to Marathi or Bengali, depending on the audiences. Thus,
this was not only modern India's first commercial urban theatre
but in a sense India's first national theatre. That it repeatedly
performed Shakespeare is merely another of colonial India's many
ironies.

The Parsi theatre not only performed English plays but literally
took over the material culture of European theatre in India: it
played in the same halls, adopted the proscenium arch with its
backdrop and curtains, Western furniture and props, mechanical
devices and props. Artists from Europe were commissioned to
paint the scenery, stage machinery was ordered from England,
playbills in the English style were distributed throughout the city
advertising the novel attractions of 'Transformation Scenes' or 'Dissolving Views' and spectators were given an 'opera book' or programme containing the lyrics of the latest songs (see Figure 1). Some
of the actors were sent to England to imbibe English acting styles,
and the companies often had an English girl at the piano. Different performers, within the Parsi theatre and in other theatres too,
were compared to figures from the English theatres: thus Ganpatrao
Joshi, famous for his performances as Macbeth, was called the
Garrick of Maharashtra; the manager K. P. Khatau was known as
the Irving of India, and Agha Hashr Kashmiri, the most prolific
adapter of Shakespeare in Urdu, was nicknamed 'Shakespeare-e-
Hind' (Shakespeare of India). The Parsi performances continued
the English practice of staging small farces at the end of the main
play, and if the latter was in English then the former would be in
local languages.

The influence of Western theatrical devices and traditions upon
Indian theatrical forms contributed to a literal re-invention of 'tradition'. For example, the representations of gods and goddesses on
stage was transformed into a new genre – the 'mythological' drama.

Stories of godly lives and miracles could now be enacted with a
new force and power which drew upon Western naturalism, melo-
dramas, new machinery and theatre props. As we can imagine, all
these lent a new meaning to the staging of the miraculous, and the
proscenium stage radically altered notions of theatrical space and
the existing relationships between actors and audiences. The new
companies also eventually introduced women on the Bombay stage,
with K. P. Khatau bringing Gohar Jan, a famous singer from
Calcutta, to act Shakespearian roles in his company (see Figures
2 and 3). Mary Fenton, an Englishwoman, and Munnibai were
other celebrated early actresses of the Parsi stage. But initially,
as on the Renaissance stage, boys (and in some cases men) acted
female roles. Jayshankar, the actor who took the part of Desdemona
(Sundari) in the phenomenally successful Gujarati adaptation of
Othello, continued to call himself by that name throughout his
career and became 'the most popular leading lady' of his day.

Shakespeare was in constant repertory on the Parsi as well as
the Marathi and Bengali stages. In the Marathi theatre, a distinct
'Shakespearian style' of acting has been identified, as opposed to
a 'Sanskrit style'.[19] Though both categories are rather imprecise, they
nevertheless indicate the way in which a revival of ancient Indian
plays co-existed, and sometimes meshed, with the staging of Western
plays. In 1934 R. K. Yajnik listed over two hundred adaptations
of Shakespeare in various languages, despite the fact that many play-
scripts were lost and surely many others were not known to him.[20]
In Urdu, Shakespeare has been the most translated foreign author
– the first Urdu translation of Shakespeare was of *The Merchant
of Venice* in 1884 called *Tajir-i-Venice*.[21] Plays were often produced
in a hurry, and adapted to suit the company's or the audience's
needs. This was no simple case of imitation. Indian theatres certainly inherited Shakespeare from the British, but just as they used
fancy Western theatrical devices to stage the exploits of local
heroes and figures from Indian mythology, so·in turn they transformed Shakespearian plays into Indian folk performances. Some
of these transformations were a matter of the material conditions
of production: Gohar Jan, after all, was a courtesan-performer of
light-classical Indian music, and her rendition of a Shakespearian
heroine was necessarily hybrid, but in a way that perhaps cannot
be understood within currently fashionable accounts of hybridity in post-colonial theory. Whereas these accounts emphasise the

psychic dislocations between black skins and white masks, and the mimicry of colonial culture by colonised subjects, the performances we are considering here were not conducted with attitudes of reverence towards Shakespeare or Western theatre, nor did they force the performers to abandon their own forms of acting.

Other changes were more deliberate, songs and dances being the most constant additions to most Shakespearian plays. Thus, *Sherdil* (*Lion-heart*), an Urdu version of *Othello* by Najar Dehlvi, performed by the Parsi Alfred Company in 1918, opens with Brabantio entertaining Othello with dance and music. Desdemona and Othello's courtship is depicted through songs. Roderigo and Iago sing in duet to awaken Brabantio and his kinsmen with the news that the 'peacock is in the house of the thief' or that Desdemona and Othello have eloped. Most of the love-scenes lent themselves easily to the insertion of songs, but these were also used in less obviously conducive situations: in a popular Marathi version of *The Winter's Tale* (*Vikalpavimocana* or *Dissolution of Doubt*; translated by Nevalakar and performed by the Natyakala Company, Poona, 1894) Hermione asks Polixenes not to depart from the court in a song. Polixenes also sings what is called 'a philosophical song' at the end of Act I. Even more startlingly, *Hamlet* in Urdu (*Khune-nahaq* or *Unjust Murder* by Munshi Mehdi Hasan, Parsi Alfred Company, Bombay 1898) was turned into a musical. *Junun-i-Vafa*, an Urdu adaptation of *Titus Andronicus* acted in 1910, incorporated an old favourite of the English music hall called 'Navaho'. In the Marathi *All's Well That Ends Well* (*Priyaradhana* or *Propitiation of a Lover* adapted by V. S. Patvardhan, Natyakala Company, Poona, 1894), Helena bewails her lot in a song, and attributes her present misery to her misdeeds in a past life, holding herself responsible for the premature deaths of her mother and her father.

Favourite songs had to be sung thrice or even five times to please the audiences. In the midst of a serious play, says Yajnik, 'the action stops, and the other characters lose all interest in the performance while the favourites are charming the audiences as in a music hall'.[22] Songs and dances were not the only demand of the Bombay audiences. During performances of *Macbeth*, which was one of the most popular productions on the Marathi stage, audiences literally could not have enough of the actor Balabhau Jog as Lady Macbeth in the sleep-walking scene (see Figures 4 and 5):

When the troupe went to Bombay, on the night of its first production the tumultuous enthusiasm of the audience reached such a high
pitch that they continued shouting 'Once more!' (meaning repeat the
sleep walking scene), declaring that they would not allow the play
to continue until they were satisfied. Then the great Ganapatrao,
who played Macbeth with distinction, came forward and lectured
the audience: 'This is not a music-hall, where you can encore a song
as many times as you like. If you still persist in your demand, realize
that such a consummate piece of acting cannot be repeated devoid
of its context. Yes, I shall start the whole play again, and will need
three more hours to reach this point. It is already one in the morning; but I have no objection if you get the necessary police sanction'.
The effect was instantaneous; the play proceeded.[23]

No wonder plays carried on for many hours: a performance of
Cymbeline at the festivities during the wedding of the Maharaja of
Baroda in 1879 reportedly lasted nearly six hours from 9.10 p.m.
till 2.55 a.m.! This performance was put on by the Itehal Karanjikar
Company in Marathi. The players here adapted to a non-urban
stage, as indeed all the Parsi and other travelling companies had
to do. A detailed contemporary account of this performance by a
visiting Englishman tells us that the

> theatre was a temporary structure of bamboo poles and canvas. The
> stage, a whitewashed sandbank forming an oval about three feet in
> height, twenty feet in breadth, and forty feet in depth, was partly
> concealed behind a drop curtain, on which an elephant-and-tiger-
> fight was depicted, and by a proscenium of canvas, adorned with
> full-length portraits of three-headed gods and mythic heroes in strange
> attire. Three uprights – one of them a growing tree – on either side
> the stage, sustained the 'foot-lights' – some twenty kerosene lamps.[24]

The performance itself was equally unorthodox for a Shakespeare
play: it opened with the *sutradhar* (the leader of the chorus in
Marathi theatre) and others presenting a hymn to the god Narayan,
and then the curtain was raised to reveal the elephant-god Ganapati
(Littledale calls him 'a vermilion-faced, elephant-trunked monster')
who directed the manager to sing in praise of the goddess Saraswati
(goddess of learning and the arts). Saraswati appeared to dance,
and then another choral hymn to the gods was sung before the
play proper began. In fact such proceedings would be less incongruous in a makeshift theatre which would be closer to traditional
performative spaces than in formal Bombay theatres whose Western

space they transformed as radically as they did Shakespeare. Littledale claims that *Cymbeline* itself was minimally changed from the original. Cloten, however, was the Queen's nephew instead of her son, since her having a child by a previous marriage was implausible in a society where widow remarriage was still largely forbidden. Also, 'the audience seemed rather horrified at the love scenes between Imogen and Posthumus, for the well-regulated Indian wife, so far from running to embrace her husband, usually veils her face at his approach'. The soothsayer in Act V was replaced by a Brahmin astrologer, who promised a victory to Iachimo's side if he took care to feed the Brahmins. The costumes were 'Indian' although this was not always the case, and it is said that for the greatly successful Urdu *Hamlet* 'the famous manger-actor, Khatau, tried his best to follow Henry Irving's model for dress and scenery'.[25] The result usually was a strangely hybrid dress, sometimes more Indian than Victorian, sometimes the other way around, and a theatrical look that was common in early Indian cinema as well (see Figure 6).

The plays were often far less respectful of the Shakespearian text than this version of *Cymbeline* was. For example, in the first scene of the Urdu *Twelfth Night* (*Bhula-bhuliaiyan* or *The Maze* acted by the New Alfred Dramatic Company, Bombay, 1905), Dilera, the princess of Baghdad (Viola) and Jafar (Sebastian) are seen escaping in a railway train from the invading army of Safdarajanga, King of Bokhara, who is in love with Dilera. The train is caught in a storm, a bridge crashes and the twins fall into the seawater below. They survive, however, and the rest of the play follows the original. The Marathi version of *Measure for Measure* dramatises the song, 'Take O take those lips away' by showing the lovelorn Goddess Parvati pining for her Lord Shiva. And the play ends with not only the message of upright government, justice and chastity but a wish for the 'uplifting of the Motherland'.[26] Thus Shakespeare is made to speak for anti-colonialism. Such a manoeuvre was not unusual, and elsewhere I have discussed the contradictions inherent in making Shakespeare speak for particular positions by subscribing to his universal appeal.[27] In comparison with some others, this was not a self-consciously political theatre. But my point here is that it eluded categories such as 'élite' or 'Westernised' on the one hand and 'nationalist' or 'folk' on the other; rather it was both the product and the producer of a hybridity that was the hallmark of urban colonial India.

Such a hybridity permeated to the other theatres which were influenced by the Parsi stage. The enormously popular Gujarati version of *Othello* changed Shakespeare's play into a tragi-comedy in three acts with songs. Othello is a handsome young prince who does not know his own identity, an idea that is more profound than perhaps the adapter intended. In the first act:

> there is an echo from *Cymbeline*, for Cloten is pining for Desdemona at instigation of his stepmother. By the favourite Shakespearian device [*sic*], Desdemona, dressed as a boy, escapes with Othello, while his friend, dressed as a boy makes love to Cloten. The true lovers ultimately find their way to the kingdom of Othello's father. The King, not knowing his son, gives him permission to marry Desdemona, and appoints him the Commander of the army by removing Iago from the post. Thus the motive for revenge is established.... A new complication is created by Iago's daughter, married to Othello's friend, who tries to save Cassio. Othello throws his innocent wife into a river after half strangling her. She is rescued in the last act by Othello's mother, who is leading a pious, retired life. Later on a farcical situation is developed by Iago's daughter trying to make love to Desdemona dressed as a boy.... In the final scene an effective curtain is secured by the sensational exposure of Iago by Desdemona, by the dramatic recognition of Othello and his mother by the King, by the installation of the hero, and the marriage of Iago's daughter and Othello's friend.[28]

It is worth noting that tragedy as a genre is not generally part of either classical or folk theatres in India – hence most adaptations of Shakespearian tragedies transform the endings to happy ones.

In a rather unusual lecture to the Shakespeare Association at King's College, London, in November 1924, C. J. Sisson, who was then a reader at the University of London and who had earlier taught at Elphinstone College, Bombay, pointed to the popular appeal of this transformed Shakespeare.[29] He indicated the vast distance between the Shakespeare trotted out by colonial educators and Anglo-Indian performers, and the Shakespeare who romped on the popular stage:

> It may be wondered whether Mr. Matheson Lang, when in 1912 he presented *Hamlet* and *Romeo and Juliet* in Bombay at the European theatre, ever spent a night at the Balliwala Grand Theatre in the

bazaar, and if so whether his Hamlet bears any traces of the resolute Indian Jehangir,[30] he would have seen, whether his Romeo stirred then his cultured or, at any rate, well-dined audience as much as the beloved Indian Khusroo would stir the populace in Grant Road. (p. 20)

At the time, Shakespeare, and Western culture in general, were at the heart of a nationalist controversy. Sisson noted this, and suggested that the declining popularity of Shakespearian adaptations after 1912 was

> a conscious reaction against European culture, and in especial, English culture . . . one of the fruits of an understandably querulous nationalism, which has had a marked repercussion upon literature and art. It is notable, for example, that Mrs. Sarojini Naidu, once a very charming poetess in English verse, is now absorbed in political agitation. Her lyre is silent in the clash of arms. And the populace of the great cities is subjected to a constant stream of propaganda such as involves Shakespeare in the enemy ranks of protagonists of an alien civilisation seeking to impose itself upon an ancient people. Nor does this take the form merely of a tacit boycott of Shakespeare in the popular theatres. It is seen in the persistent attempt to replace the study of English literature in schools and universities, hitherto compulsory, with the study of vernacular languages and literature, and in the effort to encourage their development as the general medium for expressing the aesthetic life of the people. It is seen also in a tendency to exalt Sanskrit literature at the expense of English, and to decry Shakespeare, to indulge in iconoclasm and to ridicule the long-lived and deep rooted admiration of his works among cultured Indians. Professor Legouis, in an article *La Revolte de l'Inde contre Shakespeare*, in the *Revue Anglo-Americaine* for February, 1925 . . . quotes with approval the views of Tagore, who sees in the domination of Shakespeare the danger that a feeble imitation of the West may involve the effacing of a splendid indigenous inheritance. Now all enlightened English opinion greets with satisfaction the development of Indian nationalism, the very aim and end of British rule in India, and the justification of that rule. But such arguments are mere obscurantism, the bane of the great movement. . . . *The Empire Review* for May 1925, contains an article by R. J. Minney, late Secretary of the Shakespeare Association in India. . . . Mr. Minney, like everybody else who has written on this theme enlarges complacently on the literary worship of educated Indians for Shakespeare in the original. But he has nothing but contempt for the adaptations of Shakespeare on the popular Indian stage . . . his admiration is reserved for Shakespearian

Festivals, presided over by the Viceroy, whom two thousand people come to see, at which bits from *A Midsummer Night's Dream*, with goblin dances, and from *The Merchant of Venice* presented by advanced young ladies of the Bengali society, form the entertainment. Now as long as the Shakespeare Association and its English or Indian members hold these views . . . so long will Tagore and M. Legouis be justified in their views. . . . In my vision of the true function of Shakespeare in India, therefore, I see something far more fruitful than a mere succession of devotees in the study of pious ceremonial performances before the members of an Association . . . we must not queer the pitch for Shakespeare's true work in India by practising an insular literary creed. . . . Because Shakespeare is virtuous, shall there be no cakes and ale in Bombay or Calcutta? (pp. 20–4)

Sisson here touches upon the two different Shakespearian 'traditions' that were being created in colonial India – the 'purist' and the 'appropriative' – the former was (and still is) the hallmark of academic establishments and the English-language theatre in the country. The appropriative tradition was largely wrought on various non-English language stages. The particular Shakespeare Sisson eulogised has been largely forgotten, but, as we shall see, its legacy remains visible. Not that Sisson was free of colonial zeal: if his countrymen had argued that Shakespeare and the Bible were the two essential ingredients for colonial education, in Sisson's view Shakespeare's 'true function' in India was analogous to the Christianisation of Hinduism: Shakespeare would, he argued, act as a sort of leavening and produce 'great drama bred from an existing indigenous drama in which the new seed has already been sown' (p. 24). Sisson was rather more perceptive in suggesting parallels between the popular stages of Bombay and the Tudor stage in terms of their iconoclasm, free adaptation and material conditions of production, a comparison that has been endorsed by several later critics of the Parsi drama. They point to the fact that the Bombay companies were co-operative concerns, with actors holding substantial shares. Plays were written to order and often bought outright, so that the author had no further rights in the play. Sisson writes:

The best companies maintain a paid 'kavi' or playwright, whose duties are to write new plays, to re-dramatise old and well tried subjects, to re-furbish old plays or alter or add scenes or topical matter where required. Collaboration in the writing of plays is frequent, the comic part being entrusted to one 'kavi', the serious part to another, the 'romantic' love-scenes to a third, and the songs to a fourth. . . . Bombay companies . . . too are formed, suffer defections, fuse into one another or unite for a time, move from theatre to theatre, or build theatres for themselves, and travel in the provinces, as far abroad as Rawalpindi on the Afghan Borders. . . . There are pirates at work, and there are even shorthand writers who sit in obscure corners and are at times caught and ejected in the act of stealing copy . . . for a private printer, or for a rival company to play. . . . The evidence suggests that a full text may be printed after the run of the play. The stage-copy is jealously guarded while the play is in use. . . . The more one examines the vernacular theatre and drama in Bombay, in general or with especial interest in its versions of Shakespeare, the more one feels that here we have something like the conditions of the Elizabethan stage in actual working order, and that light may be thrown thereby upon some of the problems of that stage. (p. 19)

This chapter cannot discuss the claim about these parallels between Renaissance England and twentieth-century India. On the one hand, they are not entirely fanciful, even though one must guard against the obvious dangers of positing such large cross-cultural comparisons. Both societies are in some very rough senses transitional between a feudal, rural and a urban mercantilist-capitalist economy, and while the contexts for these terms are culturally and temporally different, certain similarities in terms of urban growth and gender and class relations exist.[31] But what makes the two utterly different is the colonial factor in India – a factor that also indicates India's long pre-colonial history which would complicate any parallels we might seek to make. Nevertheless, both theatres were the first public commercial urban theatres of their cultures, and both were patronised by members of various classes. On the Parsi stage too, the rivalry between theatre-managers led them to spend more and more money on outrageous costumes and sceneries, £4,000 to £5,000 being reportedly spent during a single production both on dazzling scenic effects and on elaborate costumes. Like their Elizabethan counterparts, Parsi managers also spent money to woo actors belonging to rival companies and employed local 'gallants' to applaud their own actors, and hiss off a rival show. In any case, it is clear that the 'Shakespearian' element in Parsi theatre ran deeper than the plays themselves to embrace the conditions of theatrical production and consumption.

Shakespeare Wallah

On 7 July 1896 the first motion pictures were shown in India by agents of the Lumière brothers. Within a week they had become a mass attraction as 'the eight-anna wallahs also began to see the movies'.[32] Indians were also quick to start making their own films, even quicker than Americans – the first indigenously produced feature, *Pundalik*, was released on 18 May 1912, a couple of months before Americans saw *Queen Elizabeth*.[33] Indian cinema was to become not only the largest film industry of the world but also, very shortly after its inception, the most important pan-Indian form of entertainment, and hence central to any understanding of Indian 'national culture'. The first fifty years of its development took place under a colonial administration.[34] But although engendered in a very literal sense by the material presence of colonialism, it rejuvenated indigenous forms of entertainment like the mythological, and began to address questions of national identity. At any rate, it certainly spelt the end of the popular Bombay stage: contemporary stage enthusiasts like C. R. Shah foresaw the latter's inevitable demise:

> these 'talkies' follow the same technique and can make their shows spectacular; besides the entertainment they provide is not very expensive. They can afford to pay higher salaries to the actors and actresses; and so the modern tendency is to attract the good actors and singers of the theatres in Bombay and make them act and sing for the screen. So many well-known actors – Ashrafkhan, Bhagwandas, Patwardhan and others – have left or are about to leave the stage and sign contracts with the film producers.[35]

Sisson too saw cinema as strangling the Bombay popular theatre, which led him to characterise the cinema 'an Occidental pseudo-art [that] has here been embraced without lamentation' (ironically in opposition to a Shakespeare that he clearly regarded as Indian!).

But, at another level, there was no clash between this new love of the masses in Bombay and the old one: the Parsi theatre literally dissolved into cinema as the drama companies transformed themselves into the early film companies. Financiers, managers and actors were common to both. The sensibility and the repertoire also overlapped. Sohrab Modi and his elder brother Rustem, for example, recast their theatre group into the Stage Film Company in order to film their popular play *Hamlet* or *Khoon ka Khoon* (literally *Blood for Blood*) which was 'staged against painted curtains, several times inside the studio and photographed from different angles. . . . It was indeed a free adaptation of the classic play, with seventeen songs, characters bearing Indian names and new ones added where necessary' (Figure 7).[36] Agha Hashr Kashmiri, the Shakespeare-e-Hind, switched easily to writing screenplays and to the new kind of popular entertainment.

But Shakespeare was no longer central to this new form of entertainment in any obvious sense. The re-production of Shakespearian plots was not, as in the case of the urban theatres, a staple feature of Indian cinema. However, even when the films were not Shakespearian, the actors had often cut their theatrical teeth playing Shakespeare; thus, Kamlabai Gokhale, one of the early actresses of Indian cinema remembers having first 'gone onto the stage at the age of four with my mother Durgabai in *Vikar Vilasit*, an adaptation of *Hamlet* in Marathi. I acted as a little boy in the play-within-the-play. Our company was a prose company. We used to stage Shakespearian plays.'[37] More intangible was the impact of style – the declamatory theatrical performances of early film in India retained the features of the 'Shakespearian' stage as it had developed in India. Also, it is interesting to consider how the pastiche of song and dance, melodrama, disguise and plot reversals in the popular Bombay film are features inherited from the earlier Bombay stages, and via them from various traditions of playing Shakespeare.

However, when one thinks of Shakespeare and travelling players in India, it is not Parsi companies but Geoffrey Kendal's travelling troupe, 'Shakespeariana', made famous by Merchant–Ivory's film *Shakespeare Wallah* (1965), that comes to mind. Kendal and his wife, Laura Liddell, along with other members of their troupe, toured India extensively from the 1940s to the early 1960s. From Himachal Pradesh in the north to Kerala in the south, from Manipur in the east ('where no one had ever seen English drama before') to the urbane Bombay in the west, the geographical and cultural ambit of the company was quite extraordinary. It played before the Mountbattens, Jawaharlal Nehru, various minor royalty, in tea estates, among the Kipling-esque élite of hill stations, and most often before all kinds of school audiences. The film documents the disintegration of this troupe in the context of post-colonial India where its once ready-made audiences drawn from schools and colleges evaporated, although it was still patronised (in every way) by the occasional raja. One could stretch a point and say that the Kendals occupied a space made possible, and then vacated by the Parsi theatres. But the *differences* between the two sets of travelling players and their Shakespeares are equally important. The Kendals exported a British Shakespeare into India, although Geoffrey Kendal maintained that Indian audiences were the most receptive to Shakespeare: 'my favourite audience is Indian schoolgirls' he writes in his autobiography, 'they always got thoroughly involved in the play', or again, Indian audiences 'really are the best in the world, nothing escapes their attention'.[38] Kendal would occasionally 'use local musicians and the songs of Elizabethan England seemed to harmonise perfectly with an Indian flute or sitar. I costumed some of the productions in local dress, which had the effect of bringing the two cultures together, and from this a wonderful understanding between actor and audience developed' (p. 123). Although this is a kind of transformation in its own right, and Kendal certainly saw the troupe as avant-garde, there was nothing Indian about the Shakespeare he played. Their school audiences were fed on a steady diet of colonial literature and schooled in reverence for the Bard and the canon. Moreover, the idea that Indians 'loved' Shakespeare worked to deflect the dangers of nationalism: 'armed with Shakespeare, whose plays were so much appreciated in India we felt we could ignore the warnings about the nationalist movement and possible troubles. India was moving towards independence but we did not see that it might affect us' (p. 85).

The film *Shakespeare Wallah*, which was based on a diary kept by Geoffrey, pits the decline of the Kendals (Buckinghams in the film) *against* the growing popularity of the Bombay film. Manjula, a spoilt young film star of the Bombay cinema, played by Madhur Jaffrey, is the rival of Lizzie, the daughter of the Buckinghams, played by the Kendals' younger daughter, Felicity. Both vie for the hand of Sanju, a rich Indian played by Shashi Kapoor. But they are also professional rivals. Manjula is a typical Bombay film star, which means that she has no idea of what it takes to be a dedicated performer. Lizzie, honed by her father's training and moulded by the Shakespearian stage, is the exemplary actress. The professional contrast spills over into their personalities, their morals and the kinds of femininity each represents: Manjula is also lazy, unscrupulous and wily, whereas Lizzie is unspoilt and naive. Sanju tries to make Manjula watch Lizzie act, and constantly praises Lizzie's professional dedication. Manjula's frothy song-and-dance sequences are pitted against Lizzie's intense Shakespearian performances. Mr Buckingham himself holds Garrick as a model for Shakespearian acting. If the Parsi theatre had yoked together Shakespeare and the Bombay film, *Shakespeare Wallah* represents them as diametrically opposed.[39] In fact, it reverses the relationship posited by Sisson – Shakespeare reverts to being the Occidental, and the Bombay film becomes vulgarly Oriental, an opposition that is tellingly cast in the differences between the Western woman and the Indian one.

Neither Sisson nor *Shakespeare Wallah* captures the historical *interrelation* between the Hindi film and Shakespeare. Like the Parsi theatre, the popular Bombay film developed as a pastiche of song and dance, comedy and tragedy, evoking Hollywood films, Western plays, Indian epics and folk theatres. Brecht once suggested that the nearest modern approximation to the Elizabethan stage was the Broadway musical with its spectacle and songs. One might suggest that the Bombay film, via the Parsi theatre, claims that position for itself. But any discussion of the transformation of Shakespeare into Parsi popular theatre, and then the further transformation of this theatre into Bombay cinema, must take account of the important cultural and material breaks between them. These cultural 'exchanges' also indicate crucial ruptures. The point at which the 'cakes and ale' of the Parsi theatre are no longer Shakespeare also marks the limits of appropriation.

'National' cultures

The theatrical transformations discussed in this chapter span a whole century – from 1857 to the 1960s. No stable understanding of Indian 'national culture' can emerge from this turbulent period, which includes the first Indian war for independence in 1857, the growth of powerful movements for self-rule that outlined diverse blueprints for an independent India, the transition from British to Indian governance in 1947 along with the partition of the country, the early years of the formation of a nation-state, and the beginning of the end of the Nehruvian dream of a secular, modern yet culturally independent country. During this period intense and multiple

contests for defining and controlling an Indian nation catalysed
and spread over the country. To contextualise adequately the entertainments I have discussed here within these developments in
national politics and culture is a task beyond the scope of this
chapter. But this very difficulty indicates that a binary division
between colonial and anti-colonial, between 'Western' and 'indigenous' cultures, is not adequate to understanding any of these
cultural phenomena. Despite the differences between them, the
Parsi theatres, the Bombay film and Geoffrey Kendal's troupe all
catered to pan-Indian markets. The Parsi theatre and the Bombay
film could be said to have created the idea of a national audience;
Kendal banked on there being a national love for Shakespeare that
would transcend nationalism. But it is obvious that the concept
of the 'national' in each case is different, and its relationship to
'nationalism' is also constantly changing.

Lakshminarayan Lal points out the psychic contradictions and
schisms upon which the Parsi theatre built its popularity. From the
mid 1850s, colonial rule in India altered existing class configurations. In the urban centres particularly, it accelerated the growth
of new commercial groups, working classes, professionals and salaried people. All of these, he suggests, needed new forms of entertainment and formed 'the market' for Parsi theatres. On the one
hand, these urban audiences craved the 'new' and the foreign –
hence each company marketed itself by appending 'new' to its title,
promising fresh scripts, tales of distant shores, imported technical
devices that would facilitate a new spectacularity, as well as foreign
actresses who would make tangible the incorporation of the alien
within the familiar. On the other hand, the same audiences, cradled
by the growing nationalist movement, also responded to a reas-
surance about their hoary and weighty cultural heritage.[40] These
schisms are not simply equivalent to a colonialist/nationalist divide.
The desire for the new and the foreign cannot be seen as solely
induced by colonial culture – it was also an aspect of new class
aspirations and energy fostered by urban growth, and indeed we
can also relate it to the energy unleashed by nationalism. Indian
nationalism was itself heterogeneous, and important sections within
it articulated the right of India to move forward and embrace the
world on its own terms. The playing of Shakespeare by the Parsi
theatres is testimony to both these impulses, and is quite different from the fossilised reproduction of a more obviously colonial

AT THE

CORINTHIAN THEATRE

ETC.

THE LOVE STORY OF THE AGES

NALA AND DAMAYANTI

A Spectacle of Super-Extravagant Splendour
in Three Acts
etc.

With an All-Star Cast Featuring India's
Popular Stage-Star

MASTER MOHAN

in the principal rôle of 'Bidushak'

The Play is replete with gorgeous dresses, wonderful trans-
formation scenes and weird and enchanting effects. . . .
The entire gorgeous scenery designed and painted by
India's Greatest Living Artist

Mr. K. HUSSAIN BUKSH, of Lahore

See?   See?   See?

The Sleepy Lotuses transform themselves into Fairy visions.
The Vision of Princess Damayanti.
The bursting of a lotus and the appearance of Goddess
    'Saraswati' therefrom.
The flight of the Swan.
The 'Swayambara' of Damayanti.
Narad's descent from the clouds.
The miraculous appearance of Kali with the Flaming Sword.
The transformation of five Nalas.
The transformation of 'Karkota' in a forest fire.
The Durbar-Hall of King Nala.
The transformation of seven Fairies, etc.

1 Advertisement for a new play on the Parsi stage.

2 Gohar Jan, the singer from Calcutta, who became one of the first women on the public stage, as she appeared on a 1920s matchbox label.

3 (facing) Gohar on a picture postcard, printed in Luxenburg.

Miss Goher

4 Ganpatrao Joshi, in the role of Manjirao (Macbeth) in 1896.

5 Balabhau Jog, famous for female roles, including that of Lady Macbeth.

6 (above) Typical costumes as used in Shakespearian adaptations.

7 (left) Sohrab Modi and Naseem in their first film, *Khoon ka Khoon* (*Hamlet*, 1935).

8 (left) Actor D. Billimoria, the 'Douglas Fairbanks' of early Indian films.

9 (below) *Shakespeare Wallah*: the Maharaja and the Players.

10 (facing above) Madhur Jaffrey as Manjula the Bombay film actress in *Shakespeare Wallah*.

11 (facing below) The opening shot of *Shakespeare Wallah*.

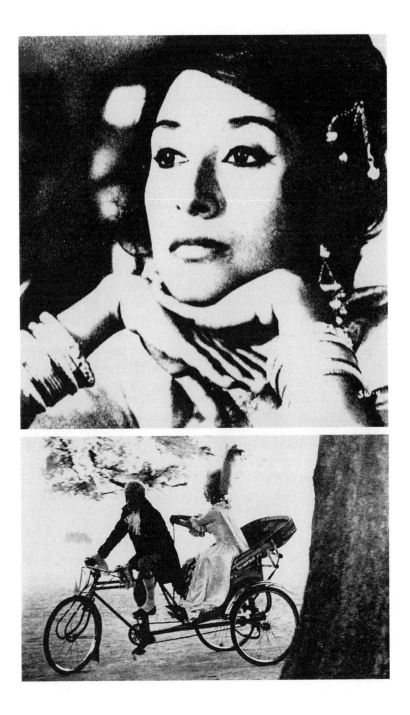

Shakespeare in Indian classrooms. Moreover audiences also demanded the familiar pleasures of older stories and the forms of
telling them. This desire allowed the public theatres, who after all
had to sustain themselves through the box-office, to transcend the
two models offered it by colonial aesthetics – those of classical
Sanskrit and Western canonical dramas.

Elsewhere I have argued that 'post-coloniality' is not an adequate term for understanding the different relationships of different sections of Indian society to colonialism and nationalism.[41]
Class, gender and region (and other factors such as religion and
caste) profoundly alter the relationship of people to Western culture, colonial education and cultural icons like Shakespeare. The
Shakespeare played in Mizoram a few years ago, the icon upheld
by some departments of English in India, the bard appropriated by
Western-educated nationalists in the nineteenth century, the dramatist presented by British players like the Kendals, the playwright
adapted by theatres in various languages across the country, are
not identical. We may also find that our own attitudes to the teaching of Shakespeare shift according to the context of the discussion. Colonialist hangovers do persist in India, but they jostle with
an increasingly militant Hinduism. Some of us who have spent
much energy canvassing for a change in the way a colonialist Shakespeare is still institutionalised within English literary studies in India
increasingly find ourselves having to argue that a simple replacement of Western literature by 'Indian' or 'Third World' texts will
not undermine existing ideological or critical orthodoxies. The binary opposition between East and West now feeds into an aggressive re-definition of the Indian nation in communal terms. In 1987
the Hindu Mahasabha stopped a play called *Shakespeare ki Ram
Leela* (*Shakespeare's Ram Leela*, a farce in which Romeo and Juliet
stumble on to a *Ramalila* performance) from being performed at
Bombay's Prithvi theatre. They interpreted the play as a slur on
Hinduism.[42] Thus, it is necessary to resist both the colonial hangovers surrounding Shakespeare and this easy polarity between 'us'
and 'them'.

In this chapter I have considered the shifting place of Shakespeare within different performative spaces that are all 'national'
to a lesser or greater extent. I have tried to show that while they
can be seen to develop from one another, their relationships to the
colonial presence as well as to nationalism are divergent. Together,

they indicate a range of considerations that emerge from the travels of Shakespeare abroad. Individually, they also lead us to locate nuances of culture and politics that cannot be sensed if one understands the 'national' to be identical to the 'anti-colonial'. In these transformations of Shakespeare we can glimpse radical changes in the relationship between the popular and high culture, the indigenous and the foreign, the original and its appropriations.

Notes

1 Thomas Heywood, *The Fair Maid of the West Part I* in *The Dramatic Works of Thomas Heywood* (New York, Russell and Russell, 1964), Act II, scene iv. This edition contains no line numbers.

2 R. R. Cawley, *Unpathed Waters: Studies in the Influence of the Voyagers on Elizabethan Literature* (Princeton, Princeton University Press, 1940), p. 178.

3 Richard Hakluyt, ed., *Principal Navigations* (Glasgow, J. Maclehose and Sons, 1905), 8, p. 47.

4 Martin Orkin discusses how the Shakespearian text itself ties in with some of its subsequent repressive deployments, 'A sad tale's best for South Africa', paper presented at the Shakespeare Association of America Meeting, Chicago, 1995.

5 Aijaz Ahmad, ' "Third world literature" and the nationalist ideology', *Journal of Arts and Ideas*, 17 & 18, p. 133.

6 William Foster, 'Forged Shakespeariana', *Notes and Queries* (21 July 1900), p. 42.

7 S. Race, 'J. P. Collier's fabrications', *Notes and Queries* (5 August 1950), pp. 345–6.

8 M. Stachan and B. Penrose, *The East India Company Journals of Captain William Keeling and Master Thomas Bonner, 1615–1617* (Minneapolis, University of Minnesota Press, 1971), p. 24.

9 Chris Baldick, *The Social Mission of English Criticism 1848–1932* (Oxford, Oxford University Press, 1983), chapter two.

10 William Foster, 'Replies', *Notes and Queries* (16 September 1950), p. 415.

11 Karen Hansen, *Grounds for Play* (Berkeley, University of California Press, 1992), p. 80.

12 Gauri Viswanathan, 'The beginnings of English literary study in British India', *Oxford Literary Review*, 9:1–2 (1987), p. 10.

13 Partha Chatterjee, *The Nation and its Fragments: Colonial and Postcolonial Histories* (Princeton, Princeton University Press, 1993), p. 7.

14 Lakshminarayan Lal, *Parsi–Hindi Rangmanch* (Delhi, Rajpal and Sons, 1972), p. 33.

15 *Jatra* literally means both 'festival' and 'journey', and is a form of travelling folk theatre long popular in Bengal and surrounding areas.

16 Performances of the Hindu epic *Ramayana*.

17 E. Barnouw and S. Krishnaswamy, *Indian Film* (New York, Oxford University Press, 1980), p. 72.

18 Chatterjee, *The Nation and its Fragments*, pp. 7–8.

19 V. S. Desai, 'Years of glory, 1880–1920' in *The Marathi Theatre 1843–1960* (Bombay, Popular Book Depot, 1961), p. 8.

20 R. K. Yajnik, *The Indian Theatre, its Origins and its later Developments under European Influence* (New York, E. P. Dutton, 1934).

21 *Shakespeare in India, an Exhibition of Books and Illustrations to Celebrate the Fourth Birth Centenary of William Shakespeare* (Calcutta, National Library, 1964), p. 10.

22 Yajnik, *The Indian Theatre*, p. 122.

23 *Ibid.*, p. 173.

24 H. Littledale, '*Cymbeline* in a Hindoo playhouse', *Macmillan's Magazine* (May 1880), pp. 65–6.

25 Yajnik, *The Indian Theatre*, p. 161.

26 *Ibid.*, p. 143.

27 A. Loomba, 'Overworlding the "third world"', *Oxford Literary Review*, 13 (1991), 164–91.

28 Yajnik, *The Indian Theatre*, p. 169.

29 C. J. Sisson, *Shakespeare in India: Popular Adaptations on the Bombay Stage* (London, The Shakespeare Association, 1926).

30 Hamlet in an Urdu adaptation by Umrao Ali in 1895.

31 A. Loomba, *Gender, Race, Renaissance Drama* (Manchester, Manchester University Press, 1989); Lakshminarayan Lal, *Parsi–Hindi Rangmanch*, p. 34.

32 F. Rangoonwallah, 'Before the beginning', *Cinema Vision*, 1:1 (1980), p. 14.

33 S. S. Chakravarty, *National Identity in Indian Popular Cinema, 1947–1987* (Austin, University of Texas Press, 1993), pp. 34–5.

34 R. Armes, *Third World Film Making and the West* (Berkeley, University of California Press, 1987).

35 Yajnik, *The Indian Theatre*, p. 251.

36 F. Rangoonwallah, *75 Years of Indian Cinema* (New Delhi, Indian Book Company, 1987), p. 92.

37 S. Bahadur and Shyamala Vanarase, 'The personal and professional problems of a woman performer', *Cinema Vision*, 1:1 (1980), p. 23.

38 Geoffrey Kendal, *The Shakespeare Wallah* (London, Sidgwick and Jackson, 1986), pp. 77 and 79.

39 In real life, the lines were not so rigidly drawn: Shashi Kapoor, a popular Bombay star, had apprenticed with the Kendals and married their older daughter Jennifer.

40 Lakshminarayan Lal, *Parsi-Hindi Rangmanch*, pp. 34–5.
41 '*Hamlet* in Mizoram', in Marianne Novy, ed., *Cross-Cultural Performances* (Urbana-Champagne and Chicago, Illinois University Press, 1993), pp. 227–50.
42 *India Today* (15 February 1988), p. 23.

Acknowledgement

Gratitude is due to Merchant Ivory Productions for their permission to reproduce illustrations from *Shakespeare Wallah* (1965).

6

✣

Whose things of darkness?
Reading/representing *The Tempest*
in South Africa after April 1994

✣

Martin Orkin

Perhaps not surprisingly, in South Africa, within the provenance of Shakespearian critical practice, 'resistance' still means resistance to an entrenched Shakespeare establishment which is often actively hostile to new historicism, feminist or queer studies and cultural materialism. This establishment remains intent on the perpetuation of apolitical readings that double up as self-improvement programmes or even as surreptitious acts of worship.[1] Thus, a relatively recent article entitled 'Shakespeare not our contemporary' asserts with breathtaking as well as embarrassing confidence or ignorance how little the 'aggrieved and materialist mentality' of the 'new historicist enterprise . . . shares of the traditionalist assumptions of the continuity of culture and the intrinsic value of the great liberating works of the imagination'.[2] It trundles on-stage, as an answer to its *bêtes noires*, certain elementary observations about rhetoric in order to conclude:

> Now that we have education, theoretically, for all, we neglect rhetorical training and thus disable most of our adults from participation in public life. To think of high school pupils as orators in training requires a certain leap of the imagination, but it is worth noting that it is still implicitly part of the public school tradition in England, where the ruling class and the entrepreneurs are groomed. . . . A nation that enjoys freedom of speech teaches its young the art of speaking well and listening with discrimination, and has its affairs debated

passionately and eloquently in public, is a nation where civilisation
has triumphed. (p. 76)

The author of this article cites as 'evidence' for his views on English and South African education and renaissance rhetoric his own
'experience at Stowe School, Buckingham, England' (p. 77), and
the editor of the journal in which this article appears, at the time
the President of the Shakespeare Society of Southern Africa, lauds
this paragraph in his general editorial introduction to the whole
journal (p. v).

Its title notwithstanding, then, this article actively propounds a
'relevance' in the study of rhetoric in the Shakespeare text for
modern South Africa of a very specific kind. Bearing in mind the
role of the South African ruling group for the last forty years and
longer in the context of multiple ethnicities, it is impossible not
to set beside it a passage from Stephen Greenblatt's well-known
exploration of the early impact of the new world upon the old:

> It is precisely to validate such high-sounding principles – 'Eloquence
> brought men from barbarism to civility' or 'All men are descended
> from one man and one woman' – that the Indian languages are
> peeled away and discarded like rubbish by so many of the early
> writers. But as we are now beginning fully to understand, reality for
> each society is constructed to a significant degree out of the *specific*
> qualities of its language and symbols. Discard the particular words
> and you have discarded the particular men.[3]

While the tenacity of this bid to 'civilise' through 'eloquence'
might strike members of a European or North American metropolis as a provincial and risible apartheid or colonialist anachronism,
within South Africa persistent establishment practitioners drawing
on such discourses, still often in positions of authority and dominance within the academy, receive implicit encouragement, as they
have also received, elsewhere, patronage,[4] from the metropolitan
centre. For example, the 1991 edition of *Shakespeare Survey* contains an article by Russ McDonald on *The Tempest* which provides a more interesting and clearly articulated version of the
concern with rhetoric to be found in the South African article to
which I have referred.[5] In the first part of this chapter, I attempt
to respond to some of the general points he makes in the course
of his argument. I will do so partly by examining certain passages

which he does not discuss in the course of his article. Then I try
to explore, in the wider context of resistance against the legacies of
apartheid and a South Africa which now has eleven official languages rather than only two, what kinds of readings of *The Tempest*, instead, might be of use since April 1994 for South Africa.

I

Miranda's opening utterance in *The Tempest* (I.ii) contains, amongst
much else, evidence of the 'repetition' that, according to McDonald,
is 'a fundamental stylistic turn' (p. 17) in the play, although he
does not himself discuss this particular speech:

> If by your art, my dearest father, you have
> Put the wild waters in this roar, allay them.
> The sky, it seems, would pour down stinking pitch,
> But that the sea, mounting to th' welkin's cheek,
> Dashes the fire out. O, I have suffered
> With those that I saw suffer: a brave vessel –
> Who had, no doubt, some noble creature in her –
> Dashed all to pieces! O, the cry did knock
> Against my very heart – poor souls, they perished.
> Had I been any god of power, I would
> Have sunk the sea within the earth or ere
> It should the good ship so have swallowed, and
> The fraughting souls within her.

> (I.ii.1–13)[6]

In tracing here the 'musical repetition' that impresses McDonald,[7]
we may find, amongst much else,[8] in the use of 'dashes' and 'dashed'
and of 'suffered' and 'suffers', evidence of *polyptoton* (*traductio*)
'the repetition of words derived from the same root'.[9] Puttenham
calls *polyptoton* the tranlacer 'when ye turne and tranlace a word
into many sundry shapes as the Tailor doth his garment, and after
that sort do play with him in your dittie',[10] and Peacham describes
it as 'a form of speech which repeateth one word often times in
one sentence, making the oration more pleasant to the ear. . . . This
exornation is compared to pleasant repetitions and divisions in
music'.[11] These definitions appear to underlie or at least anticipate
McDonald's view of the presence of lexical repetitions or, elsewhere, aural echoes or repetitive patterns in 'both the verbal style

and the dramatic structure' of the play.[12] For him, give and take some qualifications, they are 'musical and ... this music is only indirectly functional' (p. 24). The effect is to introduce 'aurally a sense of wonder' providing a strategy that 'tantalises the audience with the hope of clarification and fixity that art seems to promise, but ... also demonstrates the difficulty and perhaps, finally, the impossibility of attaining them' (p. 24).

McDonald does go on to insist that in reading *The Tempest* stylistically and in noting that the play 'valorizes ambiguity and irony' (p. 27) he is not arguing for 'another version of New Criticism' (p. 27). His argument is that the stylistic characteristics of the play lead us to 'the problems of authority and power that dominate political interpretation'. Despite such disclaimers, however, his observation that the poetry of the play 'alerts us to the delicate relation between literature and ideology' and to an awareness of 'the pleasures of the unfixed' leads him to privilege a position 'deeply sceptical about the operation of all kinds of power – poetic, political, and critical too' (p. 28). It is not surprising, therefore, that, somewhere outside this 'delicate' [clumsy?] and presumably to him unpleasurable intersection of poetry, politics and interpretation, he finds a superior 'moral and imaginative athleticism, an intellectual fitness' which is, apparently for him also, lacking in the interpretations of cultural materialists and new historicists. What he advocates, he tells us, provides 'immense pleasure' and he adds: 'At this point one of my old teachers would have said, "You know. The Keats thing"' (p. 25).

But there are of course other observations to make about the repetitive harmonies in Miranda's lines. For example, McDonald would also presumably be excited by the aural containment of the 'wild waters, in this roar' – itself alliteratively evocative – by 'art' and 'allay'. This is not merely evidence of a 'music' and 'wonder' only 'indirectly functional'. It points to and reflects, in Miranda, a profound yearning for order and fear of chaos. This, in turn, suggests what critics find everywhere in the text: on the one hand, an inevitable epistemological uncertainty, which we know from post-colonial criticism must face the traveller or colonist once she or he has left the metropolitan centre, and, on the other hand, a consequent need for an ordering presence – exemplified in the play by the patriarchal mage Prospero and his art.

Critics such as McDonald would presumably also recognise as

'exquisite' the verbal balancing of opposites in the movement in
language from sea to sky (lines 3–5) that itself reflects poetically,
amidst the threat of chaos, desire and longing for control and omni-
potence in an epistemologically uncertain world. Here Miranda's
energetic evocation of what she sees, the rhetorical handbooks
show, is evidence of her art in *hypotyposis* (*demonstratio*), the
ability to 'describe and set forth many things in such sort as it
should appear they were truly before our eyes' (Puttenham).[13] It is
moreover evidence of her skill in *deisis* (*obsecratio*), 'by which
the orator expresseth his most earnest request, petition or prayer'
(Peacham),[14] and *exuscitatio*, 'when the speaker being much moved
with some vehement affection in himself doth show it by the
utterance of his speech and thereby moveth the minds of his hearers'
(Peacham).[15] Miranda's rhetorical skill is perhaps most powerfully
and movingly evident in the use of the *polyptoton* I have already
noted – the movement from 'suffered' to 'suffer'. This communicates
not only Miranda's personal distress at the storm and the helpless-
ness of the ship's victims but, as well, her profoundly empathetic
response to their suffering, which, her father underlines, touches
'the very virtue of compassion' (I.ii.27) in her.

But again, the wonder and music of this is not necessarily all
that may be foregrounded. For one thing, the style of Prospero's
subsequent narrative in this scene set against Miranda's utterances,
as Ania Loomba amongst others invites us to understand, can pro-
fitably be explored in terms of gender relations.[16] In her opening
speech, if Miranda is eloquent she remains in every way helplessly
dependent on her father's powers, if Miranda's response is empathetic, it is also passive. For another, Miranda's repetitive patterns
and eloquence, and the sensitive response to suffering they commun-
icate, occur in a particular place at a particular moment in the play.
That this is disturbingly significant is nowhere clearer than when
it is contrasted with the kind of eloquence she goes on to practise
in her notorious *apostrophe* to Caliban, which, as Orgel notes,[17]
was often reattributed to Prospero by editors of the play:

> Abhorred slave,
> Which any print of goodness will not take,
> Being capable of all ill! I pitied thee,
> Took pains to make thee speak, taught thee each hour
> One thing or other. When thou didst not, savage,
> Know thine own meaning, but wouldst gabble like

A thing most brutish, I endowed thy purposes
With words that made them known. But thy vile race –
Though thou didst learn – had that in't which good natures
Could not abide to be with; therefore wast thou
Deservedly confined into this rock
Who hadst deserved more than a prison.

(I.ii.350–61)

Here stylistic 'eloquence' and the 'music' of repetition are put to very different use. We may briefly note, amongst the many observations that might be made, how Miranda's rhetorical patterning, which gives the same length to corresponding phrases or clauses, echoes Cordelia's use of *isocolon* in her response to her father's question about their bond (*King Lear*, I.i.95–102).[18] It includes also *epanados* or *traductio*, which Puttenham defines as 'the speedie iteration of one word with some little intermission'.[19] Miranda's patterning in 'I pitied thee', 'took pains to make thee speak', 'taught thee', 'I endowed thy purposes', like Cordelia's, with its overt or implied use of 'I' on the one hand and 'thee' on the other, also emphasises a bond, but this time it is, as critics have emphasised, the one of mistress/slave. The use of *polyptoton* here too is also significant, enabling her to privilege her version of what constitutes appropriate behaviour in the repetitive play with the words 'goodness' and 'good' set against 'abhorred', 'savage', 'ill' and 'vile'. The repetitive patterns in Miranda's language here work to reinforce existing power relations. They suggest, as well, an urge towards self-justification. This urge, with its concomitant interpellation of the subject Caliban, climaxes in the use of *polyptoton* again: Miranda's determined insistence upon the justness of Caliban's treatment in 'deservedly' is reiterated a moment later with the word 'deserved'.

Critics have suggested that Prospero's self-justifying attack upon Caliban's sexuality is a means of evading Caliban's assertion of his ownership of the land. Miranda's attack upon Caliban also has its equivocal aspect: she cannot help acknowledging, even as she insists on his inferiority, that he does have the capacity to 'learn' (in ways clearly not acceptable to these practisers of eloquence). Indeed, the contrast this speech provides with Miranda's earlier moving as well as musical expression of empathy could not itself be more eloquent in pointing to the brutality and callousness of which these travellers and settlers are sometimes capable, their eloquence notwithstanding. As Malcolm Evans has it, 'The rhetoric of complexity, maturity and exquisite riches clothes the nakedness and barbarism of the basic affirmation about masters and slaves'.[20]

The way in which rhetoric may contribute to the definition of and practice of particular power relations is evident in Prospero's language as well. On the one hand, in his initial narrative to his daughter about his previous experience as ruler in Milan, the tortuous syntax of his language suggests his present endeavour to order what was at the same time a disruptive and uncontrollable past. On the other hand he is also concerned to represent the legitimacy of his claims and the unjustness of his present situation. Interestingly here, the interaction between Prospero and his daughter again involves, amongst much else, *polyptoton*. Thus, with the words 'blessed' (I.ii.61) and 'blessedly' (I.ii.63) he invests their survival as well as, by implication, his current project, with divine patronage. Further, his sense of their 'humanity', their experience as vulnerable and suffering victims of political ruthlessness, is developed in the repetitive play of words such as 'crying' (I.ii.132) and 'cry' (I.ii.134 and 149) together with 'sigh' (I.ii.149) and 'sighing' (I.ii.150).

Moreover, Prospero's narrative of his and Miranda's suffering contrasts tellingly with the less complicated ways in which he asserts his dominance over Ariel, Caliban and Ferdinand.[21] The fact that, as Breight points out,[22] Prospero could have learned about Ariel's history only from Ariel himself makes the details of his rhetorical style in his narrative to Ariel about Ariel's past significant primarily in terms of the relations of domination and subordination pertaining between them, which Prospero works, by means of his rhetorical style, to maintain. In the final act, too, as his authority re-emerges his style loses the tortuous complexities of the opening scenes. The only notable use of *polyptoton* to be found there involves repetitive play with the word 'strange', the effects of which are to foreground his own authority and power in providing clarity for the subjects of his magical powers, as well as the resolution of his political project.

It is of course not only post-colonial critics who may help us to understand the equivocal nature of the instruments of eloquence. Humanist preoccupation with the abuse of rhetoric, as critics have often noted, is a recurrent obsession in much Jacobean drama. But the material practice of these travellers to the island, overtly evident in Prospero's often quoted reference to his and Miranda's dependence upon Caliban's labour,[23] set alongside the music of their utterances, provides a paradigmatic instance of processes which still operate within or underlie not only the article with which I began but, more importantly, many of the assumptions and practices in South African neo-apartheid education. Furthermore, here in Africa, as elsewhere – as writers such as wa Thiong'o, Baldick and Eagleton have argued[24] – large doses of mainly British literature have been injected into the educative system. Appreciation of and pleasure in the 'aesthetically' satisfying canon of masterpieces from the metropolis has always been a convenient means for the disablement and distraction of colonial subjects from any self-awareness or self-understanding. This is something, too, Evans points out, Edward Harrison indicates in his account of his experiences teaching English in the Caribbean islands.[25] Indeed, at the present moment of writing – even after April 1994 – the majority of South African students, certainly at secondary level, are still largely discouraged from the study of and awareness of most Southern African literature. The preoccupation throughout the apartheid years with Romanticism, Romantic conceptions of subjectivity and the self-absorption which certain versions of it might encourage, threatens to continue as favourite additional component in the recipe for neo-apartheid hegemony.[26] The privileging of a sensitivity to the use of eloquence and the music of rhetorical patterning, of a kind that involves a 'morally athletic' awareness of ambiguities, ironies and the numinous that, again, 'lie beyond' the pale of politics, art and criticism cannot be responded to dispassionately. The 'Keats thing' – as McDonald has it – itself, still travels, as it did in the past, to the Third World, to colonial or to 'post'-colonial contexts, as well as to Prospero's island, in ways most sinister.

II

It is sometimes argued, not only in South Africa, that Caliban is a 'thing most brutish' (I.ii.356), and Miranda together with Prospero has every right to respond accordingly. Greenblatt himself writes:

> Caliban is anything but a Noble Savage. Shakespeare does not shrink from the darkest European fantasies about the Wild Man; indeed he exaggerates them: Caliban is deformed, lecherous, evil-smelling, idle, treacherous, naive, drunken, rebellious, violent and devil-worshipping
> ... *The Tempest* utterly rejects the uniformitarian view of the human

race, the view that would later triumph in the Enlightenment and prevail in the West to this day. All men, the play seems to suggest, are *not* alike; strip away the adornments of culture and you will *not* reach a single human essence.[27]

Greenblatt's argument elsewhere in his article tempers the apparent implication here that the construction of Caliban is 'Shakespeare's', rather than that of the travellers or colonists on the island. Still, Thomas Cartelli has argued importantly that the whole play provides a seminal event in the development of 'beliefs that have characterised Western encounters with the "Other" throughout the course of colonial history'.[28] He maintains further that 'Prospero contributes . . . a culturally privileged rationale for objectifying what are really always subjective representations of the Other' thus supplying 'a pedigreed precedent for a politics of imperial domination premised on the objectified intractability of the native element' (p. 106).

Annabel Patterson, however, questions the contention that *The Tempest* is 'complicit in a mythology of benevolent colonialism, of the foreign conqueror's right to the land and labour of native peoples supposedly less civilized than himself'.[29] And, taking this as a starting point, it is particularly important for a South African audience firstly to address directly the problem of the representation of Caliban on stage.

Caliban's 'role' as a 'thing most brutish' is apparently prepared for, as everyone knows, even in the Folio's list of actors, where he is described as 'a saluage and deformed slaue'.[30] The perfect imperialist version of what this denotes is perhaps to be found in Kermode's renowned edition,[31] especially in section four of his introduction to the text. However, given some of the perspectives provided by post-colonial readings, and bearing in mind Kermode's own acknowledgement that Montaigne's 'Of the cannibals' – as Annabel Patterson also underlines[32] – is the only undisputed source for the play,[33] we may perhaps respond to his version of the text's representation of the 'other', here, with greater caution. In addition to the meanings of the word 'savage' convenient to Kermode's purposes, we may note Schmidt's gloss on Shakespeare's use of the word as denoting, in some contexts, 'uncultivated', 'unpolished', 'uncivil' as well as, in others, 'wild', 'beastly', 'brutal'.[34] Kermode has this in mind when he comments imperiously that Caliban is associated 'as were the uncivilised inhabitants of the Indies, with the wild or salvage man of Europe, formerly the most familiar image of mankind without the ordination of civility'.[35] But such meanings may as easily direct us to what Greenblatt's article as well as post-colonial criticism and social anthropologists have established about the colonial representation of potentially subject peoples: they are held to be 'naked', without culture and language of their own, lacking, specifically, cultivated and polished European versions of civility.

In his discussion Kermode also takes the term 'deformed', without question, literally. This, too, positions the 'other' from the start as abnormal and encourages literal interpretations of the fish imagery in stage make-up and costuming in performance, which itself, it may be argued, is a disguised form of racism. It is worth noting that one of the meanings which *The Oxford English Dictionary* (OED) gives for the word 'fish' is '3b. Used (with prefixed adj.) unceremoniously for "person".' Although the date of the first citation provided is 1750, use of the word to denote a person is evident in a number of proverbs all in use much earlier. *The Oxford Dictionary of English Proverbs* shows Lyly using the proverb *That fish will soon be caught that nibbles at every bait* in this way: 'Philautus, who euer as yet but played with the bait, was now stroke with the hooke (1580 Lyly *Euph and his Eng*, ii.104)' and the proverb is alluded to similarly in: 'The fish long playing with the baited hook, / At last is caught: thus many nymph is took ([c. 1612] 1633 P. Fletcher *Pisc.Eclog.*, V, Poems, ii.287)'.[36] It is interesting that *OED* gives for the word 'fish' the sense '3a. Applied *fig.* to a person (also *collect.* to persons) whom it is desirable to "catch" or "hook"' but gives as the date of its first citation, 1722. In the context of incipient colonialism and slavery, such a meaning for the word 'fish' applied by colonists to the natives whom they encountered on their travels may well have been operative earlier. Indeed, Trinculo's first encounter with his particular 'fish' encourages him very soon to think of taking it back, as other colonists had done, to earn money for him at the metropolitan centre (II. ii.18–35).

In any event, all the productions of the play which I have seen, running counter to this sense of the word, choose to present Caliban as literally half-fish or fish-like. The cover on the most recent Arden reprint of Kermode's edition of the play, reproduces Caliban, perennial representative of the 'other', in this way as literally abnormal. Is this, it must be asked, the only possible sense in which Caliban is to be understood as 'deformed'? If the play is not simply to perpetuate a version of the 'other' as, inevitably, a 'thing' that is, physically, 'most brutish', caution, here too, is essential. As Patterson tellingly points out, 'every director has to decide' for himself or herself 'what Caliban shall look like'.[37]

After all, the first time that Miranda meets Ferdinand she observes to him that he is the third man she has ever seen – though later, as earlier, she slips again into the more usual habit of constructing Caliban as sub- or non-human or, in III.i.50–2, erasing him completely. Caliban himself has no trouble about who he is: at the end of his first meeting with Trinculo and Stephano he advises the absent Prospero in song to 'get a new man' (II.ii.180). We should recall too that the word 'thing' is used elsewhere in Shakespeare not necessarily to denote physical abnormality but the expression of angry dislike or rejection. Cymbeline calls Posthumous 'basest thing' and Imogen 'disloyal thing'.[38] The compliant Ariel is Prospero's 'brave spirit' (I.ii.206) but, when he seeks to reduce his term of slavery, his master calls him a 'malignant thing' (I.ii.256). Furthermore, scholars register the fact that travellers to the New World were impressed by the strange dress customs of those with whom they come into contact. They may well have used these as a further means of dehumanising the 'other' in description.[39] The use of the insult 'monster', which begins in the joke of Stephano's discovery of the four legs, may similarly be understood as a series of proto-colonialist racist insults. Certainly, as we would expect, Prospero's direct references to Caliban's appearance are never neutral. In the final moments of the play he calls him a 'misshapen knave' (V.i.268) in the context of his implicitly self-justifying narrative about Caliban's past. A little later he tells Alonso that Caliban 'is as disproportioned in his manners / As in his shape' (V.i.290–1). What he means by this is clear in his instruction a moment later 'Go, sirrah, to my cell . . . / As you look / To have my pardon, trim it handsomely' (V.i.291–3). For Prospero what is handsome is Caliban's submissive service.

Against Kermode's literal interpretation of the meaning of the word 'deformed' may be set, as well, Schmidt's gloss of the word as not merely 'misshaped' but, in certain contexts, 'ill-favoured'.[40] We may recall here that the coloniser has mostly responded negatively to the appearance of the colonised. And in this context it is interesting to note the proverbial formulation which B. J. Whiting cites, *D154 Black Deformity is no fault with Moors*, although he provides only one citation for this, dated *c.* 1515: 'No fault with Moriens is blacke difformitie, / Because all the sort like of that favour be' (Barclay, *Eclogues*, 205.679–80).[41] This supports the possibility that the word 'deformity' may sometimes in practice have expressed merely difference from European expectations of 'norms' in appearance rather than literal grotesqueness or misshapenness. Such evidence together with post-colonial perspectives on the play combines to argue that the subsequent insults delivered at Caliban throughout the play may well be presented and performed on stage as racist reaction to, domination of and exploitation of the 'other'. A production of *The Tempest* which selected the most handsome young man available, preferably, in South Africa, black or Asian, might powerfully foreground such acts of racist representation underpinning processes of exploitation operative in the language of the travellers or colonists to the island, in ways, too, that would invite in South African and other audiences a more critical, reflective and non-conservative response. Conversely, the more usual presentation of Caliban on stage as physically deformed, grotesque, half-human half-fish, continues to reproduce and encourage racist stereotyping at the same time obscuring the extent to which such stereotyping itself is a 'thing most brutish' – likely always, to contribute to patterns of hegemonic exploitation and oppression within the social order in which this fish-like 'other' returns to give a never-ending string of repeat performances.

III

How is a South African audience to take the presentation of Stephano and Trinculo in the play? Do they provide evidence to confirm what Annabel Patterson identifies as the view that 'the Elizabethan underclasses were deliberately represented in the plays as ignorant groundlings castigated by Hamlet, licensed, dependent clowns in courtly households, and unsavoury crowds in the street',[42] demonstrating also – she quotes Coleridge as arguing for *The Tempest* particularly – 'the springs of the vulgar in politics' (p. 6)? Instead, might there not be found, in elements of their presentation, what Alan Sinfield calls 'scope for dissident understanding

and action . . . because the social order *cannot but produce* faultlines
through which its own criteria of plausibility fall into contest and
disarray'?[43]

When he first encounters Stephano and Trinculo Caliban takes
them to be 'fine things, an if they be not sprites' (II.ii.111–12) –
presumably benevolent as well as potent although he admits despite the pun on 'sprites' that these visitors might be more sinister.
It can be argued that, although the scenes involving Stephano and
Trinculo are often accounted for as primarily a sub-plot that provides a comic and lower-class parallel to the subversive impulses
of Antonio and Sebastian, at least as significant is their role as
travellers or proto-colonists. Although only minor agents, they
remain still part of the 'invading group' on the island. Indeed, it
is only towards the end of the second scene in which they appear
(III.ii) that a parallel between Stephano and Trinculo and the behaviour of Antonio and Sebastian as conspirators develops. In II.ii,
their first appearance on stage, the parallel to be identified is that
between Stephano and Trinculo on the one hand and Prospero on
the other. And one of the understandings Caliban will acquire about
Stephano and Trinculo in the course of the play – as indeed, he
has before done about Prospero – is what sort of 'things' exactly
these visitors to his island turn out to be.

In Act II both scenes present the travellers' or colonists' attempts to read or narrate the new reality of the 'desert' island in
which they find themselves. In the first scene, against the attempts
of Gonzalo to develop a pastoral, sententious and utopian lesson
– all drawn from the European discourse they bring with them –
out of the unfamiliar landscape, Antonio and Sebastian respond
more subversively and cynically with, at the same time, a European sense of *realpolitik*. The second scene largely involves the
comedy in the similar attempts of Trinculo – 'here's neither bush
nor shrub to bear off any weather at all' (II.ii.18–19) – and Stephano
to understand and 'order' the landscape in which they find themselves. Encountering a native of the island, Trinculo as proto-colonist thinks at once, after noticing his strangeness, of possible
exploitation of his find: 'Were I in England now, as once I was,
and had but this fish painted, not a holiday-fool there but would
give a piece of silver' (II.ii.27–9). But importantly he admits also
that 'this is no fish but an islander' (II.ii.35–6).[44] Stephano too
speaks, inevitably, as proto-colonist – 'do you put tricks upon's

with savages and men of Ind?' (II.ii.56–7). Their comic interrogation of what they find parallels the concerns of both Prospero and
Miranda, as travellers or colonists to impose epistemological cer-
tainty, drawn from the books and language they bring with them
from Europe upon the landscape within which they find themselves. Indeed Caliban's response to them – not only susceptible to
their drink, he promises to 'show them every fertile inch o'th'island',
he sees Stephano as a 'brave god', he is invited by the two to kiss
their particular 'book' of knowledge – parallels his earlier narration of his own response when Prospero first came to the island
(I.ii.331–9).

Act II scene ii opens with Caliban's extended speech dwelling
on the punitive powers of his master that 'hiss me into madness'
(II.ii.14). Curt Breight has helped us to understand that this, like
much of the punishment described or meted out elsewhere in the
play, does not necessarily invite a dominantly comic rendition in
performance.[45] It is therefore significant that, even as these more
recent arrivals on the island from the metropolitan centre humour
their new-found 'subject', they not only see fit to exploit and
continually abuse and mock him but speak in a way that is potentially punitive and sadistic as well: 'I shall laugh myself to death
at this puppy-headed monster. A most scurvy monster! I could
find in my heart to beat him' (II.ii.148–50).

Furthermore, Stephano and Trinculo demonstrate by the end of
the scene their intention, like Prospero, to impose their European
notions of hierarchy and possession upon this inhabitant of the
island: 'we will inherit here' (II.ii.169). We may recall that Antonio
and Sebastian cynically remark in the previous scene that Gonzalo's
European idealism (similarly) fails to dispense with traditional hierarchy (II.i.154). And this determination of the colonist to exploit
the place to which they have travelled, and to impose upon it
European forms of political hierarchy, is foregrounded again at
the start of the next scene in which Stephano and Trinculo appear.
Joking about the tottering 'state' the two now deem themselves to
rule, they stress the subordinate role of their 'servant-monster'
(III.ii.3–4 and 7), pretend to promote him to 'lieutenant-monster
or standard' and laugh at Caliban's elevation of Stephano to the
title 'lord' (III.ii.29). Stephano asserts, too that 'the poor monster's
my subject' (III.ii.33–4) and invites him to 'kneel and repeat' (III.
iii.38) his suit. It is this motive particularly that the triumphant

Prospero mocks in the final scene – 'You'd be king o' the isle, sirrah?' (V.i.287).

Aspects of their behaviour so far and aspects of Stephano and Trinculo's subsequent behaviour in the remainder of III.iii and then in IV.i suggest, moreover, an additional and significant point about the behaviour of the ruling order when situated on the periphery. In their continual obsession with drink, and in the ease with which Prospero and Ariel are able to distract them from their objectives by exploiting their greed, these travellers and proto-colonists on the periphery are shown to be unreliable, subject to debauchery, easily distracted, easily persuaded too, to undertake a disruptive project. In this they now parallel or echo, especially, Antonio and Sebastian, who as travellers are also potentially at least proto-colonists (of course of a superior hierarchical position). The parallel between Antonio and Sebastian and Antonio and Alonso at the centre has of course often been noted. Located on the periphery, and aware of the distance of the space they occupy from the centre, they decide to attempt a seizure of power for themselves. This sense of subversive potential and treachery within the ruling group itself, common in the tragedies, is identified in the colonial context, it is worth adding, also in *Othello*. There, on the periphery too, the ruling colonial class is also shown, in Iago's vicious undermining and destruction of Othello,[46] to be riven from within by destructive rivalry and ambition. In turn such tensions reflect back upon similar divisions within the ruling class at the centre whose claims to be legitimate and natural rulers, by these means too, are interrogated.

IV

If Stephano and Trinculo may partly be seen as comic versions of their more powerfully exploitative and sometimes vicious masters, representations of the underclasses elsewhere in the play work differently. As Patterson points out, 'the play opens with a chal-lenge from below: the Boatswain announces that physical danger from the elements makes nonsense of social hierarchy and equates personal worth with the willingness to work'.[47] Nevertheless, Sebastian and Antonio's verbal abuse of the Boatswain (I.i.40–5) disregards his points. At the close of the play, the Boatswain speaks with appropriate loyalty: 'The best news is that we have safely found / Our king and company' (V.i.221–2), but despite this expression of devotion, in a revealing, albeit jocular, insult, 'Now, blasphemy, / That swear'st grace o'erboard' (V.i.218), the mild and kind Gonzalo shows that he shares the more vicious Sebastian's and Antonio's class prejudice towards the sailor. Reassertion of civility and loyalty most certainly does not entail any abandonment of existing power relations, which the jest, and the implicit patronising contempt it bespeaks, is itself designed to perpetuate.

Patterson argues the presence of populist concerns in the play in other ways too, maintaining that *The Tempest* invokes 'troubling thoughts – of the ethical status of Prospero's colonialism, the enslavement and manumission of Ariel, the monopoly of power (as magic), the relation of power to education (Prospero's books), Caliban's intelligence, the relation of literary fantasy to utopian thought. The complex effect is to resubmit the *substance* of popular claims, grievances, behaviour and credos in philosophical, even allegorical, disguise' (p. 11).

In this context I would like to examine some details of the way in which Caliban's struggle to resist Prospero is presented in the text. It is however worth prefacing this discussion with the observation, firstly, that there is a repetitive preoccupation with resistance of a particular kind noticeable in the late plays. Richard Strier has argued that even earlier, in *King Lear*, before the blinding of Gloucester, when Cornwall's servant attempts to stop him the text presents 'the most radical possible sociopolitical act in a way that can only be interpreted as calling for [the] audience's approval' (p. 119).[48] Similar incidents of resistance that are likely to have won the audience's approval may be found in Cornelius's refusal in *Cymbeline* to obey the Queen and in Pisanio's growing conviction evident in III.ii and in his exchanges with Imogen in III.iv that disobedience is the best way to serve his master. *The Winter's Tale* affords repeated incidents in the behaviour of Camillo, Paulina and others of resistance to and disobedience of the misguided will of a ruler.

Secondly, *The Tempest* itself is concerned throughout not only with government but with rebellion. Ariel, Caliban and Ferdinand all challenge Prospero's authority in the first act. In succeeding acts the movement to rebellion involves not only Caliban, Stephano and Trinculo on the one hand, and Sebastian and Antonio on the other, but even on occasion Miranda. Moreover, Prospero's very presence on the island is itself the result of an act of subversion and rebellion. And finally, the equivocal presentation of Prospero as ruler in *The Tempest* is preceded in both *Cymbeline* and *The Winter's Tale* by a concern with the problem of misguided and (temporarily) destructive rulers, a concern that complements and precipitates the interest in resistance in each of these texts.

In these contexts, we may recall the crucial moment in III.ii, when the play with hierarchy in which Stephano and Trinculo indulge is redirected by Caliban who asks, 'Wilt thou be pleased to hearken once again to the suit I made thee?' (III.ii.36–7). The single-minded nature of Caliban's determination to resist Prospero, suggested here, has not perhaps been sufficiently underlined or explored by critics. Bearing in mind the work of scholars including Clare and Patterson on censorship,[49] it may be possible to argue that the text itself may be deliberately euphemistic about this dimension to his behaviour and language partly because of the demands of censorship. This may, similarly, account for the use of a comedic frame in which to set the movement undertaken by Caliban, with the help of Stephano and Trinculo, to mask the play's more interrogative import.

Even so, most critics nowadays acknowledge that Caliban's struggle has its own eloquence and power. That Caliban is more than the narratives and verbal modes of interpellation that seek to position him used by the travellers or proto-colonists, particularly Prospero, is evident, as post-colonial critics have pointed out, from the challenging moment of his first appearance. It is evident too in the tactical realism of his recognition of powerlessness in 'I must eat my dinner' (I.ii.330) and in his narrative of Prospero's response to his own naive welcome to the arrival of what proves to be his future master on the island – and which has resulted in the loss of his land. Throughout this first encounter he manifests continued readiness to confront and challenge Prospero. And the extent to which Caliban is aware of his situation is confirmed just before his exit from the stage when he remarks, demonstrating, again acute awareness of the realities of his political predicament in an aside: 'I must obey. His art is of such power, / It would control my dam's god Setebos / And make a vassal of him' (I.ii.371–3).

When Caliban meets Stephano and Trinculo, his characteristic generosity to these 'fine things' – yet to be fully understood by him

– quickly encourages his abiding desire to be rid of 'the tyrant that I serve' (II.ii.157). While it may be argued by conservative critics that his willingness to acclaim a 'new master' (II.ii.180) evidences an intrinsically servile nature, it may equally be argued not only that Caliban might here be seeking a strategic alliance against his tyrant master but also that the text cannot openly present a case for a deliberately aggressive move into 'masterlessness'. In any event, Caliban goes on to sing of 'freedom' (II.ii.181) and shows, in his subsequent struggle to resist Prospero, a far cannier sense of what is involved than either of his two newly acquired 'masters': 'As I told thee before, I am subject to a tyrant, a sorcerer that by his cunning hath cheated me of the island' (III.ii.40–2).

As earlier, here too the text acknowledges that Caliban is capable of his own narrative as well as his own thoughts, inevitably entirely different from those of Prospero. Caliban's subversive proposals in III.iii which follow are, it may be argued, of necessity contained, as I hinted, given theatre conditions and censorship, by the concealed comic presence of Ariel. Nevertheless, the comedic frame threatens to shatter whenever the violence and intensity of Caliban's view of his master is directly acknowledged in his language: 'Yea, Yea, my lord. I'll yield him thee asleep, / Where thou mayst knock a nail into his head' (III.ii.59–60) and:

> There thou mayst brain him,
> Having first seized his books; or with a log
> Batter his skull, or paunch him with a stake,
> Or cut his weasand with thy knife. . . .
>   they all do hate him
> As rootedly as I.
>
>   (III.ii.86–93)

Breight gives a fascinating account of the extent to which resistance was not only a subject for debate but a preoccupation of the Jacobean government.[50] He provides evidence for the existence of continuous 'discursive productions of treason – arrests, trials, executions, displays, pamphlets, sermons [which] pervaded the sociopolitical environment of the entire second half of Elizabeth's reign and the first few years of James's government' (p. 4). Whether or not Breight is correct about the extent to which *The Tempest* deliberately presents Prospero's own practice of his art and power to make a related point, his work confirms that Caliban's language here must have produced more than merely melodramatic or poetic impact upon the Jacobean audience. The ferocity of this language confirms the existence of a determined 'other' which the dominant order, despite its discourses and practice of power, is nevertheless unable to erase. Thus, in the following scene, despite the fact that the degenerate travellers or proto-colonists Stephano and Trinculo are easily distracted by the tricks Prospero and Ariel play on them, Caliban remains single-mindedly committed to his struggle,[51] increasingly contemptuous of their irresponsibility and greed. In the face of an apparently insuperable political power, this determination, masked by humour, remains eloquent. The impression it makes is also intensified by the extent to which, as Breight has also shown, Jacobean tactics of torture and persecution are indicated in the language used to describe the torments not only of Caliban early in the play but of Caliban, Stephano and Trinculo when their move against Prospero is exposed. Annabel Patterson argues that Caliban knows the song Stephano sings which includes allusion to the proverb *Thought is free*. The determination to resist in every way possible, set frequently in the context of language that, as Breight has shown, evokes the darkly punitive nature of the Jacobean state where difference and dissent is concerned, foregrounds, as well as his actual struggle, the courage of Caliban's intellectual will to resist throughout.

V

In the last act of *The Tempest* the knit of romance in the revelations and reconciliations achieved by Prospero's art is simultaneously implicitly unravelled. His farewell to that art is a formal recognition of the limits of human agency beyond the island, the artifice of the play, the theatre in which it is performed. Beyond this for him, by his own admission, there is only prayer. Recognitions of a less manageable world beyond the island are resonant too in the Boatswain's description of the suffering of the sailors, 'all clapped under hatches / Where, but even now with strange and several noises / Of roaring, shrieking, howling, jingling chains / And more diversity of sounds, all horrible, / We were awaked' (V.i.231–5), in the well-discussed implications of Antonio's silence and in the entrance of the three conspirators and what they resonate. This movement away from romance and recuperation into a more

uncertain and unpredictable reality includes, as the play draws to
its conclusion, Prospero's famous remark 'this thing of darkness I
/ Acknowledge mine' (V.i.275–6). It is worth recalling in this context that the English colonial project contemporary to the first performances of this play, as Peter Hulme identifies it,[52] is part of that
reality into which the text appears at this stage to be at least partly
returning its audience. Hulme points out that the English colonial enterprise remained uncertain with the failures of attempts to
establish colonies in Newfoundland and Virginia and a fiasco at El
Dorado. Stories abounded of the loss of the *Olive Branch* in 1605
and the reappearance of its crew in England years later and of the
shipwreck of the *Sea-Venture* in 1609 and the miraculous survival
of its crew and passengers. Prospero's acknowledgement of Caliban
and at the same time the imminent departure of the settlers from
the island back to Milan again take on particular resonances in
this context that work against the tendency to read some recuperation into Prospero's acknowledgement, some sense in which he is
said here to be reconciling himself to Caliban, assuming responsibility for him, even implicitly interrogating his earlier behaviour
towards him.

The two words 'thing' and 'darkness' make such readings difficult to defend. As I indicated earlier, the word 'thing' denotes
anger and rejection in contemporary usage. The word 'darkness'
clearly communicates Prospero's continuing, recalcitrant perception of him as 'other', something that lies beyond his patriarchal
and European epistemology. In this sense his acknowledgement
may be understood as simply a reassertion of mastery, one to
which Caliban in turn submits – henceforth he will 'seek for grace'
(V.i.295).[53] It may moreover be argued that the whole conspiracy
sub-plot was contrived and allowed by the mage Prospero so that
Caliban would emerge here too as irredeemably rebellious and
therefore deserving of the treatment meted out to him, as well as
the exploitation Prospero has exacted from him. In terms of this,
Prospero is thus able not only to reassert his dominance over the
'other', but, in Caliban's own submission, the text transforms his
servitude into something actively sought. As Hulme, who argues
this, puts it: 'The violence of slavery is abolished at a stroke and
Caliban becomes just another feudal retainer whom Prospero can
"acknowledge mine". This is the wish fulfilment of the European
colonist: his natural superiority voluntarily recognised' (p. 132).

Yet the lack of confidence in this assertion is omnipresent: Prospero is on his way home – the imperial endeavour in the world in which *The Tempest* is performed is not yet continuously triumphant. In the text's very presentation of the figure of the colonised on stage, and in the presentation of his submission, the audience is pulled because of the text's own movement into its own historical moment, towards recognition of the extent to which such romances, such hierarchical and patriarchal readings of 'reality', mask their own violence in power relations, translate it and hide it beneath the rhetoric of ordered, civilised and humanist compassion and acceptance.

VI

The kind of reading of particularly Caliban, Stephano and Trinculo which I have attempted here not only depends upon the work of several post-colonial critics but also draws upon and may be further examined in the context of studies by critics such as Patterson, Strier and Breight. Patterson's work, for example, enables us to set *The Tempest* in what she argues to be a tradition of social scrutiny, interrogation and resistance to be found in several of the plays preceding it. February 1611, the year *The Tempest* is commonly thought to have first been performed, saw the ending of what she describes as 'the discursive formation begun by the Midlands Rising . . . with the collapse of the Great Contract and the dissolution of parliament, which was not to meet again until the spring of 1614'.[54] Although Patterson emphasises that *The Tempest* 'virtually prohibits a topical response' of the kind she finds in *Coriolanus*, she nevertheless remarks that 'it is possible to align the play with developments in James's England, and particularly with the increasing emphasis on political liberties that appears in the records of the 1610 parliament' (p. 159). Again, while Richard Strier does not find in *The Tempest* the 'extended meditation on the kinds of situation in which resistance to legally constituted authority becomes a moral necessity',[55] the contexts of resistance he provides remain interesting for a play in which the concern is consistently and repetitively not only with subversion of the dominant order but with different kinds of resistance to dominant authority. Similarly, Curt Breight's contention that the play 'is a politically radical intervention in a dominant contemporary discourse',[56] and that, 'constructed as a series of conspiracies . . . it can be inserted into a vast discourse of treason that became an increasingly central response to difficult social problems in late Elizabethan and early Jacobean London' (p. 1), provides, as I noted earlier, fascinating information.

It is important, at the same time, to recall here Stephen Orgel's stress, in the Introduction to his edition of the play, on the 'characteristic openness' of the text, on 'the range of the play's possibilities' and the 'mutually contradictory' nature of many of these possibilities.[57] Strier, for example, argues that The Tempest 'is more conservative than the plays, from *Hamlet* on which precede it . . . the stress of the play . . . is on proper obedience rather than on proper disobedience'.[58] My discussion above has perforce not been able to include attention to the extensive investment in Prospero's perspective which the play also manifests.[59] Moreover, to foreground the treatment of Caliban and other representations of the underclasses in the play is not to suggest that what is to be found here is not repeatedly played off against the presentation and exploration of arguments drawn from dominant Jacobean discourse elsewhere in the text. The structure of the first four acts, we may recall, moves regularly from the one to the other. Thus in Act I, amongst much else, the move is from Prospero to his complex interaction with the not always compliant Ariel, Caliban and Ferdinand. Act II balances, as I noted, the reactions of the shipwrecked court party to the island, with, in turn, Stephano and Trinculo to the island and to Caliban. In Act III the loyal submission of Ferdinand to his 'master's' demands precedes Caliban's determined thrust towards rebellion, which is in turn juxtaposed against the punitive measures implemented against the court subversives. Act IV, too, balances the masque and all it signifies against the ongoing foul conspiracy.[60] Even in Act V, the apparent closure effected by Prospero has been extensively interrogated by numerous critics. The text, in important senses, remains throughout a site of repeated struggle between conflicting discourses.

What about the study of The Tempest in the post-April 1994 South Africa? Despite sporadic articles on the play, *The Tempest*, like *Othello*, has not often been used in the last four or more decades within the South African apartheid system. Even at tertiary level, study of the play has often been avoided. Were the history of the play's diverse appropriations elsewhere not sufficient, this avoidance itself, it might be argued, also warns against easy conclusions that the text is necessarily conservative or has conservative effects. And, while it may be true that the seventeenth-century dynastic politics within which the play is set may need greater attention,[61] South Africans cannot lose sight of the fact that the only certain source for the text still appears to be Montaigne's 'Of the cannibals'. Moreover, during the apartheid decades, almost no South African criticism of the play drew on post-colonial readings of *The Tempest*.[62] Assuredly, for South Africans, these readings will, accordingly, continue to be of the utmost importance.

Again, whatever the long-term future prospects of South Africa may be, its democratic moment has at last begun with a move away from past hegemonies of intolerance. This is reflected in unfolding debates about art and culture. Thus, in the embattled conditions of the late 1980s, an enlightened critic could write that 'any attempt to conceive of an oppositional "national culture" will have to . . . include working class expression as a major constituent'.[63] Concern with the identification of what was in the past marginalised sometimes developed further into strongly functionalist and determinist attitudes towards the production of or critical response to literature. But, during 1989, Albie Sachs, now a member of the South African government, initiated within the ANC a debate about how the arts might be used in a liberated South Africa and argued for the admission of dissent.[64] Current endeavours to establish a new South African constitution reflect strong commitment to the establishment of what might be called a human rights culture.

In the context of our fraught history and in the light of present endeavours, then, for South Africans in the foreseeable future, foregrounding the discursive struggles in *The Tempest* seems perhaps more imperative than pursuing the equally interesting questions as to whether the play is finally, either, as Breight would have it, interrogative of the dominant Jacobean discourses, or, alternatively, a work that itself perpetuates the hegemony of the Jacobean court. The text, identified as site of conflicting discourses, remains itself often dissident, resistant to the exclusivist demands of any one dominant discourse. It may be argued, indeed, that the inevitably dialogic or heteroglossic nature of drama makes it, in any situation, similarly, potentially transgressive of the straight privileging of particular ideological discursive formations. Different critical practices will discover different versions of how or whether the text resolves its conflicts. But the insistent presentation of a complexity that reflects material struggle and relations of power, which the recognition of discursive struggle in the text identifies, militates against anti-democratic predilections to censorship – discomfiting though this may remain to particular ruling classes and groups of whatever kind. The 'thing of darkness' that Prospero's practice in the play suggests, the complexity of discursive struggle in *The Tempest* as a whole resists.

Notes

1 See M. Orkin, 'Re-presenting *The Tempest* in South Africa 1955–1990', *Shakespeare in Southern Africa*, 6 (1993), pp. 45–60.

2 V. Houliston, 'Shakespeare not our contemporary', *Shakespeare in Southern Africa*, Grahamstown: The Shakespeare Society of Southern Africa, 3 (1989), p. 69. This number, despite its date, appeared only in the early months of March 1991 – that is, over a year after the then President de Klerk had announced a new direction in government policy in South Africa.

3 S. Greenblatt, *Learning to Curse: Essays in Early Modern Culture* (New York, Routledge, 1990), p. 32.

4 The Shakespeare Society of Southern Africa was formed in 1986 in Grahamstown. For some 'Eng. lit.' critics Grahamstown remains an island of determined anglophilia. The Society has amongst its patrons eminent scholars from abroad who may have as their primary interest the promotion of Shakespeare studies but are possibly not aware of the reactionary processes to which, in South Africa, they so easily gave and give their support. Several of them, invited to Grahamstown in the past decade or so, accepted, thus becoming travellers to South Africa at a time when contact with the apartheid state from abroad was strongly discouraged not only by the ANC but by other groups both within South Africa and abroad. In 1991 a new traveller to Grahamstown arrived: Frank Kermode.

5 R. McDonald, 'Reading *The Tempest*', *Shakespeare Survey*, 43 (1991), pp. 15–28.

6 All quotations from *The Tempest* are taken from W. Shakespeare, *The Tempest*, ed. S. Orgel (Oxford, Oxford University Press, 1987).

7 McDonald, 'Reading *The Tempest*', p. 19.

8 See the repetitive play involving words such as 'brave', 'noble', 'dashed', 'perished', 'souls'.

9 Sister M. Joseph, *Shakespeare's Use of the Arts of Language* (New York, Hafner Publishing Company, 1966), p. 83.

10 Cited in Joseph, *Shakespeare's Use*, p. 306.

11 Cited in L. Sonnino, *A Handbook to Sixteenth Century Rhetoric* (London, Routledge and Kegan Paul, 1968), p. 179.

12 McDonald, 'Reading *The Tempest*', p. 23.

13 Cited in Sonnino, *A Handbook*, p. 70.

14 Cited in *ibid.*, p. 135.

15 Cited in *ibid.*, p. 96.

16 See A. Loomba, *Race, Gender, Renaissance Drama* (Manchester, Manchester University Press, 1989).

17 Orgel, ed., *The Tempest*, p. 120 n.

18 The lines from *King Lear* are taken from *King Lear*, ed. K. Muir (London, Methuen, 1969).

19 Cited in Joseph, *Shakespeare's Use*, p. 85.

20 M. Evans, *Signifying Nothing: Truth's True Contents in Shakespeare's Text* (Brighton, Harvester, 1986), p. 73.

21 Amongst much else we may note that if Miranda was a 'cherubin' to him, when Ariel crosses him he is a 'malignant thing' (I.ii.256), a 'dull thing' (I.ii.285) to whom he threatens 'I will rend an oak / And peg thee in his knotty entrails till / Thou hast howled away twelve winters' (I.ii.294–6). Caliban, the 'poisonous slave, got by the devil himself' (I.ii.319) is promised:

> cramps,
> Side-stitches that shall pent thy breath up. Urchins
> Shall, for that vast of night that they may work,
> All exercise on thee. Though shalt be pinched
> As thick as honeycomb, each pinch more stinging
> Than bees that made 'em.
>
> (I.ii.325–30)

And Ferdinand is a 'traitor' (I.ii.461) who is warned 'I'll manacle thy neck and feet together' (I.ii.462).

22 C. Breight, '"Treason doth never prosper": *The Tempest* and the discourse of treason', *Shakespeare Quarterly*, 41:1 (1990), pp. 1–28; p. 10.

23 Evans, *Signifying Nothing*, amongst others, writes eloquently about the master/slave relationships in the play which include not only the exploitation of Caliban's labour but as well Ariel and Ferdinand.

24 See N. wa Thiong'o, *Decolonising the Mind* (London, James Currey, 1987); T. Eagleton, *Literary Theory* (Oxford, Blackwell, 1983); C. Baldick, *The Social Mission of English Criticism 1848–1932* (Oxford, Clarendon Press, 1983).

25 See Evans, *Signifying Nothing*, especially chapters 1, 2 and 4.

26 The study of Romantic poetry has usually been an important part of

the English syllabus at secondary level, and remains prominent in significant sections of the courses offered at some South African universities.

27 Greenblatt, *Learning to Curse*, p. 26.

28 T. Cartelli, 'Prospero in Africa: *The Tempest* as colonialist text and pretext' in *Shakespeare Reproduced*, ed. J. Howard and M. O'Connor (London, Methuen, 1987), p. 102.

29 Annabel Patterson, *Shakespeare and the Popular Voice* (Cambridge, Blackwell, 1989), p. 155.

30 *The First Folio of Shakespeare*, ed. C. Hinman (New York, The Norton Facsimile, 1968), p. 37.

31 W. Shakespeare, *The Tempest*, ed. F. Kermode (London, Methuen, 1966). Evans, *Signifying Nothing*, provides a superb critique of this edition in chapter 4.

32 Patterson, *Shakespeare and the Popular Voice*, p. 153.

33 Kermode's satirical reading, nevertheless at times wanting it both ways, argues: 'There are points in the play at which Shakespeare uses Caliban to indicate how much baser the corruption of the civilized can be than the bestiality of the natural, and in these places he is using his natural man as a criterion of civilised corruption, as Montaigne had done' (p. xxxviii).

34 A. Schmidt, *Shakespeare Lexicon and Quotation Dictionary* (New York, Dover, 1971), p. 1004.

35 Kermode, ed., *The Tempest*, pp. xxxviii–xxxix.

36 See *The Oxford Dictionary of English Proverbs*, 3rd edition, ed. F. P. Wilson (1970). See also proverbs such as *Like a fish out of water*, *c.* 1374 and *Old fish and young flesh do feed men best*, *c.* 1386.

37 Patterson, *Shakespeare and the Popular Voice*, p. 155.

38 W. Shakespeare, *Cymbeline*, ed. J. M. Nosworthy (London, Methuen, 1964), I.ii.56 and 62.

39 See Orgel's citation of Hugh Honour's description of a group of natives wearing feathers, in Orgel, ed., *The Tempest*, p. 33.

40 Schmidt, *Shakespeare Lexicon and Quotation Dictionary*, p. 290.

41 B. Whiting, *Proverbs, Sentences, and Proverbial Phrases from English Writing Mainly before 1500* (Cambridge, Mass., Harvard University Press, 1968), p. 127. OED quotes this citation from Barclay also, to illustrate the first meanings for the word which it provides which include the senses 'unsightliness, ugliness'.

42 Patterson, *Shakespeare and the Popular Voice*, p. 5.

43 A. Sinfield, *Faultlines: Cultural Materialism and the Politics of Dissident Reading* (Berkeley, University of California Press, 1992), p. 45.

44 A pointed contrast in production can be made between how the visitors to the island attempt to construct or represent Caliban and the literal strangeness which Gonzalo identifies when confronted by the

strange shapes, which he identifies as 'islanders – / For certes these are people of the island – / Who though they are of monstrous shape, yet note / Their manners are more gentle-kind than of / Our human generation' (III.iii.29–33).

45 See Breight, '"Treason doth never prosper": *The Tempest* and the discourse of treason'.

46 This point is made more fully in M. Orkin, *Shakespeare Against Apartheid* (Johannesburg, Donker, 1987).

47 Patterson, *Shakespeare and the Popular Voice*, p. 157.

48 R. Strier, 'Faithful servants: Shakespeare's praise of disobedience' in *The Historical Renaissance*, ed. H. Dubrow and R. Strier (Chicago, The University of Chicago Press, 1988), p. 119.

49 In addition to the work of Patterson see J. Clare, *Art Made Tongue-Tied by Authority: Elizabethan and Jacobean Dramatic Censorship* (Manchester, Manchester University Press, 1990).

50 Breight, '"Treason doth never prosper": *The Tempest* and the discourse of treason'.

51 Despite too, it may be argued, his alleged drunkenness elsewhere. This 'carnival' use of drunkenness is itself perhaps strategically necessary in view of censorship and the representation on stage of an 'other' that, as critics have argued, might indicate not only the natives of the New World and of Ireland but the popular voice of the voteless and powerless in England itself.

52 P. Hulme, *Colonial Encounters: Europe and the native Caribbean, 1492–1797* (London, Methuen, 1986).

53 It is possible to argue here, as I have argued earlier, that Caliban's reply is tactical, particularly as he is aware of the imminent departure of these 'visitors' from the island.

54 Patterson, *Shakespeare and the Popular Voice*, p. 145.

55 Strier, in Dubrow and Strier, eds, *The Historical Renaissance*, p. 104.

56 Breight, '"Treason doth never prosper": *The Tempest* and the discourse of treason', p. 1.

57 Orgel, ed., *The Tempest*, p.12.

58 Strier, in Dubrow and Strier, eds, *The Historical Renaissance*, p. 133. It seems unlikely that a series of texts, at least from *Hamlet* on – including, particularly, *Cymbeline* and *The Winter's Tale* – that present the monarch interrogatively and often critically should suddenly culminate in so extreme a volte face. It may, again, be argued that the frequency of a concern with resistance in *The Tempest* made it impossible to depict, as well, the many equivocal dimensions in Prospero's behaviour more openly.

59 Curt Breight's reading of the play supplies a convincing reason for this which does not at the same time privilege the discourses Prospero himself draws on.

60 See M. Orkin, 'Shakespeare and the politics of "unrest"', *The English Academy Review*, 8 (1991), pp. 85–97.

61 This was persuasively argued by David Scott Kastan at the Shakespeare Association Meeting held in Chicago, March 1995.

62 See Orkin, 'Re-presenting *The Tempest* in South Africa 1955–1990'.

63 K. Sole, 'Identities and priorities in recent Black literature and performance: a preliminary investigation', *South African Theatre Journal*, 1:1 (1987), p. 96.

64 See *Spring is Rebellious*, ed. I. De Kok and K. Press (Cape Town, Buchu Books, 1990) and *Exchanges*, ed. D. Brown and B. Van Dyk (Pietermaritzberg, University of Natal Press, 1991).

Part III

❖

Shakespeare at the heart of Europe

❖

7

❖

A divided heritage: conflicting appropriations of Shakespeare in (East) Germany

❖

Robert Weimann

Although recent critics have with great acumen interrogated the political uses of Shakespeare as a particularly vital export and symbol of 'Englishness' to foreign educational institutions, the Bard cannot very well be considered an alien article in the German cultural household, at least not one that needs to be 'imported' in order to be used and celebrated. Almost two centuries after Lessing, Goethe and the Romantic translations by August Schlegel and Dorothea Tieck, the horizon of expectation and reception cannot, in Shakespeare's case, reconstitute itself in terms of a contradiction between a given national meaning and its cross-cultural assimilation. In the first place, there is no longer any viable sense of a chasm separating the two national cultures in a European context of increasing exchange and co-operation. Secondly, and on a more fundamental level, the whole underlying concept of the 'export' or 'import' of cultural goods appears somewhat problematic as soon as a mercantile notion of exchange and property is suspended by unbound technologies of reproduction and such practices of assimilation as preclude any idea of national and juridical ownership *vis-à-vis* cultural texts, products and representations.[1]

In fact, it may well be said that the early assimilation of Shakespeare in a formative period of German cultural history made it possible for the reception of the English dramatist to constitute a site – viable to this day – of both intense cultural identification and deep-going division. This was so in a late mid-eighteenth-century context, when Shakespeare served as the most potent catalyst informing the national response to the then dominant theatre of classicism. With the advent of Shakespeare in Germany, there was available an alternative to neoclassical tragedy; the latter could henceforth be defined (and disparaged) in its relation to a courtly and aristocratic culture that, from the point of view of the emancipation of the German middle class, appeared unpromising in terms of its own social needs and perspectives.

Textual authority and performative agency in retrospect

At this point, the Elizabethan theatre of Marlowe and Shakespeare proved far more congenial and consequential. As Goethe's early interest in *Doctor Faustus*, culminating in his work on *Urfaust* (1772–5), witnesses, the Elizabethans, and Shakespeare in particular, richly stimulated the rise of a German drama under anti-aristocratic auspices. But while the Elizabethan theatre, with its socially mixed audiences, helped constitute a remarkably encompassing national culture, the German reception of it did not and could not quite do the same. It is true, this reception is too rich and complex to be reduced to any one barren formula. To judge by its results, there was an astonishing breadth and diversity, as for instance between the impact on the early Goethe and other 'storm and stress' dramatists on the one hand, and that on the later, classically oriented Goethe and Schiller, on the other. The spectrum of stimulation and resonance appears even wider, when the latter are contrasted with the work of Georg Büchner and Christian Dietrich Grabbe whose Shakespeare receptions followed that of the classically oriented poets within a time-span of less than a generation. The more recent assimilation of Shakespeare must be viewed as a site of even greater diversity, even perhaps a source of division itself, when German late Romantic responses are read side by side with those of the early or, for that matter, the later Brecht.

Although, then, the agencies in German Shakespeare reception themselves need to be differentiated, what they all had in common was an exclusive and, hence, divisive effect on the level of what was and what was not appropriated in the first place. In the circumstances, it was virtually impossible to assimilate one particularly vital element in the Shakespearian heritage: the strength of the performative dimension, its ties to a widely shared culture of playful entertainment, the vicinity of the ordinary word, a given repertoire of conventions as partially derived from half-forgotten ritual, as in the oral and extemporised ingredients of 'the jigging veins of rhyming mother-wits'[2] – all these could not possibly be revitalised. As far as German drama from Lessing to Grabbe can be said to have represented a new middle-class culture, this culture indeed was advanced as one speaking for the nation at large. But the paradox was that the cause of cultural identity was projected as an exclusive formation, in terms of a dividing dramaturgy. It was defined dramatically in terms of such aims of representation as would prefigure the Shakespearian impulse on a predominantly literary level, to the exclusion of its broader cultural, popular and material constituents.

There is no doubt that with rare exceptions (Rousseau's *Lettre à d'Alembert* being the most notable) the European Enlightenment everywhere tended to privilege the written culture over and beyond that of the spoken word. But in Germany, with its chequered map of reinvested feudalism and petit absolutism after the devastating Thirty Years War and the no less disastrous peace settlement of 1648, the advent of the middle class to positions of cultural sovereignty was particularly arduous and, in comparison with other countries in Western Europe, much delayed. In a situation like that, Enlightenment positions in the life of the theatre could not mature through gradual growth but, rather, had to be implanted from above; they had to be grafted on an unruly scene of semi-literary performances resounding with echoes of the *commedia dell'arte* and the more remote memories of travelling English comedians. Hence, the pivotal figure in the gradually emerging cultural politics of the early German Enlightenment was, in the theatre, that of the *Vertreibung des Harlekin*, the expulsion or banishment of the extemporal entertainer.[3] To eject the free-wheeling art of the comedian from a stage that, as leading performer, he often enough dominated was of course in aid of the enlightened reform movement of the time. Led by highly articulate men of letters like Johann Christoph Gottsched, this movement aimed at the eviction, from contemporary stages, of everything that, by the yardstick of neoclassical poetics, was judged to be offensive. No question, this reform movement was inspired by a sense of a mission, according to which all 'improbabilities' (sorcerers, ghosts and witches included) redolent of popular superstition were ostracised.

The expulsion of extemporised entertainment opened up and secured a new type of theatrical space, one that began to be dominated by a strictly literary mode of composition. Throughout the course of the eighteenth century, scriptural authority in the theatre gained ground until, by the time that Lessing and Goethe became aware of Shakespeare, generally valid uses of the stage could not be conceived except in terms of a purely literary culture aspiring to serve a nation of the educated. On premises such as these, the theatre of Shakespeare would as a matter of course be received and translated into a language that was the language of poets rather than that of actors or ordinary people. As Maik Hamburger, foremost (East) German translator of Shakespeare's plays in our time, has noted, in the Elizabethan theatre 'the art of the dramatist merges with the art of living, self-producing human beings. . . . The physical aspect of Shakespeare's dramatic language is closely linked with the basically popular nature of his theatre',[4] in consonance with which the stage could absorb 'the whole linguistic spectrum of a people'.[5] But as soon as this language, in translation, is 'raised to a plateau of educated refinement', it 'forfeited those corporeal elements'; henceforth, dramatic speech was dissociated from the living experience of colloquial speech and *gestus* and 'altogether hollowed out with respect to its innate theatrical quality'.[6]

The specific conditions of cultural reproduction in the theatre (here barely hinted at) need to be taken into account when the history of Shakespeare's reception in the German theatre is at issue. There is considerable continuity from Gottsched and his influence on such reform-minded performers as the Neuberin via the prestigious deliberations of the Mannheim Nationaltheaterausschuss (1782–4) down to the work of Friedrich Ludwig Schröder or that of Karl Immermann and the Düsseldorf *Musterbühne*. Wherever we look, the authority of the text reigns supreme. As Immermann put it, the task was 'not to make the poet bow to the stale conventions of the stage but to elevate the latter to the level of the thoughts of the poet'.[7] In order to control the *mimische Element*, poetry must be recognised and acknowledged as 'an art of speech'; hence, what matters in the theatre is, '*primo*, speech and, only *secundo*, the play of facial muscles, hands, and feet'.[8] Similarly, Schröder, more than a generation earlier, made a point of following the prescribed text of the poet (*Vorschrift des Dichters*): 'the actor can never achieve more than what the poet aims at'.[9]

This is not the place to unravel the fuller context in which the authority of the poet-dramatist was invoked to ensure unity between performer and performed. But the notion of textual authority sanctioned by the 'aims' or 'intentions' of the poet invariably went hand-in-hand with the attempt to proscribe the gap between the impersonator and the impersonated. To call for the closure of representation was, like the concomitant preoccupation with empathy, one way of keeping out 'that low stuff' (to echo Sir Thomas Hanmer's Preface to his edition, 1744) in the productions of Shakespeare.[10] If the appropriation of his plays could assume the status almost of a national shrine, a monumental medium of inspiration through which the German theatre could come into its own, the reception of that heritage was, even at the height of nineteenth-century bardolatry, a divisive one, seeking to preserve inviolate the literary art of the poet *vis-à-vis* the irreverent zest, the game, the craft and craftiness of the performer.

As far as the cultural policy behind such a pre-scribed mode of reception was authorised in terms of its refinement and enlightenment effects, this authorisation was far from being an innocent one. As today we look back upon the underlying directions of cultural and political power, it is difficult not to be struck by mid-twentieth-century analogies in the theatrical circulation of authority. Ironically yet not quite unexpectedly, a comparable version of this politics of reception was resurrected almost wholesale, on a programmatic level, in postwar East Germany. After a brief period of experimentation, this policy was institutionalised so as to keep at bay memories of avant-garde theatre practices, especially strong in both pre-Nazi Germany and pre-revolutionary and early revolutionary Russia. Although in later years, especially in the 1980s, there was an increasing margin for renewed experimentation, the more rigid observance of the faithful rendering of the classical text cannot, in the last resort, be dissociated from a cultural policy of control and consolidation. Behind it there was a 'no nonsense' strategy that helped preclude any subversive treatment of what was believed to be the essential realism and humanism in Shakespeare's plays.

Shakespeare in Weimar: ambivalent intersection of discourses

The appropriation of Shakespeare in the German postwar theatre constituted a public site on which profound intellectual and political contradictions of the time were intercepted, rehearsed or displaced. Although of course insignificant when measured by the larger political issues of the cold war period, there was a remarkable element of ambivalence in the criticism and theatrical production of Shakespeare in the former German Democratic Republic. Here, as nowhere else in the cultural landscape of state-administered socialism, was a unique space for the reception and (re)production of potentially the greatest cultural text of modern Western civilisation. This space constituted a self-challenging, conflicting location where the political discourse of Marxism–Leninism, endorsed and controlled by the state apparatus, was made to confront the foremost Western classic whose worldwide reception was embedded in entirely different discursive practices of authorisation and representation.

In order at least to minimise the area of division and discontinuity between the appropriating and the appropriated discourses, the postwar Weimar politics of reception demanded a mediation of the Bard through the literary culture associated with the European Enlightenment and the formative period of modern German drama. Through this predetermined level of intermediation, representations of Shakespeare were officially designed to provide a textbook case of cultural assimilation serving to exemplify the native strength of the links between the most progressive achievements of the Renaissance past and its Marxist–Leninist re-invention in the present. But in its institutionalised form, the canonisation of a prefigured repertoire of intermediation and reception was of course as rigid as it was vulnerable. In the circumstances, therefore, the incomplete and dogmatic definition of this prefigured space for assimilation could without too much fuss be amplified and, even, neutralised as soon as the given master-key of reception ceased to provide openings, especially after 1968, for a broader awareness of the cultural potential of Shakespeare's theatre in our time.

Thus, in the course of the late 1970s and 1980s there developed in Weimar a complex constellation of discourses that went far beyond the preordained pedagogy of interaction between the Renaissance text and its socialist/humanist appropriation. Now the mediating language of Lessing, Herder and Goethe could in its turn be redefined and intercepted by positions closer to contemporaneity, beginning with Büchner and Heine and, later, twentieth-century dramatists. In the midst of this, and for some of us as an inestimable kind of leavening, came the impact of Bertolt Brecht's theatrical and theoretical work. For reasons that will always remain difficult to understand, the dominant authorities in *Kulturpolitik* for many years, long after Lukàcs's own misgivings had subsided, persisted in turning a deaf ear to Brecht as well as to dramatists and directors like Heiner Müller, Benno Besson and B. K. Tragelehn who, at the time, seemed to uphold a Brechtian mode of distantiation and stylisation.[11] But Brecht's shadow was too large to be obliterated; if anything, he served as a catalyst in what was already an impressive intersection of discourses. What resulted was a more complex body of ideas and perspectives that, in its own turn, began to be exposed to those entirely different discourses associated with the rebellious energies of post-1968 developments such as post-structuralism, neo-Marxism and feminism.

The site of interaction of these discourses in Weimar was quite potent because the East German Shakespeare Society throughout this period sought to provide a joint platform for both an annual scholarly conference and a theatre festival. Although the undertaking was remarkable in many ways, it was of course incapable of redressing a centuries-old imbalance in the relations of textual authority and performative agency. In this respect, failure was unavoidable. But for almost thirty years, a significant selection of the country's most debatable and most talked-about Shakespeare productions were performed and/or discussed at Weimar; at the same time, there were public conferences, panel debates, student colloquia and teacher conferences. According to my rough estimate, some 120 productions were shown, about 300 scholarly or critical papers were read, and more than fifty lectures and discussions were held. Each year between 1,300 and 1,500 members and friends of the East German Shakespeare Society participated in the Weimar events. Over the years the format of the Shakespeare festival changed, but the support of the public never waned; in fact, membership kept increasing until it actually outnumbered that of the West German association.[12]

The paradox was that, although East German *Kulturpolitik* was centrally prescribed, it was possible in Weimar to neutralise its more aggressive and dogmatic applications. In the postwar period there was in the GDR, in reaction to the barbarous aberrations of the Nazi past, a sense of indebtedness, if not genuine commitment, to everything that was radically incompatible with National Socialism. This response was not an opportunistic matter; there was a shared desire to use a not discredited cultural past of the nation as guide to reconstruction, as tools of analysis and standards of comparison. Besides, the ambience of Weimar allowed of a margin of diverse choices: it was possible both in the theatre and in criticism to discuss the given cultural/political agenda of reception or, for a good many members and visitors, simply to ignore it. In any case, personal motivation for attendance varied considerably. Some came for the theatre productions, some for the conferences and lectures, some for socialising, while others came simply because they loved the local habitation and the place. After all, the *genius loci* offered an escape from stereotypes of a more predictable kind of politics and a readily accessible niche for contact with Western culture and the English language.

The intellectual fare, the standard of the proceedings and the quality of the performances cannot be described summarily; enough, when it is suggested that they varied greatly, from the dullest to the finest, from the most traditional to a renewed awareness of cultural change and experiment in later years. This was due at least in part to a wide range of international contributions: from Shakespeare productions, coming from Russia, Armenia, England and Japan, to the intellectual debates, in later years enriched by distinguished scholars and critics such as Catherine Belsey, Philip Brockbank, Stephen Greenblatt, Geoffrey Hartman, Wolfgang Iser, Murray Krieger, George Steiner and, finally, German dramatists like Heiner Müller and Volker Braun. But although all these contributions were warmly welcome (in fact, they cannot be rated highly enough), the most noteworthy and, potentially, the most productive aspect of the Weimar Shakespeare festival lay elsewhere. It had, more than anything, to do with the attempt, even if only partially successful, to approach the Shakespearian text as a performed event and, in doing so, to combine a sense of Renaissance socio-cultural history with the most burning issues and contradictions of our own time, especially as these were informing performative energies in the theatre.

This orientation, it should be noted, has not gone under in the most recent past. After the unification of the country (1990), theoretically distinct traditions in Shakespeare criticism continue to offer variegated approaches to the English classic. True enough, as the new and the old *Bundesländer* move closer together, it will be a question of time when the two traditions cease to represent geographically different socio-cultural types of experience. In this direction, the unification, in 1993, of the two German Shakespeare societies points the way. But even so, in the midst of carefully (and without haste) negotiating the terms and conditions of reassociation, there was on either side a desire, expressed in no uncertain terms,[13] that the specific orientations and distinctive achievements of each of the societies in the past would not just be respected but actually kept alive in the future. Thus, unlike almost anything else in the country, today's German Shakespeare Society continues to provide a platform for historically distinct traditions emerging out of different usable types of past in the reception of Shakespeare.

In view of its peculiar situatedness in a national but also international situation of both intense hopes and disappointments, the East German experiment in Shakespeare criticism and production deserves to be described and examined further. No doubt, three or four years is a short time in which to develop anything like a balanced perspective on so singular an undertaking under complex historical circumstances. Besides, for someone who was involved as an active participant from first to last (and who does not equally feel authorised to speak on behalf of the West German reception of the Bard in the same period, 1964–93) there is of course an obvious liability in the attempt to relate a divided reception of Shakespeare to the cultural history of the country at large. In order to confront this liability (and to foreground rather than minimise the premises of any possible bias) I propose not to abstract from my own experience and perspective. Instead I shall focus on a few critical and theoretical figurations where my own contribution may justify an attempt to interrelate and, thereby, historicise wider intellectual perspectives against the background of a peculiarly divided national and cultural experience.

'Positive heritage' versus conjunctural appropriation

Today the conjuncture of differing levels of historicity has widely come to be accepted as a matter of course in contemporary criticism. But what needs to be remembered is that the Weimar attempt to work out a conjunctural sense of history in our approach to Shake-speare's plays for a good many years preceded both the advent of post-structuralism and the recent reorientation in Anglo-American versions of historicism. Although the East German attempt was beset with deep-going contradictions and inconsistencies (easily recognisable in the light of subsequent experience and theory) yet even today both its characteristic points of departure and its latter-day mutations appear far from despicable. On the contrary, the question may be asked to what extent it is possible to speak of an achievement of a sort, both in what was said and done and in what was not said and done under the circumstances.

The irony is that the theoretical approach in Weimar aimed at a conjunctural reading of past/present correlations in cultural his-tory not by rejecting but by probing more deeply into the histori-ography associated with the work of Herder, Goethe, Hegel and Marx. In order more fully to understand the political context against which these East German versions of historicism were developed, a few references are needed. The 1964 reinauguration ceremony celebrating the resumption of Shakespeare Society activities, coin-ciding as it did with the quatercentenary, was marked by an official high-ranking government pronouncement. In his address, Alexan-der Abusch, Deputy Chairman of the Council of Ministers, proposed that the appropriation of Shakespeare in the GDR was part of, and helped to consummate, a tradition, reaching back to eighteenth-century German receptions of Shakespeare which, in their turn, anticipated the flowering of humanism and realism in contempor-ary socialist culture. Shakespeare's abiding greatness, it was thought, derived from a view of man (*sic*) which transcended the boundar-ies of class society and actually helped affirm and enrich 'socialist humanism'.[14]

From the more practical view of the contemporary producer and director of Shakespeare's plays this appeared to demand a reading of the temporal distance between then and now as con-stituting a progressively meaningful space for both affirmation and anticipation. In other words, there was encouragement as well as pressure to use historical distance teleologically, in terms of a master-key of ultimate fruition: the seeds of social revolution in the sixteenth-century transition from feudalism to early modern (bourgeois) society were taken to help prepare for and legitim-ate the ultimate process of liberation and emancipation through socialism. In the light of such ideological underpinnings, cultural workers in the theatre were expected to read and direct a Shakespearian tragic hero such as Hamlet as a truly utopian prefiguration of the socialist–humanist conscience even, as Anselm Schlösser, influential Nestor of East German Shakespeare studies and editor of the *Jahrbuch* (1964–83), put it, as 'pioneering champion' (*Vorkämpfer*) of socialist society.[15] Among other things, this reading aimed at foregrounding common ground between sixteenth- and twentieth-century versions of a revolutionary image of humankind.

While the arrogance behind this claim might elsewhere have been considered astonishing, this was not so in the given cultural context of Weimar. There it was possible for Schlösser to say in 1984 that 'we who live in real socialism know [the answers to Gonzalo's questions] more accurately, anticipating with Shakespeare, but more clearly and more single-mindedly [*zielbewusster*], the next stage in the development of history'.[16] From a position like that, it must have appeared necessary to attack the revisionist 'jungle of pluralistic arbitrariness of interpretation' by calling for a 'guiding compass' in the form of a 'working-class standpoint',[17] in order to safeguard what Schlösser elsewhere referred to as 'the concept of a positive heritage' (*positives Erbe*).[18]

The point here is not to ridicule the apparent simplicity in what was an officially endorsed concept of tradition but to reread these controversial uses of Shakespeare's text as 'heritage'. For although the language which Abusch and Schlösser employed sounds entirely discredited today, theirs was not simply an opportunistic concern with an unthinking rehearsal of party politics. Rather, what the idea of 'a positive heritage' stood for was the elimination of (un)necessary friction and the obliteration of any (un)bridgeable rupture between Renaissance values and Leninist evaluations. Seeking to emphasise areas of identity, or at least of concurrence between then and now, these positions attempted, without ever saying so, to construct tradition as a principle of both orientation and control. This, as a matter of fact, was not so far removed from T. S. Eliot's sense of tradition which, in an altogether different political connection, had disparaged, if not 'pluralistic arbitrariness', at least the liberal principle or, rather, 'whiggery' as the unprincipled promptings of 'the Inner Voice', what Eliot conveniently referred to as 'doing as one likes'.[19] For these critics (and some of the

theatre directors), the party provided what T. S. Eliot had recom-
mended for the writer as 'the existence of an unquestioned spiritual authority outside himself, to which he has attempted to
conform'.[20] If this appears as too generous a comparison (it may
sound less so when we substitute 'ideological' for 'spiritual'), it
may help to explain the surprising extent to which it was taken for
granted. Under these circumstances for East German academics to
reject the concomitant notion of tradition as 'an idea of order'
must have been difficult, especially when the distance between
then and now, between Renaissance culture and its contemporary cultural uses, was believed to have been bridged by splendid
mediations in the cultural history of the nation.

However, as Renaissance ideas of 'harmony' were foregrounded
through socialist idealisations (as anticipations of a classless society), their remoteness from the ordinary realities of life in East
Germany became more and more crippling. At this point theatre
people, a director like Adolf Dresen and a translator and dramaturge like Maik Hamburger, took the lead in questioning the
cultural uses of such a heritage. Their Greifswald production of
Hamlet (1964) refused to acknowledge unambiguous areas of identity between Renaissance ideas and contemporary ideals and, by
implication, questioned the whole notion of continuity between then
and now. Instead, the Prince of Denmark in this production was
radically (and grotesquely) marked by his 'antic disposition'; played
by an immensely talented actor, this version of Hamlet appeared
to undermine the ideological construct of a premature humanism
that anticipated a future space for harmony in the relationship
between society and the individual conscience.[21]

It was more than coincidence when, at about the same time,
Shakespeare criticism and scholarship began to probe into current
assumptions of both continuity and historicity in theatrical as well
as critical interpretations. What, on a theoretical plane, appeared
as an urgent desideratum was first of all to confront the tension
(and make distinctions) between the two levels of historicity associated with sixteenth-century productions and twentieth-century
receptions of the Shakespearian text. In order to point at areas of
(dis)continuity between the two, I proposed a terminology which
attempted to distinguish between 'past significance and present
meaning'.[22] The idea was to define historicity in the uses of the
Shakespearian text more closely on two differing levels so that

both the gaps and links between them could be viewed simultaneously, as if in a state of interaction or mutual conditioning of one another. To be sure, such definition of the object of the Shakespearian scholar as critic was, at the time, proposed within the traditional demarcations of Shakespeare studies and could not hope to address what in today's critical language would involve an approach to the dramatic text as part of a given discursive practice. Even so, the attempt was to make relative the notion of continuity (teleological or otherwise) between now and then without allowing for any diametrically opposed concept of radical discontinuity or rupture.

Accordingly, if the object of the Shakespearian critic as cultural historian was neither the four-hundred-year-old text in the hands of Elizabethan actors nor the late twentieth-century context of its contemporary reception and interpretation, it seemed necessary to chart the contradictory space of both continuity and discontinuity between now and then. Neither the postulates of *Kulturpolitik* (emphasising 'present meaning' and function) nor the standards of positivistic scholarship (emphasising 'past significance' and genesis) appeared acceptable. On the contrary, the space for both concurrence and rupture called for a more complex notion of (dis)continuity between the past world of the Shakespearian text and the present world of its reception. Once it seemed possible to show that the pastness of the text and its theatrical context cannot and must not be separated from Shakespeare as a construction in the present, the task of the cultural historian needed to be contained in the reading of the critic, and vice versa.

Thus, the very notion of (dis)continuity between then and now was one way to respond to, even perhaps to contain, cruder notions of critical teleology. It is true that these methodological counter-proposals as developed implicitly but also explicitly in the late 1960s and early 1970s continued to entertain a good many illusions about the dialectics of contingency and validity in the 'historical process'. But the idea was to correlate the text as a product of the past and its reading as an experience in, and production of, the present. To stress the connection of these two dimensions in the reception of Shakespeare was to argue for more than just expediency in the sense that, say, an awareness of history might prevent us from crude anachronisms in interpretation. The point was that these two dimensions appeared inherent in a conjunctural view of the changeful uses of the classical text itself as soon as a distinction could be made between textual representation in, and cultural function of, Shakespeare's plays. Since the two are not the same, the cultural historian as critic is confronted with a multiple frame of reference in which *Zeitlichkeit* and *Überzeitlichkeit*, discontinuity and continuity, can be made to relate and, even, to interrogate one another.

Thus, the suggestion was that in any modern reception of Shakespeare two categorically distinct locations of discourse, each articulating diverse temporal interests, would collide with or react upon one another. But the resulting intersection of these discourses was not an academic affair; for the more one thought of it in terms of a (re)productive potency of modern performances, the more stringently practical and material issues appeared to be involved. We can proceed from neither a genuine Elizabethan production (which in its irretrievable uses of space and time and place already implied an interpretation of the text) nor from one that makes us believe that, say, *Hamlet* is a contemporary (or a socialist) play. Therefore, any reception of Shakespeare has to come to terms with the difference between historically used signs and a later code of their appropriation. But to be aware of the difference in question is not necessarily frustrating; for the manner in which this difference is coped with constitutes the most far-reaching decisions for both historical criticism and serious theatrical interpretation.

Once it was established that such conjunctural reading would involve mutual interrogations, and even contestations, of radically different discourses, there was little room left for concepts of reception which sought to reaffirm classical notions of harmony, continuity and closure. For both the Shakespeare scholar and the theatre director, the question was not whether or not to accept both codes in their different worlds as points of reference but rather how to relate them towards their most rewarding intersection and mutual 'interference' (to use the word in the special sense, according to H. C. Wyld, of an 'interaction of two streams of vibrations or wave motions').

Looking back at this early project of conjunctural historicity in reception I find it difficult not to use the contemporary language of 'difference' and discourse analysis. But the language in which this project was first developed was, like the dialectic of time and timelessness, certainly not the language of post-structuralism. The irony (and, surely, inconsistency) was that it was possible to reject Goethe's dramaturgy of closure without forgoing his supreme awareness of *Zeitlichkeit*. Although this project of multiple historicity owed its greatest debt to Hegel and Schleiermacher, it was the poet who had most poignantly phrased it in what he called his 'Legacy': 'Then is the past persisting, / The future living even now. / The moment is eternity' (*Dann ist Vergangenheit beständig, / Das Künftige voraus lebendig, / Der Augenblick ist Ewigkeit*).[23]

Whatever its terminology, the project, I would like to believe, was not a mean one when it made available a notion of re-presenting a text of the past neither in its identity with, nor in its isolation from, discourses in the present. In that sense, 'timelessness' (or continuity) would result through a sense of time (or discontinuity). If the formula of 'past significance and present meaning' continued to entertain an innocent concept of what, conjuncturally, was meaningful, such 'meaning' precluded its location in either the shallow waters of topical propaganda or in the erudite memory of the museum. 'Meaning' in Shakespeare, or so I thought, could best be discovered through this past present, or that part of it which – although past – is still with us, as part and premise of a (dis)continuous difference in the intersection of two discourses each opening the other through staged performances.

Uses of gallimaufry: popular culture in the theatre

While some such theoretical groundwork for the reception of Shakespeare in (East) Germany was meant to stimulate both theatrical production and historical criticism of the Bard, there was no doubt a desire on my part, perhaps not fully conscious at the time, to privilege the balance (or at least co-existence) of socially and temporally heterogeneous elements in a culture full of flux and transition. As I suggested in *Shakespeare and the Popular Tradition in the Theater* (first published in German, 1967), it was possible for a pre-modern, pre-capitalist popular culture profoundly to enrich and be mingled with a late English version of Renaissance humanism. The resulting *mélange* was no longer an exclusively popular one, and it certainly was neither univocal nor homogeneous. Nevertheless, it was quite inclusive for all that, once the popular element could be shown to be a major constituent of a national culture, which already presupposed a unique interaction of Renaissance and Reformation elements.

At this point, the strong emphasis on 'gallimaufry,' the 'hodge-podge' or 'mingle-mangle' composition of Elizabethan culture and society was in response to, and in aid of, several circumstances.[24] In my dissertation (1955), written during the Stalinist years of unrelenting dogmatism, I had come to the conclusion that Shakespeare's theatre could not be grasped as an institution dominated by one class. Rather, as then proposed, the Elizabethan stage was sustained by a balance of socio-political forces old and new. At the time, class-consciousness was writ large and emphatically defined as the consciousness of one particular class (as opposed to an ensemble of class relationships). Along these lines, prominent Marxist historians had tended to identify the Elizabethan Renaissance with the culture of one class alone (for Jürgen Kuczynski, for example, it was that of the bourgeoisie, while for Christopher Hill elements of a late feudal and courtly society appeared to be dominant).[25]

Although my early emphasis on the 'gallimaufry' of social forces in sixteenth-century English culture was designed to serve as an antidote to the more rigid notion of an indivisible class hegemony, there were, as the years went by, a growing number of problems with this emphasis. Even though it seemed appropriate to underline the extraordinary richness and complexity of Shakespeare's own place in time, and even though the notion of an all-encompassing theatre culture could be used as a socio-historical correlative to Keats's idea of Shakespeare's 'negative capability',[26] this emphasis did tend to minimise social, cultural and political divisions actually inscribed in a good many Elizabethan discursive practices. To say that the Elizabethan public 'playhouses not only defied the emerging social divisions but actually seemed to thrive on the richness of their contradictions'[27] was one way of strengthening the case for the popular element in the theatre. Clearly this emphasis tended to play down the exposure of popular culture to the marketplace where, as recent experience has taught us, folklore can all too easily be manufactured as fakelore. At the time, however, the links between pre-modern and early modern popular culture appeared to be far more important than its proximity to market forces of exchange and circulation.

However, the foregrounding of these links did not so much

reflect a nostalgia for what L. C. Knights in *Drama and Society in the Age of Jonson* had called the 'anti-acquisitive attitude' but, rather, was a fundamental *conditio sine qua non* for taking an independent position *vis-à-vis* an unhelpful triad in contemporary cultural politics: at the time, any study in popular traditions was bound to be judged by how it proposed to cope with the threefold demand for humanism, realism and *Volkstümlichkeit* ('popularity' in the sense of an association with the cause and the culture of the people).

In the circumstances, this threefold position, championed as it was in all spheres of cultural and artistic activity, constituted a programmatic context in which a Soviet cultural politics was effectively combined with a late nineteenth-century Russian poetics. In particular, the concept of *Volkstümlichkeit* (or *Volksverbundenheit*) was directly indebted to the Russian convention of *narodnostj*, originally a nineteenth-century term invoked by pre-revolutionary artists and intellectuals seeking to serve the people. But this somewhat undifferentiated category was, as in Soviet criticism of nineteenth-century fiction, indissolubly linked with a Tolstoian notion of 'realism' that combined the epistemology of 'reflection' ('art reflecting reality') with formal criteria of lifelike representations privileging a poetics of empathy and naturalisation. At the time, Soviet Shakespeare criticism did not seem to have too many difficulties applying these concepts to Shakespearian drama.[28] But in Germany, thanks to Brecht and Expressionist drama, such a threefold platform of realism, humanism and *narodnostj* appeared to preclude a viable awareness of contemporaneity in the staging of Shakespeare; nor was it possible, I thought, for criticism on this basis honestly and unconstrainedly to stimulate a modern sensibility in the theatre.

This gap between the dogma of cultural politics and the pursuit of a living reception of Shakespeare was especially frustrating when, in a sixteenth-century context, the concept of *narodnostj* (or its German equivalent) came to be identified with basically a nineteenth-century notion of 'realism'. There was a need to explode the false claim on congruity between them by foregrounding the pre-Enlightenment standards of a theatre that privileged non-representational (and potentially subversive) forms of clowning, 'madness', disguise, wordplay, riddle, prophecy and residual uses of ritual. Thus, in my study of the popular tradition in the theatre (written between 1963 and 1966) the idea was to study the process of assimilation by which pre-modern uses of popular discourse and custom came to be adapted to a culture that either preceded modern forms of realism and empathy or accommodated them in a larger ensemble of 'mingle-mangle' forms and functions.

Again, theatre people were the first to perceive that this was *Volkstümlichkeit* with a difference.[29] Such redefinition of the popular tradition was, of course, deeply indebted to Anglo-American scholars like C. R. Baskerville, S. L. Bethell, C. L. Barber and others. In the event, this approach effectively unhinged the neoclassical and Romantic mediation (and predetermination) of the Shakespearian 'heritage'. In doing so, it brought to the fore a prehumanist, not necessarily literary emphasis on agencies of performance in the Elizabethan theatre. The emerging gulf between Enlightenment or Romantic appropriations of Shakespeare and the historicising approach through sixteenth-century uses of popular culture henceforth helped to redefine the uses of 'tradition' itself as a cultural practice potentially unsanctioned and divisive rather than univocal and affirmative. As opposed to the legitimation effect of an easily controlled intermediate form of canonisation (administered as part of a pragmatic master-key rather than a Marxist approach to cultural history), there was, to say the least, an immense complication in the order of the temporal and functional links and gaps between the classic text in its time and contemporary uses of it in ours.

This redefinition of the uses of the early modern theatre as a potential 'heritage' coincided with significant changes and experiments on the East German stage. Whereas the irreverent voices in Dresen's and Hamburger's 1964 *Hamlet* were easily muted, the theatre in the 1970s unabashedly set out to address contradictions in the current ideological language of harmony and closure. In particular, Benno Besson in his production of *Hamlet* (1977) presented a deep rift between neoclassical order in the humanist poetics of the Prince of Denmark and the sheer expertise, competence and experience of the players. Rather than neutralising these tensions in the language of the play, his production surrendered any univocal assertion of meaning in favour of a more complex projection of a divided space for socio-cultural diversity and conflict. Thus, Besson's production, which was performed and discussed in Weimar,[30] provided a welcome piece of unorthodoxy. Challenging

in no uncertain terms the adequacy of neoclassical–Romantic standards of appropriating Shakespeare's text for the modern stage,
Besson redefined the role of the Prince as that of a 'muddy-mettled
rascal', a 'John-a-dreams', who could refer to himself as 'a rogue and
peasant slave' (II.ii.502–20).[31] The idea was not to play down the
Elizabethan mingle-mangle, where 'the toe of the peasant comes
so near the heel of the courtier' (V.i.136–7), but to redefine a mobile
social relationship that appeared to affect the circulation of authority inside the theatre itself. Besson – the most talented and internationally influential of Brecht's disciples – contributed a striking
rereading of Hamlet's advice to the players. Defying the purely literary authority of the poetics of representation, as administered by
the Renaissance Prince, the First Player, slightly bored by mere theory, appeared to know more about mimesis than any disquisition
could teach him. Here we had the humanist as an all too obtrusive
Maecenas providing learned citations; his mere verbiage was to
bolster up the self-representation of the courtier's, soldier's, scholar's
image. At the same time, there were forces resisting this representation, jeopardising it through antic clowning, disguise, 'extasy' and
other audience-related forms of performative practice. The production had a sensational impact on the East German cultural scene.
Hamlet, the presumed representative of both humanism and the
people, was effectively (and without much fuss) dislodged from his
former pre-eminence as premature harbinger of idealised news
about a revolutionary future.

Here, indeed, a canonised tradition of intermediation was prac-
tically questioned in terms of both what (as Shakespeare's text)
was represented and what (in the contemporary theatre) was doing the representing and performing. Basic presuppositions of
authority and validity, hitherto governing selection and control
over a given canon, had ceased to be operative. As was the case
in Greifswald in 1964, the theatre itself challenged the politics of
canonisation through which the alleged certainties of a masterful
past were designed to control and contain whatever uncertainty
the future held.

The question, then, needed to be confronted whether there was
an alternative to an understanding of 'heritage' that, arrogantly,
claimed to institute a possessive, totalising, self-congratulatory mode
of ownership over texts and discourses of the past. Was it perhaps
possible, on the strength of the performative element in the theatre,

so to redefine the uses of Shakespeare that our reception of his plays would *not* have to be regarded as an illusory project by which some ideological consciousness (or reason, in its presumed autonomy) hoped to extend its sense of sovereignty and continuity to the events and figures of the past? In other words, was there perhaps a site on which a mutual engagement between the textual meaning of representation and the energies of performance could constitute an ever changeful, viable space for the appropriation of the classic? If ever there was such a thing as 'interference' between then and now, it would presuppose a discursive space in which textual authority – far from being given – could be suspended as part of a larger circulation of social energies, performative agencies, and play-ful rehearsals.

It was in response to this question that, I felt, the popular tradition in theatre deserved to be further studied and assessed. Clearly this tradition was unthinkable without an incommensurate ground of performative practices that could never quite be subsumed under any totalising uses of meaning. In this respect, the study of the popular tradition in the theatre did reveal a divisive potential both on the Shakespearian stage and in our reception of his plays. That stage did not contain any unified type of theatrical space: the division between symbolic *locus* and non-symbolic *platea* precluded the self-contained autonomy of any textually prescribed role. On this stage, role and actor, textual authority and performative agency would enter into a relationship that, spatially, socially and semiotically, was an open one, offering space for both continuity and division.

If this was so, the reproduction of Shakespeare's plays in our time could not possibly hope to reintroduce a unitary concept of theatrical space that by itself would compel a unifying mode in the relations of scriptural and non-scriptural signs and meanings. The appropriation of Shakespeare's text today, then, was best thinkable as the reception of a potentially divisive series of significations, as 'meanings which contradict and answer one another and which decline to annihilate themselves in a final global meaning'.[32] Although the links between Shakespeare scholarship and Shakespeare production in East Germany must not be overestimated, there was in this question at least some rudimentary room for an element of give and take between them. Brecht after all was well advised when he said that today Shakespeare's plays can best be revitalised when first of all his theatre is revisited.

In that sense, the division in the German reception of Shakespeare, officially cemented in the dark years of cold war politics, had incidentally rather than intentionally a certain unforeseen parallel in the respective directions of Shakespeare studies. Although in its own terms rich and stimulating, West German Shakespeare criticism had in these decades tended to champion the arts of verbal language;[33] the strategy of its most brilliant critic was (as John Dover Wilson put it in his Preface to Wolfgang Clemen's *The Development of Shakespeare's Imagery*) 'to elucidate the art of Shakespeare the poet-dramatist'.[34] A different emphasis on the theatre as an institution with its roots in sixteenth-century culture and society came from East Germany. It pointed in a direction that was both strangely at odds and surprisingly in consonance with the general upheaval in literary scholarship and critical theory that occurred in the late 1970s and 1980s.

Signs of authority versus the authority of signs

In the early 1980s, the new paradigm, looming ever larger in Western theory and criticism, could no longer be ignored in the humanities in East Germany.[35] From the point of view of the proceedings of the German Shakespeare Society, it was difficult to think of a more forcefully challenging body of discourses than the emerging alliance, as yet scarcely differentiated, between post-structuralism, neo-Marxism and feminism. For those who were prepared to look (and refused to follow Professor Erich Hahn, head of the Council of DDR philosophers, in his call for putting the whole postmodernism issue on the index of the Central Committee) the challenge was formidable: it comprised basic issues of epistemology, historiography and semiology, and was unsettling especially to those positions that had gone into orthodox uses of Shakespeare as 'heritage'. Not only was preferential reference to any exemplary kind of past culture (whether or not described as 'heritage') put into question; henceforth the ground was prepared for what another world citizen of Weimar, Friedrich Nietzsche, had conceived as the combined uses of both memory and forgetfulness. Together, they would serve as constituents of something larger (and more problematic) than canonicity. In this connection, the concept of 'repression' itself was a reminder of what Gayatri C. Spivak in her Preface to Jacques Derrida's *Of Grammatology* called 'the complexity of the act of choosing forgetfulness'.[36] Thus, the *oubliance* of the critic and/or the institution would have to be acknowledged as part of an active faculty relating to the not so innocent play of knowledge and ignorance in the process of cultural appropriation itself.

At the same time, certain uses of 'forgetfulness' in Weimar, so close to the horrors of Buchenwald, had an unacceptable ring. And there were other circumstances that stood in the way of an uncritical acceptance of the new paradigm, including that central part of it commonly referred to as deconstructionist. Even so, the forcefulness of postmodern theory was such that elementary notions of representation and subjectivity had to be renegotiated. The ensuing discussions were contradictory and often enough unsatisfying; but for all that their direction cannot very well be understood simply in terms of an 'impact' (or 'influence') of the critical upheaval in Western Europe and North America. What appears no less noteworthy is the extent to which, simultaneously, the East German encounter with postmodernism in the theatre and post-structuralism in critical theory was in response to indigenous needs and problems. True enough, these needs in their turn were linked, directly or indirectly, to political, cultural and technological changes on an international plane. In the circumstances, it seems fair to say that the new paradigm (here comprising new historicism and cultural materialism) immensely helped to stimulate ways and means by which the full extent of a precariously concealed indigenous crisis could be exposed and grappled with.

To illustrate these developments, it seems best in conclusion to recall at least some of the annual Weimar proceedings, especially as these gradually came to take up the postmodernist challenge. Perhaps the 1982 conference with its theme, 'Theatrical Practice and Shakespeare Scholarship', was the first to suggest the beginnings of a new kind of orientation. Again, theatre people were in the forefront of political and cultural change. The main attraction of these Shakespeare Days (as they used to be called) was a performance of Alexander Lang's radically experimental, in many ways postmodern, production of *A Midsummer Night's Dream*. As its dramaturge, Alexander Weigel, seemed to imply in his conference paper, this show had to be viewed in conjunction with important cultural 'changes in the relations of directing and acting'. To all intents and purposes, performers brought a 'new, more sovereign and active approach to rehearsals', in connection with which the production could not be 'considered as the realisation of a [preconceived] concept'. Signalling the sense of a 'crisis' in the traditional *Regietheater*, Weigel projected the theatrical process itself as the source of ultimate authority – which authority culminated in 'what was unexpected, what was not preconceived' in performance.[37]

While on this occasion literary critics and cultural historians were slow to take up this important point of departure, there was, by implication, a more adequate response to these unresolved problems when, in 1986, the theme of the conference was 'Shakespeare – History and Utopia', or when, a year later, the recent upheaval in the humanities was directly faced. Although, again, in 1987 the usual run of four or five theatre productions was shown and discussed, the conference, whose theme was 'Gender, Power, and Humanism [*Humanität*]', remained at the centre of attention. Here was a somewhat delayed occasion for the oldest literary society in Europe to come to terms with feminist criticism of Shakespeare in a context marked by the need for redefining the relations of power and discourse. This agenda, especially as it absorbed the post-structuralist and new historicist concern with relations of language and power, was, to that date, unheard of in the German Democratic Republic. It was one thing to propose to discuss epistemological questions such as might pertain to dramatic representation; it was quite another thing to open up a public platform in Weimar for such highly controversial issues as Western feminism and (non-)Marxist theories and politics of power. It is true that public access to the proceedings was to a certain extent limited: the conference was bilingual and part of the discussion was in English; but even that was a *novum*, even perhaps an achievement of a sort, one that was sure to be frowned upon by doctrinaire participants. Although the whole undertaking remained a precarious one to the last moment, circumstances were fortunate for us. Among panellists and speakers we were privileged to have some of the most distinguished names in contemporary international Shakespeare studies;[38] we had the support of at least one courageous and far-sighted representative of the Ministry of Culture;[39] and of course we had in our project the emphatic association with Shakespeare in whose sheltered space ideological postulates could at least partially be neutralised.

However, it would be wrong to overemphasise the necessary strategy of cunning and co-operation that, in the circumstances, was necessary to make these and similar occasions possible. The irony was that the borderline between nonconformity and 'complicity' could not be sharply demarcated; and, what is more, the resulting ambivalence was certainly not of an opportunistic order. On the one hand, there was no impenetrable barrier between new historicism or cultural materialism and the less dogmatic versions of an indigenous historical materialism: the area of potential assimilation, even mutual give and take, was not inconsiderable. On the other hand, disagreements were not slurred over. For instance, the concept of *Humanität* was used in reference to the notion, exemplified in Marx's *Grundrisse*, that standards and premises of humanism cannot be abstracted from material and intellectual appropriations of the world, especially those processed through socialising forms of physical or mental labour. This position, far from being a concession to anyone, was not a departure at all from what by and large innumerable GDR discussions had established. Further to develop this position served to vindicate cultural agency and event as against their textualisation or fictionalisation. In this respect, East German participants in the debate, like Hanna Behrend, Friederike Hajek, Brunhild de la Motte, Sabine Nathan, Ursula Püschel, Thomas Sorge, Günter Walch and myself, did not have to go out of their way to chart common ground with feminist criticism of Shakespeare, wherever this criticism itself affirmed the need, as Lisa Jardine phrased it, 'to retrieve agency for the female subject in history'.[40]

Still, while important positions in the feminist project could without too much difficulty be assimilated, the question of power, especially when dissociated from gender struggle, was a more highly sensitive issue in Weimar. At least part of the reason for that was a specifically national one. After the disastrous defeat in 1933 of arguably the strongest European working-class movement, the German Communist Party had pursued a popular-front type of policy, canvassing in particular artists and intellectuals who would as fellow-travellers be prepared to join an anti-fascist alliance against Hitler. Among a vanguard of distinguished names like Brecht, Becher, Seghers, Feuchtwanger, Heartfield, Piscator, Eisler, Dessau and others it was Heinrich Mann who, at the Paris congress of anti-fascist writers (1935), had formulated the need for a close bond, even 'unity' (*Einheit*), between *Macht* and *Geist*, power and intellect. After 1945, when many of these exiled artists and intellectuals decided to return to the Eastern part of Germany, this 'unity' was reaffirmed as part of a policy of alliance and co-operation.

However, as the years went by, there developed the perception of an increasing gap between the declared principles of this policy and the actual relations of *pouvoir* and *savoir* in the country. The contradiction came to a head when, upon the forced exile of dissident poet and singer Wolf Biermann (1976), a leading group of writers, including Christa Wolf and Heiner Müller, submitted a petition to the Politbureau protesting against the measure. The subsequent series of severe reprisals on those who had signed the petition tended to shatter what cautious hopes had been nourished by Erich Honecker's policy of 'no taboo' in the arts. As Franz Fühmann said in an interview in May 1978, writers now were thrown back upon themselves and forced 'to think again about questions such as the relations of literature and power'.[41]

In the circumstances, it seemed impossible to ignore the need for looking into the crisis-ridden relations of discourse and power more closely and to do so in a broadly historical perspective. No doubt there was a prehistory to these troublesome relations first culminating in early modern social, religious and technological constellations through which a sixteenth-century crisis of authority emerged in Western and Central Europe. In this period, unprecedented proliferations of discursive practices were connected with inevitable divisions between *auctoritas* and *potestas*; it was a situation when certain language uses could first be considered as in opposition to or 'tongue-tied by authority'. Shakespeare's interest in the issue of authority could easily be established;[42] he used the term about sixty times in his writings. But was there not, in the sixteenth century, a wider context in which a passionate concern with and challenge of authority was, as it were, institutionalised? The answer was the European Reformation in which a powerfully held authority was questioned on behalf of a different type of authority that largely drew on discursive practices such as the reading, interpreting and translation of Scripture. The Luther anniversary in Weimar (1983) was a fitting occasion to trace the resulting crisis of authority, one that culminated in a conflict between the dominant signs of authority (as ecclesiastical *potestas*) and that newly potent author-ity (*auctoritas*) in the uses of signs.[43]

From here, it was only one step to explore conflicting uses of authority in sixteenth-century England where, in a crucial mid-century situation, the issue emerged in its full ramifications. The conservative Bishop Gardiner attacked 'Certain printers, players, and preachers' for behaving 'as though we know not yet how to be justified' and for seeking 'to slip the anchor-hold of authority, and come to a loose disputation'.[44] Shakespeare, being of course himself a player and presumably in touch with printers, was confronted with, and involved in, some such ground swell of change and crisis in the locations of authority. As the Elizabethan gaps between the fixed exercise of power and the 'loose' authorisation of written and spoken language grew wider, a new paradigm of authority began to loom on the horizon of modern culture: no longer available through given locations of power and meaning, authority now constituted itself not so much in a pre-discursive situation or at the beginning of discourse (where given sources used to be cited as valid) but rather in the production and perception of meaning, truth, conviction, and belief as process.

In Shakespeare's time, then, important constellations in early modern culture and politics appeared to constitute a bifold court of appeal juxtaposing (as my 1987 essay phrased it) 'the authority of signs versus the signs of authority'.[45] The Elizabethan theatre was remarkably well equipped to assimilate this division in author-ity to its own specific mode of representation. The platform stage harboured the traditional difference between, on the one hand, the verisimilitude of the *locus* as a closed site of representation and, on the other hand, a *platea*-like opening for what Joseph Hall called the performer's 'self-resembled show'. Hence, there was no unitary concept of theatrical space that by itself would have compelled a unifying mode in coming to terms with textualised and performat-ive locations of authority. Under these conditions, the Elizabethan stage in its *platea*-like dimension could privilege the authority of what and who was performing; at the same time, the symbolising and localising potential of this same stage could foreground the au-thority of what and who was represented. The difference between performance and text is not of course identical with this (here very much oversimplified) division in the uses of theatrical space. Even so, the swift, socially and semiotically charged interplay between

performance-oriented actor and text-oriented role, between exis-
tential and playful parameters of theatricality, is unthinkable without the mutual engagements resulting from the institutionalising
of the division in question.

But was this 'bifold authority' (*Troilus and Cressida*, V.ii.147)
in Shakespeare's theatre anywhere consistently contiguous with
the early modern dissociation between signs of authority and the
authority of signs? This question, rich in political implications for
the East German reception of the Bard, did not permit of either an
unambiguous yes or no. Enough when here I content myself with
the observation that the antagonism between external power and
intellectual authority, although on the Elizabethan horizon, was fully
to be developed by the continental Enlightenment where it became
a cogent source of the perception of the sovereignty of self-author-
ising cultural practices. In Weimar in the 1980s, it was tempting for
me to resurrect this scenario if only to reassure one's own response
to the deepening legitimation gap in the dominant language of
ideology. But it was one thing to be tempted, in Jürgen Habermas's
phrase, by a *herrschaftsfreie Raum*, an unconstrained site of independent communicative practices; it was quite another matter to
subscribe to the scenario of an opposition between material and
intellectual locations of authority.

When I decided strictly to qualify rather than reconfirm this
scenario, the reason was both theoretical and political. Theoretically, my project was such that it sought to reassociate the issue
of authority with the early modern stimuli and technologies of
authorship as well as with the conditions of authorisation. In this
direction, I had become wary of an uncontaminated flow of *Geist*.
More recently, any concept of the self-sufficiency of knowledge
and meaning seemed especially problematic after Jacques Derrida
in *Writing and Difference* had exposed unsuspected areas of complicity between force and signification, violence and metaphysics;
similarly, an innocent view of purely virtuous uses of language
appeared untenable after Michel Foucault in *The Order of Discourse* had conceived of discourse as by itself powerful, as a cultural practice that can forcefully intervene in, violate and reorder
the world of objects.

The confrontation with these relentless readings of the uses of
language and culture was brought to a head by the political events
of 1989. It is true that, when in November of that year the wall

came down, the oppositional relation between discursive and powerful locations of authority appeared for one long hour to be triumphantly confirmed. But after the moment of celebration was over, too many things happened that began to contradict the premises on which the critical intellect sought to overcome the bastions of petrified power. Dissident writers in particular were soon disillusioned; but then for intellectuals to have defied the regime of authoritarian power was, through a strange process of inversion, to participate in the circulation of awards and prestige resulting from, paradoxically, both the existence and the negation of the same established authoritarian power. This, precisely, was the uncanny threshold between unorthodoxy and complicity: the intellectual power of nonconformity itself thrived upon, in fact presupposed, the external enforcement of conformity. Hence, on several levels doubts appeared justified whether it was possible, then as well as now, to grasp relations between the authority of external power and the power of an internal or discursive authority in terms of a dichotomy or opposition pure and simple.

From the point of view of the Bard's reception in our time, it was these political events of course that brought the study of Shakespeare in the German Democratic Republic to an unspectacular conclusion. But this conclusion, far from conclusively answering the question of authority in the representation of the classic, may well be conducive to new perspectives on the validity of difference in Shakespeare studies. These of course are beyond the scope of the present chapter. Still, after the topography of partition in the reception of Shakespeare is radically altered, our own divided experience past and present (including that in the world at large) may well serve as an eye-opener for dissociative energies which have never been sufficiently acknowledged in Shakespeare's theatre itself. Here, the recently perceived area of discontinuity between textual authority and performative agency may be only a pointer in this direction. It is a direction in historical criticism that complements, on the international level of reception, the strange but not unfamiliar spectacle of an inheritance that, conjoining the world's family of nations into acts of cultural appropriation, results in unequal possessions.

If, at this late date, 'negative capability' may be translated into the authorisation of difference and diversity, Shakespeare is destined to answer the demand, in the reception process, for diversity as well. This diversity is behind the need for all our changeful *inter-pretations* of Shakespeare; but, even in answering this need, there is something beyond division that this huge performance-text gives and conjoins – something which is behind all our diverse inter-pretations of *Shakespeare*. Thus, the divisions of the past, like those in the future, can best be coped with when transmuted into a dis-criminating awareness of what, in each particular place and time, an appropriation of the English dramatist can and cannot give us. Inseparable from all our yesterdays, this awareness may spe-cifically inform the work, the play, the 'imaginary puissance' that this performance-text demands and that *we* in this hour can or cannot give.

Notes

In several sections this chapter draws on a (here thoroughly reworked and substantially augmented) fragment of a draft first written for a collection of East German Shakespeare studies and production interviews, *Shake-speare Redefined*, ed. Lawrence Guntner and Andrew McLean, forthcom-ing. My thanks go to Lawrence Guntner for invaluable help with the language of the draft. Although here much revised, this whole chapter might not have been written except for the initiative, encouragement and patience coming from him, Andrew McLean and my present editor, John Joughin.

1 This concept of reception *qua* appropriation complements, I assume, Werner Habicht's critique of nationalist versions of Shakespeare in the German imagination; see his *Shakespeare and the German Ima-gination*, International Shakespeare Association Occasional Papers, No. 5 (Hertford, Stephen Austin, 1994), where the important literature on the subject is conveniently listed (p. 23, n. 1). Such versions are not, of course, a specifically German phenomenon; see, e.g., Balz Engler, 'Shakespeare in the trenches', *Shakespeare Survey*, 44 (1992), pp. 105–11. On the concept of appropriation, as here proposed, see my essay 'Appropriation and modern history in Renaissance prose narrative', *New Literary History*, 14 (1982/3), pp. 459–95, esp. pp. 461ff. The most detailed and, I think, perceptive study of postwar German Shake-speare reception East and West is Ruth Freifrau von Ledebur, *Deutsche Shakespeare-Rezeption seit 1945* (Frankfurt, Akademische Verlags-gesellschaft, 1974) with full bibliography for the years 1945–72.
2 Christopher Marlowe, *Tamburlaine the Great*, ed. J. S. Cunningham (Manchester, Manchester University Press, 1981), p. 113.

3 For more recent reconsiderations of this reform movement, see Rudi Münz, *Das 'andere' Theater: Studien über ein deutschsprachiges teatro dell'arte der Lessingzeit* (Berlin, Henschelverlag, 1979) and Hilde Haider-Pregler, *Des sittlichen Bürgers Abendschule: Bildungsanspruch und Bildungsauftrag des Berufstheaters im 18. Jahrhundert* (Wien, Jugend und Volk, 1980).

4 Maik Hamburger, 'Gestus and the popular theatre', *Science and Society*, 41 (1977), p. 37.

5 *Ibid.*, p. 38.

6 *Ibid.*

7 Karl Immermann's letter to Graf von Redern; cited by Martin Linzer, *Die Düsseldorfer Musterbühne* (Studienmaterial für die künstl. Lehranstalten) (Berlin, 1956), p. 77.

8 *Ibid.*, p. 79.

9 Cited in Dieter Hoffmeier, *Ästhetische und methodische Grundlagen der Schauspielkunst Friedrich Ludwig Schröders* (Studienmaterial) (Berlin, 1955), p. 18.

10 *Eighteenth Century Essays on Shakespeare*, ed. D. Nichol Smith (Oxford, Clarendon Press, 1963), p. 86.

11 In the Introduction and Epilogue to *Shakespeare und die Tradition des Volkstheaters* (Berlin, Henschelverlag, 1967) I had identified my approach with Brecht's postulate, 'to start from the stage for which Shakespeare wrote' (p. 30). Juxtaposing Brecht's position with that of Goethe, my suggestion was that neither empathy nor alienation could provide a fully balanced approach to Shakespeare today. But in these years repeated requests in Weimar to discuss the Brechtian reception of Shakespeare met with stubborn opposition.

12 For a fairly reliable record of the Weimar 'Shakespeare days', see *Shakespeare-Jahrbuch* (Weimar), 100/101 (1964/5) to 128 (1992).

13 See the second issue of the reassociated yearbook (1994) where, on the eve of the unification of the German Shakespeare societies, the two presidents (Suerbaum and Weimann) bid farewell to their respective constituencies (1994, pp. 9–16).

14 See Alexander Abusch, *Shakespeare, Realist und Humanist, Genius der Weltliteratur* (Berlin, Dietz Verlag, 1964).

15 Anselm Schlösser, 'Über das Herangehen an *Hamlet*', *Shakespeare-Jahrbuch*, 120 (1984), p. 112.

16 Anselm Schlösser, 'Von Fremden, Eingeborenen und Barbaren bei Shakespeare', *Shakespeare-Jahrbuch*, 114 (1978), p. 21.

17 Schlösser, 'Über das Herangehen an *Hamlet*', p. 112.

18 On this concept and the reception of *Hamlet* in Germany, see Manfred Pfister, 'Hamlet und der deutsche Geist: Die Geschichte einer politischen Interpretation', (Shakespeare) *Jahrbuch* 1992 (West), pp. 13–38.

19 T. S. Eliot, 'The function of criticism', *Selected Essays 1917–1932* (London, Faber and Faber, 1932), p. 27.

20 *Ibid.*, p. 29; Eliot's italics.

21 On the Greifswald production of *Hamlet*, see Lawrence Guntner's admirable survey, 'Brecht and beyond: Shakespeare on the East German stage', *Foreign Shakespeare: Contemporary Performance*, ed. Dennis Kennedy (Cambridge, Cambridge University Press, 1992), pp. 109–39.

22 See 'Past significance and present meaning', *New Literary History*, 1:1 (1969), pp. 91–109. A German version under the title 'Gegenwart und Vergangenheit in der Literaturgeschichte' first appeared in *Weimarer Beiträge*, 5 (1970), pp. 31–57.

23 J. W. Goethe, *Sämtliche Werke* (Jubiläums-Ausgabe) (Stuttgart/Berlin, 1903ff.), II, p. 246 (my translation).

24 Full documentation of the mingle-mangle (and related metaphors of mixture, as here taken from John Lyly's prologue to *Midas*) was central to the thesis of my dissertation, *Drama und Wirklichkeit in der Shakespearezeit* (Halle, Niemeyer, 1958), esp. pp. 13–180.

25 For a critical dialogue with both historians, see *ibid.*, pp. 26–7, 54–5. Cf. Ledebur, *Deutsche Shakespeare-Rezeption seit 1945*, p. 89; citing Joachim Krehayn (1955): 'To view Shakespeare's position as between . . . the classes must be rejected as non-Marxist' (my translation).

26 See my essay 'The soul of the age: Towards a historical approach to Shakespeare' in *Shakespeare in a Changing World*, ed. Arnold Kettle (London, Lawrence and Wishart, 1964), pp. 17–42 (p. 42).

27 *Ibid.*, p. 34.

28 As Alexander Anikst, distinguished Russian Shakespeare scholar-critic noted, Soviet criticism since the mid-1930s supported 'Shakespeare's claim to the title of a people's poet and an exponent of the folk tradition' (*Shakespeare in the Soviet Union*, ed. Roman Samarin and Alexander Nikoljukin (Moscow, Progress Publishers, 1966), p. 113). As E. Kornilova seems to suggest, once 'a conception of Shakespeare as the expression of the people's soul . . . became a cornerstone' in Soviet criticism, it was possible to reject and go beyond a 'vulgar sociological tendency' that had dominated Shakespeare studies until the mid-1930s. (E. Kornilova, 'Marxist paths in Shakespeare studies', *Shakespearovski Sbornik* (Moscow, 1961), p. 369; cf. pp. 44–51).

29 As indicated in the German edition, the first critical reader of the manuscript was Maik Hamburger; the English edition was dedicated to Benno Besson and Manfred Wekwerth who had used the book in their productions.

30 As consultant to this production, I was proud to introduce it at the Weimar conference; see 'Eigenes und Fremdes in Hamlet', *Shakespeare-Jahrbuch*, 114 (1978), pp. 87–91.

31 Here and in what follows, my text is William Shakespeare, *The Complete Works*, gen. eds Stanley Wells and Gary Taylor (Oxford, Clarendon Press, 1994).

32 Patrice Pavis, *Theatre at the Crossroads of Culture*, trans. Loren Kruger (London, Routledge, 1992), pp. 59–60. This is said in reference to the work of Peter Brook, distinguished director of Shakespeare's plays in our time.

33 However, this differentiation is relative as soon as the pioneering forays of Rudolf Stamm and the more recent splendid work of Manfred Pfister is taken into consideration.

34 Wolfgang Clemen, *The Development of Shakespeare's Imagery*. Preface by J. Dover Wilson (New York, Hill and Wang, 1962), p. vi; see the same author's *Shakespeare's Dramatic Art: Collected Essays* (London, Methuen, 1972).

35 I first drew attention to the need for coming to terms with the challenge of post-structuralism in 'Der Poststrukturalismus und das Produktionsproblem in fiktiven Texten', *Weimarer Beiträge*, 31 (1985), pp. 1061–99; 'Text und Tätigkeit in *Hamlet*', *Shakespeare-Jahrbuch* (Weimar), 121 (1985), pp. 30–43; 'Mimesis zwischen Zeichen und Macht: Neue Perspektiven (am Beispiel Shakespeares)', *Zeitschrift für Germanistik* 9 (1988), pp. 133–55. These studies at least in part prepared the way, critically and conceptually, for a series of international conferences in Weimar (1985, 1987, 1989, 1991), which sought to come to terms with the new paradigm in Shakespeare studies. The history of the assimilation of post-structuralism in (East) Germany has scarcely begun to be studied, except in such pioneering essays as that by Utz Riese, 'Postmodern culture: Symptom, critique or solution to the crisis of modernity? An East German perspective', *New German Critique*, 57 (1992), pp. 157–69.

36 Jacques Derrida, *Of Grammatology*, trans. Gayatri Chakravorty Spivak (Baltimore, Johns Hopkins, 1976), p. xxxi.

37 Alexander Weigel, 'Das Erbe und das Theater der Schauspieler von heute', *Shakespeare-Jahrbuch* (Weimar), 119 (1983), pp. 67–8.

38 Among panellists and contributors, there were Susan Bassnett, Walter Cohen, Marion O'Connor, John Drakakis, Stephen Greenblatt, Graham Holderness, Zdenek Stríbrný, Henryk Zbiersky and others.

39 The representative was Willi Schrader without whose co-operativeness (and integrity) this conference would have been inconceivable.

40 Lisa Jardine, *Still Harping on Daughters*, 'Morningside Edition' (New York, 1989), p. viii. Among many other voices, see Jean Howard,

'Cross-dressing, the theatre and gender struggle in early modern England', *Shakespeare Quarterly*, 39 (1988), p. 435.

41 *Die Zeit* (12 May 1978); see *Dokumente zur Kunst-, Literatur- und Kulturpolitik der SED, 1975–1980*, ed. Peter Lübbe (Stuttgart, 1984), p. 543.

42 For an early outline of the problem, see 'Shakespeare and the uses of authority', *Shakespeare, Man of the Theatre: Proceedings of the Second Congress of ISA, 1981*, ed. Kenneth Muir *et al.* (Newark, University of Delaware Press, 1983), pp. 183–99.

43 Cf. my Festvortrag of 1983, 'Shakespeare und Luther: Von neuzeitlicher Autorität und Autor-Funktion', *Shakespeare-Jahrbuch*, 120 (1984), pp. 7–24.

44 John Foxe, *Acts and Monuments*, ed. S. R. Cattley, 4th ed. rev. by J. Pratt (London, Seeley and Burnside, 1877), 6, pp. 31 and 40.

45 'Autorität der Zeichen versus Zeichen der Autorität: Statussymbol und Repräsentations-problematik in *König Lear*', *Orbis Litterarum*, 42 (1987), pp. 221–35. There is an English translation under the title 'The authority of emblems versus the emblems of authority in *King Lear*', *The Aligarh Critical Miscellany*, 3:1 (1990), pp. 1–16. Cf. my *Shakespeare und die Macht der Mimesis: Autorität und Repräsentation im elisabethanischen Theater* (Berlin, Aufbau, 1988) where 'the power of representation' throughout is shown to engage and disengage the representation of power.

8

✦

Past and present Shakespeares: Shakespearian appropriations in Europe

✦

Thomas Healy

I

While walking through the streets of Sofia in May 1991 Boika Sokolova told me about a recent production of *Romeo and Juliet* by a group of young Bulgarian actors. What was most striking about the performance was that it was largely silent. The players mimed the parts, presenting the play through performed actions occasionally punctuated with a few of the most significant speeches delivered at breakneck speed. When I expressed surprise at this, wondering how an audience would respond to Shakespeare with hardly any language and, indeed, whether they would obtain any idea of *Romeo and Juliet* from a mostly silent production, she explained to me the play's history in Bulgaria. I had assumed that *Romeo and Juliet* would not be especially familiar to Bulgarian audiences, a view emerging from my almost complete ignorance of a country I had heard about as a shady client state of the Soviet Union. In fact, *Romeo and Juliet* is probably a more important play within Bulgarian cultural history than it is in British experience.[1]

During the mid nineteenth century, as many countries in Central and Eastern Europe developed nationalist movements to counter the empires of Austria and Turkey, Bulgaria remained firmly dominated by Ottoman Turkey. European-oriented culture was viewed with suspicion by the authorities, and European drama which represented state events – regardless of whether they took place in fictitious or long-vanished regimes – was banned because it was perceived as potentially intervening in current politics. Thus, while sharing in Eastern Europe's developing passion for Shakespeare, the energies directed toward *Hamlet* or *Macbeth* which were prominent elsewhere were repressed in Bulgaria by an occupying power which perceived such plays as politically dangerous. The domestic tragedy of *Romeo and Juliet* was, however, allowed, if not liked, by the Turks. The result was that the play became politicised through emphasising its links with a European culture which was seen as opposing a dominating Ottoman one. Further, *Romeo and Juliet* readily fitted with an emerging Bulgarian nationalist literature which frequently emphasised the tragic consequences of love, for instance the long poems *Stoyan and Rada* (1840) and *The Fountain of the White-Footed Maiden* (1873), the first dealing with love destroyed by family prejudice, the second with a society which defends itself against external threats by developing a love cult but which cannot contain its own self-destructive impulses.[2] Shakespeare's play in which two lovers are doomed because of the intractable hostilities of their families became symbolic of the Bulgarian struggle for national self-determination against a controlling power, and performing it was an act of defiance against a repressive regime. After Bulgaria acquired political independence, the play (in Bulgarian translation, of course) was rapidly prescribed for study in schools along with Greek, Latin, French, German and Russian classics which were seen as the new defining context for Bulgarian culture.

Under the postwar communist regime, the established national importance accorded *Romeo and Juliet* allowed it once again to take on a politically symbolic role as a protest play. A production at the National Theatre in 1954 stressed the tragedy of the lovers crushed by their hostile families, emphasising the plight of individuals seeking to make their own choices in a tightly controlled order. Despite state-sponsored reviews damning its quality and antagonistic murmurings in the controlled press, the production was an enormous popular success, playing to full houses over several seasons and being successfully revived up until 1964. As a drama recognised to be nationally important to Bulgaria, *Romeo and Juliet* was too established, and Shakespeare too much celebrated in the

Soviet world as a heroic representative of the progressive historical will, for the play to be banned, or for the state to act in a
manner which acknowledged that a production exposed the current
government performing the same culturally repressive role the Otto-
mans had a century earlier. The play's established pre-eminence in
Bulgarian culture allowed it a certain autonomy, permitting it to
function as an expression of dissent through productions proposing alternative perspectives to those sanctioned by the state.

Thus, a challenging production of *Romeo and Juliet* was not
unexpected in the new democratic Bulgaria of the new Europe
following the 1989/90 revolutions. What, though, was the significance of a virtually silent production, a mimed *Romeo and Juliet*
produced in an absurdist setting of collapsing plaster columns and
dismembered dummies? This was not clear to the Bulgarians I
spoke with at the time. Boika Sokolova suggested it was like the
hole in the Romanian flag during the revolution of the preceding
year. In their fight against Ceaucescu and his securitate forces, the
Romanians had cut the communist coat of arms out of the centre
of the flag, a visible sign of their rejection of the old order. However, this signal of change was beginning to look increasingly
suspect even a year later, as the old order appeared in new guises.
What was the significance of the hole in the flag: a declaration of
change; a denial of the past; a window on to the future; or, literally, an acknowledgement of absence, a space whose implications were not clear?[3] The mimed *Romeo and Juliet* was similarly
uncertain in meaning. Did it indicate a questioning of a previous
national icon, or a culture waiting for a new language for its new
future? Perhaps it merely suggested experiment for experiment's
sake in an artistically freer environment (though one discovering
its art being emptied of its function as a politically challenging
force)? Certainly this production was a sign of absence, something
missing (the text), but also something still there (the expected
recognition by the audience that this was *Romeo and Juliet*). This
largely silent production exemplified a past no longer complete, a
future still undecided, and, most prominently, a present where
known theories and structures for understanding social happen-
ings were displaced, yet where nothing had confidently replaced
them. It seemed that *Romeo and Juliet* was no longer functioning
as a representative text speaking for Bulgaria, but there was, at
present, nothing to put in its place.[4]

Certainly, this sense of changes bringing gains and losses was apparent walking in 1991 through Sofia, perhaps best encapsulated by the transformation of a Stalinist monumental civic building into the Sheraton hotel. There was an excitement about political transformations, tempered by a realisation of practical difficulties: there had been severe food shortages the previous winter because of economic uncertainty. Yet, despite confusing social, economic, political and cultural signals, and the apprehensions, ironies and even euphoria they generated, Shakespeare was still being performed. His drama had once more been appropriated to reflect present national concerns. Here was a further instance of the seemingly endless ability of Shakespeare's drama to transform itself into significant cultural commentary and provide a vehicle to intervene within any nation's cultural life.

This example of a mimed *Romeo and Juliet* in Bulgaria, however, made me question how much of this was Shakespeare and whether it was, in any respect, significant that this production enacted in only the vaguest manner a play originally conceived in the 1590s. Shakespeare studies in the last decade have become familiar with the idea of Shakespeare wearing different guises in different social and historical contexts, and have accepted that there are many Shakespeares rather than one. Critical studies with titles such as *Shakespeare Reproduced, The Shakespeare Myth, That Shakespeherian Rag, The Appropriation of Shakespeare, Reinventing Shakespeare* all testify to how complex interplays between texts, histories, readings and performances are recognised as precluding a stable Shakespeare.[5] The conservative world of textual editing has come to accept that the Shakespeare canon is not firmly set and that many plays exist in different versions, even within the period of their origins. The image of Shakespeare as a historically situated agent staring out from the title page of the First Folio and laying claim to the texts within it has been replaced by the protean Shakespeare: a body of artefacts (texts, performances, visual images, accounts) whose limits are unfixed and which is able to appear in apparently endless guises, each one capable of proclaiming a Shakespearian authenticity because, no matter how many shapes Shakespeare is pursued through, there is no final state in which 'he' may be proclaimed as resting. Where the British might feel that Shakespeare is most present in his dramatic language and that Shakespeare without words is oxymoronic, the

Bulgarian *Romeo and Juliet* indicates a Shakespeare able to transcend language, whether spoken in English or in translation.

II

What are the implications of this multitude of Shakespeares, an
assemblage refusing the imposition of any limits set on it by one
or other national community, interest group, collection of audiences or readers? One obvious effect has been the displacement of
claims to a single dominating perspective of what Shakespeare can
mean. An awareness of multiple possibilities has made possible
opposition to attempts by any one group to promote a hegemonic
Shakespeare. As John and Jean Comaroff have recently noted, 'the
more successful any regime, the more of its ideology will disappear into the domain of hegemonic practice; the less successful,
the more its unspoken conventions will be open to contest'.[6] In
Britain, the attempts by government bodies during the early 1990s
to manipulate the National Curriculum in schools so as to examine Shakespeare in specific ways were met with howls of protest
from teachers and academics, causing most of the proposals to be
dropped.[7] For instance, the anthology of poetry originally prescribed for secondary schools opened with Jaques's 'All the world's
a stage' speech from *As You Like It*, intended, it seemed, to promote a vision of universal humanity – or at least the British version
of it.[8] The speech's prominence at the beginning of the anthology appeared to suggest that it, and by implication Shakespeare,
could be viewed as proclaiming a quintessential human model
rather than a Western, affluent, socially élite and masculine life.
Instead, though, of being greeted as a straightforward example
of Elizabethan 'Golden Age' verse, as I suspect it would have been
thirty years ago, the passage was perceived as politically interventionist, exemplifying Shakespeare as representing long-established
verities of ideal British life, ones it was in the ideological interests of
the dominant Conservative Party to promote. Through an awareness
of what may be termed the Caliban perspective in Shakespearian
studies (views situated against the grain of controlling discourses),
however, British readers were able to witness Jaques's speech as
emerging from a class-based, partisan, gendered, Western European character. The presence of a multitude of Shakespeares,
and their consequent varying perspectives, has made it possible for

readers within one national or social group to gain access to the Shakespeares of different cultural locations and, thus, in this instance, to develop interpretative frameworks to counter attempts to regulate what the speech might legitimately mean in the schools of England and Wales. Knowledge of plural, protean Shakespearian identities helps prevent Shakespeare's appropriation by those who wish to impose a uniformity on him or seek to limit interpretation of what his writing represents.

The enduring tradition of Shakespeare adulation, as Jean Marsden notes, 'once established . . . becomes self-perpetuating'.[9] For different reasons in different communities Shakespeare has been adopted and adapted as a cultural resource and it increasingly seems that one of the principal functions of Shakespearian criticism is to account for these histories of incorporation by national or other groupings. Certainly, there is no evidence that Shakespeare's multitude of guises in different national communities is diminishing. Thomas Sorge has powerfully argued for the importance of recognising these intercultural encounters and discursive negotiations which Shakespeare generates as offering a social and critical space for negotiating the anxieties of cultural modernisation:

> From such a perspective, Shakespeare criticism with its rich heteroglossia of critical intervention, with its immense reservoir of elements of stability and change along with its huge transnational corpus of texts, may not be one of the most negligible places from which to contribute to the process of the always risky project of cultural modernization.[10]

Should we, though, admire unreservedly this protean plethora of Shakespearian representations? Aijaz Ahmad's *In Theory: Classes, Nations, Literatures*, notes how

> one is impressed by how very much the increasing dominance of the poststructuralist position has had the effect . . . of greatly extending the centrality of *reading* as the appropriate form of politics, and how theoretical moorings tend themselves to become more random, in this proliferation of readings, as much in their procedures of intertextual cross-referentiality as in their conceptual constellations.[11]

Ahmad is rightly concerned with the apparent randomness of the politics which emerges from such readings because of critical refusals to engage with location – in space and time – when determining cultural and theoretical perspectives for reading. His book is a vigorous critique of the ways recent commentary on 'Third World writing' actually celebrates texts produced in metropolitan centres, ones which fashion the category they purport to discover elsewhere. Thus, documents produced among immigrant communities in metropolitan locations are heralded as the authentic exemplars of post-colonial literature at the expense of texts actually produced in locations previously colonised. The determination of what 'Third World writing' is, has been and should be, in Ahmad's view, has been misappropriated by a metropolitan-based criticism divorced from the actualities and histories of the spaces it claims to represent:

> As the elite immigrant intelligentsia located more or less permanently in the metropolitan countries began appropriating this counter-canonical category [texts recouped from pre-colonial times or against the colonial grain] as their special preserve and archive, the emphasis kept shifting, from the epochal to the modern, erasing in the process the difference between documents produced within the non-Western countries and those other which were produced by the immigrant at metropolitan locations. (p. 91)

In a detailed assault on the contradictions and inconsistencies he perceives in Edward Said's *Orientalism*, Ahmad reflects how a metropolitan domination of 'Third World literature' turns counter-canonical texts into items of consumption. Readings of selected texts by a metropolitan criticism, and the belief that such readings are an engagement in politics, are misplaced and indeed help nullify the potentialities of some texts for actual social interventions. Rather than directing new conceptual directions to achieve real political results, what emerges is simply a First World metropolitan culture manifesting fantasies of political participation in Third World issues through their consumption of products which are increasingly stripped away from distinct cultural locations:

> Rarely in the latter half of the present century has one come across so unabashed a recommendation that the world . . . should be consumed in the form of those fictions of this world which are available in the bookshops of the metropolitan countries; the condition of becoming this perfect consumer, of course, is that one frees oneself from stable identities of class, nation, gender. Thus it is that sovereignty comes to be invested in the reader of literature, fully in command of an imperial geography. . . . This is the imperial geography not of the colonial period but of late capitalism: commodity acquires

universality, and a universal market arises across national frontiers and local customs. . . . When cultural criticism reaches this point of convergence with the universal market, one might add, it becomes indistinguishable from commodity fetishism. (p. 217)

This is not the place to assess Ahmad's claims about Said and a metropolitan control of 'Third World literature'; but his remarks are challenging in considering the question of the many Shakespeares. Part of the problem with Shakespeare is that his protean qualities across histories, cultures and languages are still critically conceived as possessing a type of homogeneity. Despite a recognition of disparities and even confrontations in what 'Shakespeare' means, the perception remains that the multitude of ideas and uses his writings have been appropriated to serve all contribute to an entity called Shakespeare. Those joining in the Shakespearian enterprise – editors, critics, directors, performers, readers or audiences – imagine themselves somehow linked through participation in this Shakespearian occupation; one ill-defined but, nevertheless, believed to exist.

What, though, is being Shakespearian? I have given one instance of how an awareness of multiple and contending perspectives of Shakespeare may help counter the attempts of restrictive ideological imposition. However, there is equally a danger that by embracing the placeless Shakespeare – seemingly adapted and adaptable within all cultures – participants in the Shakespeare enterprise are merely revealing themselves as consumers of a cultural resource which offers the fantasy of cross-cultural participations or understandings. Rather than furthering engagements with national or cross-national concerns in culture and politics, Shakespearian ventures may be perceived as the politics of randomness, developing a belief in a common resource which offers a structure to explore virtually all cultures, but which ignores or elides issues remote from those generated by Shakespearian readings (if Shakespeare is not involved with it, it is somehow not a central issue) and, most crucially, displacing commitment to, or opposition against, one reading.

III

Considering political appropriations of Shakespeare between the Restoration and the 1740s in England, Michael Dobson notes how

> One of the most striking and paradoxical results ... was that in topically and contingently rewriting his plays, Shakespeare's adapters helped to promote them to a status 'above' politics, cumulatively seeming to demonstrate the transcendent value of the texts to which they laid their ideologically specific claims.[12]

According to Dobson, this process promoted 'a trend away from adaptations of Shakespeare's plays which present them in the light of contemporary politics ... toward present[ing] contemporary politics in the light of Shakespeare plays' (p. 21). Dobson's observations are applicable beyond Enlightenment England, for one result of the trend he marks out is to reinforce the perception that Shakespeare is apparently able to intervene in all politics, so that, curiously, it can appear that specific politics are authorised by Shakespeare. But such a belief is fantastical, convincing only to those who imagine a universal Shakespeare from their location in the metropolitan milieu Ahmad delineates, or who are striving to participate in such a milieu. If Shakespeare is credited with a capacity to play all roles, in another sense he is capable of playing no role but that of a fetishised cipher through which varying groups claim authenticity or legitimacy for particular social or cultural platforms. When the response of Shakespearian criticism is to credit all Shakespearian appropriations as legitimately Shakespearian we are left with the dilemmas of a random politics of reading, one sharing many of the features Ahmad's notes in the vague category of 'Third World literature'.

Thus, while the recognition of a plurality of Shakespearian perspectives may temper the attempts of ideologues from the right-wing Centre for Policy Studies to control Shakespeare in British schools, this critical opposition is based on countering exclusivity with multiplicity. Since all deployments of Shakespeare become seen as somehow Shakespearian, there are no agreed critical mechanisms to reject, as illegitimately Shakespearian, any appropriation of the plays. A bizarre but useful illustration of this can be drawn from the film *Star Trek VI* where at a dinner between the largely earth-born crew of the starship Enterprise and representatives of the hostile, wholly non-terrestrial, Klingon empire a common subject for conversation is found to be Shakespeare! The Klingons express surprise at their antagonists' interest in Shakespeare, but take satisfaction that Shakespeare cannot truly be appreciated until read in the original Klingon. Even the resourceful Captain Kirk has no reply to this seizure of Shakespeare's origins because his Shakespeare, too, has been wholly devolved from history and location. To whom Shakespeare rightly belongs is finally decided in a starship shoot-out at the film's end, with the Klingons being blown up in a flurry of Shakespearian misquotation.

The multiple Shakespeares generate problems, however, even among more serious critical endeavours which attempt to match Shakespearian interventions in current cultural issues with those of the plays' original histories. A recourse to cultural and historical specificity does not automatically enable claims for the authenticity of Shakespearian perspectives, as is illustrated by Alan Sinfield's recent *Faultlines: Cultural Materialism and the Politics of Dissident Reading*.[13] In his candid opening chapter Sinfield notes that for 'many literary critics, including feminists and affiliates of ethnic and sexual minorities, the breakthrough of the 1970s was . . . the possibility of relating English teaching and writing to left-wing political concerns' (p. 8). Cultural materialism, to use Sinfield's definition, 'seeks to discern the scope for dissident politics of class, race, gender and sexual orientation, both within texts and in their roles in cultures' (p. 10). It achieves this by apprehending 'the strategic organisations of texts – both the modes by which they produce plausible stories and construct subjectivities, and the faultlines and breaking points through which they enable dissident reading' (p. 9).

The faultlines, however, which Sinfield produces in his illustrative study of *Julius Caesar* result from what he himself terms 'the New Reductionism' because, 'reorienting the action will require some violence to the received text' (p. 20). The justification for this formally signalled critical manipulation resides with Sinfield's recognition that his determined reading matches similar, but unsignalled, right-wing manipulations, and even Shakespeare's own 'political license with his sources' (p. 20). The critic becomes free to re-shape the play to provide a reading which is the critic's directorial desire, in Sinfield's case 'to check the tendency . . . to add Shakespearean authority to reactionary discourses' (p. 21). Dissident cultural materialist critics may now offer canonical texts to be 're-read . . . so as to produce *acceptable* political tendencies, and propose that formal properties inscribe a progressive politics . . . . So dissident critics may join and perhaps take over the Englit game [my emphasis]' (p. 21).

Sinfield argues that we should place texts back into their contexts and understand them as 'cultural interventions produced
initially within a specific set of practices' (p. 22); but his attempts
to recapture a text's first significances within the culture which
produced it are largely undertaken to demystify the text, repudi-
ating its transcendent qualities so as to force it to yield, against the
grain of previous canonical strictures, to an 'explicitly oppositional
kind of understanding' (p. 22). If there is something of a *realpolitik*
to Sinfield's designs with texts and history, there might also be a
recognition that even E. M. W. Tillyard had the candour to warn
readers in the preface of *The Elizabethan World Picture* that 'some
of the facts are only approximate'.[14] By acknowledging an arbitrariness in his selection of texts and issues for his cultural materialist project, even if such manipulations are no worse or better
than other distortions, Sinfield seriously limits a claim to represent
Shakespeare more appropriately. As a result, his readings largely
provide comfort to those already ideologically committed to his
critical project. While both British cultural materialism and American new historicism have helped to release a politics of dissidence
into Shakespeare, one that confronts previous conservative orthodoxies including those masquerading under formalist projections,
they offer little to convince the uncommitted or politically opposed
reader of the validity of their claims, when their assertions of having recovered an inescapable historicity so readily allow charges of
arbitrariness to be levelled against them.

The dangers of this in a British political context are apparent
through comparison with another selective appropriation of Shakespeare, one which claims a strange material base behind Shakespeare's agency to argue a very different form of politics. In an
article in *The Independent* in 1992 William Rees-Mogg, ex-editor
of *The Times*, argued that the economic depression of the 1570s,
which saw Shakespeare's father John lose most of his prosperity,
had the benefit of releasing his son's energies into the theatre.[15]
Similarly, the economic depression a couple of hundred years later
depressed the Lichfield bookselling business of Michael Johnson,
father of Samuel:

> Who knows whether the one would have gone to London as a
> common player and the other as a bookseller's hack if their fathers'
> businesses had continued to prosper.... With no depression, we

might have had a larger leather business in Stratford and bigger bookshop in Lichfield, but no Hamlet and no Johnson's Dictionary.

By proposing that economic depressions following periods of excessive credit continue to be an (inevitable?) quality of English life, with the nation currently continuing a pattern founded on centuries-old 'traditions', the social and political insecurity recession causes is made to appear less worrying. Indeed, economic instability may have released the genius of Shakespeare, an enormous contribution to national self-definition. Rees-Mogg's curious defence of the recession of the 1990s is not one that provokes any need for a considered refutation; but it illustrates how a selective use of Shakespeare's history to mesh in with current preoccupations can lead to strange representations of both past and present. In fact, Shakespeare is lost to history by claiming he is in every history. The difficulty with Sinfield's dissident strategy is that while it can readily confront Rees-Mogg's understanding of texts and history, it appears to be doing so on the same overly selective grounds which Rees-Mogg himself oppositionally employs. You takes your pick. Both critical practices have collapsed history and text into story, motivated by stated desires to present Shakespeare's early modern world as readily intelligible to the late twentieth century, both periods being seen as episodes in a continuing narrative. By stressing continuities between Shakespeare and current social and political questions, whether relating to issues of nations or individuals, critical teleologies are developed. A slippage occurs allowing texts of the past to appear as available and willing to enter into a ready dialogue with the present, as though Shakespeare, somehow, naturally leads to us.

For most twentieth-century criticism, even when Shakespeare as an English writer who represented Elizabethan and Jacobean culture is acknowledged, this cultural agent is imagined negotiating relations between literature and politics which largely unproblematically equate with present cultural environments. The most spectacular example of this to date is undoubtedly parallels created between Shakespeare and the endeavours of the true socialist artist, particularly as formulated in the Congress of Soviet Writers in 1934 and debated in the following decades. 'Shakespeare' became a vehicle to explore questions of historical progress within an Eastern European Marxist framework, almost without exception differing emphases within this framework accepting that there were important similarities between Shakespeare's age and the present.[16] This assumption of historical parallels had portraits of Shakespeare appearing side by side with Lenin in newspapers (their birthdays are close together), with eulogies celebrating Shakespeare's heroic endeavours against the oppressive forces of his time as exemplary for the present:

> Our people turns a grateful gaze to the work of the great writer because it has given wings to its inspiration from the Revival down to our own day, because we are living through a historical period when, as in Shakespeare's time, a social formation is doomed to die, so that another one should triumph, the most just, the most humane in history – Communism.[17]

Richard Wilson, following Leah Marcus, proposes a modification of the cultural materialist agenda, 'examining not what makes Shakespeare our contemporary, but what makes him an Elizabethan, looking at his writing not for relevance, but difference'.[18] This restoration of locality – in history and place – to critical inquiries into Shakespeare is important, helping to combat the political randomness Ahmad similarly ascertains in the placeless environment constructed for Third World literature. However, in dealing with a Shakespeare of the Elizabethan and Jacobean past we are confronting a culture alien and different to current ones. By articulating the difference of the past, there is a danger of developing the new antiquarianism, representing a Shakespeare who is unlikely to stimulate the same critical dynamism generated by the Shakespeare who can be absorbed by every place and age. In moving to a critical position which acknowledges the profound difference of the early modern past, and which questions its dialogue with the present, Shakespeare criticism needs to maintain a commitment to the idea of past texts culturally intervening in the present. The question is how to achieve this so that past differences are not completely distorted in order to make them fit present desires.

IV

At the start of his *Shakespearean Negotiations*, Stephen Greenblatt playfully proposes the critic as a 'salaried middle-class shaman';[19] but his subsequent presentation of this role is confused. Greenblatt denies his shamanistic model by acknowledging he is conducting his dialogue with Shakespearian ghosts on his own terms, selecting traces from the past, rearranging them and making them coherent so that they sound comprehensible when they emerge from his own voice. In contrast, real shamans are expected, are culturally allowed, to speak in riddles and fragments, mix languages of madness and sense, or sometimes sit silently immobile in trances for long periods. Literature professors are expected to speak coherently, to demonstrate reasonable hypotheses and, as Greenblatt so skilfully does, to construct critical narratives which are intellectually consistent, compelling and convincing. But, in many respects, the critic as real shaman more accurately reflects our relation with the past: the figure liminally placed between familiar and unfamiliar worlds, whose access to the unknown is limited; a figure allowed only glimpses of the other, contacts which do not necessarily translate into easily grasped knowledge within familiar categories for understanding. For all Greenblatt's romanticised self-imagining, he does recognise that the past is gone and that attempts to reintroduce it involve a critical ventriloquism, a reconstruction of what past texts may have been saying to their original hearers which, inevitably, involves us presenting the past in present voices.

This should not automatically imply, however, that our translations or ventriloquism of the past must automatically represent it on our terms. The self-consciousness in some recent anthropological writing of other cultures provides useful models through which to undertake a critique of dealing with the past.[20] The growing realisation that the questions anthropologists have asked determined the answers that are given has led to reassessments of cultural 'otherness'. Where previously anthropology automatically assumed a stance of cultural superiority, seeking to write the exotic other so as to make it knowable within a Western organisation of knowledge, there is a growing recognition of 'the other' as something potentially to embrace, providing new models through which to challenge and, ideally enlarge, our existing cultural orders. The anthropological observer starts to see she is being observed, that in the contacts established between differing cultures, both are, in some slight degree, never going to be as they were. The ability of past writing to enlarge our cultural categories through its otherness, to indicate present restrictions and challenge our organisations for understanding, is an important part of the difference of the past. An exchange continues to take place between past voices and present listeners, but one, importantly, which is less on the present's terms; our ventriloquising voices begin to sound strangely unfamiliar.

Homi Bhabha has noted that the impact of the foreign on a culture activates mechanisms within the culture to assimilate it.[21] Bhabha argues that this never entirely happens, rather the alien is drawn into the in-between, a zone of intersection in which all culturally determined significations are called into question. In proposing an importance to witnessing a Shakespeare of the past as alien, a foreign other from a foreign place, in contrast to the placeless Shakespeares of the present, Bhabha's framework offers some helpful possibilities. The present possesses mechanisms to absorb its foreign past and to familiarise it by resisting the past's claims to be alien. Yet the present's assimilation of the past is never complete, so that an apparent unresolved cultural hybridity results, a dispute between accommodating the strange to the familiar and a destabilisation of the familiar through its inability to absorb the unexpected alienness of the past. Bhabha abandons the concept of mirroring (which has been fundamental to new historicist critical practice) in favour of the split-screen, creating a crisis of authority by continuously doubling our perspectives of both texts and their histories. It is certainly the case that Bhabha's concept of hybridity is problematic by too readily allowing an occupation of a critical borderland, a position of postmodern dislocation which suggests an estranging ambivalence as the only possible critical stance. It is precisely that Bhabha's sense of hybridity makes us aware of the potentials for mere contingency, however, that his ideas have such appropriateness for the exchanges we attempt between past and present, where the presence of contingency always lurks in what 'the past' which is recreated in historical narrative might actually have been. Rather than an endless deferral of a commitment to history, hybridity can sharpen our resolve to test our assumptions and not rely on easy approximations.[22] Bhabha's ideas help a historicist criticism counter the idea of an easy dialogue with early modern texts without rejecting the possibilities of any exchange between their original historicity and their current appropriations. Importantly, they help reveal as a cultural consumerist fantasy the possibility of an easy chiastic circulation between past and present Shakespeares, one which promotes a ready exchange among his protean identities.

The potentials for early modern writing confronting readers with their own 'alienness' or 'otherness' is important for a criticism which both acknowledges Shakespearian origins as a means of combating a randomness in appropriation, and remains committed to the active interventions of Shakespearian texts and performances in addressing present cultural issues. What is required is the type of historically localised reading Richard Wilson proposes, but one placed in a critical framework alert to cultural otherness as a means of confronting the categories and organisations of knowledge familiar to the present. Emphasising discontinuities and unexpected strangeness in Shakespeare's original cultural preoccupations, structures for understanding, through which cultures try 'to make sense of themselves', are shown to be subject to history and, therefore, exposed as partial, changeable and, perhaps most importantly, not prescriptive across history. This critical process involves neither an overly determined selectivity nor a new reductionism but a firm historicism which is suspicious of easy dialogues between past and present. Confronting Shakespeare as a corpus of early modern writing defamiliarises our sense of the past, not to assert its vanished status but in order to interrogate our current organisations for knowledge and critical understanding, potentially surprising us with unfamiliar selves.

V

In the second edition of his *Imagined Communities*, Benedict Anderson concludes his book with a chapter on 'Memory and forgetting'.[23] Nations, Anderson argues, forge their biographies 'up time'. They create their imagined beginning in the present and then reverse conventional genealogy to fashion their history running back towards a supposed moment of origin: 'The nation's biography snatches, against the going mortality rate, exemplary suicides, poignant martyrdoms, assassinations, executions, wars and holocausts. But, to serve the narrative purpose, these violent deaths must be remembered/forgotten as "our own"' (p. 206). A recent collection of essays, *European Shakespeares: Translating Shakespeare in the Romantic Age*, exemplifies a Shakespearian dimension to Anderson's process, revealing how certain national cultures claimed participation in a Shakespeare they had already

made their own.[24] Brigitte Schultze notes how Shakespearian translation built Czech nationalist confidence:

> The fact that Shakespeare's rich verbal textures could then be repro-
> duced in Czech meant that the Czech language had become a much
> more versatile and adequate instrument. . . . And this had strength-
> ened the Czech's confidence in the central European future of their
> culture.[25]

Schultze perceives a similar design with Polish translations; but
she also points out that it was rare for any of these translations
to refer to the original English texts. In the Polish case, rival
schools of Shakespearian translation developed between those
favouring a French classical model and those devoted to a German
Romantic one. Because few in these Slavic cultures had opportunities to learn English, there was seldom a question of reading
Shakespeare in the original and the German translation of Schlegel
and Tieck became the shaping version of Shakespeare for Eastern
Europe. In another of the collection's essays, Weiner Habicht shows
how the German Romantic tradition emphasised the placeless
Shakespeare.[26] Schlegel had not been trying to turn Shakespeare
into a contemporary, but he had little concern with the original
historical contexts, and worked to translate historically conditioned
idioms into supposedly timeless ones.

In considering the absorption of a Shakespearian tradition into
Hungary, Peter Davidhazi discovers a similar reliance on the
Schlegel–Tieck German translation in producing Hungarian Shakespeares.[27] Davidhazi also considers how late eighteenth-century
promoters of Shakespeare did so to emphasise the superiority of
Hungarian culture. Joseef Peczeli conceived a battle of the books,
with Hungarian writers recreating foreign writers in the vernacular in ways that would surpass the 'originals'. Davidhazi suggests
that some of the most vocal adherents of Shakespeare may never
actually have read a line:

> Those Hungarian writers of the period who initiated their reading
> public into the ritual of Shakespeare worship wanted to exert a
> civilising influence. Invariably, they sought to prove that the English
> reverence for their Bard is but one example among many that shows
> how intellectuals and volumes should be respected if Hungarian
> culture is to be raised to the level of the most advanced countries of
> Europe. (p. 159)

A current example of this long-standing trend of naturalising Shakespeare to individual national concerns is provided by Janja Ciglar-Zanic in 'Recruiting the Bard: onstage and offstage glimpses of recent Shakespeare productions in Croatia'.[28] The essay concludes with a consideration of a 1992 Croatian production of *Titus Andronicus* which Ciglar-Zanic notes raised considerable controversy by transforming the text – cutting scenes and shifting around others – to address a contemporary Croatian political and social climate. Here is another illustration of the debate between those who feel that altered versions of the plays, rather than betraying Shakespeare, fulfil his plays' promises by leaving them open to adjustment to present circumstances, refusing to accept them in a sealed, finished textual form, and others who express unease at these rewritings and recruitment of 'Shakespeare' to specific social-political agendas.

What is particularly disturbing about this essay, however, is Ciglar-Zanic's own recruitment of Shakespeare: this essay illustrates the dangers of the protean, placeless Shakespeare who is open to co-option to every history. Claiming that Western Europe – Peter Brook is cited as the principal representative of this Western European perspective – has never appreciated or allowed Central Europe's participation in 'a common cultural homeland', and that the West has dismissed, as a failure to understand Shakespeare, Central European attempts to re-inscribe Shakespeare as part of its cultural heritage, Ciglar-Zanic proposes a tragedy in the West's failure to perceive unity in anything but political geography. In contrast, she argues that Central Europe maintains the idea of cultural unity not in geographical terms but in spiritual ones: a common European culture which is shared with a West which has apparently forgotten its existence and therefore denies Central Europe proper readmission to it. This note of tragic regret prefaces her consideration of the Croatian *Titus Andronicus*, where the scholarly community apparently approved the reconstructed version of the play and 'stood up for a justified rearrangement of priorities and the right of cultural communities in times of suffering to use some of the best-recognised cultural symbols to formulate their outcry'.

Superficially, this claim to use *Titus Andronicus* as a legitimate vehicle to explore contemporary Croatian problems raises no hackles, and I would be surprised if there were Western reviewers who condemned the production on the grounds that Croatia had no right to appropriate the Bard in this way. What actually underlies Ciglar-Zanic's argument, however, is a desire to have a Croatian use of Shakespeare seen as evidence of this country's proper participation in 'a common European cultural unity', allowing this nation's perspectives to be legitimised as being authentically European. Her use of 'Central Europe' is significant here. For all this essay's suggestions of a need to recognise 'political realities' in Shakespearian appropriations, what it does not once explicitly address is the context of this distinctive Croatian *Titus Andronicus* being forged by a Serbian–Croatian war which divided a previously proclaimed common national/cultural identity, that of Yugoslavia. Croatia uses a Shakespeare play to demonstrate a tragedy befalling its youth. The Shakespearian resource which, until 1991, had been appropriated for Yugoslav interests becomes 'forgotten' and Shakespeare becomes a vehicle for a Croatian 'remembering' of their place in Western European culture.

Ciglar-Zanic's language proposes a shadowy and culturally apocalyptic conflict. Croatia employs Shakespeare to articulate its suffering, it belongs in a Central Europe which has a common cultural unity with Western Europe, one which, by implication, Europe to the East does not share in. Western Europe's failure to recognise this brings this common culture into crisis. It appears that the only ones who actually understand this European culture are those in its supposed borderlands, where the struggle between civilisation and darkness is genuine, and where 'the reality' of this struggle actually generates an understanding of Shakespeare which may be absent among those in the common culture's lost centre – the West. This is the protean Shakespeare at its most confused and, at the same time, at its most insidious. Shakespeare is recognised at one level as being insufficient to modern political and cultural needs: his plays must be consciously amended, transformed, added to or selectively ignored. Yet this process is carried out not through a formal admission of Shakespearian insufficiency but through claims at recovering the 'true Shakespeare', the spirit of what he was actually trying to express. Shakespeare is recruited to a specific national platform because it is hoped this gives European, or even universal, cultural approval to its politics: civilisation is on our side.

If this seems a rather exaggerated account of Ciglar-Zanic's perspective, you have only to turn to the essay she acknowledges as the principal inspiration for her view about the loss of a common European unity based on a shared culture: Milan Kundera's 'A kidnapped West or culture bows out'.[29] Written in the mid-1980s in historical circumstances which perceived the continuation of the Soviet Empire, Kundera's piece is a lament about a dying Central Europe as a consequence of Western indifference and Eastern aggression. Even a decade ago it appeared curious, registering the dissatisfaction of an émigré, who finds his new home in the West unsympathetic to the European literary culture he feels he participates in; going as far as to express a type of nostalgia for the vanished Austrian empire! But what is unsettling, in the new cultural and political faultlines of the 1990s, is Kundera's analysis of 'the error of central Europe'. This was the 'ideology of the Slavic world', one 'invented in the nineteenth century' as a defence against German aggressiveness (pp. 102–4). By claiming pan-Slavic identity, Central Europe played into Russian hands, a nation which claims above all to represent the interests of the Slavic world. Further, this false creation of a common Slavic culture served to ease (from the West's perspective) the separation of Central Europe from its proper cultural homeland. For Kundera, Central Europe is Western Europe, an area 'rooted in Roman Christianity' (pp. 95–7). Kundera's true border emerges, one in which the Poles, Hungarians, Czechs, Slovaks, Romanians, Slovenes and Croats belong to the West, opposing the Orthodox Slavs – the Serbs, the Bulgarians, and above all else, the Russians: 'on the Eastern border of the West – more than anywhere else – Russia is seen not just as one more European power but as a singular civilisation, an *other* civilisation' (p. 100). The fatuousness of this line of argument can be instantly glimpsed by realising that in Kundera's cultural geography the Greeks have no real claim to be European either.

Interestingly, towards the end of Kundera's essay he recalls walking in Prague with a philosopher friend whose manuscript had just been seized by the police:

> We talked about the possibility of sending an open letter abroad in order to turn this confiscation into an international scandal. It was perfectly clear to us that we shouldn't address the letter to an institution or a statesman but only to some figure above politics, someone who stood for an unquestionable moral value, someone

universally acknowledged in Europe. In other words a great cultural
figure. But who was that person?

Suddenly we understood that this figure did not exist. To be sure,
there were great painters, playwrights and musicians, but they no
longer held a privileged place in society as moral authorities that
Europe would acknowledge as its spiritual representatives. Culture
no longer existed as a realm in which supreme values were enacted.
(p. 114)

For the Croatian Ciglar-Zanic the answer to this vanished European authority is to invoke Shakespeare. Shakespeare becomes
the place where European culture is supremely discovered, but a
Shakespeare, a Europe, which is now recalled 'up time' (to recall
Benedict Anderson), which is fashioned, remembered as 'our own',
and which can indeed be identified with the nation precisely because Shakespeare has become the nation's possession. For Ciglar-
Zanic, Shakespeare has become not only a means by which the
tragedy of present war can be, somehow, enacted but an indica-
tion of Croatia's wider abandonment by its cultural homeland in
Western Europe. This greater tragedy rests with a politically and
economically strong but culturally diminished West's failure to
recognise that this country at the margin of Europe has 'remembered' Shakespeare properly, when the West has forgotten him. In
this perspective, Shakespeare provides high cultural approval for
a distinctive politics which, if it were not so serious, might recall
the Klingons battling it out with Captain Kirk through Shakespearian misquotation. It is a pity that *Shakespeare in the New
Europe*, where Ciglar-Zanic's essay appears, does not contain a
piece on Shakespeare in Serbia.

VI

The dominant history for Shakespeare which has been forged
throughout Europe demonstrates a continuity of civilisation for a
world of readers and audiences, a history which creates a paradox
by promoting national identities ('our' Shakespeare) while claiming to ignore regional, ethnic or national differences (participation
in the common civilisation which Shakespeare represents). Of
course, one may find in a Shakespeare located in Elizabethan and
Jacobean culture similar rhetorics of civilised unity through which
the English nation may be defined: rhetorics which, as recently

Mervyn James, Ian Archer and Richard Helgerson have shown, were the projections of divided societies.[30] One of the features of such language is the identification of unacceptable 'others' and their exclusion, placing them outside the borders of the civilised pale which defines the nation. Memories of Shakespeare forged 'up time' tend to stress inclusion and have 'forgotten' that the local history of much early modern writing is its participation in sectarianism, promoting precisely the regional, ethnic, national and religious identities many current participants in the Shakespeare enterprise have critically repressed or evaded. Shakespearian texts, and the author himself, are 'remembered' examples of a cultural force which confronts and counters a violence of exclusion which Shakespeare's original aesthetic may be shown as promoting.

'The more successful any regime, the more of its ideology will disappear into the domain of hegemonic practice; the less successful, the more its unspoken conventions will be open to contest.'[31] The multiple Shakespeares have helped to counter attempts to create a restrictive unified Shakespeare of the one. Yet, at the same time, the multiple Shakespeares have developed their own hegemonic practices which silently assume Shakespeare as a civilising force whose continuing presence, whether drawn from English Renaissance, French Enlightenment or German Romantic traditions, illustrates cultural advancement. Asserting a Shakespeare of the past could entail exploring how a Shakespearian aesthetic in its original cultural location developed rhetorics of unity through careful strategies of exclusion, defining the limits of its civilised pale in culturally palatable fashions: for example, how Prospero's acknowledgement of Caliban as his 'thing of darkness' actually prepares for his abandonment.

In emphasising alterity in the Shakespearian past, 'Shakespeare' can confront current dominant cultural categories, and the current mechanisms through which they are understood, extending our ability to recognise the cultural organisations to which we belong and even suggesting possibilities for alternatives. We should not, however, imagine that this enlargement is simply an idealistic one: we do not discover the early modern identities we might wish to remember. Yet, we should not resist them. There is no role for a criticism which exposes the otherness of the past only to condemn and attempt to nullify its effects through dismissal.

For Benedict Anderson, those creating their nations in the present and reading back to an imagined sense of origins were participants in the print-languages which he argues laid the basis for modern national consciousness. They were, like most current Shakespearians, the professional, educated, intellectual and administrative classes who, Anderson proposes, became linked to one another through print and formed the embryo of new nationally imagined communities (in the community of letters this might be extended to a transnational, metropolitan community), a process, he argues, which was fundamentally made possible by three important institutions: census, the map and the museum – domains of the educated.[32] The problem we poignantly confront today is the backlash of those who, with new vigour, believe they are reforging their communities 'down time' – restoring those organisations of ethnicity, religion and regionalism as means of recovering self-definitions which have survived the attempts of modern national or international movements to replace them through census, map and museum. Indeed, the reformed census, the redrawn map, the reselected museum, along with a re-presented Shakespeare, become instruments to assert the new nation on sectarian lines. I propose that my argument for a criticism which recovers an alien otherness in the past in order to render unfamiliar our imagined present is given new urgency by the strange return of these 'forgotten' sectarian communities.

The recovery of a Shakespeare of the past, one located in the places and histories of his original cultural agency, should not, then, be imagined as some vain attempt to reclaim Shakespeare for the English, or to dismiss subsequent appropriations of him by other nations and histories as misguided. Such a critical programme would, indeed, be to create a pointless new antiquarianism and a new authoritarianism. A Bulgarian *Romeo and Juliet* which portrayed the Montagues as Ottoman Turks and the Capulets as Bulgarian communists, with Romeo and Juliet not as crossed lovers tragically but heroically confronting their hostile community but as participants, even willing ones, in the histories which forged their identities, might, for example, be a possible product of the critical direction I have described. Central to such a production, and the perspective lying behind it, is a recognition that this *Romeo and Juliet* is not Shakespeare's but Bulgaria's. Along with the relocation of Shakespeare to a past which is different from the present is the recognition that the agency which is still sought from him is not part of a timeless project of cultural continuity: Shakespeare as an unquestioned civilising authority no longer remains valid. Instead, Shakespeare might become a force to develop recognition of European or wider cultural differences, viewing the transformations of Shakespeare in different locations and politics as nullifying claims of participation in a common civilisation; recognising instead the sectarian positions the multiple Shakespeares occupy. Within these different Shakespearian discourses, criticism would seek not to authorise their separations and exclusions but to witness how they operate and to challenge their rhetoric of inclusiveness. Such a project rubs against the gain of what Shakespeare is held to be, and it appears to counter art's traditional role as an oppositional force which confronts, rather than acknowledges, sectarian limitations. My reasons for wishing this new role for Shakespeare are suggested by appropriating for our current position remarks of Walter Benjamin from 1940:

> The current amazement that the things we are experiencing are 'still' possible in the twentieth century is *not* philosophical. This amazement is not the beginning of knowledge – unless it is the knowledge that the view of history which gives rise to it is untenable.[33]

Notes

1 Boika Sokolova subsequently presented much of this information about *Romeo and Juliet* in Bulgaria in a paper at Birkbeck College in 1992 and published some of it in: Alexander Shurbanov and Boika Sokolova, 'From the unlove of *Romeo and Juliet* to *Hamlet* without the Prince: a Shakespearean mirror held up to the fortunes of new Bulgaria' in Michael Hattaway, Boika Sokolova and Derek Roper, eds, *Shakespeare in the New Europe* (Sheffield, Sheffield Academic Press, 1994), pp. 24–53.
2 *Ibid.*, pp. 27–8.
3 One thing it did clearly recall was the similar removal of the centre of the Hungarian flag during the 1956 uprising.
4 Considering three Bulgarian Shakespeare productions of *Much Ado About Nothing*, *The Merchant of Venice* and *The Tempest* in 1992 which similarly radically modified the plays' texts and stage performances, Evgenia Pancheva comes to the optimistic view that these modifications indicate active rethinkings of cultural identity: 'This is a Shakespeare hushed down, borrowing from himself and others, trimmed to alleviate – or exacerbate? – the wounds of a guilty, slanderous,

politicizing, revengeful, sexually aroused, banished and reacknowledged, thinking Bulgaria'; Evgenia Pancheva, 'Nothings, merchants, tempests: trimming Shakespeare for the 1992 Bulgarian stage' in Hattaway, *et al.*, eds, *Shakespeare in the New Europe*, p. 260.

5 Jean Howard and Marion O'Connor, eds, *Shakespeare Reproduced: The Text in History and Ideology* (London and New York, Methuen, 1987); Graham Holderness, ed., *The Shakespeare Myth* (Manchester, Manchester University Press, 1988); Terence Hawkes, *That Shakespeherian Rag: Essays on a Critical Process*, (London and New York, Methuen, 1986); Jean I. Marsden, ed., *The Appropriation of Shakespeare: Post-Renaissance Reconstructions of the Works and the Myth* (Hemel Hempstead, Harvester Wheatsheaf, 1991); Gary Taylor, *Reinventing Shakespeare: A Cultural History from the Restoration to the Present* (New York, Weidenfeld and Nicolson, 1989; Oxford: Oxford University Press, 1991).

6 John L. and Jean Comaroff, *Ethnology and the Historical Imagination* (Boulder Colorado, Westview Press, 1992), p. 8.

7 Lesley Aers and Nigel Wheale, eds, *Shakespeare in the Changing Curriculum* (London, Routledge, 1991). This collection demonstrates the diversity of ideas around Shakespeare and approaches to teaching him in British schools.

8 English Anthology, Schools Examinations Assessment Council (London, HMSO, 1993).

9 Jean I. Marsden, 'Introduction' in *The Appropriation of Shakespeare*, p. 2.

10 Thomas Sorge, 'Tradition and modernization: some thoughts on Shakespeare criticism in the new Europe' in Hattaway *et al.*, eds, *Shakespeare in the New Europe*, pp. 321–2.

11 Aijaz Ahmad, *In Theory: Classes, Nations, Literatures* (London and New York, Verso, 1992), pp. 3–4.

12 Michael Dobson, 'Accents yet unknown: canonisation and the claiming of Julius Caesar' in Marsden, ed., *The Appropriation of Shakespeare*, p. 21.

13 Alan Sinfield, *Faultlines: Cultural Materialism and the Politics of Dissident Reading* (Oxford, Clarendon Press, 1992).

14 E. M. W. Tillyard, *The Elizabethan World Picture* (Harmondsworth, Penguin Books, 1963), p. 8.

15 William Rees-Mogg, 'Bright lights shine out from the gloom', *The Independent* (30 November 1992), p. 17. I am grateful to Richard Wilson for drawing this to my attention. See his *Will Power: Essays on Shakespearean Authority* (Hemel Hempstead, Harvester Wheatsheaf, 1993), p. ix.

16 See for example Thomas Sorge's discussion of Shakespeare in the German Democratic Republic, 'Buridan's ass between two performances

of *A Midsummer Night's Dream*, or Bottom's telos in the GDR and after' in Hattaway *et al.*, eds, *Shakespeare in the New Europe*, pp. 54–74.

17 Cited in Shurbanov and Sokolova, in Hattaway *et al.*, eds, *Shakespeare in the New Europe*, p. 26. The piece originally appeared in the Bulgarian journal *Narodna Kultura* in April 1964.

18 Wilson, *Will Power*, p. ix; Leah S. Marcus, *Puzzling Shakespeare: Local Reading and its Discontents* (Berkeley, Los Angeles and London, University of California Press, 1988).

19 Stephen Greenblatt, *Shakespearean Negotiations: The Circulation of Social Energy in Renaissance England* (Oxford, Clarendon Press, 1988), p. 1.

20 See for example James Boon, *Other Tribes, Other Scribes: Symbolic Anthropology in the Comparative Study of Cultures, Histories, Religions and Texts* (Cambridge, Cambridge University Press, 1982); Marshall Shalins, *Islands of History* (Chicago and London, Chicago University Press, 1985); James Clifford and George E. Marcus, eds, *Writing Culture: The Poetics and Politics of Ethnography* (Berkeley, Los Angeles and London, University of California Press, 1986).

21 Homi K. Bhabha, *The Location of Culture*, (London and New York, Routledge, 1994), especially pp. 107–16.

22 For a cogent counter-argument about the dangers of hybridity as a critical tool see Aijaz Ahmad, 'The politics of literary postcoloniality', *Race and Class*, 36:3 (1995), pp. 1–20.

23 Benedict Anderson, *Imagined Communities: Reflections on the Origin and Spread of Nationalism*, revised and extended edition (London and New York, Verso, 1991).

24 Lieven D'Hulst and Dirk Delabastita, eds, *European Shakespeares: Translating Shakespeare in the Romantic Age* (Philadelphia, J. Benjamins, 1992).

25 Brigitte Schultze, in D'Hulst and Delabastita, eds, *European Shakespeares*, p. 62.

26 Weiner Habicht, in D'Hulst and Delabastita, eds, *European Shakespeares*, pp. 45–54.

27 Peter Davidhazi, in D'Hulst and Delabastita, eds, *European Shakespeares*, pp. 148–65.

28 Janja Ciglar-Zanic, 'Recruiting the bard: onstage and offstage glimpses of recent Shakespeare productions in Croatia' in Hattaway *et al.*, eds, *Shakespeare in the New Europe*, pp. 261–75.

29 Milan Kundera, 'A kidnapped West or culture bows out', *Granta*, 11 (n.d.), pp. 95–118. The essay also appeared as 'The tragedy of Central Europe' in *The New York Review of Books* (26 April 1984).

30 Mervyn James, *Society, Politics and Culture: Studies in Early Modern England* (Cambridge, Cambridge University Press, 1986), esp.

pp. 22–3; Ian W. Archer, *The Pursuit of Stability: Social Relations in Elizabethan London* (Cambridge, Cambridge University Press, 1991); Richard Helgerson, *Forms of Nationhood: The Elizabethan Writing of England* (Chicago and London, University of Chicago Press, 1992).
31 John and Jean Comaroff, *Ethnology and the Historical Imagination*, p. 8.
32 Anderson, *Imagined Communities*, pp. 163–85.
33 Walter Benjamin, 'Theses on the philosophy of history', *Illuminations*, trans. Harry Zohn (London, Fontana Press, 1992), p. 249.

9

✤

Nationalism, nomadism and
belonging in Europe: *Coriolanus*

✤

Francis Barker

There is a world elsewhere!

I

In 1935, when Europe was again on the threshold of rapid and violent transformation, Martin Heidegger asked the most radical of questions: 'Warum ist überhaupt Seiendes und nicht vielmehr Nichts?'[1] His translator into English, Ralph Manheim, has to coin a word, 'essent', for Heidegger's use of the neologism *Seiendes*, but renders the question, adequately enough, as 'Why are there essents, why is there anything at all, rather than nothing?'[2] In any case, the general meaning, direction and import of the question is clear, in either language: 'Why are there things which are; why is there anything; why isn't there simply nothing at all?' The profundity of the question is also emphatic: Heidegger himself refers to it as the question which is 'broadest and deepest' (p. 6), and as the one which is 'first in rank – first, that is, in the order of questioning within the domain which this first question opens'. This question 'is the *question* of all authentic questions' (*ibid.*).

Part of what many have experienced as the *fascination* of reading the Heideggerian text – politically the pleasure turns out to be a dubious one – consists in the expectation of 'this most fundamental of all questions' (p. 6) receiving an answer, and in following the stages of the argument in the suspended hope of such an

answer.[3] For surely, were it to be provided, such an answer could
re-endow a relativised world with meaning, and, in a situation
beyond 'cultural pessimism' – as Heidegger (incorrectly, in my
view) argues his own stance to be – could become the basis of the
philosophical and political effort which could render the world
once more susceptible of habitation and belonging, of *dasein* or
'being-there', as those abiding preoccupations of Heidegger's life-
work have it.[4] Indeed, it would allow us nothing less than 'to win
back our roots in history' (p. 39), surely something to be desired
in the chaos and near-chaos of contemporary Europe?

But if such a gratification is sought, it is also destined to remain
deferred. Instead of an answer to the authentic question, 'Why are
there things, why isn't there nothing at all?', the question itself
undergoes – in a manner quite characteristic of Heidegger's writing as a whole – a number of transformations and displacements.
Firstly, the form of the question is questioned, both for its origin
(*ur-sprung*) and its ground. Then a digression into a reflection on
the true purpose of philosophy (and a refutation of two common
misinterpretations of its true purpose) follows, leading to a posi-
tioning of the question asked as the first question of metaphysics.
The necessity of the pendant sub-question 'rather than nothing' is
next explored. The question of the 'essent' – although primary and
fundamental – is then displaced by another, 'preliminary', question
which must be asked first – 'How does it stand with being?' (p. 32).
This in turn is then subjected to the post-Nietzschean interrogation of Being as no more than a disappearing 'vapor and a fallacy'
(p. 36). And so on. A discussion of ontology (which Heidegger
understands in an opposite way to the philosophical tradition)
follows, followed in turn by a discussion of the historical demise
of Being, which is itself followed by chapters on the 'grammar and
etymology of the word "Being"', on 'the question of the essence
of Being' and on the 'limitation of Being'. And so on. A reader in
search of an answer to the question 'Why are there essents, why
is there anything at all, rather than nothing?' will read in vain.

But if that satisfaction remains elusive, at least a context for
dissatisfaction (and for the very questioning of Being) *is* quite
rapidly provided. It is an important one for our present purposes
in this volume. But again, if contextualisation is arguably the *only*
way of genuinely solving philosophical questions, that is somewhat
different from the *mere displacement* of the question by means of

substituting the invocation of context for a real thinking through to a philosophical – and contextualised – answer. In fact, a world of difference lies between these two quite distinct strategies. Some quotations will illustrate the process of displacement and substitution in Heidegger.

In the first place, a repetition of the insistence on the importance of the question of Being is inflected in such a way as more is made to hang by its outcome than the solution of a philosophical puzzle: ' "How does it stand with being?" – a sober question perhaps, but assuredly a very useless one. And yet a question, the question: is "being" a mere word and its meaning a vapor or is it the spiritual destiny of the Western world?' (p. 37). This is then followed up by an invocation of 'Europe, in its ruinous blindness forever on the point of cutting its own throat' (p. 37). It is a Europe, Heidegger says, which 'lies today in a great pincers, squeezed between Russia on one side and America on the other. From a metaphysical point of view, Russia and America are the same; the same dreary technological frenzy, the same unrestricted organization of the average man' (p. 37). Again, on the immediately following pages (of an 'Introduction to Metaphysics', no less):

> We are caught in a pincers. Situated in the center, our nation incurs the severest pressure. It is the nation with the most neighbors and hence the most endangered. With all this, it is the most metaphysical of nations. We are certain of this vocation, but our people will only be able to wrest a destiny from it if within itself it creates a resonance, a possibility of resonance for this vocation, and takes a creative view of its tradition. All this implies that this nation, as a historical nation, must move itself and thereby the history of the West beyond the center of their future 'happening' and into the primordial realm of the powers of being. If the decision regarding Europe is not to bring annihilation, that decision must be made in terms of new spiritual energies unfolding historically from out of the center. (pp. 38–9)

Or again:

> That is to say: it is crucial for the first asking of the fundamental question that in asking its preliminary question we derive the decisive fundamental attitude that is here essential. That is why we have related the question of being to the destiny of Europe where the destiny of the earth is being decided – while our own historic being-there proves to be the center for Europe itself. (p. 42)

The claim is then made that the question of Being is in fact a historical question.[5]

Holding within itself, Heidegger asserts, 'the historical destiny of the West', the question of Being 'to many ears . . . may sound violent and strange' (p. 42); but, even so:

> we have not yet come to the essential reason why this inherently historical asking of the question about being is actually an integral part of history on earth. We have said that the world is darkening. The essential episodes of this darkening are: flight of the gods, the destruction of the earth, the standardization of man, the pre-eminence of the mediocre.
>
> What do we mean by world when we speak of darkening of the world? World is always world of the spirit. The animal has no world nor any environment – Umwelt – Darkening of the world means emasculation of the spirit, the disintegration, wasting away, repression, and misinterpretation of the spirit. (p. 45)

And again, in the same figure of the pincers as above: 'Europe lies in a pincer between Russia and America, which are metaphysically the same, namely in regard to their world character and relation to the spirit. What makes the situation of Europe all the more catastrophic is that this enfeeblement of the spirit originated in Europe itself' (p. 45). The catastrophe was already prepared when the collapse of German idealism in the first half of the nineteenth century meant that

> The lives of men [*sic*] began to slide into a world which lacked that depth from out of which the essential always comes to man and comes back to man, so compelling him to become superior and making him act in conformity to a rank. All things sank to the same level, a surface resembling a blind mirror that no longer reflects, that casts nothing back. The prevailing dimension became that of extension and number. Intelligence no longer meant a wealth of talent, lavishly spent, and the command of energies, but only what could be learned by everyone, the practice of a routine, always associated with a certain amount of sweat and a certain amount of show. In America and in Russia this development grew into a boundless etcetera of indifference and always-the-sameness – so much so that the quantity took on a quality of its own. Since then the domination in those countries by a cross section of the indifferent mass has become something more than a dreary accident. It has become an active onslaught that destroys all rank and every world-creating impulse of the spirit,

and calls it a lie. This is the onslaught of what we call the demonic (in the sense of destructive evil). (p. 46)

Flabbergasted as we may be by the idealist hyperbole of this, we should be none the less ill prepared by our weariness for what follows when finally Heidegger rehearses something from his inaugural Freibourg address of 1929: a definition of what spirit is as distinct from its contemporary misinterpretation. In particular:

> the inquiry into the essent as such and as a whole, the asking of the question of being, is one of the essential and fundamental conditions for an awakening of the spirit and hence for an original world of historical being-there. It is indispensable if the peril of world darkening is to be forestalled and if our nation in the center of the Western world is to take on its historical mission. (p. 50)

When even 'the destiny of language is grounded in a nation's relation to being' (p. 51), it is clear that a culturalist account of European history leads to a definition of the philosophical *and political* project in terms which are significantly nationalist both in principle and in practice. This emerges with crystalline precision later in the text, when, in a dismissive – and now much discussed – account of the recent proliferation of philosophical works on the question of value, Heidegger sneeringly remarks that they 'call themselves philosophy', but 'the works that are being peddled about nowadays as the philosophy of National Socialism . . . have nothing to do with the inner truth and greatness of this movement' (p. 199).

The 'inner truth and greatness' of National Socialism becomes the measure of philosophical achievement and the touchstone of value. The original, primary question, the fundamental question of metaphysics – 'Warum ist überhaupt Seiendes und nicht vielmehr Nichts?' – finds its own belonging at last. 'Why are there essents, why is there anything at all, rather than nothing?' The question receives no answer. 'Why are there things which are; why is there anything; why isn't there simply nothing at all?' But if the repetition of the question fails of an answer, it does none the less announce a destination for the questioning of Being: Nazism.

II

To be faced with this is to face a dilemma.

On the one hand there are compelling thematics of Being and

belonging, of place and *existenz*, (however inflected with nostalgia, with what Adorno calls Heidegger's 'ontic longings').[6] And the compelling quality of that language feels in some quarters renewed and empowered today. But on the other hand there is the lethal, rightist – Nazi – nationalism of its political context (both in history and as a context is invoked by the text), and of its philosophical development. Then as now the theme of being, belonging, of rootedness in history (undoubtedly a historical force) becomes articulated in terms of nation, and fuels a corresponding nationalist politics.

Nationalism, when viewed across a sweep of history and a variety of different cultures, has been somewhat ambivalent – if not polyvalent – politically speaking. It has been conventional to speak positively of the emergence of modern nation states from the pan-European, medieval institutions of the Roman Church and the Holy Roman Empire (and before that, the Roman Empire as such); and of movements of national liberation from colonial occupation and oppression, and imperial and neo-imperialist domination. The (re)emergence of nationalist sentiments in Eastern Europe today in the wake of the break-up of the Soviet bloc, of COMECON and the Warsaw Pact Organisation – not to mention the many resurgent nationalisms within the former USSR itself – have also been welcomed by many.

But if there are potentially liberating forms of solidarity which may be organised by senses of national belonging – and I grow increasingly sceptical of this – there also are, and have been, forms of domination which constitute via the signifier of nation the oppression of some by others – whether the many by the few (as is usually the case in terms of class oppression), or the few by the many (which is most frequently the case with ethnic or racial discrimination and oppression). These processes operate by forms of subordination to allegedly national ideals, images, myths, symbols and constructed histories. The so-called national character or temperament may set a normative standard of behaviour; the national traditions a coercive and exclusive instrument for policing what is deemed to be permissible in political practice and social life, and for demonising and legitimating the elimination of what is not; and the national culture may set a narrow and privative agenda for what is to count as being authentic and valuable in artistic matters and in cultural activities at large. These may, at the limit, also provide the criteria by which decisions concerning genocide are made.

Equally, there is the historical experience in the modernity of the First World of the 'nation' of the ruling class or classes; and in the so-called 'Third World' the experience of the national bourgeoisie acting in concert with the colonial or former colonial powers is not an unfamiliar one. And there are, sadly, too many examples of post-communist nationalism taking the form of ethnic violence, religious hatred and emergent or resurgent fascism in countries which – despite some media myths[7] – had no, or at best very fragile, pre-communist democratic traditions (Weimar Germany, monarchist Romania), and which in some cases, during the war in and after which communist regimes and Soviet-leaning governments were installed throughout Central and Eastern Europe (whether by the Red Army, or by indigenous political developments), were actually fascist: Croatian, Romanian and Hungarian wartime fascism, and, of course, (East) Germany itself, are but the most prominent examples. There is also the troubled national history of Poland to be considered, with successive periods of prewar annexation and independence, marked by forms of Romantic nationalism and intense and often cultic Catholicism (and the anti-semitism which has, regrettably, survived through the communist period into contemporary formations of Polish civil and political society). And there are many other examples of what is at best an ambivalent history of nationalism as a political and cultural force for good or ill.[8]

And yet, once again, significant – and significantly – empowered expressions of communitarian solidarity and the insistent pressure of belonging are being expressed in terms of nation and of national identifications. To restate the dilemma: on the one hand the need of belonging as against what is at best the dreadful indifference of modern Europe; and on the other the – to me – unacceptable articulation of that inexhaustible drive as nationalism.

What is needed, I believe, is a critique of this situation. Not, certainly, a simple denunciation of nationalism – seemingly such a potent protagonist in, but perhaps not of, the new Europe (in as much as this last term denotes any kind of unity at all) – but a critical reflection on the way in which, increasingly today (and perhaps we should say 'again'), it appears that the desire for place and belonging is being articulated in such terms. And perhaps what follows will contribute to a transvaluation of that appearance. It is meant to.

III

In this light, perhaps it *is* instructive to turn back to the 'threshold culture' of the early modern moment: to turn back in particular to a 'Shakespeare'[9] who at the beginning of European modernity played such an important part (at first in the English tradition, and subsequently throughout a wider English-speaking world as well as in a number of European countries), in the foundation of an empowered cultural discourse of nation, nationalism and of national belonging.

In a context of English aspiration in the period – whether an allegedly popular sentiment, or some more contrivedly official ideology connected with the consolidation by the Tudor dynasty of the authority of the Crown at home, and the prosecution of its military and diplomatic policies abroad – it is clear that the Shakespearian text is committed – in its particular moment of a somewhat parochially imagined English history – to insistently nationalist formations of cultural value. Indeed much good work has been done recently on what has been called 'the Shakespeare myth',[10] not only on the interpretation of the patriotic discourse which Shakespeare fashions as a mythical English history but also on the way in which that has itself facilitated the turning of 'Shakespeare' into a myth and an institution, the national poet embodying and signifying an essential Englishness – with all its subliminal projection of essentially conservative values and perspectives – of which the Shakespearian mythological English history – the image of a past that is, despite the wars of the Histories, eventually 'picturesque, familiar and untroubled'[11] – is in turn a component part, confirming, in a fully circular way, the mythical history itself.[12]

However, I shall make a distinction between the patriotism of the nationalist discourse of the History plays, of Shakespeare's 'England', and that of the complexity of the fashioning of his 'Rome', of the more tensed mappings of national identity in a text like *The Tragedy of Coriolanus*. Much of the rest of this chapter will be devoted to a discussion of the significance of this.

There are relatively familiar and accessible instances of the more clearly patriotic discourse in Shakespeare. John of Gaunt's 'scepter'd isle' speech in *Richard II*, for example, draws a magical line around a non-existent island – 'this earth, this realm, this England' – and

endows the island-realm – 'This precious stone set in a silver sea'
– with Edenic and blessed sanction, charging it with the mysti-
ficatory aspect of the gentle domicile – 'in the office of a wall, /
Or as a moat defensive to a house' – and, in the same gesture of
symbolic and territorial definition, it simultaneously and partitively
demonises those envious others in 'less happier lands', subject to
'infection and the hand of war' (*Richard II*, II.i.40ff.). Or we
could examine Henry V's speeches before Harfleur (*Henry V*, III.i.1–
4) and at Agincourt (IV.iii.20–67), and remind ourselves of their
rousing invocations of English custom which seem to draw on a
tradition even as they create one: sturdy and martial English yeo-
men, St Crispin's day, the brotherhood of arms, etc.[13] And, to be
sure, nor are fairly straightforward emphases on and appeals to
patriotic feeling entirely absent from *Coriolanus*: witness the six
repeated emphases on 'country' in Volumnia's speech at V.iii.94–
124,[14] when she tries to prevent Coriolanus's invasion of Rome by
appealing to the rhetorically unquestionable signifier of the homeland, and its charged inviolability, of which the following – in the
very overtly gendered language of the text – is but the most compelling instance:

> *Volumnia:*   thou shalt no sooner
>   March to assault thy country than to tread –
>   Trust to't, thou shalt not – on thy mother's womb
>   That brought thee to this world.
>
>   (V.iii.122–5)

But the simplicity of this appeal is deceptive, for the structure of
the figuration of the discourse of national belonging in *Coriolanus*
is more ambivalent than this address to country suggests. Compared with the more rhetorical appeals to patriotic feeling in the
history plays, and even in such instances in *Coriolanus*, there is a
more problematic nationalism in the tragedy, and it is the complexity of the articulations of a discourse of national belonging
in *Coriolanus* which is, under the circumstances of the present
renewal of nationalism, more worth the excavation when it comes
to an archaeology – even an aetiology – of the discourse of nation
than the more rhetorical appeals to patriotic feeling in the history
plays or of such instances as this in *Coriolanus* itself. Or at least,
that will be the main strand of argument in what follows.

IV

At a crucial juncture in the unfolding of the narrative, Coriolanus pronounces the words 'I banish you' (III.iii.123). Apparently – and actually – banished from Rome, Coriolanus none the less speaks as the authority with the power to banish. This simple, defiant assertion focuses, in turn, an important current in the play so far, which is to do with the embodiment of national tradition. This involves the idea that the play is at least in part in the business of finding figurations of the nation by the mapping of the idea of national value (expressed often, as in the patriotic discourse, as defined and symbolically charged territory), on to the body of the emblematic hero. Many have noticed how representational transactions between the body of the sovereign and the embodiment of the national terrain, the realm, are significant in the organisation of the figural economy of the Shakespearian text.[15] Here in *Coriolanus* sovereignty in that sense is not, of course, at stake (although the charge that he aspires to tyrannical monarchy – 'affecting one sole throne' (IV.vi.33) – is laid against him), and there are, as I have suggested, some significant differences between the kind of nationalism at work in its incorporations compared with the patriotism of other Shakespearian instances. But none the less, there is an important sense in which the centralisation of what is Roman in the figure of Coriolanus, and the essentialisation of that figuration in the foregrounding of the wounds and the blood, gives rise to a mapping of the national idea of Rome on to the body of the hero which has connections with sovereign incorporation, but is, if anything more, rather than less, nationalistic than embodied and territorialised Shakespearian kingship. If this is so, the body of the representation of the embodiment of Rome, repays careful attention. Let us examine it in some detail.

The first thing to notice is that, as a figure, Coriolanus is very fully *embodied*. Throughout the early scenes, especially those of the battle for Corioles and its aftermath, there is a repeated invocation of his powerful corporeality, especially in the emphases on the blood Coriolanus sheds, and the wounds he receives in the fighting. It hardly matters whether it is an example like the description of Coriolanus's single-handed invasion of Corioles – by which

> He was a thing of blood, whose every motion
> Was tim'd with dying cries: alone he enter'd

The mortal gate of th'city, which he painted
With shunless destiny.

(II.ii.109–12)

– whether it is one of the myriad references to his bloody body
such as that of Cominius to the 'blood' which on his 'visage dries'
(I.ix.91) (and there are many more such references that could be
cited); or whether it is a call to arms like that addressed to those
'If any such be here . . . that love this painting / Wherein you see
me smear'd' (I.iv.67–9): in each case the wounds, the body and the
blood become the absolute marks of Coriolanus's impersonation
of himself. It is these same wounds, of course, whose significance
Coriolanus can later negligently diminish (perhaps this is a form
obsession): 'I have some wounds upon me, and they smart / To
hear themselves remember'd' (I.ix.28–9); or again, 'The blood I
drop is rather physical / Than dangerous to me' (I.v.18–19).

So charged is the incorporation of Coriolanus that sexual dimension inflects the marking of the body in ways which, as I shall argue
below, the dominant discourses of the play cannot mainly tolerate.
Here, however, it serves merely to notice this inflection as further
evidence of the extraordinary degree of Coriolanus's embodiment,
and in particular the homoerotic inflection in the metaphors which
characterise the bloody wounds and the emblems of the male bonding of the battlefield. Certainly when Caius Martius (as Coriolanus
still at this stage is) needs to invoke that bonding, those significant
senses of the purity of the war (to this, too, I shall return below),
this is the metaphor (and the site of metaphoricity, indeed) that
comes to his mind:

By all the battles wherein we have fought,
By th'blood we have shed together, by th'vows
We have made to endure friends.

(I.vi.56–8)

And witness the terms of the following exchange between Cominius
and Caius Martius at a point when the outcome of the battle
hangs in the balance:

Martius: Come I too late?
Cominius: Ay, if you come not in the blood of others,
  But mantled in your own.
Martius: Oh! let me clip ye
In arms as sound as when I woo'd; in heart

> As merry as when our nuptial day was done,
> And tapers burned to bedward.

(I.vi.27–32)

The numinous blood is there, of course; but so are terms of endearment and sexual desire which associate the masculinity of the war with wedding and bedding; in significant ways, of course, Coriolanus is married to the war, and to his comrades in arms. For if there is a homoerotic bonding here, this sexual charging of the marking of the hero's body is reinforced (in terms which themselves need examination), by such passages as those of his mother's fierce scoffing at Valeria's concerns for her husband's physical safety by famously valorising loyal and military mutilation over the pleasures of erotic and sexual embrace:

> If my son were my husband I should freelier rejoice in that absence wherein he won honour, than in the embracements of his bed, where he should show most love.... had I a dozen sons, each in my love alike, and none less dear than thine and my good Martius, I had rather had eleven die nobly for their country, than one voluptuously surfeit out of action.

(I.iii.2–5, 22–5)

A noble death – for country, significantly enough – is juxtaposed unfavourably to what is devalued into peaceful surfeit, as the keenness of sexual pleasure and maternal or matrimonial affection is displaced and subsumed by the alleged sublimity of war and its reflected glory. And in such a case, similar transpositions affect the sexed and gendered representation of the hero's body and its bloody wounds:

> *Volumnia*:   The breasts of Hecuba
>   When she did suckle Hector, look'd not lovelier
>   Than Hector's forehead when it spit forth blood
>   At Grecian sword contemning.

(I.iii.40–3)

Indeed, in terms of the extent to which bodily properties, and in particular the thematics of blood and wounds, fashion what we have of his identity in the early part of the play, it would probably be proper to speak of fetishisation as the mode of the play's impersonation of the hero. Certainly the invocation of the wounds often has the arbitrariness of the expression of something obsessive;

see for example Volumnia's acontextual ejaculation at IV.ii.28: 'Good man, the wounds that he does bear for Rome!' (IV.ii.28), a remark which is, in context, unmotivated, but which forces to the surface again in this late part of the play an insistent – indeed compulsive – motif from its beginning.

I shall return to the fetish of the warrior's body, and to its sexual component in particular, below. Here the central point, however, is that the getting and bearing of wounds, and the shedding of blood, are insisted upon, not only as the marks of martial valour, nor merely as the signs of Coriolanus's near-transcendent martial ability but as the signs of the fact that he is quintessentially Roman: 'We thank the gods / Our Rome hath such a soldier' (I.ix.8–9); or again, 'Rome must know / The value of her own' (I.ix.20–1). Or better, perhaps, to say that he is quintessentially *Rome*. The link between Coriolanus's military exploits and Roman authenticity is repeatedly made, and indeed, in the subsequent matter of the *showing* – and the display is important if we are speaking of representation and fetishisation – of the wounds to the populace in the scenes both of Coriolanus's triumphal return to Rome and of his reluctant, awkward suing for their voices in the matter of the consulship,[16] they become the corporeal oxymorons for something which can hardly be described as merely loyal service to Rome. To be sure, as Volumnia and Menenius eagerly await the return of Coriolanus in formal triumph, for example, their discourse contrives an anatomy of the hero as an assemblage of the scars which will become the site and the instances of the discourse of his fitness for consular power:

> *Menenius*: Where is he wounded?
> *Volumnia*: I'th'shoulder, and i'th'left arm: there will be large cicatrices to show the people when he shall stand for his place. He received in the repulse of Tarquin seven hurts i'th'body.
> *Menenius*: One i'th'neck, and two i'th'thigh – there's nine that I know.
> *Volumnia*: He had, before this last expedition, twenty-five wounds upon him.
> *Menenius*: Now it's twenty-seven: every gash was an enemy's grave.
> *A shout and flourish*
> Hark, the trumpets!
> *Volumnia*: These are the ushers of Martius: before him he carries noise, and behind him he leaves tears:

> Death, that dark spirit, in's nervy arm doth lie,
> Which, being advanc'd, declines, and then men die.
> *A Sennet. Trumpets sound. Enter Cominius the General, and Titus*
> *Lartius: between them Coriolanus, crowned with an oaken garland;*
> *with Captains and Soldiers, and a Herald.*
>
> (II.i.144–60)

But beyond even consular pre-eminence in formal leadership, this triumphal and fetishised corporeality in turn denotes not so much an achieved greatness as a rendering visible through material signs on the body of the hero, the always-already pre-givenness of his aptitude so to embody Rome. In this anatomy the cicatrices become, rather than badges of service, the near mystical signs, metaphysical metonyms, in a grammar of – symbolic – value, for Rome and the national ideal itself. The bodiliness – the wounds, the blood and the scars – becomes the marker of both. That Coriolanus is Rome's foremost servant in the wars, and its most authentic representative in peace, grows over into a sense that he is the very embodiment of its values, its tradition, its national idea.[17]

Indeed, if the text's 'marking' of Coriolanus, blood and wounds – his very 'embodiedness' – connects backwards to a Christological figuration of the body (as that of the Shakespearian sovereign often does),[18] it may also reach forward, as many contemporary readers have felt, towards a twentieth-century representation – often a kind of collective erotics[19] – of the charisma of the leader, and the fascist fantasy of such national embodiment in particular. Among Coriolanus's claims that, compared with the cowardice of the foot-soldiery (let alone the draft-dodging turpitude of such non-combatants as Sicinius Velutus and Junius Brutus), his military service most compellingly represents the Roman virtues and traditional behaviour (political and civic as well as martial), are the particular claims that he is steadfast where they are self-serving, variable and fractious, and that he is committed – this is probably the most significant factor for our purposes – to the aggressive pursuit of Roman interests, while the plebs and their tribunes seek merely the advantage of their class. His excoriation of the fickleness of the people, and ultimately also his rejection of his patrician family and friends, is connected to the fetishisation of the body of the warrior as the authentic national body via the figure of male bonding in what appears to Coriolanus as the transcendent 'purity' of the war:

> *Volumnia:*   I have heard you say,
>   Honour and policy, like unsever'd friends,
>   I'th'war do grow together.
>
> (III.ii.41–3)

As compared with the flexibilities and compromises of peacetime when policy is partisan and interested, in war the companionship of arms, honour and national policy are identical. This is at the basis of Coriolanus's and the play's militarism and nationalism (and of the militarist–nationalist equation). In war politics appear to cease to be political – that conservative dream – and becomes national instead, expressed and heroically embodied, in a unifying and incorporative transcendence of the 'merely' political, of the complexity and 'inefficiency' of quotidian process which all authoritarians despise. And to be sure, whether or not it is appropriate to speak of *Coriolanus* as containing proto-fascist discourse, certainly in the twentieth century the experience is not an unfamiliar one of the coup d'état or the 'revolution' carried out by and in the name of the armed forces as the conscience – moral and, of course, 'spiritual' – of the nation, representing the most authentic national traditions and embodying the purest examples of the national values of which they are themselves, of course, the most vigilant guardians.[20]

V

If the text has thus far been freighted with claims overt and subtle that Coriolanus truly embodies, and so 'represents', Rome, these claims culminate in the key words, 'I banish you', at that pivotal moment of the play, the moment of the epitome of the embodiment of the nation. But it is also a moment of separation. The more that Coriolanus is identified, or identifies himself, with Rome, the more this becomes a partitive and separating motif, further widening the distance between Coriolanus and the claims of'others to make up or represent Rome. I am reminded of Adorno's remark about how 'the Führer rises above an atomized nation, as he thunders against social prejudice and, to perpetuate himself, will change the guard on occasion'.[21] Coriolanus too, the more he comes to embody the nation, the more he is distanced from either its idea or its personnel, and the more violent must be the means adopted for maintaining the illusion of national embodiment. This is to say that

as far as a reading of the play – rather than the representation of
Coriolanus and his aspirations – is concerned, we begin to perceive
some systematic ambivalence – if not simply contradiction – in the
text's ability to sustain its own nationalistic ideal. We should explore
this ambivalence, and aggravate the contradiction.

There is in the play, if not a struggle for Rome, a struggle to
speak for Rome, certainly a problematical dimension to the question of who may speak for Rome and how. And significantly it is
the wounds and the scars which provide the site and emblem of
this contestation. For if wounds and the body of the hero are the
parts of speech of a powerful discourse of national identity, it is
not one without its questions and paradoxes:

> *First Citizen*: Once, if he do require our voices, we ought not to deny
> him.
> *Second Citizen*: We may, sir, if we will.
> *Third Citizen*: We have power in ourselves to do it, but it is a power
> that we have no power to do. For, if he show us his wounds and
> tell us his deeds, we are to put our tongues into those wounds and
> speak for them. So if he tell us his noble deeds, we must also tell
> him our noble acceptance of them. Ingratitude is monstrous, and
> for the multitude to be ingrateful, were to make a monster of the
> multitude; of which we being members should bring ourselves to
> be monstrous members.
>
> (II.iii.1–13)

A sense of how the power of the populace is thwarted if it buys
into the fetish of incorporation does not finally inhibit, at the most
energetic moments of confrontation between the patricians and
the plebs, the articulation of a more autonomous discourse of
collective identity:

> *Sicinius*: What is the city but the people?
> *All Plebeians*:   True,
>   The people are the city.
>
> (III.i.198–9)

But if the people are the city, then this sense of popular autonomy
runs directly counter to the empowered discourse of embodiment
of the play's opening gambit. If there is a contestation for representation, for voices and voicing, for who will speak for Rome and
who will articulate the identity of Rome and the authority of
Roman tradition, initially it is also a contest for form. It is, of

course, 'deep-structural' to the play that the national identity cannot be, or even appear to be, fissiparous or multiplex (the equivalent in terms of the expression, or giving voice, to social class, of
what we now call 'multicultural') but must be decisive, unified and
singly embodied. And the received, dominant formation – despite
Coriolanus later (and according to traditional practice) having to
sue for plebeian voices in the matter of establishing who may
speak for, or represent, Rome – is not conceived in any democratic
sense, of course, but rather through an idea of representation as
embodiment, the incorporatist implications of the mode of political and cultural thought most explicitly articulated in Menenius's
opening 'fable of the belly'. In other words, it involves neither
plurality nor solidarity but incorporation, and subsumption into
embodiment.

And yet the discourse of the text is made problematical not least
by the fact that, when the confrontation comes, it is not between
corporate patrician paternalism and popular (and populist) claims
to national identification, but among both of these and Coriolanus's
altogether more decisive impersonation of national identity, who
takes a very different view of the constitutedness of Rome and
the nation even than that inscribed in Menenius's fable. Where
received patrician wisdom would incorporate, Coriolanus, ever 'a
very dog to the commonalty' (I.i.27–8), would put the plebeians
to the sword:

> *Martius*: Would the nobility would lay aside their ruth,
>   And let me use my sword, I'd make a quarry
>   With thousands of these quarter'd slaves, as high
>   As I could pick my lance.
>
> (I.i.196–9)

And if not simply to be slaughtered, the people are, of course, in
the name of Coriolanus's belief that it is he and his tradition
which most authentically represents Rome, deracinated (and, in an
important sense, 'deterritorialised').[22]

> *Coriolanus*: I would they were barbarians – as they are,
>   Though in Rome litter'd; not Romans – as they are not;
>   Though calv'd i'th'porch o'th'Capitol.
>
> (III.i.236–8)

In that familiar and powerful language of simultaneous identification and disidentification (with an age-old Western history behind

it), the very people of Rome are turned into the barbarian aliens whose inferior but threatening and monstrous nature (in this case quite strictly bestial – 'litter'd,' 'calv'd') provides, in the very porch of the Capitol itself, the defining otherness against which true (Roman) civility is articulated. And yet, in the same language of the creatures, Sicinius catches well both the genocidal violence and the overweening – unnatural, *indifferent* – solipsism of Coriolanus's absolute substitution of himself for Rome:

> Where is this viper
> That would depopulate the city and
> Be every man himself?
>
> (III.i.261–3)

This is a thematic current which is summed up by the famous remark of Volumnia's to, and about, Coriolanus, 'You are too absolute' (III.ii.39). And it is the one where we can easily discover the ambivalence of the text as two quite different senses of the embodiment of the nation and the national tradition are uneasily turned upon each other. Compared with Menenius's inclusive aristocratic corporatism, there is the far more decisive martial embodiment of Coriolanus with its partitive and hypostatising figuration of national unity.

Not least is this ambivalence (and here we can properly begin to talk of contradiction) registered in the tension that this engenders in the play between the Shakespearian anathema on civil disorder, on the one hand, and, on the other, profound, even catastrophic, disorganisation (from the point of view of the text's most fundamentally conservative drives) in the body politic: 'Go get you home, you fragments!' (Martius, I.i.220). 'Fragments' is a key word here: it is precisely the factious, fractious, fissiparous character of the plebeians – as Coriolanus (and the dominant ideology of the text) represents them – which contrasts so detrimentally with the drive to unificatory incorporation. Dominantly the text will not tolerate, as the Shakespearian text widely does not, 'fragmentation'. And even though we may be able to see that this is no more than what it calls the result of it itself having represented in pejorative form any popular dissent from its own drives to coercive, unitary mastery, its characteristic representation of the general populace is of an unruly mob, representing the people, independently of Coriolanus's views, as fickle and partisan, and their leaders as cynically manipulative and self-serving. These representations accord closely with Coriolanus's characterisations of the plebs. But on the other hand, the confrontation between Coriolanus and the people, especially in the 'political' scenes of popular suffrage when the hero's inability to be pliant to his friends and accommodating to the people in suing for their voices, escalates into civil commotion and a near break-down of law and order (anathema, as I have said, to the text). This produces an odd dislocation of the text from itself. In that it cannot convincingly make the unruly people sole cause of the tumult – for Coriolanus's absolutism is plain (so clearly of the party of order, his will is also too unbending, so that when finally it flexes, it also snaps, with disaster as its consequence) – the text is distanced from its own representation of the 'many headed multi-tude', and from the protagonist in which its ideologically pejorat-ive account of popular aspirations is otherwise centred. Coriolanus, a servant of Rome the state, if hated (and grudgingly admired) by Rome the people, increasingly identifies himself with Rome, the city, the nation, the state. But, at odds with the received patri-cian corporatism, his impersonation of the state takes the form of treasonous partition from it, by identifying its interests against itself. And, more fundamentally, it is clear that repressive unifica-tion produces the civil disorder it is designed first to forestall and then to quell. With the anathematic catastrophe as result.

This is, at one and the same time, the assertion of a discourse of tyrannical mastery and a significant failure to make cohere either patrician paternalism or – more signally – the nationalist fixation of meaning and value on the heroic leader.

And just as surely as he is distanced from the people, so the gulf becomes unbridgeable between Coriolanus and the rest of the patrician class in general, and its political leaders, his friends, and his family (his mother especially) in particular. Of the consequences for the national idea of Coriolanus's 'political' obduracy they say:

> *Menenius*: This is the way to kindle, not to quench.
> *First Senator*: To unbuild the city and lay all flat.

> (III.i.195–6)

There results an overturning of the erstwhile stable and defining categories of compatriotism, class solidarity, familial affinity and military companionship. As patrician Rome is also deracinated, friendship and enmity is reversed –

> *Cominius*: For his best friends, if they
>   Should say, 'Be good to Rome', they charg'd him even
>   As those should do that had deserv'd his hate,
>   And therein show'd like enemies.
>
> (IV.vi.112–15)

– and Rome descends into mutual recriminations and fear. The fragmentation which once Coriolanus had alleged exclusively against the plebeians becomes the general character of all Roman identifications, as the unexpected portability of the metaphysic of nation inherent in the very figure of its most renowned and corporeal embodiment begins to tell against the residual and disidentified nation lacking its most potent symbol. At one level Coriolanus's 'I banish you' was patently absurd. But at another it is seen as only too cogent inasmuch as the Imaginary of his class (and even the enmity of his opponents) has introjected its territorialist desire into just such a psychopathic killing machine as he, and is correspondingly bereft when the automatic man walks away with the national idea, indifferent to those who feel they have the most affective and original claim on it. 'When he walks, he moves like an engine' (V.iv.18–19).

VI

If Coriolanus's 'I banish you' is the culmination of his assumption of the authority and identity of Rome, at the same time it is the outcome of a process of deracination, and of one that divides the 'nation' from itself and from the national idea. The more, it is worth repeating, Coriolanus becomes Rome, the more he is divided from it, and the more, in other words, Rome is divided from itself:

> *Menenius*:   Proceed by process,
>   Lest parties, as he is belov'd, break out
>   And sack great Rome with Romans.
>
> (III.i.311–13)

The more Rome is embodied, the less and less it is able to be embodied, unified and essentially represented. Indeed, if the relation of Coriolanus, and the figure that he is, to the play's wider figurations of nation and national territory, is gathered together in that heroic (and perhaps also somewhat pathetic) counter-sentence

'I banish you', the words of the sentence also focus sharply the complexity of the problematic of nation (as distinct from the velleities of patriotism). For if Coriolanus assumes the authority of the Rome he has always embodied (and in so doing adopts the tyrannical posture of which the people and their tribunes have accused him, gathering to himself solely the authority to dictate Rome's will), yet it is a strange authority which at the moment of its fullest and clearest identification and articulation, is, in the same instant, expelled from the City, and becomes a renegade power in the camps of the enemy, 'Like to a lonely dragon that his fen / Makes fear'd and talk'd of more than seen' (IV.i.30–1). What is revealed here, then, is a powerful assertion of identification, but an equally powerful displacement of the embodied figure of national identity.[23] For if the nation, or the ideal of the idea of the nation, is figured as embodied and metaphysically charged, is it not also somehow mobile and portable, nomadic, anonymous and exiled? Absolute – too absolute – Roman identity departs in Coriolanus, but in a process of disidentification. If once he had acquired a name – the name of a city moreover – Coriolanus abandons it again in the time of his exile:

> *Cominius*: I urg'd our old acquaintance, and the drops
>   That we have bled together. 'Coriolanus'
> He would not answer to; forbad all names:
> He was a kind of nothing, titleless,
> Till he had forg'd himself a name o'th'fire
> Of burning Rome.
>
> (V.i.10–15)

The bonding of the blood was hitherto definitive, but now it appeals in vain to the strange, disidentified, non-presence of a man with no name. Martius is, transcendentally, the Rome which is deracinated without him, and therefore he stands not in need of distinctions and honorifics. And yet, because of the slippage in the text away from the solidity of such identifications into a nomadic anonymity, he is the bearer of the emptiness of the drive to national identification he once had championed. Even the name that he threatens to cast in the fire of Rome will be a forg'd one, both manufactured, counterfeited and incandescent with the conflagration of the Rome, the national identity, which he himself none the less still embodies. Identical and yet nameless, exiled and yet the

whole of Rome, the body of Coriolanus, and the metaphysical location of the City and the national idea are both doubled over each
other, at once superimposed and at a distance from themselves.
'As if', the text has it, 'a man were author of himself' (V.iii.
35–6).

This autonomy (which turns out, of course, to be penultimate)
rehearses the figuration of Coriolanus as the embodiment of Rome,
but also disseminates that figuration. Even such remarks from
exile in Antium as 'My birthplace hate I, and my love's upon /
This enemy town' (IV.iv.23–4), or a reference to Rome as now
'th'city of kites and crows' (IV.v.43), are – subject to a logic of
opposites – no less than restatements of the essential truth that
it is Coriolanus who '*is*' Rome, and that Rome's authentic tradition is wherever he is. But at the same time it points up the displacements of a text which proves incapable fully of fixing the national
idea with the degree of solidity and surety of identification that
its militaristic nationalism demands. The signifier of nation and
national territory seems to be an individual and general caravan
of displacement and disidentification.

In arguing (and the argument is designed to have a wider implication) that if Rome, the nation and the territorialist identification
at large, is *embodied* in *Coriolanus*, it is wholly problematically
embodied by way of a profoundly ambivalent correspondence
between the body of hero and the identity of the nation, a number
of other factors need then to be taken into account, each of which
serves to destabilise any interpretation of the national apotheosis
as an ascertained fact, with the achieved character of which the
text – or we the 'readers' – can be content to rest.

There is, of course, the bodily fetishisation itself (and this word
seems to earn its place in the critical description of *Coriolanus*
when we have seen how sexually charged – and how ambivalently
so – the incorporation of the hero is, and his relations with his
women and his men) and in particular the complex erotics of
masculinity and femininity, both the sexing and the ambivalent sexuality of the body of the nation. This is connected in turn to the
ambivalence of the gendering of a passage like that in which Cominius remembers Coriolanus's youthful exploits in the wars. The boy
warrior had an 'Amazonian chin', and 'In that day's feats, / When
he might act the woman in the scene, / He prov'd best man i'th'field';
indeed, he was 'man-enter'd' – no less (II.ii.91, 95–7, 99). And

probably this must then be linked with the critically notorious passages which associate Coriolanus so intimately with his mother, 'There's no man in the world / More bound to's mother' (V.iii.158–9); or with something like the terms of Aufidius's denunciation of Coriolanus for having sealed the eventual peace with Rome: 'at his nurse's tears / He whin'd and roar'd away [the] victory' (V.vi.97–8). These examples hinge, in turn, on the striking emphases in the very last part of the play on Coriolanus as but a boy:

> *Coriolanus:*   Hear'st thou, Mars?
> *Aufidius:* Name not the god, thou boy of tears!
>
> (V.vi.100–1)

'Boy' (V.vi.104). 'Boy' (V.vi.116). It echoes through his – and the text's – last words.

But the idea of such quintessential national embodiment is also further troubled by the fact that the paramount figure of Coriolanus is curiously doubled in the text by that of Tullus Aufidius his Volscian opposite. Commentators have frequently noticed the duplicity and complicity of the figuration of Coriolanus and Aufidius as mighty opposites: there is in this design both a mutual recognition and a reciprocal identification. But in terms of the apotheosis of the national idea, this seems not only to serve the process of hypostatisation of the nation, but also a kind of dissemination by doubling of the specificity of the national personification. At the same moment as Coriolanus and Aufidius are made special, they are also deprived of their uniqueness; and vice versa. In doubling Coriolanus, Aufidius becomes his Hegelian other and identical opposite – the contrastive identity of the territory. Louis Althusser remarked some time ago on Hegel's account of the doubling of the tragic hero: the analysis is wholly relevant to a text which will have the epitome of Rome say, 'And were I anything but what I am, / I would wish me only he' (I.i.230–1); and have his opposite and double say, 'I would I were a Roman, for I cannot, / Being a Volsce, be that I am' (I.x.4–5), or 'He's mine, or I am his. Mine emulation' (I.x.12). And indeed, when Coriolanus – the incarnation of Rome – will say to Aufidius, of whom he is the 'great opposer' (IV.iii.35), 'I'll fight with none but thee, for I do hate thee / Worse than a promise-breaker' (I.viii.1–2), it is clear that such an idiom, with its suggestion of the amorous meaning of breach of contract (or at least of a lover's vow given and then scorned), evokes a relationship between the heroes which is as erotic as it is martial; or rather, in one the other and vice versa. When they meet in peace it is with an embrace, sealed by no less than this from Tullus Aufidius:

> Know thou first,
> I love the maid I married; never man
> Sigh'd truer breath; but that I see thee here,
> Thou noble thing, more dances my rapt heart
> Than when I first my wedded mistress saw
> Bestride my threshold.
>
>   (IV.v.114–19)

The eroticism of their meeting is inherent, I am arguing, in the fabric of the text, and in any case observed by all. For example: 'Our general himself makes a mistress of him, and turns up the white o'th'eye to his discourse' (Third Servant, IV.v.199–202). I have mentioned above the militaristic homoeroticisation of the national impersonation of Coriolanus and the connection of this with and to the erotics of fascism. It does not need to be rehearsed again here. Suffice it to say that in these substitutions of sexual and familial metaphors for those of national and military solidarity, in a way that feels like illegitimate and uncertain displacement rather than strongly illuminated reciprocity, the text is certainly unable to incorporate the national idea in a symbolic body whose sexuality is secure, stable and conventionally acceptable.

The taut transactions in *Coriolanus* between the underlying desire of mastery and fixity, and dissemination of forms *both* of fixation *and* of slippage[24] in the signifiers of national identity and territorial possession (actual and symbolic) which I have been discussing in the play, turn out to admit something disidentified, alien and nomadic instead of what should otherwise have been the very epitome of embodied and emplaced identity.[25] For this, ultimately, is what the present reading of the text concerns: the extraordinarily emphatic way in which its nationalism has always already turned into its opposite, and, in that turning, turned against such constitutive, *ideologically* incorporative oppositions.

VII

There is no conclusion, ever. But I want to end this chapter by asking an extravagant, and perhaps impertinent, question. It is

this: If there is to be a 'new Europe', either in terms of a sup-
ranational unity, or separative and centrifugal, newly energised
nationalisms, what 'place' in it will there 'be' for a gypsy non- or
anti-territorialism? I will try to explain what I mean.

Despite the attractive appeal of the ideal of a sure and grounded
sense of belonging and habitation, there is, to recall the Heideggerian terminology, no single ground of Being. For if, along with
the emphasis on the essential question of ontology – 'Warum ist
überhaupt Seiendes und nicht vielmehr Nichts?' – comes a – not
so – secret assumption that cultures are essentially whole, this in
turn reinforces his unreadiness to think – even philosophically –
the possibility that there is in fact no 'being as such', no single
ground on which to locate the more restricted question of the
essent, let alone the more detailed and effective questions concerning the history and the historicity of societies, and even that of
their cultural and political spheres. In this context Adorno's critique of the 'philosophy of Being' remains appropriate, and coincides closely with my own sense of the repressive unity smuggled
into the founding question of Heideggerian metaphysics: 'what',
in effect, Adorno asks, 'can count as singularity, when the only
essential thing about historical societies is their historicity?' To
which I would add that the tragic dynamic of such historicity,
especially the violence of its incommensurably antagonistic tempor-
alities, stands wholly unreconcilable with the primacy, or even the
derivative character, of any single ontological question of being
'as such'. And nor could any correlated sense of nation or project
of national salvation. The very ambivalences of national embodiment and territorial fixation which I have sought to describe in
Coriolanus themselves counter the drives of the text's most superficially patriotic levels and, in their disseminated and contested
dispersal, undercut the very project of the ontic longing and the
political obscenity both of the Heideggerian text and of the re-
awakened rightist nationalisms of our contemporary Europe.

At the theoretical level, the underlying proposition here derives
from work I have done recently not on space but on temporality.[26]
For some time I have been convinced that the value of historical
criticism lies in the complexity of the relations of identity and
difference between the historicity of the past and the 'history of
the present',[27] which produce a kind of parallax effect by which a
properly critical purchase on both moments may be achieved. This

effect is most pronounced, and its critical value most highly articulated, when the 'past' moment in question is that of the threshold
– in the early modern period – of the epoch of our own modernity
itself. Hence the significance – national myths apart – of the study
of 'Shakespeare', and the importance of extensive debate concerning problems in the theory of historical interpretation which has
in recent years been focused on his work in particular and on early
modern English culture more widely. However, among the things
which makes the recent resurgence of historicism so regrettable is
the argument that a proper historicity resides in a fully diacritical
sense of historical time 'hollowed' and inlaid by multiple temporal-
ities, with past and future turnings, qualifying the historicity of
the present (rather than the filled and essentially static time of
historicism).

I have tried to argue in this chapter that the figuration of nation
in *Coriolanus* is the subject of a critical ambivalence. Or better, it
is the site of a quite radical textual and ideological contradiction:
as I have said, the more unified, the more resisted and disperse.
But certainly – and despite an extant, if somewhat dated, tradition
of learning political lessons from Shakespeare (which is exactly
not, if I may be permitted a little irony here, what I have in mind)
– it seems that, looking back to the early modern moment, we see
thus the instability of the national ideal at that early stage of the
nationalist idea, and this may help us to reflect on the means of
what I believe is a necessary resistance to, and unsettlement of,
that idea today.

In concluding the present discussion of national embodiment, I
now wonder whether an analogous figuration of territorial space
– both geographical and symbolic – isn't appropriate if the desire of
belonging is not to become expressed solely in terms of the kinds
of dominatory and fixated nationalism I have been discussing.

To cite, in this context, at the other pole of the past–present
dialectic, the image of the life world of Romany and Sinti people
is thus, counter those fixities, to evoke the best sense of a strong
communal identity which – whatever claims it may have on place
and belonging – is without nationalist sedimentation: travelling. And
a key point here is that I am arguing not against a sense of place,
habitation and belonging, but that these should not be imagined
either in terms of the lethal nationalisms or those of the supra-
national, and quite cynical, pragmatisms of 'respectable' European

politics. But if history – or better, historicity – is inscribed in complex, diacritical, time, should not a new – post-national – geography (a geography of criticism as well as of physical place) inhabit an equally complex, transactional space, travelling not in hyper-reality (as the postmodernists would have it) but perhaps in a logic of critical, transactional space: even an in-principle nomadism, or what I am calling post-territorialism?

These questions are doubtless asked in the spirit of a certain idealism, one which will surely find no hearing in the councils of Europe. But is it not important now to recall the figures of the gypsy and the Jew – travellers and wanderers in myth and often in historical practice – and victims (in both cases on an industrial scale) of the period of European fascism, when at least the former (and for all I know, the latter), have become again today the renewed objects – with other groups, to be sure – of genocidal projects, of 'ethnic cleansing'.

The task is to find the discourses – and the practical policies – of place and belonging, without falling back into defining the legitimacy of such desires or demands in the territorialising drive to establish boundaries – whether geographical or moral – that are exclusionary rather than inclusive, and which describe a space that is essentialised and pure, rather than welcoming and provisional. To imagine community must not be in the same instant to begin the war against the others.

And the challenges, then, for criticism? Criticism has been overtly nationalistic, and has secreted nationalisms within itself, by turns. A full examination of the means of identifying and overcoming such traits would demand another chapter again. But surely the greatest challenge in the New Europe will be for criticism to learn to read 'against the grain'[28] of the texts and the social practices and ideologies with which the texts are in contact. When necessary, it will have to be a task of aggravating contradictions; but also one of seeking to imagine and explore forms of the enriching complexity of cultural transaction which a meeting of peoples and traditions ought to engender.

In the last stages of the drafting of this chapter I was surprised and pleased to come across an article by Günter Grass which addresses some related problems in terms very similar to my own. In 'What have you done to my country?'[29] Grass writes of his feelings as a German for whom the loss of his own homeland (pre-war Danzig) has liberated him in various ways ('I am curious about the world and delight in travelling'); and as one critical of the pace and modes of German reunification, when, in the summer of 1992, news of the fighting in Sarajevo was overlaid by that of the repeated firebomb attacks by massed neo-fascists, in front of passive onlookers and an acquiescent police force, on a hostel for refugees in Rostock-Lichtenhagen. He remarks of what he calls this 'German recidivism' that 'the past has tapped us on the shoulder', and links this to the appalling resonances of the agreement by Rudolph Seiters, the then Interior Minister, with the Romanian government for the repatriation of gypsies (a version 'of the slogan that presently unites all Germany: "Foreigners out!"'). Grass ends his essay with these appropriate and moving words, which I quote at length:

> Perhaps we lack the very people we're afraid of, because they are foreign to us and look foreign. Those whom, out of fear, we meet with hatred, which now daily turns to violence. And perhaps those we most lack are the ones we think of as the lowest of the low, the Romanies and Sinti, the gypsies.
>
> They have no allies. No politician represents their case, whether in the European parliament or the Bundestag. No state they can appeal to would support their demands for compensation – pathetic isn't it? – for Auschwitz, or make them a national priority.
>
> The Romanies and the Sinti are the lowest of the low. 'Expel them!' says Herr Sieters and gets on the line to Romania. 'Smoke them out!' shout the skinheads. But in Romania, and everywhere else, gypsies are bottom of the heap as well. Why? Because they are different.
>
> Because they steal, are restless, roam, have the evil eye and have that stunning beauty that makes us ugly to ourselves. Because their mere existence puts our values into question. Because they are all very well in operas and operettas, but in reality – it sounds awful, reminds you of awfulness – they are antisocial, odd and don't fit in. 'Torch them!' shout the skinheads. . . .
>
> Let half a million and more Sinti and Romanies live among us. We need them. They could help us by irritating our rigid order a little. Something of their way of life could rub off on us. They could teach us how meaningless frontiers are: careless of boundaries, Romanies and Sinti are at home all over Europe. They are what we claim to be: born Europeans!

Notes

I am grateful to my research assistant, Diane Bignell, for her patient and conscientious help in the preparation of this chapter.

1 Martin Heidegger, *Einführung in die Metaphysic*, Gesamtausgabe II Abteilung: Vorlesungen 1923–44 Band 40 (Frankfurt-am Main, Vittorio Klostermann, 1983), p. 3.

2 Martin Heidegger, *An Introduction to Metaphysics*, trans. Ralph Manheim (New Haven, Yale University Press, 1959), p. 1.

3 The pomposity of the seeming interrogation notwithstanding, this is not actually a *new* question, of course, but rather one of the founding questions of Western metaphysics. Its antiquity – Heidegger's fetishisation of an often pseudo-antiquity – lends *aura* (in Benjamin's term) to the *fascination*. I am indebted to Professor Klaus Reichert for his celebration – in conversation – of this antiquity.

4 *Dasein*, and *da-sein*, in Heidegger's usage, are also notoriously difficult to translate. Manheim opts for 'being-there', rather than the more everyday term, 'existence'; see his 'Translator's Note': see *An Introduction*, pp. vii–x, and *ibid.*, p. 9n.

5 This is the best defence of Heideggerian displacement of the deferral of a *philosophical* answer into context. Arguably all philosophical questions are rooted in the historical problematic, and need – if they are real questions – historical solutions. This is not usually admitted by professional philosophers with such explicitness. Whether or not Heidegger's construction either of the historical context or of the political answer is acceptable, is, of course, another matter. The problem of what Heidegger means by historicity is beyond the immediate scope of this paper.

6 See Theodor Adorno, *Negative Dialectics*, trans. E. B. Ashton (London, Routledge, 1990).

7 The commentaries at the time on the Romanian revolution against Ceaucescu's regime were startling for their historical ignorance.

8 Commentary on political and cultural nationalism, and the problem of the progressive character (or otherwise) of nationalism and national movements would include especially Benedict Anderson's *Imagined Communities: Reflections on the Origins and Spread of Nationalism* (London, Verso, 1983).

9 The inverted commas around Shakespeare denote as much the cultural institution as the allegedly individual playwright.

10 See especially Terence Hawkes, *That Shakespeherian Rag* (London, Methuen, 1986) and Graham Holderness, *Shakespeare's History* (Dublin, Gill and Macmillan, 1985), and Holderness, ed., *The Shakespeare*

Myth (Manchester, Manchester University Press, 1988); and Simon Barker, 'Images of the sixteenth and seventeenth centuries: as a history of the present' in Francis Barker *et al.*, eds, *Confronting the Crisis: War, Politics and Culture in the Eighties* (Colchester, University of Essex, 1984).

11 See Francis Barker and Peter Hulme, ' "Nymphs and reapers heavily vanish": The discursive con-texts of *The Tempest*' in John Drakakis, ed., *Alternative Shakespeares* (London, Methuen, 1985), p. 191. This then feeds, in turn, the fetishisation of the 'places' of his life – Stratford-upon-Avon, Anne Hathaway's cottage, The Globe; and of everything that takes part in the production of 'Shakespeare's England'.

12 In particular Shakespeare is a significant figure in the establishment of what is historically speaking a strange kind of cultural duplicity: on one hand the archetype of the national (or nationalistic) poet; on the other the universalistic transcendence of anything so local or partisan: does this oddity in the formation of a particular cultural nationalism have anything in the way of a wider purchase? Or is there some understatement in the British formation of this figure, connected until quite recently, no doubt, not so much with any alleged reserve in the famed national temperament as with the fact that the national poet of the nation which controls a global empire can be made to seem in fact universal in achievement, preoccupation and 'values'? The first time it was possible to take exams in Shakespeare was as entrance qualifications for natives wishing to join the Indian Civil Service under the Raj.

This connects, in turn, to the current renewal of cultural nationalism in English (and, of course, Welsh) education – the very notion of a 'national curriculum' carries more with it than the merely administrative sense that it will apply to the whole country (although this is invasive enough). An intensification – which has been officially 'legitimate' since, I think, the invasion of *las islas Malvinas* – of 'respectable' rightist nationalism (that of the National Front and other neo-Nazi groups having been partly incorporated into mainstream Conservatism in the form of official Thatcherite populism, *and halted on the streets by anti-fascist actions of the left*) has put into play a peculiar combination of renewed Churchillian Atlanticism and rabid Little-Englandism. Both are forms of national posturing (and supplication) that egregiously inflect the entire current discussion of England's membership of Europe in cultural, diplomatic, institutional, legal and political senses, as well as economic and financial ones. The very painful transformation of 'Britain' from a world power into a weakness 'at the heart', as John Major's facile and hypocritical phrase has it, 'of Europe', has even engendered symbolically coterminous 'debates' such as the apparently ludicrous, but actually quite significant, discussion of whether 'Shakespeare was a Tory'. (Of course he 'was'; or rather 'is', in the sense of having been institutionally constructed to conservative design, and is in the process of being yet further entrenched in the educational system as well as in other important cultural and ideological apparatuses.) The New Europe?

13 However constituted by difference the imagination may be. Note how the English Histories – especially such arch-patriotic examples as *Henry V* – constitute a symbolic, political topography, in which the bringing to representation of a national enemy (it is, in fact, 'the French', but 'who' it is doesn't really matter) provides at least the backdrop, and at its strongest the constitutive otherness, against which the stirring and strident rhetoric of the English national myth is effectively pronounced.

14 All quotations are from the Arden edition of *Coriolanus*, ed. Philip Brockbank (London: Methuen, 1976).

15 See my *The Culture of Violence* (Manchester, Manchester University Press, 1993) where I argue this at length.

16 Note especially that peculiar combination of displaying and hiding with which Freud classically associates the sexual fetish in particular: for example, unable to 'entreat them / For my wounds' sake to give their suffrage' (II.ii.137–8), nor to 'Show them the unaching scars which I should hide' (II.ii.148), Coriolanus is none the less constrained to 'entreaties' as truncated as this: 'I have wounds to show you, which shall be yours in private' (II.iii.76–7), and so on.

17 Even to the extent of near-religious – if morbid (and anachronistic) – sanction coming to seem appropriate:

> *Menenius*: The warlike service he hath done, consider: think
> Upon the wounds his body bears, which show
> Like graves i'th'holy churchyard.
>
> (III.iii.49–51)

18 Cf. the figure, and the ideological and symbolic figuration, of Duncan in *Macbeth*, and the language of his body as 'the Lord's anointed temple', and its violation a 'sacrilege'.

19 Cf. the manipulation of mass desire, the fetishisation of display, uniforms and mass rallies, of torchlight procession, of purity and pogrom; architectural monumentalism; the politicisation of black, red, silver and gold; demagogic rhetoric, and the nationalist and often primitivist cultural formations coupled to ethnic and ideological cultural policies; the cults of youth, motherhood, of the race and the fatherland, and the demonisation and domination of ethnic and racial aliens as inferiors and slaves; and so on.

In connection with Coriolanus's eroticised fascist body, see Klaus

Theweleit, *Male Fantasies* (Minneapolis, University of Minnesota Press, 1987–9).

20 In such circumstances, as in *Coriolanus*, a homoerotic component is not unknown: as well as Nazism and fascism themselves, one thinks of various related regimes such as that of the colonels and later the generals in Greece, or of various Latin American military governments, howsoever officially homophobic and indeed energetically repressive of sexual 'deviance'.

21 Adorno, *Negative Dialectics*, p. 90.

22 There is a whole sub-structural matter involved here, concerned with the fact that beneath 'nation' as political and cultural form – even possibly beneath imagined community based on ethnic belonging – there is a more fundamental 'drive' at work: that toward territorialisation. Deleuze and Guattari venture a rather obscure critique – if such it is – of capitalism in these terms.

23 The sanction of banishment is itself interesting and complex. In one register it involves the sanction of expulsion beyond the defining community. In another it involves a strange torsion in the mapping of the limits of the community by use of human and animal form. If Coriolanus's body in some important sense '*is*' the national territory, how *can* it be expelled *from* the nation?

24 I have written previously about the historical precision of the event of. combinations of, on the one hand, forms of fixity and ascertainment as the ground and instrument of textual interpretation, and, on the other, the imputation – to text and interpretation alike – of almost anthropological properties of the dissemination and departure of meaning from itself. See 'In the wars of truth,' in *The Culture of Violence*, pp. 121–42. Here, as there, the issue is not that of a choice (in any case false) between historicist objectivism and neo-liberal intepretability but the significance of the occurrence – *as event* – of the combination of these forms.

25 In this context, perhaps it is not too far-fetched to suggest a connection with what the discourse of Elizabethan social control called 'sturdy beggars'. In the spirit of what I call critical parallax, we might recall the moral panics in Elizabethan England stemming from the anxiety of the rulers and possessors which, when confronted even with the imagination of an unfixed population, manifested itself in threatening images of loss of power. And if the anxiety of the powerful in Elizabethan England feared and demonised in turn the rootless poor, the so-called 'masterless men', I suspect that this is an anxiety to which the dialectic of fixity and displacement in *Coriolanus* responds.

26 See *The Culture of Violence*.

27 To cite Michel Foucault's now-classic phrase for the expression of this

idea: see in particular *Discipline and Punish* (London, Allen Lane, 1977), p. 31.

28 In Walter Benjamin's resonant phrase; see the 'Theses on the philosophy of history', *Illuminations* (New York, Harcourt, Brace and World Inc., 1968), p. 259.

29 *The Independent* (13 February 1993).

Part IV

✤

Shakespeare and transnational culture

✤

10

❖

Shakespeare, national culture and the lure of transnationalism

❖

John J. Joughin

> To insist on the absolute absence of tradition is as naive as the
> obstinate insistence on it.
>
> (Theodor W. Adorno, 'On tradition')[1]

A volume entitled *Shakespeare and National Culture* cannot easily
countenance the end of nationalisms. Yet, predictably perhaps, at
the moment of its emergence, the tremors of the academic *Zeit-
geist* are brinkful of these very prognostications. Beyond national
culture the small and large worlds of the academy register this
shift accordingly. Some would impel us towards the actualisation
of the event of 'the new international', while others, more modest
in their expectation, merely moot a move beyond 'Eng. lit.'.[2] To
take stock of this situation is to be struck at once by the extreme
hybridity of orthodoxy and radicality which keeps close company
as nationalism begins and ends again. Yet there is simultaneously
an urgency about those injunctions which would urge our orientation toward the future – albeit one which is curiously dated in the
delivery – to which we will need to respond.

It is evident that 'Shakespeare' and the criticism which attempts
to construe its significance has more than accommodated the spatio-
temporal dislocations of the current conjuncture. Indeed, as it
transits between a variety of locales, some real, some increasingly
desired or imagined, the all-pervasive syndication of Shakespearian
culture – academic or otherwise – secures the familiar contemporary aura of any other transnational corporation: a phenomenon

which Gary Taylor has termed 'Shakesperotics' and which Terence Hawkes has characterised more succinctly as 'Bardbiz'.[3] In a changing world the global currency of Shakespeare's cultural capital and the permanent revolution of the critical trends which it helps to underwrite offers further evidence, if we required it, that amidst what Marx once termed 'free competition within the realm of knowledge' the price to be paid for accelerated intellectual exchange is that more often than not it entails a fatal association with the market forces it seeks to oppose. The same metaphorics which locate Shakespeare in a global marketplace also indirectly acknowledge our complicity in a form of joint venture, and remind us that, in its facility to unleash new ideas and to open up new means for their communication, capitalism will happily service even its most radical opponents.[4]

That the 'free' exchange of academic thought barely conceals a complicity with the implacable market logic which continues to negate both freedom and its possibility presents cultural criticism with a considerable dilemma. Currently critical discourse in the humanities registers this predicament in a strain which situates itself somewhere between disorientation and regret. The tenor is a direct symptom of its context and it is prompted by the awareness that we find ourselves inextricably enmeshed within at least two forms of culpable presentness. Each in its own way is impeachable on different counts of the violent contradictions that late capital continues to make possible. On the one hand there is, increasingly, a realisation of the remove between literary theory and political practice: the failure of our re-readings of culture to impact on their immediate surroundings and the accusation, if not the admission, of a form of academic dereliction as we continue to witness the shortfall of reflexive thought in its inability to make an impression on the world. On the other hand there is also an emergent awareness that within this impasse there lurks what might well be the key dilemma of late modernity itself: the feeling (resurgent in English departments) that disenchantment is no longer enough – and the need for something more than the cosy post-metaphysical assurance that old aesthetic sensibilities just don't count any more.

The co-existence of these extremes simultaneously drags us away from and back towards crucial assumptions informing our complex relation to the question of literary tradition. As, for all their sense of contemporaneity, pronouncements from the metropolitan centre of new conditions of uncertainty configure themselves as that most staple of literary-historical mutations – the perennial clash between continuity and innovation. We need, I think, to re-acknowledge something of the parochiality of these concerns. It is little wonder that critics from other traditions regard the inflated claims for the growing internationalisation of 'British' cultural studies and its satellites with a mixture of frustration and perplexity.[5] Even in its most liberationist currents the pressure to abandon universalising claims for Shakespeare tended to apply itself in an exclusively Western context; yet, as it did so, in its rejection of liberal humanism and its constraints, it tended to ignore still unresolved questions at the heart of those traditions themselves. Amidst its affirmation of the deterritorialisation of institutional 'English' and an acceptance of its evacuation as a guarantor of formerly unified conceptions of enclosure and identity, there was a failure to construe these normative assumptions on their own ground as well as a failure to appreciate the extent to which a national aesthetic is customarily secured by the productive and disintegrative dissental culture which surrounds it.

Whither Shakespeare then? It seems clear to me that, in considering a future for the discipline of English or one that lies beyond it, we will need first to re-raise the question of national identity as it has informed and reproblematised the immediate past of institutional variants of Englishness. The current turn to nationalism offers an opportunity to focus on the particular configuration of British cultural materialism; both in its emergence as an oppositional formation which would break with traditional dogmatics, yet also in its current failure to move beyond 'Eng. lit.' and in its ongoing struggle to come to terms with all that its inheritance might entail.

The dead hand of 'English'

In the first enthusiasm of political criticism, literature and Shakespeare especially were deployed by some as a conduit of everything reactionary – capital, patriarchy, nation and empire.
     Alan Sinfield, *Cultural Politics – Queer Theory*[6]

With the benefit of hindsight Alan Sinfield feels able to mark a remove from the critical formation he was so influential in shaping. In the early days of cultural materialism, as his remark suggests, there was, indeed, a tendency to reimpose a false degree of homogeneity on the past. In practice this often saw an all too easily identifiable rainbow alliance of mainstream Englishness – Eliot, Leavis or Tillyard – doubling for what became abbreviated as the 'institution of literature', a straw target which was then ritually bowled over in its various forms as it was re-read and de-essentialised. In its assimilation of a post-structuralist approach to Renaissance studies, cultural materialism effectively exploited the tense relation of the 'early modern' as a site for interrogating the emergence of modernity itself; and as a vantage point from which to affirm the dissolution of metaphysical totalities past and present. Superficially this also helped to dislodge the relation which had been forged between idealised notions of literature's value as a standing representative of a national culture. Yet it quickly became apparent that the event of this rupture was less than seismic; and tended in any case to operate a methodological shorthand which, whilst it expressed and exposed a direct and eminently deconstructible relation between 'Eng. lit.' and its former claim to transcendence, was also prone to dismantle orthodox conceptions of truth and meaning only to reinstall the canon by other means. Something of the dangerous hermeneutic insularity of this strategy and its unwitting complicity with residual forms of institutional entrenchment was actually remarked at a relatively early juncture. So that in his introduction to *The Shakespeare Myth*, one of the formation's founding texts, Graham Holderness already voices reservations concerning the 'dead hand of "English"',[7] urging in its stead a willingness to situate 'Shakespeare' within its broader and often extra-literary configuration where it continues to inform the more public, though often less tangible, notions of his embodiment of national character.

Of course the breach envisaged here was explicitly anti-élitist and intentionally provocative. And its democratising spirit had also been strongly signalled from the outset. So that at its initiation a 'Political Shakespeare', in breaking with the traditional concerns of 'Eng. lit.', also registered its commitment to 'the transformation of a social order which exploits people on grounds of race, gender and class'.[8] The focus here was as much on the present as the past. Indeed the hope was that the divide between high and low culture would be reconciled and overcome and that in the remix of the former with the latter something of the praxial potential of contemporary popular mass culture would even be released, rechannelled and reciprocated. This was a move which envisaged an irreverent re-configuration of all forms of exclusivity and gestured toward a break between the institutional inside and its outside. So that artefacts and practices which had 'traditionally been prized within the evalu-ative idea of culture' were now resituated as 'one set of signifying practices among others' to be read alongside 'the cultures of sub-ordinated and marginalised groups like schoolchildren and skin-heads' and 'forms like television and popular music and fiction'.[9] In the transformative meshing of cultural studies to literary tradition the most 'startling' effect was to be secured in the detradition-alisation of 'Shakespeare' not merely just as guarantor of essential humanism but as the still prevailing long-term functionary of a system of cultural hierarchy which sought to maintain a sense of difference between 'us' and 'them'.

This sense that we must push beyond the boundaries of institu-tional English is confirmed by a strain within cultural materialism which if anything has continued to grow more grandiose in its claims. In what is in many ways an excellent essay on 'Lear's maps' Terence Hawkes offers the following justification which is worth quoting at length:

> At this stage, my strategy will be clear enough. By focusing on those 'cultural meanings' that we generate now, in our own historical context – meanings which can hardly be separated from our percep-tion of those generated then, in the text's historical context – I have invoked an aspect of the 'historicism' mentioned earlier. Such an analysis might seem merely practical, in a traditional British mode, at best only of so called 'academic' interest. But it can also reason-ably claim to have broader horizons. In focusing on the way in which different readings of texts compete for the power to generate cultural meaning, and in aiming to see how ideological positions are formed and sustained through their use; how, more specifically, dis-cursive stratagems operate in the criticism and performance of Shake-speare's plays, and on behalf of what and of whom, this sort of analysis commits itself to intervention in matters traditionally thought to lie beyond the walls of the academy. Add an overt concern with the material historical and economic implications of literary criticism itself, together with a focus on the relation between the academic subject called 'English' and the cultural power of the Englishness which it often upholds, and the sense of Cultural Materialism's in-volvement, at its furthest reach, with larger matters of politics and public policy is unavoidable.

For the British, after all, 'English' never was and never could be just another academic subject. On the contrary, its larger dimension grows directly out of the fact that it was always intended to be *the* subject, both at home and, with perhaps greater significance, abroad: the sacred repository of national values, standards and identity, the crucible in which a whole way of life was to be reverently concocted, shaken and occasionally stirred. And yet, as recent and continuing stirrings amongst non-English communities in Britain have shown, those on the periphery of this civilising arrangement, perceived as the non-civilised or Brutish, have a disconcerting habit of periodically dashing that cup from English lips. In the process, perhaps, they remind us of the complexity of our inheritance from Brutus, and in its Brutish/British name offer to break free from the smoothing-over process to which a particularly narrow version of 'Englishness' seems committed.

A literary criticism which responds – beyond the boundaries of 'English' – to those peripheral Brutish dimensions might not unreasonably, as I have suggested, find a sort of rallying point in the work of the late Raymond Williams: a Welshman from the periphery, not an Englishman from the centre, with a lifelong interest in mapping those dimensions of the symbolic boundary-ridden British terrain which his finest novel calls *Border Country*.[10]

In its rejection of homogeneities of the type noted by Sinfield, Hawkes's intervention is exemplary in its willingness to rehistoricise tragedy as a complex form of nationhood. Yet even whilst attending to the problems of unification that *Lear* conjures forth or as Hawkes himself puts it earlier in the essay, the play's 'multi-level sense of nationhood',[11] the moves between domains which subsequently serve to confirm its contemporary relevance become so rapid and dizzying as to secrete a degree of geographical occlusion in the process. As problems in *Lear* with the Union or 'Englishness' in its Brutish/British context are implicitly yoked to concerns of the present – specifically recent 'stirrings' of post-colonialism and multi-culturalism – the sleight of hand which wants to recruit a conjuncturally productive awareness of historical otherness to a more contemporary form of marginality is in danger of simultaneously eliding something of the authority residing in otherness which enables it to carry out this manoeuvre – even and especially as it protests its own concern with marginality. In its ability to unsettle the discipline of English from within, tragedy's traditional eccentricity is coterminously conflated with the extra-literary, explicitly

in its extra-institutional call for a 'literary criticism which responds
– beyond the boundaries of "English"', even as the scare quotes
acknowledge 'English' as our own construction – a distinction it
remains simultaneously willing yet unable to dispense with. Current trends of detraditionalisation confirm a cultural criticism in
separation from society and even as its affirmation of critical difference also 'protests' the remove, its ability to do so is bound to
remain in relative confinement – to the extent that the limit and
range of its innovation are predetermined by the very forms of
institutional embeddedness which continue to guarantee the effect-
iveness of their break with tradition in this form. In ways that we
will need to return to remark, the dead hand of 'Eng. lit.' does still
partially maintain its grasp, and a radical criticism is still indirectly sustained by the relation.

Culture wars and the culture of dissent

It was of course beyond 'Eng. lit.' that cultural materialism continued to reach. Yet as it did so, and as it pursued an increasingly
interventionist strategy in matters of public policy, in its willingness
to narrativise away its centre, it found itself facing the by now
familiar predicament of any other postmodernist cultural theory,
in danger of being co-opted to, and subsumed by, the broader
reaches of a dissentual culture of protest which towards the end
of the 1980s confirmed a split between political and intellectual
worlds, which registered the very loss of its critical purchase in
its frantic need to make a difference.

   In this context (despite its own early awareness of something
of the pitfalls of such a strategy) it is evident that the premature
affirmation of a break with institutionality in its attenuated form
continued to have debilitating effects for a radical criticism. Indeed
from the moment of the break onwards it was as if the mere act of
disaffiliation from the established literary tradition had itself both
displaced as well as replaced a form of 'political' activity. On the
one hand, even as the collision between past and present proved
conjuncturally productive in its ability to relativise the old dogmas,
within the wider reaches of the academy it was always in danger
of being accommodated as a matter of harmless ambivalence: different in its political inflection no doubt, but even in its disruptive effect capable of rubbing shoulders with what by now was, in

practice, emerging as a broad church of 'textual analytics' within which Marxism was reassimilated only to figure as one reading among many others.[12] On the other hand, forestalling recognition of the dangers of this form of pluralistic incorporation, in a related move, the localised alienation effect which a radicalised literary criticism could still muster tended to be arrogated in the direction of its immediate constituency. And here the danger was that dissidence began to be discharged and indeed measured in terms of its ability to cause localised friction in individual departments or rekindle old flames across broader collegiate rivalries. Again of course in this form cultural materialism traded off the very hierarchical tensions it would otherwise deny. Yet rather than forging a connection with, or articulating any form of accountable relation to, actual social transformation, institutional in-fighting now circulated within a rarefied academic circuit and served to facilitate rather than prevent the actual detachment of the critic from society. The 'broad political objectives of the movement' had not been realised.[13] And in its transposed form just as internal dissidence began to double for 'struggle' it also served to confuse even as it confirmed a crucial distinction – that the break from the institution of literature was also a break within its confines. In a curious *volte face* cultural materialism – a critical formation whose claim had been to exploit the oppositional potential remarked in a renewed awareness of bourgeois criticism's claim to ignore the context of its production – had suppressed the question of its own determination. The consequent inability to distinguish between a form of oppositionality which was intra- rather than extra-academic prevented a more reflective form of engagement which would have weighed an enclosure within 'Eng. lit.' against as well as alongside its own unwitting collusion in sustaining the actuality of the ongoing division it continued to maintain. Ironically, the formation now found itself to be at its least grounded when it had claimed to be at its most politically engaged. And rather than being able to put theory into practice this most materialist of formations began to mark its failure to impact on the materialities which surrounded it.

As those same forces of fragmentation which served to make a market out of education in the 1980s insisted on the reinstatement of more traditional unities (including the imposition in England and Wales of a national curriculum), the suspicion dawned that, amidst the apparent deregulation provided by the new forms and permutations of cultural criticism, we had greatly underestimated the ongoing capacity of these new media to interarticulate with residual structures of institutional and corporate conformity, and, indeed, to be overtaken by them. For all its scaremongering topicality, a dangerously decentred critical orthodoxy had not come to pass even whilst key areas of an 'English' system of education were now consolidated in their most divisive form. As beyond 'Eng. lit.' it was precisely 'Eng. lit.' that was in the ascendant.

During the early 1990s this discrepancy between theory and practice was seized upon, by a reactionary formation which was only too willing and able to remark its shortfall.[14] By way of consolidating the considerable material gains it had accrued during the preceding decade, the ideological offensive of neo-conservatism was now well under way. And as base and superstructure shifted place, the so-called 'culture wars' ensued. Amidst the fallout, the productive output of a radical criticism from the mid-1980s was now effectively remobilised and dustjackets which had claimed the emergence of a newly revolutionised critical field were misrepresentatively recited by the moral re-armers as evidence for the defence. The language of conflict, confrontation, takeover, systematic offensive, was intellectualised, editorialised and fetishised – everywhere endlessly iterable. That this 'struggle' and its rhetoricisation of a crisis in the 'cultural consensus' turned out to be something of an elaborate stalking horse did not prevent a radical criticism from playing into the hand of its entrapment. In Britain, within its wider dispersal it was the liberal left intelligentsia who rushed to pick up the gauntlet first. Whether it was the academic journalese of the *Times Higher Education Supplement* addressing the 'complex debate about literary canons' and inviting authors and academics to provide a list of 'essential reading for an educated person' (with appalling irony some of the latter obliged by providing a theorist's top ten, you know the sort of thing – Derrida, Foucault, Barthes etc.), or *The Late Show* pondering PC, or, again, the re-arrival of Fukuyama's declaration of 'the end of history'.[15] Meanwhile in the academy itself so long as the right were continuing to set the agenda it did not take long for those liberals on the right of centre who were unwilling to engage in the theoretical debates of the recent past to seize their opportunity. Predictably, just as a return to the Renaissance had configured something of a strategic move to appropriate the professional high ground in the theorisation of literary studies, an anti-theoretical retrenchment now sought to occupy the same terrain, the fact that radical approaches began to be traduced with alarming ease only serving to locate the strength of the current status quo of liberalism, a 'consensus' which for all their innovation the new formations of cultural materialism and new historicism had failed to displace.

The Shakespearian heterotopia

In the fullest reaches of their constituency the culture wars are often configured as a form of stand-off between the protested cultural disempowerment of the right and the political/critical discontent of the left. In its representation of what amounts to a form of interarticulation between inverted authority and non-authorised alterity this rhetorical polarisation secretes its own forms of alliance. Amidst currently resurgent notions of a leftist pedagogy and discussions surrounding the so-called political correctness of Shakespeare criticism, it is possible to see just such a process at work, whereby under the guise of pluralism, and airing the debate, difference may eventually equal domination, not merely in the sense of producing a flexible superiority between Shakespeare left and right but by the constitution of the oscillation itself.[16] The play-off between these two positions in their various permutations produces a kind of Shakespearian heterotopia which keeps its place through placelessness, whilst the elaboration of its topology protests a lack of hierarchisation which is then simultaneously complicit with the brands of conformity it also serves to underwrite.

Nowhere is this vulnerable complicity more crudely exposed than in its re-inscription within the British press. Yet we should not for this reason alone dismiss its significance. For it is within the confines of this form of commonplace dissemination that, as Benedict Anderson reminds us, the national imaginary customarily locates perhaps its most influential expression of placelessness and belonging:

> the newspaper reader, observing exact replicas of his own paper being consumed by his subway, barbershop, or residential neighbours, is continually reassured that the imagined world is visibly rooted in everyday life. . . . [F]iction seeps quietly and continuously into reality, creating the remarkable confidence of community in anonymity which is the hallmark of modern nations.[17]

It is within the groundless domain of this form of mediatisation especially that (as a number of contributions to the present volume aptly demonstrate), despite an energetic engagement with various strains of the eponymous Shakespeare myth, radical criticism remains unable to contest its own misappropriation amidst the complex of cultural processes which function to safeguard the Bard effectively as *the* guarantor of Englishness – both, simultaneously, as a representative of a conservative populism *and* as an exclusivist icon of high culture. By way of corroboration we might briefly return to Terence Hawkes's work and compare its reception within the middlebrow broadsheets.

Doubly irked no doubt by the institutional legitimation and international profile afforded by the relocation of the critic's essay on *King Lear* within the sacred pantheon of a new series of the British Council's 'Writers and their work' imprint, James Wood, a long-term opponent of cultural materialism, decides to 'tackle' the critic about this accordingly. By-line reads: 'James Wood thinks Shakespeare is great. But he tried telling that to Terence Hawkes, who thinks any "greatness" is our own invention.' Wood proceeds to shorthand Hawkes's position in the following terms:

> Professor Hawkes has likened Shakespeare to a black hole, into which we throw our meanings, a writer of 'no necessary distinction'. Last year he told the Guardian that he would rather watch *The Bill* on TV than go out to see Shakespeare, and that while jazz makes him jump for joy, Shakespeare does not.[18]

Throughout the piece the formal inference of Wood's position is clear. The 'danger' of Hawkes's brand of cultural relativism is that it is unsecured. At this rate the centre will not hold. Rejecting *Lear*'s status as a 'masterpiece', as Hawkes's essay announces it will do, ill befits its place in the ranks of what should remain a front-line representative for educational Englishness abroad – the British Council. This at once of course confirms Hawkes's point about *King Lear*'s substantial imbrication within the civilising mission of Englishness. Yet strikingly, the debate is never for a moment in danger of being pitched or still less grounded in these terms. There's no direct mention here of imperial Englishness at all. And though Wood's soundbite summary of Hawkes's position barely represses a host of anxieties concerning potential forms of dislocation – the imminency of Shakespeare's potential misplacement at the heart of darkness, the breakdown of law and order which sees *The Bill* supplementing for an abbreviated form of William, Hawkes's enjoyment of such hybridities (no doubt confirmed by his proclivity for jazz, that most miscegine of forms) etc. – these horrors never come to pass, even as in their turn they serve to confirm in displacement the fertile placelessness which constitutes the national imaginary of which they are intrinsically a part. Yet the interview itself is conducted solely within restrictively familiar lines of engagement as Wood insists on Shakespeare's strong endorsement of traditional aesthetic verities – a claim which by a final twist of irony he actually secures by co-opting to his cause one of the affiliated forefathers of the Yale School of deconstruction, Harold Bloom, a critic who had something to say of greatness and its invention. Meanwhile very much on the receiving end of all this Hawkes finds himself cornered and conducting the closest of close readings concerning the valency of individual phonemes in key speeches from *The Winter's Tale* and *Antony and Cleopatra*.

Only days earlier, presumably on the scent of the same story, Brain Masters in *The Mail on Sunday* had already broadened the offensive against Hawkes but this time in a very different setting. On returning to his alma mater he is not pleased with what he finds. Headline reads:

> There is an English course where the professors regard Shakespeare's plays as no better than the writing on a cornflakes packet. Where the students assess the lecturers. And where women undergrads refuse to read books written by men. Is this life on some kookie Californian campus? No. This is University College, Cardiff.[19]

Although we're nominally in Wales here we are also clearly simultaneously closer to home and dealing with English for the English. Amidst Masters's tirade the high-cultural integrity of 'Eng. lit.' in what should be its most traditionally exclusive domain – the groves of academe – is formally breached on a number of fronts. A form of topsy-turvydom ensues – students assess lecturers, women refuse great white males, whilst the Shakespearian tome itself is little better than something you would prop your newspaper against (*The Mail on Sunday* presumably). These are signs of invasion to be sure. Yet here the enemy is not so much within as without. If we were in any doubt, the conflation of Cardiff and California as sanctuary of West Coast Kookiedom holds the key. For little

England is on the receiving end here of nothing less than the cultural imperialism of an ever-expanding global Americanism. And in the process the American academician now becomes the enemy. For as Masters assures us: 'Nearly all these influences the whole rag bag of prejudice and empty gesture started in the US were imported here'.[20]

As it stage-manages a confrontation it shorthands as 'critical theory versus traditional humanism' we might note that the mainstream media are quick to recognise two cultures of eccentricity within the academy which simultaneously secure 'Eng. lit.''s position as the most vulnerable and the most impregnable of formations. Masters's piece provides as good an example of this as any other. On the one hand he carefully litters his piece with complaints concerning the dangerous strains of abstraction and 'jargon' which the new formation propagates – here again the inference is clear enough: we would be far better served by plain English and British empiricism. In this form the objection is again a familiar one and is reminiscent of a tradition of attacks on the élitist pretensions of 'lit. crit.' – ranging from the unacceptable continentalism of the Bloomsbury Group to French structuralism and the MacCabe affair. Yet the rejection of exoticism in this form is carefully interarticulated with an acceptance of other more acceptable forms of exclusivity. More precisely, the cosy provincial permissible Englishness of a fondly remembered past – the spectre of one Professor Heywood Thomas who taught Masters himself. So important is its provenance that Masters opens his account with it:

> Thirty-five years ago I was an undergraduate at University College, Cardiff, reading French and Romance Philology under a delightfully anachronistic old man called Professor Heywood Thomas. Grey and stooped, with his half-moon reading-glasses perched on the very tip of his nose, he would shuffle into the lecture room as if he had forgotten to take off his bedrooom slippers and could barely find the energy to mount the rostrum. He would say 'Good morning' in a timid, hesitant voice, arrange his notes, then suddenly burst into a French fluent throughout his whole body, arms flailing, back straight, eyes burning, and with the voice of a robust 20-year-old. At the end of the lecture he'd resume the skin of the shy little Welshman he had abandoned an hour earlier.[21]

So it is that the pastoral groves of academe can still house the memory of respectable forms of decentredness and shelter the impression of the sleepy anachronism to which one day it will return. Secured in the present instance by a shy Welshman from the periphery, fluent in continentalism, but still the truer patriot for all that, not only despite, but also precisely because of his current dislodgement: 'I doubt', Masters ventures to add, 'whether anyone like Heywood would be welcome at Cardiff these days. Too eccentric. Too brilliant. And he loved literature too much.'[22] There are doubtless numerous permutations of the Shakespeare heterotopic and many other media for its dissemination. Yet the recurrent pattern of its *modus operandi* is striking in its ability to assimilate and mobilise a dizzying irreducibility of contexts, an array of Englishness – it hardly matters which. Amidst the upheaval, 'Eng. lit.' stays in place, even as it is seized upon by popular media only too happy to confuse and remix the distinction between discrete forms of institutional Englishness on their own terms. As within the fuller spread of its misrepresentation, the demarcation between Shakespeare as 'repository of transcendent values' on the one hand and as the embodiment of the national character and territorial integrity on the other is often deliberately and wilfully obfuscated.[23] Yet the net effect of this undecideability should not be misconstrued as insubstantial, or as mere black hole. For the heterotopia claims its place within placelessness. And in this respect, as Foucault reminds us, it is 'concrete and abstract at the same time'.[24] In the examples cited above it clearly reconfirms a ritualised space of compensation in its public articulation of a strain within the English national imaginary which is almost beyond contestation. The populist profile of these 'cultural' debates and the arrogation of scholarly discourse to the same domain are symptomatic of a process of pluralistic incorporation which now pervades the sector we work in – and it is difficult to see how we might oppose them on these same grounds.

In contemplating the move beyond 'Eng. lit.' Hawkes quite reasonably locates a 'rallying-point' for its future orientation within the work of Raymond Williams, who was as he reminds us 'a Welshman from the periphery, not an Englishman from the centre'.[25] Here again of course the invocation of a political peripherality is explicitly anti-national and goes to the very heart of a radical heritage, to be remarked between high and low culture, as it settles its origin in the nineteenth century as a response to the move away from a rural community. As a form of decentring written against the grain of the emergent need for unification and the construction of an imagined community of nationalism, this traditional polarity between the country and the city is most memorably reproblematised within Williams's own work in his exemplary refusal of a map of Englishness which in its selective metropolitan incorporation would silence the claims of the marginalised and oppressed. Yet it's unclear where the sustainable roots for such a populist radicalism lie in the current political conjuncture. In their British context the culture wars point up the lack of a role for public intellectualism and we need to remark the consequence of this. If we are ever to realise a unified and integrated transformation of English within the current atomisation of 'struggle', we need a topology of Shakespeare studies which will hold the centre in order to accommodate the constitution of an oppositional identity within the contingencies of situational change. A dialectical Shakespearian criticism must both acknowledge the debilitating dimensions of its current dissentual insularity and simultaneously refuse to abolish the distinction between the institutional inside and outside in more critical terms. The recognition that nonconformity is often already compromised by what it opposes is merely the first step towards a critique of the conditions which continue to produce indisciplined conformity and thereby partly preserves a weaker brand of critical difference in its place – a difference we must continue to work within even as we struggle to detach ourselves from its constraint. In this respect, if, for the time being, the interpretative act cannot take its place as a free role, then so much the better.

Eccentric belonging

One never inherits without coming to terms with some specter.
(Jacques Derrida, *Specters of Marx*)[26]

On reflection, it is not surprising that the most central of decentred formations – tragedy – attracts so much attention in the British variant of the culture wars, as, amidst their misrepresentation, the media attacks are nevertheless unerringly accurate in their ability to locate the residual legacy of a crucial faultline within the deep memory of 'Eng. lit.' itself, wherein the generic partition of tragedy serves to situate a crucial point of orientation within its own uneven development as a discipline. In its more orthodox form,

Reg Foulkes has usefully resurrected the term *Hamletism* to describe this process of assimilation wherein a tragic criticism has
long located 'the liberal intellectual paralysed in will and incapable of action', yet still somehow occupying the ethical and cultural
high ground.[27] In its affirmation of an unacceptable degree of
solipsism, in the form as well as the content, of its critical practice,
at moments of national crisis academic detachment is all too readily recast as dereliction of duty, and so too by association is tragedy.[28] *Hamlet* and *Lear* resist appropriation as straightforwardly
patriotic figures precisely because of their stature as high culture
which in this context now re-emerges as an approximation of
nationalism's other. Yet in its very vacillation on the margins, Shakespearian tragedy also serves here in its ambivalence to confirm the
reinstalment of a masculinist warmongering centre and, if performed
at all, as Hawkes reminds us in the essay that's caused all the
rumpus, the map will be redrawn so that a more heroic form of
individualism prevails.[29]

Such a genealogy should serve to remind us that the deep entwinement of Shakespeare with a particular national culture is
seldom straightforward even as it often takes the most 'traditional'
forms. Unsurprisingly perhaps at moments of crisis rifts within
this symbolic geography begin to open up and disconceal their
complicity with forms of demonisation which are still pretty much
engrained within the national psyche. In its own indirect negotiation of the changing relationship between literature and nationalism a radical criticism is bound to be ensnared in the process. If
the turn to history conventionally repels the threat of invasion,
then tragedy can also locate a potentially disruptive enemy within.
A potentiality perhaps indirectly remarked, even in its displacement, by cultural materialism itself. We might remember that at
the outset it was a radical tragedy rather than a radical history
which carried the day.

Whatever the legacy, we might note in passing that the generic
exclusivity of cultural materialism's earliest disaffiliation from tradition was striking in its uniformity. It was as if the disjointure and
eccentricity of seventeenth-century tragedy attracted and unified a
critical movement.[30] And in this regard an articulation of critical
dissent not only facilitated a particular break with the past but also
indirectly fostered a degree of reconciliation. In a double move,
and often by its own admission, it was as if the interrelationship

between critical theory and Shakespearian and Jacobean drama, and the shared sense of dislocation articulated therein, was in the fullest sense a formative one, serving to engender a form of consolidation which not only finally located a methodological affinity but also regrounded a formerly disparate sense of political and personal alienation. Suddenly displacement made a fondly anticipated homecoming possible. Jonathan Dollimore speaks for a generation of scholars when he restates the case in the following terms in his introduction to the second edition of *Radical Tragedy*:

> Why did I write this book? . . . I first read Jacobean drama while studying English at University. . . . There was a perversity about it which attracted me and which resisted the staid and narrow attitude with which literature was usually taught at that university. This drama seemed to cross conventional boundaries, or require that I did so in reading it. . . . At Sussex . . . the desire for something else found an intellectual direction. Critical and cultural theory enabled me to make political sense of my own past; it also enabled me to articulate and explore what I found challenging in Jacobean drama as well as clarifying the reasons why traditional literary criticism seemed inadequate – for me personally, and, as I soon found out, for others too.[31]

Dollimore's admission of eccentric belonging is resonant, and is consistent with a tradition of nonconformity within the institution in which he serves. If the tragic self-consciousness of a recent radicalisation of 'Eng. lit.' configures an anxious survivorhood – a tragic formation – then it is because it locates two aspects of desire, each serving the other: on the one hand the felt need to bear witness, to establish a relation, to return, to belong; on the other, the need to make a difference, to uproot, to repudiate the staid ground of potential disendowment. The institutional genealogy is complex, and the inheritance heterogeneous, yet the draw back to belonging is strong and cultural materialism is not the first formation to locate the sense of its attraction. At its best its work often indirectly registers this dialectical entwinement with the past as a more grounded sense of groundlessness than perhaps I've allowed for above – a sense of participation in non-participation. Yet in the current conjuncture this often also accommodates a resource only of disorientation and regret, mourning even, a melancholic traversing between the past and the present – textually productive no doubt, but unable to formulate a usefully coherent understanding of its own current historical and cultural situation, let alone mobilise an integrated strategy for the oncoming struggle, or, indeed, for all its forward thinking according to its own critique of identitarianism, often unable to identify the ground *beyond* where such a confrontation would take place.

In keeping with many other literary radicalisms which emerged after 1968, the configuration of this remove from actual transformation took a characteristically activist and iconoclastic form. As in its break with the aesthetic essentialism which preceded it and in its continued determination to forge a relationship to the social process, cultural materialism became producer of a mode of so-called epic or revolutionary criticism which focused on producing textual dissonance rather than harmony. Symptomatically at this point the relativisation of the question of the aesthetic had taken a quasi-aesthetic turn, which, in its ability to secure displacement within the very authority it sought to transform, now also denied the non-exclusivity of the breach between culture and politics it simultaneously claimed to secure. In its various permutations a post-aesthetic employment of art against the vantage point of its own dislocation confirms a formation which cannot cut its ties with the past without indirectly reconceiving something of the deeper realisation of loss that this separation entails. In its attempt to move beyond 'Eng. lit.', cultural materialism's productive break with metaphysics simultaneously served to endorse in its displacement nothing more or less than a form of metaphysical need. And we will need to return to consider the consequence of this.

Shakespeare and transnationalism or culture's future heritage

The new is the longing for the new, not the new itself.
(Theodor W. Adorno, 'The new, Utopia and negativity')[32]

Meanwhile, in its second phase, as the drive beyond 'Eng. lit.' continues to gather momentum, there can be little doubt that it will continue to wager on the future and the progressive potentiality of the new spaces of groundlessness opened up by a restructuring of the global and the possibilities for intervention therein.[33] Yet here too, it is striking just how much of a familiarly small world is in danger of being confirmed in the compass of the one-way street which leads away from, but always back to, the metropolitan centre. In this context 'politicising' a global Shakespeare runs an even greater risk of re-inscribing many of the forms of corporate conformity we have already noticed above. Yet as the pedagogical concerns have become more pressing, cultural materialism has sought once again to insist on the emancipatory possibilities of an 'affirmative' postmodernist culture, suggesting that the commercialisation of Shakespeare unwittingly contributes to the delegitimation of the very traditions it is expected to uphold. Amidst the dissolution we are provided with a new opportunity for 'cultural struggle and change', as Shakespeare's mediatisation celebrates a form of forbidden utopic impulse – a progressive potential we ought to exploit.[34]

Yet in truth the Bard rubbing shoulders with *Beavis and Butt-Head* will offer us a fairly superficial deepness with which to oppose instrumentalism: the sad supplement of a shock effect, which in its preconceived transgression of aesthetic niceties calculates a critique of contemporary culture, yet duplicates in the complexity of its remove the consolidation of the very process it would seem to transform. The counter-claim that would affirm a form of emancipatory potential in the forms of the internal confliction that capital takes, and which amidst the clash of discourses and ideologies disconceals new sites of resistance and productive possibilities, is a form of condescension. The danger of a critical practice which imports cultural difference, in order to celebrate ghetto sensibility, is that, as Jay Bernstein shrewdly observes, in its attempt to break with tradition such a postmodern practice 'alters the empirical world without transforming it'.[35]

The vague hope that capital might be hoist by its own petard must be read alongside its undoubted proclivity for the continued reinstalment of hierarchisation. Just as for some, in its more liberated forms, capitalism seeks to preserve the rights of citizenship and the individual against forms of sexual and racial discrimination which are regarded as unrepresentative, for others (the unrepresented), capital's expansion only ensures a reproduction of the ever more exotic forms of deprivation that they must endure. That these forms and identities are relentlessly garnered and reassimilated by a media culture, which in its hunger for difference would reprocess degradation as difference, is remarkable to be sure. And that such images are also in their turn redeployed to seduce, comfort or socialise us undoubtedly registers something of our increasingly schizoid participation in a form of detachment which makes ever more eccentric forms of belonging possible. Yet it also continues to ensure, in its dislocation, that the location of the difference we can make via the interpretative acts which would seek to understand these phenomena is conditional upon our actual institutional remove from this same brand of difference. With its over-reliance on new figures of hybridity and/or ambivalence, the current forms of radicalism sheltering in departments of English literature under a range of interpellatives often betray a kind of displaced ontic longing for the solace of an unmixed or unchanging present which is not wholly dissimiliar from historicism.[36]

The appearance of these 'alternative' formations and their insistent affirmation of dynamism and change during the reactionary consolidation of Reaganism and Thatcherism itself betrays a complex relationship between criticism and its social reality. Yet for as long as we prioritise the abolition of borderlines within the academic and between the academic and the everyday, then by the same token if the only available radical alternative produces a fetishisation of struggle as a form of non-hierarchised dispersal or peripheral singularity, it will remain an impoverished substitute for the real thing, especially while those in power are in the business of shaping unities of transformation. Often it has to be said in the name of liberalism's less fashionably radical but still complicitly relativist celebration of a still weaker brand of alterity and non-hierarchisation which would finally declare 'all spaces, all grounds, all formations, equivalent'.[37] On either count, the liberal or the radical deregulation of traditional academic obligations must be read alongside the continued separation of inside and outside. It is a form of conditional which any mute acceptance of the post-modernisation of Shakespeare studies arguably helps to occlude but fails to alleviate, a separation of domains which a dialectical criticism cannot afford to falsely reconcile. Yet so long as Shakespeare continues to figure for the 'First World' in a global context, or at least helps to articulate its so-called 'realm of uncertainty', it is just as likely to be solicited to still more spurious forms of the brands of 'politicisation' which would offer to free us from these very constraints. Most recently of course it is none other than Jacques Derrida who in his *Specters of Marx* has secreted Shakespeare in such a solution and within the wider reaches of a 'new International', which in its less than tangible constituency would call us to reconcile our differences without uniformity:

> The 'New International' . . . is an untimely link, without status, with-
> out title, and without name, barely public even if it is not clandes-
> tine, without contract, 'out of joint', without coordination, without
> party, without country, without national community (International
> before, across, and beyond any national determination), without co-
> citizenship, without common belonging to a class.[38]

Derrida's sudden turn to Marx is characteristic in its unexpected-
ness, if by his own admission somewhat dated in its claim to
topicality. Yet as his argument develops, a degree of novelty is still
imparted by the form of the return – the remix of Marx and Shakespeare. The suspicion lingers that Derrida's invocation of no less
a spectre than Hamlet shelters a covert form of significance – and
that the unsettling discordance it is able to secure is at one with
its exclusivity.

Nowhere is 'culture's future heritage' more secure than in these
permutations of its present dislodgement in the here and now[39] –
yet only so, we might note, in its oppositional acceptance of a form
of defeat. The future/past can be retrieved but only as a spectre. This
'is' the promise, the limit of its possibility. That it will never arrive.
And just as Derrida's Shakespeare (though no doubt he would
answer Shakespeare is *plus d'un* – both more than one and no longer
one) offers an unsitable site from which to mediate the negotiation
between past and future, we might note that this is a form of exclusivity which is so valid in its lack of validity to the present that
it need not bother itself with questions of the depredation of culture
in its relation with commerce. But it offers instead another type of
plenty, as in moving between places, from its metropolitan centre
it confirms in its close-kept distance the spectral lure of corporate
transnationalism itself, in the very fullness of its present emptiness.

In forgoing the seduction of Derrida's future now, we need to
remark what might be at stake in Shakespeare's inclusion in this
longer-term empty time, this future heritage. And in remembering
the future in this form, we will need to recall in advance, that
wherever homogenous history continues it will never cease to be
written by the victors. Of the present, and in the future.

Afterthought: Shakespeare and the aesthetic

In their negotiation of post-Marxism via a tragic aesthetic, cultural materialism and deconstruction take different forms. Yet

whether the spectral symptomatises an historicist *dispositif* redolent of defeat or remarks philosophy at the limits of its disenchantment;[40] read either way, in its lack of direction, the current crossing
point locates a potentially dangerous lacuna. As a withering Shakespeare admits and dispels spectres it also configures a dissociation
of sensibility which a 'bad' ontological or humanist solution will
happily rectify.[41] So it is that, in either form, while we're busy
remembering and forgetting, tragic post-Marxism is in danger of
both occluding and making possible capital's move to the far right,
not to mention the nationalisms it spawns in the process.

In these circumstances it is not a question of choosing between
high and low culture, still less of collapsing their distinction or
dissolving their differences. Nor should it be a choice of dispens-
ing with English as a reductive idealism on the one hand or returning to formerly abandoned aesthetic verities on the other. The
challenge to criticism is not that Shakespeare is guarantor of conservative cultural values, although of course the signification of
'Shakespeare' continues to sustain this relation, but that, in the
process, Shakespeare has become 'alienated' from truth and moral-
ity. In their attempts to move beyond 'Eng. lit.', new historicists,
cultural materialists, feminists, queer theorists, acknowledge this
loss in different ways, but only still so far by failing to acknowledge the degree of their complicity in securing the institutional
separation of domains, which continues to guarantee its productive non-availability. On various levels, and in its different constituencies, it is becoming apparent that we have only succeeded
in breaking with metaphysics in forms which indirectly confirm its
continued claim upon us.

For Theodor Adorno, as Jay Bernstein reminds us, 'The division
of high and low art as a division, reveals the fate of particular and
universal in contemporary society.'[42] In this form at least Shakespeare also continues to suffer the fate of its exclusion, but in
doing so also runs the risk of being co-opted to reconcile itself
around the figure of its own refusal. Properly reconceived, an
aesthetical understanding of Shakespeare would be wary of such
an enchanted form of disenchantment and would clarify the necessity of continuing to think the unknowable within the constraints
of its conditioning. For it is in its admission of continued separation that Shakespearian division itself contains the seeds of its own
dissolution, or, as Bernstein puts it in another place, 'Hibernating

within aesthetic discourse is another discourse, another meta-physics, the very one we apparently need in order to cognise and transform the one we routinely inhabit.'[43] If we are to meet the claim of art we will need to acknowledge the absence of a truly political praxis in our current problematic. We will also need to resist the politics of style which is currently afforded by the supplement of anti- or indeed quasi-aestheticism.

Will Shakespeare continue to mark the separation of high and low culture even and especially amidst these strenuous attempts to deny the distinction? I think so. I hope so. For the moment, whether it reconfigures itself at the limit of philosophy or indeed as the exemplary text of philosophy's born-again new demise, Shakespeare, so often displaced as mere synecdoche for Englishness, might also return to help us think through the relationship between philosophy and nationalism. No doubt in its own form the permanent revolution in Shakespearian studies obliquely registers something of this potentiality, yet, read within these confines alone, the frenetic activity is perhaps less a mark of the complex evolution and self-conflictual morphology of institutional Englishness itself than the ongoing index of our failure to come to terms with the full extent of our direct implication in what so far, radical critics are in agreement, has been the continuing legacy of its domination. Yet in remarking our prevailing intellectual situation and its own inevitable implication in the process it would seek to overcome – the commodification of thought and the shortfall therein – a reconceived interrogation of the Shakespearian aesthetic might simultaneously locate a 'last hope for thought', not merely in facilitating the denial of a separation between 'high art' and commerce but by helping us to articulate our critique of its non-availability from within what's left of the divide itself.

In this sense alone Shakespeare's refusal to be redeemed in the here and now must be weighed with a refusal to forsake the promise that one day the future might be fulfilled, and that somehow it must be.

Notes

1 Theodor Adorno, 'On tradition', *Telos*, 94 (1993/4), pp. 75–82 (p. 78).
2 On the 'new international', of which more later, compare Jacques

Derrida, *Specters of Marx: The State of the Debt, the Work of Mourning, and the New International*, trans. Peggy Kamuf (London, Routledge, 1994). The need to secure an oppositional relation beyond 'Eng. lit.' is provocatively argued in Alan Sinfield's *Cultural Politics – Queer Reading* (London, Routledge, 1994), cf. esp. pp. 60–82.

3 See Gary Taylor, *Reinventing Shakespeare: A Cultural History from the Restoration to the Present* (New York, Weidenfeld and Nicolson, 1989; Oxford, Oxford University Press, 1991), pp. 298–372; and Terence Hawkes, *Meaning by Shakespeare* (London, Routledge, 1992), pp. 141–53.

4 It is Marshall Berman of course who provides the classic exposition of the subsumption of revolutionary thought within the process of modernisation in his *All that is Solid Melts into Air: The Experience of Modernity* (London, Verso, 1982), cf. esp. pp. 111–14.

5 See especially Aijaz Ahmad, *In Theory: Classes, Nations, Literatures* (London, Verso, 1992); also compare Saba Mahmood, 'Cultural studies and ethnic absolutism: comments on Stuart Hall's "culture, community, nation"', *Cultural Studies*, 10:1 (1996), pp. 1–11; and Kuan-Hsing Chen, 'Not yet the postcolonial era: the (super) nation-state and trans*nationalism* of cultural studies: response to Ang and Stratton', *Cultural Studies*, 10:1 (1996), pp. 37–70.

6 Sinfield, *Cultural Politics*, p. 31.

7 Graham Holderness, ed., *The Shakespeare Myth* (Manchester, Manchester University Press, 1988), p. xiv.

8 Jonathan Dollimore and Alan Sinfield, eds, *Political Shakespeare: New Essays in Cultural Materialism* (Manchester, Manchester University Press, 1985, 2nd. ed. 1994), p. viii.

9 *Ibid.*

10 Terence Hawkes, 'Lear's maps' in *Meaning by Shakespeare*, pp. 121–40 (pp. 133–4). Also compare *King Lear*, Writers and their Work series (Plymouth, Northcote House in association with the British Council, 1995), wherein relevant sections from the essay on *Lear* are also partially reincorporated.

11 Hawkes, 'Lear's maps', p. 123.

12 Again, Aijaz Ahmad effectively makes the point for us in his excellent *In Theory*, cf. esp. pp. 1–42. I draw on his analysis here and throughout this section of my argument

13 Holderness, *Shakespeare Myth*, p. xiv.

14 Amongst others Richard Levin's campaign was particularly strident. For an early taste of his vitriol compare 'The politics and poetics of bardicide', *PMLA*, 105 (1990), 491–509.

15 *The Times Higher Education Supplement* (24 January 1992).

16 A condition confirmed to some extent by the volume of that same name, compare Ivo Kamps, ed., *Shakespeare Left and Right* (London,

Routledge, 1991). Though I should note that it is *Shakespeare Left and Right*'s hard-won saving grace that it registers the danger of its own entrapment. Indeed, resisting the spurious options on offer, more than one contributor actually suggests silence as the best strategy, compare Sprinkler, p. 127; and Woodbridge, p. 292.

17 Benedict Anderson, *Imagined Communities* (London, Verso, 1991), pp. 35–6.

18 *The Guardian* (8 March 1995), p. 10.

19 *The Mail on Sunday* (5 March 1995).

20 *Ibid.*

21 *Ibid.*

22 *Ibid.*

23 I should note an indebtedness here to Simon Frith whose 'Literary studies as cultural studies – whose literature? whose culture?', *Critical Quarterly*, 34:1 (1992), offers several useful corrective distinctions concerning the shifting complex of relations between literature and national identity within a populist reconstruction of an English curriculum.

24 Michel Foucault, 'Of other spaces', *Diacritics*, 16 (1986), 22–7. I'm grateful here for Edward Soja's exposition of the ambivalent spatiality of heterotopias in his *Postmodern Geographies: The Reassertion of Space in Critical Social Theory* (London, Verso, 1989), pp. 16–21, cf. esp. pp. 17 and 18.

25 Hawkes, *Meaning by Shakespeare*, p. 134.

26 Derrida, *Specters of Marx*, p. 21.

27 R. A. Foakes, *Hamlet versus Lear: Cultural Politics and Shakespeare's Art* (Cambridge, Cambridge University Press, 1993), p. 6.

28 Foakes reminds us of the verdict of G. Wilson Knight, voice of patriotic 'lit. crit.', who even in peacetime regards Hamlet as 'undermining by his sickness "the health of the state"', *Hamlet versus Lear*, p. 34.

29 Hawkes, *Meaning by Shakespeare*, pp. 129–33.

30 As well as Jonathan Dollimore, *Radical Tragedy: Religion, Ideology and Power in the Drama of Shakespeare and His Contemporaries* (Brighton, Harvester, 1984), compare at same conjuncture Francis Barker, *The Tremulous Private Body: Essays on Subjection* (London, Methuen, 1984) and Catherine Belsey, *The Subject of Tragedy: Identity and Difference in Renaissance Drama* (London, Methuen, 1995).

31 Jonathan Dollimore, *Radical Tragedy: Religion, Ideology and Power in the Drama of Shakespeare and his Contemporaries* (Hemel Hempstead, Harvester Wheatsheaf, 2nd ed. 1989), pp. xi–xii.

32 Theodor Adorno, *Aesthetic Theory*, trans. C. Lenhardt (London, Routledge and Kegan Paul, 1982), p. 47.

33 This rhetoric of unsituated intervention is now of course all-ascendant within cultural studies more generally: for a representative sampling compare David Morley and Kevin Robins, *Spaces of Identity: Global*

Media, Electronic Landscapes and Cultural Boundaries (London, Routledge, 1995), pp. 1–2.

34 Compare Alan Sinfield, 'Heritage and the market, regulation and desublimation' in Dollimore and Sinfield, eds, Political Shakespeare: New Essays in Cultural Materialism, pp. 255–79 (p. 279). For an excellent critique of the affirmative strain in postmodernist cultural theory compare Jay Bernstein, 'Introduction' in The Culture Industry: Selected Essays on Mass Culture (London, Routledge, 1991).

35 Bernstein, 'Introduction', p. 22.

36 I borrow the notion of the 'unmixed' and some sense of its implication in negation within 'current intellectual politics' from Fredric Jameson's discussion of the same in 'Marx's purloined letter', New Left Review, 209 (1995), pp. 75–109, cf. esp. pp. 90–5. The dilemma of the potential entrapment for a criticism that considers itself an anti-hierarchical postmodernism is amply suggested by Jürgen Habermas's summarisation of the condition itself, as he observes that 'The new value placed on the transitory, the elusive and the ephemeral, the very celebration of dynamism, discloses a longing for an undefiled, immaculate and stable present' as cited in David Harvey's The Condition of Postmodernity: An Enquiry into the Origins of Cultural Change (Oxford, Basil Blackwell, 1989), p. 325. For a more detailed and in many ways exemplary critique of postmodernism as a form of historicism and the ramification of these concerns for a reconfiguration of tragedy and history compare Francis Barker's 'Nietzsche's cattle' in The Culture of Violence: Tragedy and History (Manchester, Manchester University Press, 1993), pp. 93–115.

37 Compare S. P. Mohanty, 'Us and them: On the philosophical bases of political criticism', Yale Journal of Criticism, 2:2 (1989), pp. 1–31, for a lengthier and more illuminating interrogation of the collusion.

38 Derrida, Specters of Marx, p. 85.

39 I owe the phrase to Donald Hedrick who used it to situate a seminar on 'Shakespeare and modern commercial culture, or learning from LA' at the Sixth World Shakespeare Congress 'Shakespeare and the Twentieth Century', 7–14 April 1996, Los Angeles, where a version of this section of the paper was offered in a truncated form.

40 To borrow the expression from the title of Peter Dews, The Limits of Disenchantment: Essays on Contemporary European Philosophy (London, Verso, 1995).

41 Again compare Jameson in 'Marx's purloined letter' on this point.

42 Bernstein, 'Introduction', p. 6.

43 J. M. Bernstein, The Fate of Art: Aesthetic Alienation from Kant to Derrida and Adorno (Oxford, Blackwell, 1992), p. 9. I am indebted here and above for his incisive elucidation of the fuller implications of aesthetic alienation and the post-aesthetic condition.

11

✠

Elizabethan world pictures

✠

Curtis Breight

Sitting on a bullet,
Thinking of power,
Every hour.
Being in space,
Controlling the world,
With a different face.
Paris, New York, Moscow, Tokyo.

(Hans in My Own Private Idaho)

You noble diggers all stand up now
you noble diggers all stand up now
the wast land to maintaine seeing Cavaleirs by name
your digging does disdaine and persons all defame
   Stand up now stand up now
Your houses they pull down: stand up now, stand up now
your houses they etc.
your houses they pull down to fright poore men in town
but the Gentry must come down, and the poor shall wear the Crown.
   Stand up now diggers all.

(Anonymous, 'The Digger's Song')[1]

All men have stood for freedom . . . and those of the richer sort of
you that see it are ashamed and afraid to own it, because it comes
clothed in a clownish garment. . . . Freedom is the man that will turn
the world upside down, therefore no wonder he hath enemies. . . . True
freedom lies in the community in spirit and community in the earthly

treasury, and this is Christ the true manchild spread abroad in the
creation, restoring all things unto himself.

(Gerrard Winstanley, 1649)[2]

'The onely Shake-scene in a countrey' (Robert Greene, 1592)[3]

In 1989, in *The Price of Empire*, the late and former United States
Senator J. William Fulbright wrote that America's 'militarised
economy' is a 'politically forbidden topic'.[4] I begin this chapter by
citing Fulbright because one could argue that American (re)cannon-
isation in the 1980s, especially construction of President Ronald
Reagan's six-hundred-ship navy followed by President George Bush's
pronouncement of a 'New World Order',[5] goes hand in hand with
(re)canonisation on film of the West's most famous author, William Shakespeare. Beginning around the time of Kenneth Branagh's
Henry V, filmed in 1988 probably as some kind of tribute to the
four hundredth anniversary of England's engagement with the Spanish Armada,[6] and continuing in the 1990s often fragmentarily in
movies such as *Moon 44* (1990), *The Russia House* (1990),[7] *Antonia
& Jane* (1991), *Star Trek VI: The Undiscovered Country* (1991),
Hard-boiled (1992), *Last Action Hero* (1993), *Tombstone* (1993),
Interview with the Vampire (1994), *The Lion King* (1994), *The
Madness of King George* (1994) and *Renaissance Man* (1994),
Shakespeare has returned to the big screen with a vengeance. Only
a few years earlier Shakespeare had been rendered an icon of high
British culture in the sometimes boring BBC version of *The Complete Works*, too oft featuring frozen actors uttering immortal verse
shot from about two camera angles.[8] But now popular audiences
are having Shakespearian greatness globally thrust upon 'em in
lively films, clever adaptations and subtle allusions.[9] There is, of
course, a long and indeed unbroken history of Shakespeare on film
– especially on silent film[10] – but what makes the current period
so interesting is the sheer variety of cinematic representations: for
example, a Japanese version of *King Lear* (Akira Kurosawa's *Ran*,
1985), a Finnish parody of *Hamlet* (Aki Kaurismaki's *Hamlet
Goes Business*, 1987), Jean-Luc Godard's *King Lear* (1987), Franco
Zeffirelli's *Hamlet* (1990),[11] a Mafia version of *Macbeth* (*Men of
Respect*, 1991) recalling an earlier gangster version (*Joe Macbeth*,
1955), Peter Greenaway's mind-bending adaptation of *The Tempest*

(*Prospero's Books*, 1991), Branagh's *Much Ado About Nothing* (1993)[12] and the even more recent *Othello* and *Richard III*.

One kind of critical response to this resurgence would be to call it a renewed form of cultural imperialism, an attempt by Anglo-America to (re)impose its stories on a world long accustomed to imperial domination and practices of *realpolitik*; moreover, to retell those stories at a time when various forms of imperialism are being scrutinised anew.[13] Such a response might focus on the largely American (Hollywood) and British origin of Shakespeare films. But to respond thus, to locate only a 'British' Shakespeare or what Michael Bristol calls 'America's Shakespeare',[14] would be to neglect the multi-national quality of the resurgence. As film becomes increasingly international on the cusp of vast changes in whatever we call the new information industries *in toto* (including but not limited to satellites, telecommunications, film, video, music, computers, CD ROMs, books, animation etc.), Shakespeare is being used as both a means of global communication and a touchstone for struggle within tumultuous societies such as the USA. The fact that US and British film industries have recently reinvigorated popular Shakespeare perhaps indicates a neo-conservative impulse to recanonise the Bard for a still relatively democratic educational system – to the exclusion of alternative 'Anglo' voices. But on the other hand, the national and international flavour of the last decade's 'Shake-cinema' (adapted from Robert Greene), as well as the fact that even Hollywood displays multiple attitudes to Shakespearian raw materials, might indicate that Shakespeare is not just some ideological tool by which a single dominant group reproduces its own cultural and economic hegemony. *Interview with the Vampire*, for instance, features Tom Cruise quoting part of Othello's speech before the murder of Desdemona, uttered as he drains the blood of a young black woman. This moment ironically reverses the play's racial roles in a socio-political environment revealing total institutional exploitation of Africans. Since the time period for most of the film bridges the turn-of-the-nineteenth-century Atlantic world, the vampire's 'murder' of a poor black girl pales in comparison to an international slave trade generating atrocious casualties.[15]

Across the Pacific, John Woo's Hong Kong 'action' movie *Hardboiled* is even more suggestive in its fragmentary use of Shakespeare.[16] An early sequence linking Shakespeare and weaponry affirms – all the more powerfully given the long-standing struggle between China and the British Empire, the history of Hong Kong and the realities of 1997 – that Britain's national poet and the 'illegal' arms trade are somehow inseparable. Alan, working for the police under deep cover as a Triad hitman, goes to the public library to do a job on an arms dealer named Jimmy. Accompanied by a great jazz soundtrack, he walks casually through the stacks until he reaches section 400, 'Literature', where he selects the middle volume of a three-volume set. He joins Jimmy at his table, opens the volume which conceals a gun with silencer, asks him why he betrayed Uncle Hoy, and then shoots him in the forehead. When the detective hero Tequila later locates the volume replaced by Alan after the hit, he is amused that its title is *Complete Works of Shakespeare*. At the garden of his estate, dotted with Chinese as well as Western classical statues, Uncle Hoy congratulates Alan by saying: 'Smart work you did in the library'. Later Alan 'betrays' Uncle Hoy in a scene reminiscent of Brutus's betrayal of Julius Caesar. Alan feigns being seduced by the cash offer of Johnny, a rival gangster who runs a worldwide arms operation and does business in a room featuring a huge imitation mural, a Renaissance painting of the Three Graces. This gangster's motto is – 'where there's war there's Johnny. Most things will go in and out of style. That is, except war, my friend.' When Tequila realises that Alan is working undercover, he screams at his boss: 'You better tell us which are the cops and which are the thieves. And why you want us to kill each other.' Alan is so befuddled that he forgets his own birthday, explaining – 'so busy being a gangster, I don't know which me is real'. The story is so like an Elizabethan revenge tragedy that Tequila says 'woe betide' anyone who tries to stop him from getting Johnny, whom Tequila holds responsible for the death of his partner in the opening sequence. Woo's strategy of deploying the *Complete Works* handgun, thematic reference to *Julius Caesar*, and 'Elizabethan' language in a contemporary 'colonial' yet potent city state surrounded by powerful land and naval forces of numerous countries captures the continuous violence of imperial history and culture. Since Johnny is very 'Anglo' in appearance, we are encouraged to think that his global business is linked to the 'legal' trade in weaponry recently dominated by the USA (in 1995 France), accompanied by Britain and now many other countries (including China) as major arms manufacturers.

Woo puts the handgun inside the *Complete Works* because in the nineteenth century, at least, the British Empire used lots of military hardware in opium wars against China;[17] and beginning around the same time, according to Leela Gandhi relying on Gauri Viswanathan, the worship of Shakespeare, or 'bardolatry', was linked to 'empire building and curricular strategies in colonial and "decolonised" India'.[18] Woo highlights divided loyalties, betrayals, friendships and unbridled killing in a 'gansterised' world whose only shared code, except for the most ruthless, is to spare women and children. Given imperial legacies we cannot help but be reminded that the current and massive global small arms trade – 'legal', 'illegal', who cares? – is destroying entire economies while enriching only a few. For Woo, weaponry and culture are co-extensive. We might adapt Caliban's line from one of Shakespeare's colonial plays for this movie: 'You taught me weapons, and my profit on't / Is I know how to shoot.'[19]

In brief, an already quasi-globalised Shakespeare of the nineteenth century has become a different kind of international phenomenon through twentieth-century cinema – and a phenomenon generating large amounts of economic as well as cultural capital. *The Lion King* alone grossed hundreds of millions of dollars. Although still dominated by Hollywood and England, Shakespeare's nigh universality in the Anglophone world, availability in multimedia and lack of copyright make 'him' a fit subject for global film. Moreover, Shakespeare's globalisation of his own drama, extending a tradition established in the brief yet brilliant career of his contemporary Christopher Marlowe, makes him additionally attractive to an International Shakespeare Industry covering books, films, videos, audiotapes and numerous educational tools and games. The economic impact of the Shakespeare-on-film resurgence is considerable, so consequently there must be ideological and political issues at stake. The resurgence coincides, for better or worse, with a call mostly by right-wingers such as Pat Buchanan for cultural wars in the USA.[20] It is thus important for critics to acknowledge the revival of Shakespeare on film and try to account for what's going on in the cultural wars. For regardless of one's critical and/or political persuasion(s), the combination of diverse cultural production and right-wing declaration of cultural wars – including recent statements by US Republicans such as Bill Bennett and Senator Bob Dole attacking Time Warner in particular and

Hollywood in general – forces any teacher/scholar and critic committed to Shakespeare on film to take some position on the complex uses of cinema.

For example, in 1989 and 1990 Warner Brothers produced *Lethal Weapon II* and *Hamlet*, both starring Mel Gibson. A few critics have noted similarities between the 'crazy' gun-toting Detective Martin Riggs and the wild-eyed sword-wielding Hamlet played by Gibson. But no one (so far as I know) has written that *Lethal Weapon II* includes other allusions to *Hamlet* and sends a distinct political message. Riggs is an avenging black-suited Hamlet against a corrupt 'court' (or government) symbolised by the Claudius-like South African consul (Arjen Rudd). Riggs dates the Ophelia-like Rika Van Den Haas, secretary to the consul, who dies by drowning. Riggs is on the verge of death after a knife fight at the conclusion, cradled by Horatio-like Danny Glover (Detective Murtaugh) on a stage-like, shipboard platform. A political message involving race relations and international criminality under the guise of diplomatic immunity is sent to a South Africa that has rapidly evolved between 1989 and 1995. Likewise, in *The Lion King* the message about Africa, partially symbolised by the ghostly, Old-Hamlet-style return of the murdered King Mufasa, involves a call for new leadership and responsibility in a long-ravaged land. As for *Tombstone*, references to the 'Faust' story (Marlowe, Goethe, the whole legend) and to Shakespeare's *Henry V* – framing a bloody struggle between the Earps/Doc Holliday and the 'Cowboys' watched by silent onlookers including Chinese immigrants – suggest any number of contemporary political messages: one plausible interpretation is that the 'West' of the film is today's West (the Pacific Rim), and that a battle between 'Western' groups (one wanting to make money peacefully, the other to exert control through violence) is occurring; given complex US/Asian histories throughout the twentieth century and earlier, the film may be speaking allegorically via silent Chinese onlookers matched by equally quiet American flags hanging in the background of numerous frames.[21]

Shakespeare on film has thus become not one but many different discourses serving distinct interests. While a radical director such as Derek Jarman entered one discourse precisely by shifting much energy from screening Shakespeare (for example, *The Tempest*, 1979) to adapting Marlowe's *Edward II* (1992) for explicit contemporary gay concerns, an equally radical director such as Gus Van Sant turns Shakespeare's *Henriad* upside down in *My Own Private Idaho* (1991; hereafter *Idaho*).[22] Jarman and Van Sant present a cinematic, political and ideological challenge to directors such as Branagh and Zeffirelli, whose 1989 and 1990 films are relatively straight narratives. Branagh and Zeffirelli focus on the seeming dilemmas of central characters while mostly erasing Shakespeare's empathy for English and other people during Elizabethan wartime, symbolised by the ubiquitous yet diverse commoners of the *Henriad* and *Hamlet* (for example, in the *Henriad*: gardeners, all the inhabitants of the so-called 'tavern world', ostlers and carriers, Falstaff's draftees, all other common soldiers who die or get maimed, women driven to the poor house and/or prostitution, boys killed in battle; and, for example, in *Hamlet*: royal guards loyal to Hamlet not Claudius, Horatio, Young Fortinbras's adventurous soldiers, Rosencrantz and Guildenstern, travelling players boldly willing to alter their performance for Hamlet despite a dangerous atmosphere, Fortinbras's soldiers marching on Poland, who probably reappear as the Danish commoners backing Laertes's near palace coup in the following scene, 'Seafaring men', clowns, court onlookers who do nothing to prevent the wounded and dying Hamlet from killing Claudius). Jarman and Van Sant keep faith with the spirit of Renaissance drama by including numerous scenes of poor or vulnerable people in revolt against the 'norms' of contemporary society.[23]

Many contemporary Shakespeare films deserve extensive analysis, but I would like to focus on *Idaho* as an unusually creative instance of using Shakespeare to construct a modern political film that simultaneously illuminates the heart of the Shakespearian text. *Idaho* is *not* a postmodern fragmentation but a coherent interpretation of Shakespeare's *Henriad* relevant to a global audience. Although *Idaho* cannot be categorised – even the director asserts that the script was cobbled together from 'three different screenplays' including a 'modernised version of *Henry IV*', and thus 'it's like being in a plane where there are six different channels' – nevertheless Van Sant provides one key to interpretation: 'it's much better if you see it more than once. There are all sorts of things that become apparent on multiple viewings – I still see stuff that I didn't know was there: serendipitous things that are there for a purpose, that are put in, ultimately, by my subconscious.'[24] I call

Idaho an 'interpretation' of the *Henriad* because it reverses what are traditionally conceived as Shakespeare's main and sub-plots (high political world versus tavern world). As David Kastan affirms, the 'comic plot' of *1 Henry IV* 'voices what the unitary state would repress, indeed exactly what the unitary plot would repress'. Kastan shows that the supposed sub-plot could share top billing with the supposed main plot from the play's inception, citing the title page of the 1598 quarto as well as seventeenth-century references to the play as *'Falstaff'*.[25] Van Sant goes one better than this, privileging the lower-class world to reveal its inhabitants as social victims of institutional power. In this respect he captures what mainstream criticism of the *Henriad* tends to suppress – Shakespeare's increasing concern with human casualties of élite struggle and military violence. For between *Richard II*, which has almost no concern for the people, and *Henry V*, which gives face and voice to both lower- and middle-class casualties of militarism evoking relentless Elizabethan wars from 1585 to 1604, Shakespeare compiles a litany of victims: men, women and children.

Van Sant's interpretation is brilliant because it not only valorises the victims of a given social order (contemporary America) but also suggests how this order is the end-product of imperial history. The film speaks globally and historically because it connects American imperial power to the early modern dawn of European imperialism, the Renaissance, which in turn was ideologically based upon the Roman Empire. As Edward Said claims about American criticism in *Culture and Imperialism*,

> to read most cultural deconstructionists, or Marxists, or new historicists is to read writers whose political horizon, whose historical location is within a society and culture deeply enmeshed in imperial domination. Yet little notice is taken of this horizon, few acknowledgements of the setting are advanced, little realisation of the imperial closure itself is allowed for.[26]

Consequently a film such as *Idaho* cannot be seen in its political guise because it is easier (and safer) to see it as merely a personal quest by a disenfranchised character.[27] To understand the politics of *Idaho*, and also to grasp this film as a radical reconfiguration of how it is possible to screen Shakespeare today, we can begin by juxtaposing its subtle anti-imperialism to an amazing moment in Stanley Kubrick's *Spartacus* (1960). Immediately after a homoerotic

scene between Laurence Olivier's Crassus and Tony Curtis's
Antoninus, cut in the film's first release and put back only in 'The
Restoration' (1990), Crassus utters a speech on the Roman army
(six cohorts of the Roman garrison) as it marches against rebel
slaves on Mount Vesuvius:

> Antoninus, look, across the river. There is something you must see.
> There boy, is Rome. The might, the majesty, the terror of Rome.
> There is the power that bestrides the known world like a colossus.
> No man can withstand Rome. No nation can withstand her. How
> much less a boy. Hm? There's only one way to deal with Rome,
> Antoninus. You must serve her. You must abase yourself before her.
> You must grovel at her feet. You must love her. Isn't that so
> Antoninus? Antoninus! Antoninus!

Meanwhile Antoninus has fled to join the slave revolt. *Spartacus*
– produced between two bloody Asian wars rooted in the imperial
legacy – bears indirect witness to deep cultural anxieties in the
USA. Crassus's speech bodies forth the Roman Empire through a
line adapted from *Julius Caesar*, embodying empire through militarism.[28] In *Spartacus* the actors playing Romans are British and
the slaves are Americans. The film thus displays a kind of schizophrenia, failing to reconcile contradictions between an America
conceived as revolutionary and a contemporary America which
had inherited much of the British Empire. Despite outgoing President Eisenhower's 1961 warning about the unwarranted influence
of a newly constructed 'military-industrial complex', *Spartacus* is
unable clearly to speak the problems of contemporary empire.[29]
Idaho, however, uses a converse strategy: whereas *Spartacus* hides
Shakespeare under nascent imperial militarism, *Idaho* slyly points
to imperial decline under a modern adaptation of Shakespeare's
Henriad – itself a kind of people's epic showing many casualties
of medieval and contemporary, domestic and foreign war. Van
Sant's imperial theme becomes apparent by gradual accretion of
images, allusions, jokes and songs – a strategy akin to carnivalesque
practices in Shakespeare's tavern world, including robbery, practical jokes, songs, drinking and entertainments mocking the king.
   Idaho battles Branagh's *Henry V* in the cinema wars. Recent
critics (including myself) have argued that *Henry V* is politically
reactionary.[30] Our collective position is all the more validated by
the fact that Branagh's film is lionised by right-wing Shakespearians

such as Kenneth Adelman, 'Reagan's Missile Man', who teaches
'Popular Shakespeare' at Georgetown University while holding a
pointer with a hand giving the finger: 'he loved' *Henry V*, 'especially the movie's "enticing" depiction of the Battle of Agincourt
that made him sorry he wasn't there'.[31] The institutionalisation of
Branagh in today's (Popular) Shakespeare on film canon, at least
in the USA, is demonstrated by Mobil Corporation's sponsorship
of a 'Masterpiece Theatre' screening of the film on American television on 26 April 1992, about two years after the film was
released on video. The screening was supported by a 'Teacher's
Guide' mailed and addressed to the 'English Department Head'
in US secondary schools; its first page features a letter from Allen
E. Murray, the 'Chairman of the Board, President, and Chief Executive Officer' of Mobil Corporation.[32] Murray mentions 'Henry's
struggle in handling the reins of leadership', thereby ushering secondary school teachers and their students into a view of the play
stressing royal responsibility. Given Hal's threats of execution by
hanging against thieves and even his own companions in *1 Henry
IV*,[33] as well as the enactment of Bardolph's hanging in Branagh's
film, it is somewhat ironic that the address of Mobil Corporation
is 'Gallows Road'.

The old main drag

Idaho interprets the *Henriad* as a timeless story about dispossessed people. Mike as Poins, Scott as Hal, Bob as Falstaff are just
the main actors in this larger story. *Idaho* excoriates certain key
institutions and ideologies underlying Western society (such as the
nuclear family) while celebrating victims who survive and even
love one another under oppressive structures. The most obvious
target of critique is contemporary America on the whole, ironically blasted by multiple repeats of 'America, the Beautiful' at key
moments in the film, played slowly and fragmentarily. But an
America in which wealthy suburbanites use poor youngsters for
sex (and sometimes emotional comfort) is not the sole target.
When Mike first appears on the road in Idaho at the film's outset,
wearing a gas-station attendant's shirt with the name 'Bob' sewn
on the front (which thus links him with the Falstaff character who
will shortly appear, significantly 'back from Boise', Idaho), we
learn that the road is unique and has a 'fucked-up face'. But it is

also a road that Mike has been on before: 'I always know where I am by the way the road looks. Like I just know that I've been here before, I just know that I've been stuck here, like this one fucking time before, you know that, yeah.' Mike's first attack of narcolepsy – defined for us in a dictionary in the film's initial frame, and perhaps emblematic for an entire generation rendered somnolent – occurs on this road.[34] The road is both personal and political, or rather a road in which the personal and political necessarily intertwine. Mike's first narcoleptic 'dream' includes an image of himself as an innocent adolescent sleeping in his imaginary Mother's lap, wearing what looks like the 'Stars and Stripes' of the US flag – minus the stars. The image is repeated a few frames later on a street corner in Seattle, when Mike almost lapses into another fit at the sight of a woman who reminds him of Mom. These opening frames, combined with the first complete song on American ranch life ('Cattle Call'), locate the film specifically. But once the location seems to be fixed, it begins to be unfixed by multiple references to different nationalities and periods of history.

Idaho takes us back in history to reveal how we got here, how we're stuck on this road. America the Beautiful is gradually exposed as a decaying American Empire, built on the same old grim story of exploitative class relations and destruction of native cultures. The film often seems merely a bewildering montage, but the imperial theme links the personal to the political: Mike's frequent narcoleptic fits are not simply a personal struggle to remember his own Mother but a kind of 'political unconscious', a need for the Mother of all Empires to give an accounting for the damage done to her children.[35] This is why Mike seeks Mom first in the American heartland (Idaho) and later in Rome – the cradle of Western imperialism – but discovers only portraits of presumably shattered families on the walls of his father/brother's trailer, and Roman street boys identical to those he left behind in the Pacific Northwest. It is also why numerous characters (but especially Mike) are 'Jesus' figures, crucified by history in a steady stream of religious images.[36] The Mother who cradles a partially flag-draped Mike in two early frames is matched by Scott cradling Mike on arrival in Portland, imitating Michelangelo's *Pietà* under a statue of a Native American riding a large buck: the caption below reads 'The Coming of the White Man'. Allusions to and inclusion of Native

Americans recur in this film because they were the first victims of
European imperialism in the Western hemisphere. Since Scott, even
more acutely than Shakespeare's Prince Hal, knows better – seeing
through the hypocrisy of his father and the social relations of the
well-to-do – his 'mothering' is no better than that of Mike's Mom.[37]
Like Hal, Scott announces that he is calculating a change, a betrayal of friends such as Mike who believes he will 'fall back when
Scott inherits his money':[38] 'When I turn twenty-one, I don't want
any more of this life. My mother and father will be surprised at
the incredible change. It will impress them more when such a fuck
up like me turns good, than if I had been a good son all along.'
Earlier Scott told Mike: 'I love Bob more than my father. I'd say
I love Bob more than my mother, and my father.' But Scott himself is already a 'mother' equivalent to the exploitative political
'mother'.

Some reviewers mistakenly view the Shakespearian subtext as
merely part of *Idaho*, and solely comprised of *1 Henry IV*. Lyons
claims that the 'whole halfway house' of *1 Henry IV* 'is shaky;
better for Van Sant to have filmed the Shakespeare (with actors
who could speak it) or reimagined the entire thing'.[39] Such reviewers miss the film's use of the entire *Henriad* and fail to see that a
focus on *1 Henry IV* can divert even the diligent viewer from the
extensive yet sly treatment of Shakespeare and Renaissance culture. The 'Renaissance' scenes begin when Mike is picked up by
Alena and taken to an upper(-middle)-class neighbourhood. He
enters her house, strolling past a stained glass image of Madonna
and Christ Child into a wood-panelled living room evoking the
riches of Renaissance aristocratic domesticity.[40] First Mike sits in
front of latticed bookshelves, and then peers out of a Tudor-style
latticed window from a bedroom. Here, while trying to embrace
Alena, he succumbs to a narcoleptic fit that 'really scared the shit
out of that lady', so fellow hustlers Gary and Scott dump Mike
outside. They initially drop him at the base of a tree with a mock-
Tudor house in the background, an image shown more clearly
when Scott enters a waiting taxi. But meanwhile Scott drags Mike
across the street into another yard and delivers a Renaissance-style
speech. While a vicious domestic fight occurs behind the thinly
veiled curtains of another bourgeois house, Scott tells us that he
'grew up in a neighbourhood like this'. He refers bitterly to his
'dad', whom we later learn is local politician Jack Favor, Mayor

of Portland: 'he has more fucking righteous gall than all the property and people he lords over, and those he also created, like me his son.' Scott and Mike travel to Portland so that Scott can confront his two fathers, Bob and Jack. Scott's search for his 'true father' mirrors Mike's search for the personal and political Mother.

The 'Renaissance' is thus established well before the supposed Shakespearian 'halfway house', both visually and verbally, yet it is a Renaissance tied directly to the USA. When Mike explores Alena's bedroom, 'Home on the Range' hums in the background as though emanating from a charmbox that is winding down (perhaps in Mike's brain). When Scott delivers his big speech over Mike's prostrate body 'America, the Beautiful' plays distinctly in the background. Alena and Scott's dad seem to represent modern ladies and lords of imperial America. Ironically, the next scene occurs at 'VIDEO FOLLIES', an adult store featuring '1200 ADULT VIDEOS RENT & SALES MAGS. AND NOVELTIES 25c VIDEO BOOTHS'. The store is framed between two venues of presumably temporary accommodation, since three street boys hover outside in the cold: 'Hotel Gatewood' and 'St. Regis Hotel' evoke, by their very names, both American and British culture. The 'talking magazine' sequence that follows is perhaps the most striking moment in the film, but it is preceded by crucial frames that are easy to miss at first view. As the camera tracks across gay magazines we briefly glimpse the 'Fall' edition of '*Torso*' with two males on the cover, a long-haired teenage boy being caressed from behind by a slightly older male. The teenager, whom we shortly come to know as 'Digger', is wearing what appears to be a Renaissance hat and holding a golden wine goblet in his left hand and an old ornamental sword in his right. The captions on the cover mock Shakespearian titles: 'KING LEER' is most prominent, with 'Two Gentlemen of Pomona' (a suburb of Los Angeles) and 'Pleasure for Pleasure' below it.[41] Slantwise across Digger's mid-section is 'Julio and Ron Dewet'. The Renaissance, Shakespeare and modern America are thus fused together. This sequence, not the artificially cordoned off *Henry IV* scenes, is the first Shakespearian moment, and it is used to help establish imperial and sexual connections across two millennia. Scott's magazine, '*Male Call*', mockingly says 'Homo on the Range' (also 'Ready to Ride' and 'Cowboys & Indians All Tied Up', the latter announced on the cover of '*Honcho*' magazine as well). '*G-String*' features Mike in a pose evoking the crucifixion,[42] captioned by 'Pillars of the Roman Empire', 'Go Down on History', and 'Hard Evidence'. Near the end of the sequence six magazines are framed together, with Digger's '*Torso*' and Mike's '*G-String*' above and flanking Scott's '*Male Call*'. This single frame – static yet speaking, past yet present – unites Rome, Renaissance England and modern America in a bizarre politico-sexual triad.[43]

Since ensuing frames show Mike waking up in the rich neighbourhood it seems worth asking if he dreamed the magazine sequence. If so, such a dream is all the more 'real' because it is the fantasy/nightmare of imperial history, the road we've been on before. The magazines set us up for an even deeper plunge into the Portland underworld. After Scott and Mike discuss their hopes of seeing Bob, two street boys give first-'date' narratives in documentary style. During his narration Digger wears a British flag T-shirt appropriately linking him to the Renaissance images and Shakespearian mock titles of his magazine cover. Carl relates how his 'buddy Scott' had betrayed him, running off with the money from a john while he had to 'do the (unwanted) date'. A brief sequence in between the two narratives shows Scott comforting a distraught girl, framed with a wall clock above their heads featuring an 'RC' or Royal Crown (Cola) advertisement. The 'buddy Scott' seems to be the film's Scott, already having abandoned a poor pal to be 'screwed' well before his ultimate betrayal of his companions. The magazine sequence and first-date narratives are linked scenes: the sequence displays an aesthetics of homoeroticism bearing little relation to the reality of sexual power and terror for teenage street boys disclosed in the narratives. Moreover, the following movement into the obvious Shakespearian episodes suggests that a traditional view of the *Henriad* stressing the 'comic' life of the tavern world obscures the equally menacing forms of power and terror exercised by Prince Hal and Falstaff in *1 Henry IV*.

Thus when Bob and Budd (a kind of Pistol character) show up the next morning quoting Shakespeare (for the first time in the film) the camera looks straight down at them from the roof of a presumably derelict building, and captures them walking amidst thousands of yellow leaves (American 'Fall').[44] Appropriately, Budd keeps repeating a line adapted from the decrepit Justice Shallow in *2 Henry IV* – 'Jesus, the things we've seen' ('Jesu, Jesu, the mad days that I have spent!'; 'Jesus, the days that we have seen').[45] The 'things' (not 'days') they've seen are memorable because shocking.

Bob retorts – 'We have heard the chimes at midnight' (III.ii.209) – perhaps a socio-political *consummatum est*.[46] It is less interesting to analyse the whole Shakespearian 'halfway house' than to notice how mere moments problematise the 'Education of the Prince' interpretation enshrined in traditional criticism. When Scott gives his 'fuck up' speech, Bob listens carefully and snorts: 'Huh, you'll become a headroller, a hatchetman for your old man.' Scott replies: 'No. You will be the hatchetman, Bob. That will be your job. And so there will rarely be a job hatcheted. It will all be just one endless party, won't it?' Van Sant thus captures a key issue from *1 Henry IV*: Prince Hal is just as adept as his father, King Henry IV, in converting followers into henchmen. Just as Henry IV made the Percy clan into henchmen facilitating his seizure of the crown in *Richard II* – even Hotspur views his Percy kinsmen as 'the agents, or base second means, / The cords, the ladder, or the hangman rather' (*1 Henry IV*, I.iii.163–4) – so too does Hal symbolically make Falstaff a 'hangman' (I.ii.56–65). By giving Falstaff a military command later in *1 Henry IV* Hal literalises the symbol, enabling the indebted Falstaff to exploit his royal commission to draft men for the wars: 'A mad fellow met me on the way, and told me I had unloaded all the gibbets and pressed the dead bodies' (IV.ii.36–8). Falstaff received some £300 from the King's Exchequer to press able soldiers, but instead he drafted petit bourgeois 'toasts-and-butter' who 'bought out their services' by bribing Falstaff to release them (20–2). And so now his 150 troops consist of 'discarded unjust servingmen, younger sons to younger brothers, revolted tapsters, and ostlers trade-fallen . . . the most of them out of prison' (27–9; 41–2). Later Falstaff leads these 'scarecrows' (38) to the slaughter in a battle in which 'not three' survive (V.iii.36–8). He does this in order to pocket the men's pay, reflecting familiar complaints about Elizabethan captains.[47] Commenting on the murderous disorders of Elizabethan wars repeatedly evoked in the *Henriad*, in which at least a hundred thousand poor men were drafted and then frequently sacrificed by their own impecunious and greedy commanders, even an apologist for the Elizabethan hierarchy wrote: 'In these disorders it is not fit, that others should be imployed in warres, then such as now are. which some call pressed men, for that they go as willingly to service, as to hanging or pressing.'[48] The economic dislocation of Falstaff's draftees helps to explain why Mike wears the gas-station attendant's shirt naming him 'Bob' at the opening; finding 'linen enough on every hedge' (the presumably stolen shirt; IV.ii.48), Mike 'enlists' under 'Bob', joining a legion of contemporary American (and global) youth – the homeless, unemployed, underemployed – vulnerable to economic 'restructuring'. When Mike enlists under Bob he also enlists under Scott, voyaging abroad (as in *Henry V*) yet coming up empty-handed while the mayor's son returns home grasping his new bride and his new inheritance (compare *Henry V*).

But all is not horrible in Van Sant's lower-class world. In fact, this world is valorised. The derelict hotel where the group gathers, run by Jane Lightwork, is juxtaposed to Alena's sanitary neighbourhood. The warm atmosphere of Welles's festive tavern world in *Chimes at Midnight* is harnessed for these scenes. As in Welles, there are 'normal' dogs in the derelict hotel, anticipating the campfire conversation between Scott and Mike over the issue of 'normal' dogs and dads. The hotel offers family, unlike the veiled violence of bourgeois suburbia. Here is affection, drinking (of 'Falstaff' beer), reefer, laughter and dancing in shared community. The 'criminals' dance in harmony like the Three Graces after they agree on the robbery plot. When Scott and Mike rob the other thieves they use what appear to be 'Easton' aluminium baseball bats, an expensive symbol of suburban athletic boyhood and American 'Little League' baseball. The effect is bittersweet. Scott says to Bob, 'there's no reason to know the time, for we are timeless', and we grasp the paradoxical misery and joy of their situation. Scott calls Bob 'Santa Claus' because this generous magical figure arrives in the winter of our discontent.

After the robbery Mayor Favor wheels into his office to the tune of 'America, the Beautiful' (again), asking about and commenting on his son in lines drawn from *Richard II* (see Welles's similar sequence).[49] Like Alena's house, the office is richly wood-panelled. A picture of a much younger Jack Favor on a mantel is flanked by two golden statuettes of armed medieval knights, and one of the mayor's plaques is in the form of a military shield traditionally used for coats of arms.[50] The cut to Scott and Mike on a motorcycle is interrupted by Scott's question: 'Hey Mikey, how long have I been here on the streets, on this crusade?' They take off into traffic while the camera pans from one side of the street to the other in a key sequence. On the left side is an American flag hanging limply on an unknown building designated only in bold letters 'IMPERIAL', and as the camera pans right we see two news-paper boxes, one the now ubiquitous box containing the national conservative paper spawned in the 1980s, *USA TODAY*. Shake-speare's Henry IV frequently and publicly calls for a pious crusade from the end of *Richard II* almost to the point of death in *2 Henry IV*, yet expires in a room ironically called 'Jerusalem'. But in private, on his deathbed, Henry informs Hal that his manoeuvres were designed to 'cut off' his previous henchmen, and that he 'had a purpose now / To lead out many to the Holy Land, / Lest rest and lying still might make them look / Too near unto my state' (IV.v.209–12). Henry's 'realpolitikal' advice to the prince is thus 'to busy giddy minds / With foreign quarrels, that action hence borne out / May waste the memory of the former days' (214–16). *Idaho* was produced at the same historical juncture as the United States and Britain led their 1990/1 crusade to the Middle East, reinforc-ing boundaries imposed mostly by Britain and France earlier this century. Thus again, as in the magazine sequence, fragments of multiple histories are fused to reaffirm imperial realities.

The casualties of contemporary institutional exploitation are not just the youngsters of the derelict hotel. *Idaho* constantly jux-taposes images of nature (a rabbit, salmon swimming upstream) against artificial representations (the painting of rabbits or hares in Alena's living room, the metal fish on a mantel in her bedroom, the fish on the wall of Hans's hotel room at 'The Family Tree'). When Scott confronts his father at the Mayor's office (see *1 Henry IV*, III.ii) Jack Favor criticises him while 'America, the Beautiful' plays yet again in the background:

> I don't know whether it is God trying to get back at me for some-thing I have done but, your passing through life makes me certain that you are marked, and that heaven is punishing me for my mistreatings. When I got back from France ... and saw what your cousin Bill Davis had done at his family's ranch, I thought, by my soul, he has more worthy interest to my estate than you could hold a candle to. And being no older than you are, he organizes opera-tions for state senators, lobbies for the small businessman, and has an ambitious five-year plan for the forests that even I would like to support.

In the *Henriad* royalty and nobility wreak havoc, but in *Idaho* even the lowest levels of the socio-political hierarchy destroy the environment: the plan for the forests is a plan to cut them down.

Native Americans who briefly appear in the film, if only as statue or policeman, are none the less a constant ideological presence. Salmon, forests – indeed, the whole natural world – are sacred to these people. The young dispossessed and native inhabitants are thus ironically victimised by mere mayors, state senators, small businessmen and ranchers.[51]

Even as Scott and Mike journey to Idaho in what seems a purely personal quest to see Mike's brother/father and find his Mom, Van Sant never relinquishes his larger socio-political concerns. For Richard lives in 'Globe, Idaho', as indicated by the address on the bloody postcard – a pun alluding to both the world and Shakespeare's Globe Theatre. The boys search for Sharon at 'The Family Tree' inn yet encounter Hans, whose song quoted as an epigraph above encapsulates one strong political message of this film: the faces may change but the institutional organisation is recalcitrant, and the organising principle is violence (or the threat of violence). Imperial history illuminates the otherwise incongruous shift from Idaho to Rome. The Roman street boys are little different from those in Portland. The only difference is that the Roman boys hustle in an architecturally beautiful location. But Van Sant shows us less beauty than a thin tourist brochure of Rome. The finest shot in the film occurs immediately after Scott has abandoned Mike to run off with Carmella, who relinquishes her normal dog. Mike joins the same Italian boys from the opening Roman shot in a tree-studded park with the ruins of the Colosseum in the background. The boys lean against trees, another subtle reference to crucifixion. Two thousand years of imperial history are captured in a single frame. The Roman adventure helps to explain why Van Sant begins and ends his film with roads. Roman roads were notoriously straight, just like the road on which Mike stands and passes out at beginning and end. 'This road will never end. It probably goes all the way around the world', Mike says near the conclusion, because nothing seems to change. History is circular. When Scott and Mike arrive in Idaho they stop on this same road, and Mike attempts to show Scott how he sees it. But the 'fuck up' cannot discern the 'fucked-up face' of this tired old road.[52]

Scott's rejection of Mike and his other street friends is not a betrayal of what some critics perceive as his homosexual identity.[53] Scott is not gay, as early scenes repeatedly suggest. Our first view of him is at Alena's house, where he tells Mike about her sexual proclivities; he rejects being a 'fairy' in the magazine scene; he physically comforts and kisses a street girl; he tells Mike at the campfire that 'two guys can't love each other'.[54] Scott's affair with Carmella may just be a gesture of normalcy to prepare him for his new role as a rich member of the establishment (although he tells Mike he 'fell in love'), but this is not betrayal. Scott understands the hypocrisy of the rich, and thus his facile assumption of his father's mantle constitutes the personal and political betrayal of his street life and friends. This is why Scott's first public appearance as his father's heir occurs in 'Jakes', the Elizabethan word for a privy: Scott rejects Bob in a shithouse filled with the well-to-do.[55] Many of the drinks being consumed, including most of those delivered to Scott's table, are martinis containing little plastic swords, a mockery of the ultimately fruitless militarism characteristic of King Henry V – and perhaps a sardonic reflection on Scott's prospects as a future politician at the three-martini lunch. Van Sant alludes to *Henry V* even before adapting Hal's notorious rejection-of-Falstaff speech from *2 Henry IV* (V.v). When Scott enters 'Jakes' he is greeted by a sycophantic guy who introduces him to 'Tiger Warren'. The credits claim that Tiger is playing 'himself', encouraging us to believe that he is an actual restaurant tycoon. He says – 'Scotty, you ever considered a political career?' Scott's smiling glance suggests willingness to become a(nother) 'vile politician' (*1 Henry IV*, I.iii.238) and in this respect we are reminded of Henry V's rhetoric to his troops at the siege of Harfleur – 'imitate the action of the tiger'.[56] Scott's initiation into the ruling bourgeoisie is curiously bathetic. But now he is in the *tiger warren*, a contrast to the rabbit warren of the first scene in which Mike associates himself with an innocuous bunny – 'Where do you think you're running, man? We're stuck here together, you shit.'

Deep night

The subsequent death scene also imitates *Henry V* (II.i.82ff. and II.iii). Like Shakespeare's send-off for Falstaff, Bob's wake is serio-comic. But Van Sant's slickest touch is the contrasting funeral scene for Scott's two fathers. While some religious authority mutters Biblical platitudes over the coffin containing Jack Favor (yet relevant platitudes on the futility of laying up earthly 'treasures'), Bob's

funeral on the edge of the cemetery quickly shifts from a solemn
to a riotous occasion. The 'mourners' pile on top of Bob's pine
box for a kind of drunken orgy. Their laughter, or more likely an
extra-terrestrial laugh floating through the trees, concludes the
scene. The importance of this sequence cannot be underestimated.
For despite the serious political quality of the film as argued above,
what makes *Idaho* so enthralling is that it's funny. As the director
admits, 'I like things that are frightening and funny at the same
time.'[57] Van Sant seems less interested in denouncing than in mocking the rich, meanwhile representing how the destitute – like salmon
swimming up-river to spawn – struggle, endure and have orgasms.
They also live and laugh. The salmon image occurs near beginning and end. Like a few other images such as Richard's paintings
it is irreducible, or at least multiple in its possible significations.
The salmon is sacred to Native Americans; the salmon's struggle
to return to the place of its birth, then spawn and die, suggests
Mike's search for his origins; the salmon's tenacity indicates the
strength of the doomed. But the salmon image is also a sexual
joke: Mike seems to be thinking of it when trying to come during
a blowjob administered by a bizarre client; and the image recurs
immediately after the dispossessed grope each other on Bob's coffin
– 'deep in the arms of love' (from 'Deep Night').[58]

The whole movie is filled with funny moments, usually verbal:
Mike's story to Walt about his dad's second suicide at 'Boxcar
Canyon'; Mike's retort to his john's extended numerical calcula-
tions about being luckily born on 4/4/44 – 'you know your math'
– and, indeed, the entire 'Dutch Boy' scene; Mike's comment on
Alena's appearance smoking a cigarette in her Mercedes – 'this
chick's living in a new car ad'; Mike's exchange with Alena on
entering her mansion – 'This is a nice home. Do you live here? /
Yes. / I don't blame you'; and Alena's gesture and retort to the
dishevelled Mike's comment about never being picked up by a
'pretty rich girl' – 'They don't! I don't know why that is'; Scott's
mockery of Bob's girth before the robbery – 'How long has it been
Bob since you could see your dick?'; Mike's terse reply to Scott's
comment about what they'd do if a bomb fell on the city – 'take
shelter?'; a policeman's question when trying to break into the
derelict hotel – 'if we're looking for a fat man, why don't we just
get one under the bridge?'; the laconic police exchange with Scott
about looking for a 'large fat man', 'fat as butter'; the mayor's

aide's comment on apparent *coitus interruptus* – 'sorry for the interruption'; Mike's response to the bizarre picture of Hans's mother – 'she looks just like you', and Hans's gratitude – 'thank you'; the narcoleptic Mike being twice unable to fall asleep while Scott and Carmella have loud sex in the room above him. The result is a film whose positive quality cannot be epitomised by a single adjective. Most of the good emotions are felt by characters in difficult circumstances, while the well-to-do almost never laugh or smile. Mayor Favor, for instance, is always sour-faced. Even Bad George who appears at 'Jakes' brings 'great tidings' and 'much joy', while Bob comments on the 'jingle bells' on his shoes. This evocation of Christmas and revelling helps to transfigure the crucifixion images. George is the Renaissance fool wearing bells evoking popular culture, perhaps morris dancing, and when he calls for 'hardcore fun' we get the pun and imagine a Fool appropriate to 'King Leer'.

'America, the Beautiful' plays slowly yet again for the final scene, in which Mike passes out on the Idaho road. The victimisation of the sleeping Mike followed by an apparent rescue matches the two songs played as the credits roll, 'The Old Main Drag' and 'Deep Night'. Van Sant leaves us with ambiguity, and this seems appropriate for a conclusion that displays a deeply guarded optimism.[59] The old main drag is that imperial road going all around the world as a kind of noose strangling the globe, but it is always possible for the victims – like Mike tenderly placed by a stranger into his (nostalgic) 1950s American sedan – to find themselves 'deep in the arms of love'.[60]

Epilogue: 'Who talks of my nation?' (*Henry V*, III.ii.125)

One of the obituary articles for River Phoenix, who died under mysterious circumstances of apparent drug overdose on 31 October 1993, attributes his 'gradual introduction to hard drugs' to his role in *Idaho*: 'To get into character as a druggie gay hustler, Phoenix and others who worked on the movie hung out with heroin-using street kids until the lines between the junkies and the actor slowly started to blur.'[61] Such an attribution attempts to make this radical film somehow responsible for Phoenix's death, and thereby to discredit the film itself. By isolating the individual, the magazine obituaries never broach the far more important issue of the socio-political conditions under which alienated people seek solace – whether in drugs, communal solidarity or something else. Van Sant's film uses Rome, the Renaissance and Shakespeare to critique the modern imperial nation for its production or mothering of the destitute, and to suggest that the only way such outcasts can find a 'home' is in alternative conceptions of the nation. In *Idaho*, and in his more recent production of *kids* (1995), Van Sant represents at least part of the nation as young people intensely passionate and intensely victimised. Both films visually 'talk' about the dubious kind of nation that is produced by and produces such passion and victimisation.

In the epilogue to *Henry V* the Chorus informs us that

> the world's best garden he achieved,
> And of it left his son imperial lord.
> Henry the Sixth, in infant bands crown'd King
> Of France and England, did this king succeed;
> Whose state so many had the managing,
> That they lost France and made his England bleed.
>
> (7–12)

In the previous Chorus we are encouraged to imagine a general (probably Essex) 'from Ireland coming, / Bringing rebellion broached on his sword' (V.Chorus.30–2). As Patterson suggests, the word 'broached' could signify either 'spitted' or its reverse – the idea of broaching rebellion against England – in this case leading rebellion from Ireland to London.[62] Fifty years after *Henry V*, in 1649, the civil war obliquely prophesied in the play's epilogue came to a symbolic head with the decapitation of Charles I. In this same year a group of revolutionary sectarians called 'Diggers' attempted to seize waste land on 'St George's Hill . . . just outside London'.[63] These communist, socialist or communal Diggers were put down by force, but their 'colony' was 'merely one particularly well-documented example of a trend which was repeated in many other places'.[64] Diggers believed in economic as well as political freedom, supporting extensive cultivation of land held in common while opposing 'lords of the manor' who cut down 'common woods and trees' for 'private use'.[65]

The figure who most corresponds to Mike in *Idaho* is Digger, whose British flag T-shirt matches Mike's American flag T-shirt. The linkage between British and American imperialism is thus challenged by a different connection between British and American commoners. By reversing the supposed main and sub-plots Van Sant turns the world upside down. Although *Idaho* critiques the continuum of imperial history it none the less evokes alternative practices and conceptions such as the Digger movement to promote optimism and hope. The wheatfields of Idaho, 'the potato state', recall the Digger vision of the earth as a 'common treasury'.[66] The Digger Utopia is pantheistic and hence materialist, including a notion that Christ inheres in all people: 'The second coming is "the rising up of Christ in sons and daughters"; the worship of any other Christ but the Christ within man must then cease.'[67] In such a vision all the cross and crucifixion images of *Idaho* take on a far different resonance, a positive (e)quality of human dignity for all. In this Utopia of 'King Leer' the symbolically crucified Edgar/Poor Tom would 'have enough' after 'distribution' undid 'excess'.[68]

Notes

I would like to thank countless students at the University of Pittsburgh and University of Newcastle, Australia, for wonderful reflections, information and essays influencing my discussion. This chapter is dedicated to the late River Phoenix and whatever we call the global generation surrounding him.

1 *The Penguin Book of Renaissance Verse*, ed. D. Norbrook and H. R. Woudhuysen (London, Penguin, 1992), pp. 464–5.

2 Cited by C. Hill, *The World Turned Upside Down: Radical Ideas During the English Revolution* (London, Penguin, 1972), p. 107.

3 R. Greene, *Greene's Groats-Worth of Witte* and *The Repentance of Robert Greene*, ed. G. B. Harrison (Westport, Greenwood, 1970 rpt; orig. 1923), p. 46. The present essay is part of a current book project entitled *Elizabethan World Pictures*.

4 J. W. Fulbright, *The Price of Empire* (New York, Pantheon, 1989), p. 131.

5 See D. Rosenberg, 'Process: The realities of formulating modern naval strategy' in *Mahan is not Enough: The Proceedings of a Conference on the Works of Sir Julian Corbett and Admiral Sir Herbert Richmond*, ed. J. Goldrick and J. Hattendorf (Newport, Naval War College, 1993), pp. 158–9 for analysis revealing that American assessment of Soviet naval strategy as wholly defensive led President Reagan's naval planners to adopt a staggeringly expensive and offensive maritime strategy. This book is especially valuable for drawing linkages between Renaissance and modern naval operations.

6 See A. Sinfield, *Faultlines: Cultural Materialism and the Politics of Dissident Reading* (Berkeley, University of California Press, 1992), pp. 2–3 for another kind of anniversary, a reproduction of a 'Royal Ordnance' weaponry advertisement – featuring lots of hardware and a small offset picture of the 'Globe Theatre' – which claims that 'since Shakespeare's work played at the Globe Theatre in 1588, Royal Ordnance's products have been in action in every major event of Britain's military history'. As Sinfield notes, since the Globe only started seeing action in 1599 (p. 4), the anniversary is a bit screwed up: 'We helped protect the Globe in 1588' (p. xii); 'After 400 years, Royal Ordnance still plays the Globe. All of it' (p. 3).

7 Films based on John Le Carré novels include both fragmentary use of Shakespeare and, in the case of *The Deadly Affair* (1967), extensive use of Christopher Marlowe's *Edward II*; the conclusion features the torture and murder of King Edward II performed on stage while the espionage plot unravels in the audience – a kind of play-within-a-film strategy.

8 I owe this description to a former student who shall remain anonymous. I do not mean to denigrate the BBC series, which includes some wonderful versions of plays neglected in mainstream and alternative cinemas, e.g., *Measure for Measure*, *Coriolanus*, *Titus Andronicus* and *Pericles*. Indeed, without the BBC we would have no film versions of many Shakespeare plays. Nevertheless, experience teaches me that for American and Australian undergraduates (and probably for other undergraduates studying English across the globe) BBC Shakespeare is less interesting as a pedagogical and aesthetic experience than sampling an equal or higher number of now easily available Shakespeare (and Marlowe, and historical) films produced internationally between the 1930s and 1990s.

9 My favourite subtle allusion is from *Hard Times* (1975), in which Strother Martin (Poe) explains to Charles Bronson (Chaney, a bareknuckle fighter during the American Depression 'managed' by James Coburn, 'Speed') how opium prevented him from completing medical school: '*Poe*. Well in my third year of studies a small black cloud appeared on campus. I left under it. *Speed*. What he's trying to say is that he's a dyed-in-the-wool hophead. *Poe*. I have a weakness for opium. *Chaney*. That's a habit that's hard to quit. *Poe*. Some are born to fail. Others have it thrust upon them.' See W. Shakespeare, *Twelfth Night*, ed. H. Baker (New York, Signet, 1965), II.v.144–5.

10 R. Ball, *Shakespeare on Silent Film: A Strange Eventful History* (New York, Theater Arts Books, 1968). W. Uricchio and R. Pearson, *Reframing Culture: The Case of the Vitagraph Quality Films* (Princeton, Princeton University Press, 1993). I owe the second reference to John Nichols.

11 See also Zeffirelli's opera of Giuseppe Verdi's *Otello* (1986).

12 Shakespeare on film has always been hard to categorise, and perhaps this is why there are so few good discussions of the subject, especially by film specialists. One big problem involves distinguishing among adaptations, parodies, fragments, and so forth. Another involves recognising how Shakespeare, especially in Hollywood, has been screened through other traditional film genres such as the Western (e.g., *Jubal*, *McLintock!*), the musical (e.g., *Kiss Me Kate*, *West Side Story*), science fiction (*Forbidden Planet*) and the gangster movie. 'Cold War' US Shakespeare films could be said to compete with great non-US films by directors such as Kurosawa (*Throne of Blood*, 1957), and Grigori Kozintsev (*Hamlet*, 1964, and *King Lear*, 1971). As for today, how do we categorise movies such as *Rosencrantz and Guildenstern Are Dead* (1990)? Recent films which use Shakespeare in what seem to be meaningful ways include *My Dark Lady* (1987), *Withnail and I* (1988), *The Addams Family* (1991), *Frankie & Johnny* (1991), *JFK* (1991), *L.A. Story* (1991), *Soapdish* (1991), *Jennifer 8* (1992), *The Playboys* (1992), *The Man Without a Face* (1993), *True Romance* (1993) and *D.O.A.* (1988) – my favourite, since an English department professor is outquoted on Shakespeare by a student who is subsequently murdered; and then the professor is subjected to Jacobean-style poisoning by a junior colleague. See also the HBO Animated Shakespeare Series broadcast over the last several years in the USA on cable. For a good recent listing of films that includes all varieties see L. McKernan and O. Terris, eds, *Walking Shadows: Shakespeare in the National Film and Television Archive* (London, BFI, 1994).

13 *Shakespeare's Books: Contemporary Cultural Politics and the Persistence of Empire*, eds P. Mead and M. Campbell (Melbourne, Melbourne University Press, 1993); E. Said, *Culture and Imperialism* (London, Chatto & Windus, 1993); M. Egnal, *A Mighty Empire: The Origins of the American Revolution* (Ithaca, Cornell University Press, 1988); *Cultures of United States Imperialism*, eds A. Kaplan and D. Pease (Durham, Duke University Press, 1993).

14 M. Bristol, *Shakespeare's America, America's Shakespeare* (London, Routledge, 1990).

15 See also *Souls at Sea* (1937), whose early use of *Hamlet* in relation to the slave trade is more optimistic, since the film features Gary Cooper as an American waging one-man war against slavery on the high seas until British intelligence recruits him for its wider campaign.

16 I owe my introduction to John Woo films to Andrew Buck.

17 Said, *Culture and Imperialism*, p. 126.

18 L. Gandhi, 'Unmasking Shakespeare: The uses of English studies in colonial and postcolonial India' in Mead and Campbell, eds, *Shakespeare's*

Books, p. 81; G. Viswanathan, *Masks of Conquest: Literary Study and British Rule in India* (New York, Columbia University Press, 1989). See the Indian film *Shakespeare Wallah* (1965), discussed in Ania Loomba's chapter above, for one representation of 'Shakespeare' in India.

19 W. Shakespeare, *The Tempest*, ed. S. Orgel (Oxford, Oxford University Press, 1987), I.ii.362–3. See also *The Dogs of War* (1980), featuring Christopher Walken in 'private' war against an entire African state run by a military dictator (title adapted from W. Shakespeare, *Julius Caesar*, ed. A. Humphreys (Oxford, Oxford University Press, 1984), III.i.273). At the conclusion Walken kills the dictator and his would-be heir, installing as head of state a former prisoner who helped him recover from a brutal beating by the dictator's troops. The film has a much closer thematic connection to Political Shakespeare than appears at first glance.

20 See, for example, Michael Medved, co-host of the American 'Sneak Previews' programme ironically produced on the supposedly left-leaning Public Broadcasting System (PBS). Medved's address at the 'Center for Constructive Alternatives' in a seminar entitled 'Culture Wars' beckons Hollywood back to the presumed 'mainstream' of American values partly by citing the example of the Bard: 'Was William Shakespeare alienated from the Tudor monarchy? He wrote play after play glorifying Elizabeth's antecedents and became a court favorite. He was part of the establishment and proud of it.' M. Medved, 'Hollywood's poison factory: Making it the dream factory again', *Imprimis*, 21 (1992), p. 5. I owe this reference to Cy Salowe. Buchanan announced cultural wars during his 1992 campaign for the presidential nomination of the Republican party, and revived the call during his 1996 campaign.

21 See G. Vidal, *Screening History* (Cambridge, Harvard University Press, 1992), for a terse discussion of historical films that seems to herald a spate of similar new books as well as new historical films: e.g., *Braveheart*, *Rob Roy* (a remake of the 1954 *Rob Roy, the Highland Rogue*), *Queen Margot* (1994), *Orlando* (1993; from Virginia Woolf's novel) and *Pocahontas* (1995). Excellent historical films seem to crop up at the same time as excellent Shakespeare films, e.g., in the period 1966–71: *Chimes at Midnight* (1966), *The Taming of the Shrew* (1967), *Romeo and Juliet* (1968), Peter Brook's *King Lear* (1971), *Macbeth* (1971); *A Man for All Seasons* (1966), *The Lion in Winter* (1968), *Anne of the Thousand Days* (1969) and *Cromwell* (1970). It is interesting that historical films tend to be upbeat (or at least not too downbeat), whereas decades of ongoing revisionist historiography have witnessed much 'negative' or critical analysis. See *Index on Censorship*, 3 (1995) for a topic entitled 'Rewriting history'. There is, or

should be, some kind of connection between revisionist scholarship and the film industry, especially if we continue to increase the use of multi-media in classrooms.

22 For a good discussion of Jarman's film see C. MacCabe, '*Edward II*: throne of blood', *Sight and Sound* (October 1991), pp. 12–14.

23 See G. Holderness, 'Shakespeare rewound', *Shakespeare Survey*, 45 (1992), pp. 64–5 for a smart critique of a ' "Shakespeare on film" canon' apparently underpinning the 'authority of a hegemonic critical discourse'. I would extrapolate and say that recent film-canon struggles include Branagh versus Jarman/Van Sant, Zeffirelli versus Kaurismaki/Woo. The politics and economics of film distribution – i.e., a system in which Branagh and Zeffirelli are relatively available worldwide, while Kaurismaki is not – play a huge role in how any film-canon competition transpires.

24 A. Taubin, 'Objects of desire', *Sight and Sound* (January 1992), p. 13.

25 D. Kastan, ' "The king hath many marching in his coats," or, what did you do during the war, Daddy?' in *Shakespeare Left and Right*, ed. I. Kamps (London, Routledge, 1991), p. 244.

26 Said, *Culture and Imperialism*, p. 66.

27 D. Lyons, 'Gus Van Sant: lawless as snow-flake, simple as grass', *Film Comment* (September/October, 1991), pp. 6–12. H. Greenberg, 'Review: *My Own Private Idaho*', *Film Quarterly*, 46.1 (1992), pp. 23–5.

28 See *Julius Caesar*, I.ii.135–6: 'Why, man, he doth bestride the narrow world / Like a colossus.' Olivier, of course, starred in many Shakespeare films: *As You Like It* (1936), *Henry V* (1944), *Hamlet* (1948), *Richard III* (1955), *Othello* (1965) and *King Lear* (1984).

29 See I. R. Hark, 'Animals or Romans: Looking at masculinity in *Spartacus*' in *Screening the Male: Exploring Masculinities in Hollywood Cinema*, eds S. Cohan and I. R. Hark (London, Routledge, 1993), p. 161 for the function of the gaze in *Spartacus*, which tends to make the audience 'suspiciously Roman-like moviegoers'.

30 C. Breight, 'Branagh and the Prince, or a "royal fellowship of death" ', *Critical Quarterly*, 33.4 (1991), pp. 95–111. C. Fitter, 'A tale of two Branaghs: *Henry V*, ideology, and the Mekong Agincourt' in *Shakespeare Left and Right*, pp. 259–75. M. Fortier, 'Speculations on 2 *Henry IV*, theatre historiography, the strait gate of history, and Kenneth Branagh', *Journal of Dramatic Theory and Criticism*, 7.1 (1992), pp. 45–69.

31 L. Grove, 'Kenneth Adelman, into the arms of Shakespeare: Reagan's missile man bombards his students with a literary passion', *The Washington Post* (1 October 1991), p. E1. See K. Adelman, 'The blast of war', *Policy Review*, 52 (1990), pp. 80–3, a title which signifies in popular American parlance that war is fun ('war's a blast'). Right-wingers

who never saw combat such as Adelman – precluded from enlisting in the Marines for the Vietnam war 'because of chronic eczema that prevented his wearing a wool uniform' (Grove, p. E3) – tend to fantasise about the joys of war. The extended battle sequence in Orson Welles's *Chimes at Midnight* is far better than either Branagh's or Olivier's *Henry V*. See Welles's witty remark on his great predecessor in O. Welles, *Chimes at Midnight*, ed. B. G. Lyons (New Brunswick, Rutgers University Press, 1988), p. 260: 'In *Henry V* . . . you see the people riding out of the castle, and suddenly they are on a golf course somewhere charging each other.'

32 Mobil Corporation, *A Teacher's Guide for William Shakespeare's Henry V* (Bedford, W. E. Andrews, 1992). The ideological bias of this publication is evident throughout its seventeen pages, but a few examples from an early section entitled 'The literary context of Henry V' will establish my point (pp. 4–5): 'The Welsh, the Irish, and the Scots present a constant threat of revolt' to Henry IV, as though somehow this medieval monarch were king of an imaginary British UK *c.* 1400 (there was no 'Britain' in 1599 either); both Hotspur and Hal are said to 'grudgingly admire the other's prowess and bravery', which Hotspur precisely does not because Hal has displayed no such qualities; 'the young king faces the awesome responsibility of the throne', struggling 'to become a strong, moral king, to heal the scars left over from the rebellion, and to expand his empire into France'. 'The Themes of Henry V' are said to be: 'King Henry's moral and emotional growth', 'The burdens of leadership', 'The nature of power', 'Patriotism' and 'War' (p. 6). I owe this reference to Erin Barrett and Alette Cox, who also provided wonderful information on the teaching of Shakespeare in secondary schools. See also K. Branagh, 'Henry V', *Players of Shakespeare 2*, ed. R. Jackson and R. Smallwood (Cambridge, Cambridge University Press, 1988), pp. 93–105 for a largely emotional view of the character Henry V.

33 W. Shakespeare, *The First Part of King Henry IV*, ed. A. R. Humphreys (London, Methuen, 1967), I.ii.56–65; II.iv.315–21. Further citations in the text.

34 Narcolepsy, I suspect, is also at least partially indebted to the complex politics underlying this exchange among Cassius, Casca and Brutus in *Julius Caesar*, I.ii.249–54:

> *Cassius*: But soft, I pray you; what, did Caesar swoon?
> *Casca*: He fell down in the market-place, and foamed at mouth, and was speechless.
> *Brutus*: 'Tis very like; he hath the falling sickness.
> *Cassius*: No, Caesar hath it not; but you, and I,
>   And honest Casca, we have the falling sickness.

35 F. Jameson, *The Political Unconscious* (Ithaca, Cornell University Press, 1981). See Steppenwolf's song 'Monster' for the idea of America as a disastrous mother.

36 Multiple images of the cross include: one on Mike's Mother (repeated for the woman on the street corner in Seattle, who wears the same clothing); the long prominent light hanging below a crossbeam in Mike's first outdoor 'dating' scene, and below which he is recumbent near the end of the film; the window frame as cross directly behind Daddy Carroll in the Dutch Boy scene; Gary's cross; the street viewed from above as a cross in the first motorcycle scene (recalling *Cool Hand Luke*); the crosses in the derelict hotel during Bob's post-robbery narration; the cross in Little Richard's left ear. Cf. Zeffirelli's *Hamlet*, in which the cross image is not ironic but used to signify Hamlet as phallic Christian avenger. See also *The Ninth Configuration* (1979), which contains a complex Shakespearian current (especially *Hamlet*), and crucifixion frames suggesting that the inmates of the military asylum (mostly Vietnam veterans) and their possibly insane ex-Special Forces psychologist are 'Jesus' figures.

37 Van Sant also writes himself into the character of Scott. See R. Rugoff, 'Walking on the wild side', *Premiere* (October 1991), p. 35. Gus Van Sant = Scott Favor, ten letters in each name, four the same. Van Sant also mocks himself in relation to northern European johns and other 'phenomena': Hans, Dutch Boy cleanser, Porsche, Mercedes. Van Sant thus links himself to the wealthy suburbanites.

38 Mike's plan may be indebted to the Nurse's dead husband's punch line to the child Juliet: 'Thou wilt fall backward when thou hast more wit, / Wilt thou not, Jule?' W. Shakespeare, *Romeo and Juliet*, ed. D. Bevington (New York, Bantam, 1988), I.iii.43–4.

39 Lyons, 'Gus Van Sant', p. 8. Yet cf. Greenberg, 'Review', p. 25.

40 See also the Madonna and Child painting in the Italian john scene.

41 I thank David Boyd for helping me to identify 'Pomona' in the frame, and for numerous other conversations about film.

42 See L. Loud, 'Shakespeare in black leather', *American Film* (September/October 1991), pp. 32–3 for information that this scene was originally shot as a far more explicit 'Jesus' scene: the magazine was called '*G-String Jesus*' and Mike was in an explicit crucifixion pose; Flea (Budd) commented, 'They're trying to avoid *The Last Temptation of Christ* syndrome'.

43 '*Honcho*' directly above Scott also includes 'He Came and He Went', a mockery of what Scott will do to his companions as well as a sexual pun, and perhaps a glance at Julius Caesar's legendary 'veni, vidi, vici'. It also coincides with 'The Coming of the White Man' statue.

44 Yellow leaves on the trees and dead leaves below Mike's head are also very prominent in the Native American statue scene.

45 W. Shakespeare, *The Second Part of King Henry IV*, ed. A. R. Humphreys (London, Methuen, 1966), III.ii.32–3 and 214. Further citations in the text.

46 Van Sant admits that he was influenced by *Chimes at Midnight* (Taubin, 'Objects of desire', p. 13). Juxtaposition of the two films reveals that Van Sant heavily adapted and borrowed from Welles, taking a cue from Welles's largely heterosexual preoccupations in his tavern scenes and translating that sexual energy into a 1990s, mostly homosexual scenario.

47 Sir J. Smythe, *Certain Discourses Military*, ed. J. R. Hale (Ithaca, Cornell University Press, 1964).

48 M. Sutcliffe, *The Practice, Proceedings, and Lawes of Armes* (London, Christopher Barker, 1593), p. 64.

49 W. Shakespeare, *King Richard II*, ed. P. Ure (London, Methuen, 1961), V.iii.1ff.

50 The box stolen from the rock promoters also features a coat of arms and the words, 'League of Spiritual Discovery'.

51 For just one example of how Native Americans relate to the natural world, see the Mayan lamentation over the demise of their culture in *The Destruction of the Jaguar: Poems from the Books of Chilam Balam*, trans. Christopher Sawyer-Laucanno (San Francisco, City Lights Books, 1987), p. 7: 'Know that in the new era / the jaguar will have a rabbit's body, / broken teeth, / a spear of sorrow piercing its side. / The rulers will lose their mats, / their white clothes, / will wander the streets as mangy dogs. / The people will gnaw roots, / eat the leaves of weeds / and in the cities / the vultures will grow fat / on the cadavers.' I owe this reference to David Noble.

52 The Idaho road as 'fucked-up face' is also a sexual joke: it's a straight hard road directly into a 'face'. At the conclusion Mike says, 'I'm a connoisseur of roads. I've been tasting roads my whole life' – which adds to the oral joke. The concluding frame – 'have a nice day' – and the smile faces pasted on Dick's overhead light extend the irony of overlapping images of the 'face'.

53 Taubin, 'Objects of desire', p. 12.

54 Note that the campfire scene corresponds to *2 Henry IV*, II.ii.33–7, in which Hal and Poins have a conversation including jokes that imply a sexual relationship between the two.

55 See the discussion of Harington's late Elizabethan texts on Ajax/a jakes in D. H. Craig, *Sir John Harington* (Boston, Twayne, 1985), pp. 66–83. See also Thersites' probable mockery of 'Ajax' as 'a jakes' in W. Shakespeare, *The History of Troilus and Cressida*, ed. D. Seltzer (New York, Signet, 1963).

56 W. Shakespeare, *King Henry V*, ed. J. H. Walter (London, Methuen, 1954), III.i.6. Further citations in the text.

57 Rugoff, 'Walking on the wild side', p. 34.
58 'Deep Night' is one of two concluding songs on the soundtrack. See also W. Shakespeare, *Measure for Measure*, ed. J. W. Lever (London, Methuen, 1965), I.ii.83: 'Groping for trouts, in a peculiar river'.
59 Jarman's *Edward II* has a similar conclusion.
60 The lyrics of 'Deep Night' include 'stars' and 'moonlight' (images shown in the film), and 'whispering trees' – which may correspond to the laughter in the trees over Bob's orgiastic funeral.
61 D. Kennedy, 'Dark side of the high life', *Who Weekly* (6 December 1993), p. 50. Other moralising obituaries preoccupied with the flawed tragic individual include W. Cole and J. Ressner, 'His own private agony', *Time* (15 November 1993), p. 70; and S. Levitt *et al.*, 'River's end', *Who Weekly* (15 November 1993), pp. 50–6.
62 A. Patterson, *Shakespeare and the Popular Voice* (Oxford, Basil Blackwell, 1989), pp. 86–7.
63 Hill, *World Turned Upside Down*, p. 110.
64 *Ibid.*, p. 118.
65 *Ibid.*, pp. 121, 128–9, 131.
66 *Ibid.*, p. 145.
67 *Ibid.*
68 W. Shakespeare, *King Lear*, ed. K. Muir (London, Methuen, 1972), II.iii.15–16; IV.i.69–70.

❖

Afterword

❖

John Drakakis

At the beginning of the final act of *Love's Labour's Lost*, the pedant Holofernes and the curate Sir Nathaniel engage in a dia-logue whose prime object is the ridicule of the extravagant Span-iard Don Armado. Sir Nathaniel confides, something in the manner of a thesaurus, that he did 'converse this quondam day with a companion of the king's, who is intituled, nominated or called, Don Adriano de Armado' (V.i.6–8). This prompts the following response from Holofernes:

> *Novi hominem tanquam te*: his humour is lofty, his discourse per-emptory, his tongue filed, his eye ambitious, his gait majestical, and his general behaviour vain, ridiculous, and thrasonical. He is too picked, too spruce, too affected, too odd, as it were, too peregrinate, as I may call it.
>
> (V.i.9–14)

Don Armado, it seems, is one of those 'rackers of orthography' who distort the written language when they convert it into speech. Holofernes complains:

> He draweth out the thread of his verbosity finer than the staple of his argument. I abhor such fanatical phantasimes, such insociable and point-devise companions; such rackers of orthography, as to speak dout, fine, when he should say doubt; det, when he should pronounce debt, – d, e, b, t, not d, e, t; he clepeth a calf, cauf; half, hauf; neigh-bour *vocatur* nebour; neigh abbreviated ne. This is abhominable,

which he would call abominable, it insinuateth me of insanie: *ne intelligis domine*? to make frantic, lunatic.

(V.i.16–25)

The trenchant comic irony arises here out of the stark clash of linguistic opposites, as the oral language of theatre is made to collide with the language of writing at one level, at the same time as it is a vehicle for the ridicule of the speech of the 'foreigner'. In his evidently misguided privileging of writing over speech, and the peppering of his own speech with Latinate phrases and constructions, the teacher Holofernes seeks to elevate English to the status of the classical language; but his demand for an absurdly literal standardisation of pronunciation, set against what he perceives to be the distorting variety of this unusual instance of the spoken language, carries with it an ideological charge: it asserts a national order of language in the face of a foreign and hence risible linguistic variation, in this case embodied in the figure of the Spaniard Don Armado. Whether the model for Holofernes was Richard Mulcaster, author of *The Elementarie* (1582), the linguistic reformer who believed that the perfection of English was deeply related to the maintenance of social and political order, is in some ways secondary to the issue of a national standardised language which *Love's Labour's Lost* raises, locates, curiously, in the court of Navarre, positions between the court and the 'low' characters, and in part ridicules.[1]

Of course, from the perspective of the later twentieth century, we may inflect this exchange differently. Shakespearian texts have now become the standard by which competence in the English language, and universal literacy may be judged, where the question of standardisation is taken for granted. As the Leeds-born poet Tony Harrison puts it in a humorously self-denigrating poem entitled 'Them & [uz]', 'Poetry's the speech of kings. You're one of those / Shakespeare gave the comic bits to: prose.'[2] Holofernes judges merit according to the criteria of a standardised orthography which derived its grammatical models from Latin, and its models of pronunciation from an absurd literalness. In what has become something of a historical irony, a manifestly vernacular writer, of the sort that Shakespeare is often claimed to be, is now, in the modern world asserted to be the *fons et origo* of the English language itself, an English 'classic'. This is a claim that is sustained through the education system, which has become an important, some would say the most important, channel for the production of a linguistic community.[3] Etienne Balibar has observed that both the 'school' and 'the family' fulfil more than functional roles in so far as they subordinate 'the reproduction of labour power' to what he calls 'the constitution of a fictive ethnicity through the construction of a "linguistic community"'; although he does go on to distinguish carefully between the essential 'openness' of a linguistic community, and the fundamentally 'closed' nature of what he terms 'racial ethnicity'.[4] Balibar argues that by its very nature the linguistic community 'possesses a strange plasticity' in that it permits appropriation, and the refashioning of individual identity: 'One's "mother" tongue is not', he argues, 'necessarily the language of one's "real" mother':

> The language community is a community *in the present*, which produces the feeling that it has always existed, but which lays down no destiny for the successive generations. Ideally it 'assimilates' anyone, but holds no one. Finally, it affects all individuals in their innermost being (in the way in which they constitute themselves as subjects), but its historical particularity is bound only to interchangeable institutions.[5]

We may detect here, of course, a version of the concept of 'hybridity' which now figures prominently in colonial and post-colonial critical discourse. It may also go some way towards accounting for the different reception that a canonical writer such as Shakespeare has elicited from different cultures – although even here there may be something of a problem in that, as we shall see, much depends upon the extent to which some of those cultures are historically predisposed to the treatment of 'English', and to English political institutions as exemplary, and to literary icons such as Shakespeare who are asserted to embody such values.

But in the late sixteenth century the question of a literary canon had yet to be posed in what we might recognise as its modern form, nor can we assume, despite the advances of print technology, and the development of a book market, a stable language which might function as the basis of a national culture. As John Guillory has recently pointed out, it was because the Latin and Greek classics functioned 'as the rarest and most expensive form of cultural capital' that Renaissance humanists were concerned to imitate them. But Guillory goes on to argue that the institution of a vernacular canon 'belongs to a nationalist agenda, quite distinct from the multilingual cultural internationalism of the Renaissance humanists'.[6] That Shakespearian texts now occupy pride of place in what Guillory calls a vernacular canon raises a question about the extent to which that canon generally, and Shakespeare in particular, are touchstones of a more general literacy whose structures inscribe 'the entire system by which reading and writing are regulated as social practices',[7] in the modern world. We may in some ways, of course, recognise the political claims made on behalf of a universal literacy to permit democratic access to a full range of social institutions, but this in itself, as Guillory again points out, masks a contradiction; the language of 'participatory democracy' is none other than 'the speech of the professional-managerial classes, the administrators and the bureaucrats'.[8] In the second poem which comprises Harrison's 'Them & [uz]' the demotic voice struggles with the demands of a 'received' grammar and a received pronunciation:

> You can tell the Receivers where to go
> (and not aspirate it) once you know
> Wordsworth's *matter/water* are full rhymes,
> [uz] can be loving as well as funny.
> My first mention in the *Times*
> automatically made Tony Anthony![9]

To return to the case of *Love's Labour's Lost* for a moment, the play was published in a quarto in 1598, and then again in the First Folio of 1623, and so it enjoyed circulation in print as well as in performance. Benedict Anderson has shown convincingly that in the combination of print technology and capitalism lay the foundations of a national consciousness. He argues that through capitalism, 'mechanically reproduced print-languages' functioned to assemble and disseminate 'related vernaculars' in such a way as to lay the foundations for 'national consciousnesses'.[10] These 'print-languages' accomplished this in three ways: firstly, 'they created unified fields of exchange and communication below Latin and above the spoken vernaculars', secondly, 'print-capitalism gave a new fixity to language, which in the long run helped to build that image of antiquity so central to the subjective idea of the nation', and thirdly, it created 'languages-of-power of a kind different from

the old administrative vernaculars'.[11] Of course, as a slight modi-
fier to this view we may cite the empirical evidence of the relative
instability of dramatic texts during this period, variations in spelling within and between copies, considerable orthographic variety,
and variations in general typographical layout, all of which are
present in some form or other in *Love's Labour's Lost*. In the late
sixteenth to early seventeenth century we are at the beginning of
a process which accelerated into the very 'imagined community'
that Anderson describes, and possibly beyond. Indeed, that notion
of an 'imagined community' may well be one of the things negotiated in the second tetralogy of history plays, as Willy Maley
argues cogently in his essay in this collection.

Yet here again, the position is further complicated in the case of
Shakespeare, since, in addition to his having become the 'national'
poet, he is also regarded as a figure of international significance,
a symptom of a particular historical trajectory. Indeed, one German Romantic critic could extol Shakespeare's history plays because they were part of a larger British history, in which it was
thought that 'Europe might find its own history reflected in coherent and idealised form'. The writer, Adam Muller, subscribing to
what has become a very powerful myth, sought to remind his
audience in Dresden in 1806 of what he describes as

> the dramatic character of the British constitution, which has been
> praised from time immemorial because it can no more be termed
> despotic, i.e. monological, than democratic, i.e. dialogical; rather,
> the monological element in the shape of king, clergy and aristocracy
> is united with the dialogical element in the shape of the lower house,
> to form a single beautiful dramatic whole.[12]

In thinking of Shakespeare and national culture, therefore, the title
of this wide-ranging volume of essays, we need also to think, as
a number of contributors have emphasised, in a European dimension, as well as in those more problematical areas of colonial and
post-colonial cultures where a residually imperialist 'English' jostles
continuously, as Ania Loomba and Martin Orkin show, with indigenous languages and cultural experiences. Indeed, the difficulty is
now in thinking Shakespearian texts, the embodiment of a sovereign national culture, in the bewildering context of the fragmentation of those 'imagined communities' of which Benedict Anderson
speaks. In the words of Homi Bhabha:

The great connective narratives of capitalism and class drive the engines of social reproduction, but do not, in themselves, provide a foundational frame for those modes of cultural identification and political affect that form around issues of sexuality, race, feminism, the lifeworld of refugees or migrants, or the deathly social destiny of AIDS.[13]

Once we reach this point then a serious clash of methodologies becomes evident as those, such as Bhabha, who champion a sophisticated and inherently nomadic postmodernism, engage with those who are still struggling to secure the material benefits of modernity.[14] This is in part the subject of Tom Healy's provocative account of 'Shakespearian appropriations in Europe'.

In the chapter which opens this volume, Graham Holderness and Andrew Murphy insist, rightly, that 'Shakespeare has *always* been the subject of appropriations of one sort or another' (p. 21). It is, of course, historically the case that the impulse to unify Shakespearian meanings has in some ways been bound up with a process of cumulatively ascribing cultural authority to a particular collection of texts. But, as Alan Sinfield, following Raymond Williams, has pointed out, forms of dissident Shakespearian criticism can often find themselves assimilated into the 'mysterious protean power' of the very cultural authority which they seek to question.[15] Sinfield proposes a strategy of 'self-consciously impudent anti-reading; a creative vandalism' which might undermine the very capacity of the Shakespearian text to assimilate every challenge into itself. But the point that Holderness and Murphy insist upon is that the text has no 'self', no identity, no internal coherence which can be separated from the practices in and through which it is constituted. These are not opposed positions, so much as differences of historical emphasis; Sinfield is concerned at this point in his argument with an already constituted cultural authority which is the product of a protracted historical process, whereas Holderness and Murphy wish to retrace the steps of that history in an attempt to track it down to a series of myths of origin, and then to project it forward again into the educational arena of universal literacy. It is here that the concept of an 'imagined community' is constructed, although once that essentially *nationalist* project is exported to other cultures, new and complex political configurations emerge.

The suggestion that modern readers read Shakespearian texts 'in

modern translation' (p. 25) raises a host of questions which challenge the very foundations upon which the artificially stabilised
claims to a national cultural authority are based. Not only are these
texts mediated through the normalising protocols of editorial practice but they are also sustained through a network of secondary
critical texts of which Simon Barker provides both an eloquent
taxonomy, and a critique. His account of the disempowering pressures under which many radical British secondary schoolteachers
work, along with his articulation of the domestication and subsequent disabling of serious alternative accounts of Shakespearian
texts, makes salutary reading. In the face of so ubiquitous a challenge, what Barker calls a 're-loading of the Shakespearian canon
itself' (p. 50) may well involve breaking free from a familiar list
of prescribed Shakespearian texts, or learning 'new ways with them';
and yet, as we have seen, simply contesting the space occupied
by élitist ideologies, or liberal humanist readings, cannot (except
through the deployment of Sinfield's 'creative vandalism' which
seeks explicitly to confront rather than to share in the text's
accretions of cultural authority) but become annexed to the very
project to which it is ostensibly opposed. Much depends upon the
recognition that Shakespearian texts, like all texts in this respect,
either can be the objects of mastery or alternatively can be recognised as sites of struggle where questions of freedom displace questions of mastery. Nor will the situation be changed unless there is
some positive resistance across the board to those mealy-mouthed,
finance-led plans specifically designed to fracture political consensus, to foster compromise, and to ensure political mastery. In
this respect, Sinfield's metaphor is a telling one, and points more
directly than the comfortable ethos of academe can usually tolerate to an oppressive violence which displaces its concerns into the
act of interpretation itself. Set against this, Richard Wilson's witty
exposure of the medicinal function to which directors have co-
opted Shakespeare, invites us to contemplate the deep affinity
between effects of administering Shakespeare to those thought by
successive directors of the RSC to be culturally impoverished, and
a laxative manufactured by the father of the director Peter Brook.

The challenge of reading Shakespearian texts 'otherwise', however, is not simply a matter of disclosing the 'real' Shakespeare
beneath the accretive surfaces of ideology. If we pose the question
in this starkly positivistic manner, then two complex issues emerge.

Firstly, there is, as Robert Weimann astutely observes, the question involved in any reception of Shakespeare of coming to terms with 'the difference between historically used signs and a later code of their appropriation' (p. 186). His reiteration of the multiform semiotics of Elizabethan theatrical space which permitted both the representation and the questioning of 'authority' leads him to identify 'a new paradigm of authority' which signals the onset of the early modern. He concludes:

> no longer available through given locations of power and meaning, authority now constituted itself not so much in a pre-discursive situation or at the beginning of discourse (where given sources used to be cited as valid) but rather in the production and perception of meaning, truth, conviction, and belief as process. (p. 198)

In a very poignant moment, Weimann uses Shakespeare to articulate the dilemma of the displaced East German intellectual tempted towards 'an unconstrained site of independent communicative practices', but faced with the stark political consequences of subscribing 'to the scenario of an opposition between material and intellectual locations of authority' (p. 199).

In some ways, Weimann's carefully circumscribed move into the arena of post-structuralism dovetails with the second issue: the move away from what Homi Bhabha has labelled dismissively 'identikit political idealism'.[16] Here, in a move reminiscent of Greenblattian new historicism, *negotiation* replaces the more familiar *negation* and is designed, so Bhabha argues, 'to convey a temporality that makes it possible to conceive of the articulation of antagonistic or contradictory elements: a dialectic without the emergence of a teleological or transcendent History, and beyond the prescriptive form of symptomatic reading where the nervous tics of ideology reveal the "real materialist contradiction" that History embodies'.[17] Here progressive reading comes not in the guise of 'a pure avenging angel speaking the truth of a radical historicity and pure oppositionality' but in the full theoretically charged awareness that 'our political referents and priorities – the people, the community, class struggle, anti-racism, gender difference, the assertion of an anti-imperialist, black or third perspective – are not there in some primordial naturalistic sense. Nor do they reflect a unitary or homogeneous political object.'[18]

These are the two differently nuanced positions to which some of the chapters in this volume grouped around the title 'Contesting the colonial' offer something of a response. It is also picked up in a more extended form in Francis Barker's philosophical investigation of nationalism, nomadism and belonging. 'Englishness' is a question of an imagined community whose fictive ethnicity is capable of being projected on to other cultures; this imperialism is at the heart of the question of the split colonial subject for whom hybridity and nomadism become a *modus vivendi*. But this fictive ethnicity is also capable of being folded back into itself through displacement into the area of class affiliation. At home Shakespeare becomes the touchstone of class loyalty and/or class aspiration, but it is also the site upon which the 'nation' reaffirms its fictive ethnicity. Willy Maley detects this 'British problem' as a thematic concern in the second tetralogy, where marginal Welsh, Scots and Irish, not to mention the French, are symbolically central to the construction of an emergent British identity.

The identification of the colonial as 'other' opens up a space for resistant reading very much in the founding moment of the formation of Britishness. Such resistance, of course, presupposes some degree of cultural affiliation, if not exactly the continuities of a nationalist tradition against which colonial power might be read. More difficult, because more complex, is the case of a colonised culture absorbing into its already fissured institutions a canonical writer such as Shakespeare. Here cultural identity is 'negotiated' and 'translated', to use Bhabha's terms, 'in a discontinuous intertextual temporality of cultural difference'.[19] But, as Ania Loomba astutely points out, it was the clash between what had become an élite, Westernised theatrical tradition and a popular Indian colonial tradition that was both the *product* and *producer* of a hybridity that she claims was 'the hallmark of urban colonial India' (p. 122), for example. If we set this alongside Martin Orkin's timely reminder of the politically anaesthetising power which 'the "aesthetically" satisfying canon of masterpieces from the metropolis' (p. 149) can exert by way of distraction from the process of critical self-awareness of the colonial subject, then we are afforded a glimpse of the political complexities involved in the process of negotiation and translation which Shakespearian texts undergo 'transnationally'.

It is to a 'global' Shakespeare that John Joughin and Curt Breight speak. The *theatrum orbis terrarum*, exemplified in Shakespeare's

Globe, and parodied in the Sam Wanamaker replica currently under construction in London, is now nothing less than a form of global cultural capital. Shakespearian texts have become the unified and unifying discourse in which cultures are encouraged to define their experiences globally. They are also the site upon which those experiences may be contested, rethought, reread. But it is curious that at a time of postmodern fragmentation it is the Shakespearian quotation, now *de rigueur* in popular film, that proffers some semblance of coherence, offering a fantasy, as Tom Healy suggests, of cross-cultural understanding.

We need go no further than two recent examples to demonstrate this fantasy in operation. In October 1995 as the annual Tory Party conference drew to a close, the Secretary of State for Education, Mrs Gillian Shepherd, announced a new committee which would promote the use of 'better English'. The national newspaper *The Guardian* for 12 October reported that the group 'which will include Sir David English, chairman of Associated Newspapers, and the Tory MP Gyles Brandreth, would aim to empower people "to express themselves clearly and appropriately"', and would be given a two-year budget of £250,000. The chairman of the committee was to be the television newsreader Trevor McDonald, the boy who 'learnt new words daily and modelled his elocution on the tones of the late radio cricket commentator John Arlott', and who became 'Trevor McDonald OBE, voice of the nation and benchmark of impeccable speech'. McDonald, a black Trinidadian immigrant who as a schoolboy in Trinidad was taught by Presbyterian missionaries from Canada, had learned by heart passages from Dickens, Trollope, Lamb and Hazlitt, Tennyson (his favourite) and, of course, Shakespeare. McDonald, noted apparently for his 'effortless skill in dropping citations into his news scripts' was subjected to the 'Victorian moral values' advocated by his father, and taught himself to speak perfect English 'by reading the Oxford Dictionary and emulating the mellifluous cadences of the BBC'. To seek authority in the fantasy of authentic origins is one thing, but to submit, through an act of impersonation, rather than mimicry, to so complete a logic of the signifier is an altogether different matter. This inversion of the politics of mimicry, from the desiring to the disciplined, or the desire for discipline, represents an attempt by authority through the display of its cultural capital to reinforce its power. And yet, McDonald is almost the same, but not white, and in this crucial difference lies an irony that forces us back to a consideration of the question of the cultural roots of national identity.

Meanwhile, authority is constantly seeking to renovate itself. The first week of November 1995 saw the release of a double compact disc of a series of readings from Shakespeare's plays, 'The Prince's Choice', in which the heir to the throne has out-grown the desire to become an intimate item of female sanitary wear, for the more substantial identity of Shakespeare's Prince Hal. Charles's (Hal's) rejection of Sir Robert Stephens (Falstaff), 'I do, I will', was, according to the producer of the CD, Glyn Dearman, given a new authenticity: 'In the rehearsal I said to Prince Charles, I said, "Sir, you are in the unique position of being the only person in the world who can say that line knowing what it feels [like] and what it means". And there was a long pause and he said "Right". And when he came to do it it was spine-tingling.' The Prince of Wales, a seasoned campaigner in the 'cause of the Bard' and the cause of the English language (the two are perceived as synonymous by him) seems blithely unaware of the cultural significance of his own 'choice' in this instance. While Prince Charles reads Shakespeare, Shakespeare 'reads' Prince Charles, and the convergence of the two readings is enough to set the spine tingling indeed in terms of future monarchical strategy.

In these two examples, 'national' culture is shown to be con-siderably more complex a phenomenon than their surface appeal would suggest. The colonised subject, now on display as a mani-festation of the efficacy of the imperial endeavour, aligns with the manipulative future king in a fantasy of ethnic coherence. *Shake-speare and National Culture* demonstrates in a number of ways both the powers and the dangers of such fantasies.

Notes

1 See Darrell Hinchliffe, *The Writing Masters: A Critical Account of the Relationship between Writing and Speech in the Orthographic Reform Debate of the Sixteenth Century with Special Reference to Rich-ard Mulcaster's The Elementarie (1582)*, unpublished Ph.D. thesis, University of Strathclyde (April 1994), pp. 198–9.
2 Tony Harrison, *Selected Poems* (Harmondsworth, Penguin, 1984), p. 122.

3 Etienne Balibar and Immanuel Wallerstein, *Race, Nation, Class: Ambiguous Identities* (London, Verso, 1991), pp. 102–3.

4 *Ibid.*

5 *Ibid.*, p. 99. Balibar concludes this argument with the suggestion that changing circumstances allow the language community to 'serve different nations (as English, Spanish, and even French do) or survive the "physical" disappearance of the people who used it (like "ancient" Greek and Latin or "literary" Arabic)'. He concludes: 'For it to be tied down to the frontiers of a particular people, it therefore needs an extra degree [*un supplement*] of particularity, or a principle of closure, of exclusion' (p. 99).

6 John Guillory, *Cultural Capital: The Problem of Literary Canon Formation* (Chicago, University of Chicago Press, 1993), p. 76.

7 *Ibid.*, p. 77.

8 *Ibid.*, p. 79.

9 Harrison, *Selected Poems*, p. 123.

10 Benedict Anderson, *Imagined Communities: Reflections on The Origin and Spread of Nationalism* (reprinted London, Verso, 1994), p. 44.

11 *Ibid.*, pp. 44–5.

12 Jonathan Bate, ed., *The Romantics on Shakespeare* (Harmondsworth, Penguin, 1992), p. 85.

13 Homi K. Bhabha, *The Location of Culture* (London, Routledge, 1994), p. 6.

14 Cf. Aijaz Ahmad, *In Theory: Classes, Nations, Literatures* (London, Verso, 1994), pp. 68–9.

15 Alan Sinfield, *Faultlines: Cultural Materialism and the Politics of Dissident Reading* (Oxford, Oxford University Press, 1992), p. 24.

16 Bhabha, *The Location of Culture*, p. 25.

17 *Ibid.*

18 *Ibid.*, p. 26.

19 *Ibid.*, p. 38.

Index

Note: Plays are listed under their titles. Page numbers in *italic* type indicate illustrations.